MASKED DECISIONS

The Triangular Life of
Dick 'The Destroyer' 'Doctor X' Beyer
From American Athlete to International Icon

Vincent Evans with Dick Beyer

Vince Evans Publishing

The opinions expressed in this manuscript are solely the opinions of the author and do not represent the opinions or thoughts of the publisher. The author has represented and warranted full ownership and/or legal right to publish all the materials in this book.

Masked Decisions
The Triangular Life of Dick 'The Destroyer' 'Doctor X' Beyer; From American Athlete to International Icon
All Rights Reserved.
Copyright © 2012 Vincent Evans with Dick Beyer
v5.0

This book may not be reproduced, transmitted, or stored in whole or in part by any means, including graphic, electronic, or mechanical without the express written consent of the publisher except in the case of brief quotations embodied in critical articles and reviews.

Vince Evans Publishing

ISBN: 978-0-9835548-9-9

PRINTED IN THE UNITED STATES OF AMERICA

Acknowledgements

To bring this story of a gifted athlete and his remarkable family and friends to print required the support and contributions of my equally remarkable family and that of many friends, some old, some new, but all fully vested in the outcome. From the hand-written notes, newspaper articles, publications, archives, family accounts, and Dick Beyer's personal recollections, this project began as a puzzle with each piece methodically placed in time to recapture a life, and legacy, long overdue. My friendship with Dick Beyer started simply with an interview for a story in Buffalo's Living Prime Time Magazine owned by the late Jerry Flaschner, who was more than a friend – he was my Yoda. Dick was pleased with the story I wrote about him and said "Vinnie, when it's time to write my book I'll call you." I didn't put much stock into his comment, but I didn't know the extent of Beyer's loyalty or his veracity until after his induction into the Greater Buffalo Sports Hall of Fame, an organization I was privileged to serve as an officer and board member. It was then that Dick said to me "Remember what I told you? Let's get cracking." So began a sojourn that took more than four years to complete, but the one constant, driving force that kept it alive and together was the uncanny, vivid, and detail-rich memory of Dick Beyer, who retold story after story as if they occurred earlier in the day not sixty years ago. Whatever the ultimate outcome this project engenders, my love and appreciation for Dick Beyer will forever be told. Thanks, Dick, for the opportunity of a lifetime.

So many other people to thank from across the United States, Canada, New Zealand, Japan yet so little space. My early drafts were drawn from family notes given me by Dick Beyer's sisters, Jean, Shirley and Dorothy; their deep love for their brother evident in every word and recollection. Clarification and conversations were provided by Kris, Rich and Kurt Beyer, and this project would not have been nearly as complete nor as interesting without their input and expectations for accuracy; in loving ways, they continue to protect their father; many thanks to all three of Dick Beyer's children and special thanks to Kurt for details, edits, and translations; you were more important to the story than you realize. My love and thanks to Wilma, Dick's wife and all-everything, who knew where to locate the photo, article, or note among the family treasures in their home and was ever-present to help her husband with a story; the times you and Dick spent at my home in Florida were truly enjoyable; you are the embodiment of devotion.

Steve Yohe's detailed ring record of Dick Beyer, The Destroyer, and Doctor X proved invaluable to the timeline; Steve is the consummate Destroyer fan and wrestling historian and his work deserves special recognition. In addition, I extend thanks to John Capouya, Mike Tenay, Rick Azar, Rip Morgan, Scott Teal, Mike Lano, Art Williams, Marty and Gary Youmans, John Hansen and Dan Westbrook for your journalistic advice. To all the 'Boys' who took time for telephone or in-person interviews in Las Vegas including the late Billy 'Red' Lyons, Ed Albers, Nick Bockwinkel, Don Leo Jonathan, Harley Race, Terry Funk, and Ilio DiPaolo's son Dennis, my appreciation for your comments. To Dick Easterly for your recollection of Syracuse football stories, Hank Olejniczak for details on Buffalo's Central Terminal, and to special contributor Maggie Minenko in Los Angeles, thanks for giving color and dimension to the work. To Dan Westbrook, thank you for the color photo of The Destroyer on the front cover; you have become a good friend. For their generosity of time, a warm round of thanks to the 'Japanese circle' including Mitsuaki Tanimura, Master and Masako Hada, Tokio Tsukata, Nobuyoshi Seo in Asahikawa for hosting me in your city, Toshiyuki Kuramuki, Horst at the X Bar in Tokyo, Marty Keuhnert for your superb contributions, and the Destroyer's crew at the Azabu Juban Festival – you made my stay in Japan unforgettable and you brought to life the iconic stature The Destroyer holds in your country; I am forever grateful to you and the world holds you and your countrymen in thoughts and prayers; Japan will return stronger.

It would be a grievous omission if I did not thank all the extraordinary teachers from St. Mary's School and St. Vincent High School in Plymouth Pa., King's College in Wilkes-Barre Pa., and at the State University of New York at Buffalo; I am grateful to Sister Jane Frances who recognized something in a recalcitrant fourth grader and especially to Howard B. Fedrick who, intellectually and creatively, moved my mind and soul to such dimensions that they never returned to their original shape – he is missed by many.

I've been gifted with a family, not unlike Dick Beyer's family, that has nurtured and sustained me and that never has forgotten its roots in the Evans, Murray and Mrugal traditions. My brother Blayne, sisters Michelle Evans Prokarym and Rene Evans Congdon and their families – you have always been there for me during highs and lows and I am eternally thankful. To my kids Jeffrey and Megan – my love for you remains unconditional and you will always be my proudest accomplishments. To their partners Tiffany and James, you have made our family only better and blessed us with Grayson and Haylee – being a grandparent is an exhilarating experience. Thanks also to my blended family of Mike and Jennifer Mayes, Kathy and Patrick Laboe and their son Jacob – your early support meant so much.

During my formative years my mother, Fran Evans, instilled in me a love of words – in any language. Despite limited schooling, Mom is the most intelligent woman I've ever known and provided four children happy childhoods without letting on how desperate times were for the family. She remains the most giving and loving woman who thinks only of others and how she can be helpful. Mom, you are the gravity in our world and my love for you is eternal. You are also the queen of comedy and everyone is happier around you and your sense of humor.

Finally, to Patrice Evans, my partner on this journey – your support and encouragement moved this project to its conclusion. During my darkest hours you held constant and believed in the story. More importantly, you believed in me. As you read the manuscript for the first time, and I saw you cry, I knew it was a good story; you always cry when you read something that connects and moves your spirit. Oddly, I gained confidence from your tears. Throughout the course of writing – across our life in New York, Florida, and California – we made whatever we had work for us. You showed me how good life can be and I admire and respect you in so many ways. Patrice, with you, all my decisions are easy ones...that's what real love does.

Contact the Author at vinevans@gmail.com.

Additional details and photos can be found at www.thedestroyer.com

"You will find Dick Beyer highly charismatic with true athletic expertise...This story will amaze you."

-Dan Westbrook, Pro Photographer, *Tokyo Sports Press*

"Why did I become a wrestling fan? Two words - The Destroyer."

-Mike Tenay, Wrestling Historian, Broadcast Announcer for *Total Nonstop Action Wrestling* (TNA)

CHAPTER 1

HE REMOVED FROM inside his jacket the tattered, well-thumbed copy of the little book and glanced at the inscription written by his father, with thoughts firmly fixed on building an exciting and memorable body of work, this time on the west coast. After all, he had established a compelling presence in Hawaii the first four months of the year, alternating as hero and villain in his business and connecting with his audience in both roles. Prior to his popularity in the Pacific, he garnered rave reviews almost from the start of his career in Columbus Ohio, in Western New York, the Chicago, Tennessee and Kentucky territories, and was selected "Rookie of the Year" by *Wrestling Life Magazine* in 1955. In each territory, with every match, on punishing, unforgiving surfaces, he had given up his body and his full measure of skill and showmanship, so that fans sitting on sticky bleachers or wooden seats in smoky, brummagem arenas, small dimly-lit school gyms, and foul-smelling activity halls vicariously fought with or against him – either way, they were engaged. That was important to him; it became so the same day his dad gave him the book, the two inextricably joined. The airplane from Hawaii taxied to a complete stop followed by his wife's voice "Can you carry him down the steps?" Walking off the plane and onto the tarmac toward the Los Angeles airport terminal building with Willy, his wife of three years, and holding two year-old son Kurt, an upbeat Dick Beyer was thinking that Dick Beyer, professional wrestler, was about to make as big a name for himself as the Hollywood sign in the hills high above L.A. He did not know how wrong - and right - he was to be.

Beyer and his wife weaved their way through the crowded airport terminal that was packed with April travelers, picked up their luggage, and darted to the ground transportation area for a taxi ride downtown. After checking into a hotel and settling his family, Beyer left the premises and hailed another taxi for himself. As was the custom in the business, he needed to report to the wrestling commission office in Los Angeles and obtain a license to work in the territory. Before he left Hawaii, Beyer was told that the license would be ready when he arrived in California. Jules Strongbow, the Los Angeles territory match maker, had personally phoned Beyer to invite him to wrestle on the west coast. Beyer gained the attention of Strongbow through a phone call from World Wrestling Alliance and well-known L.A. territory champion Freddie Blassie. Said Blassie "Jules, you need to see this guy Beyer; he's the best baby face (wrestling good guy) in the country." Beyer had befriended the sardonic, biting Blassie several years earlier in Tennessee, and recently wrestled him in Hawaii in a losing effort for the WWA title; later, as a newly converted heel (wrestling bad guy) Beyer was in Blassie's corner for his match against popular islander Neff Maiava. After that match, Blassie again told Strongbow "You can bring Beyer into the L.A. territory as either a baby face or a heel…he's that good." While in Honolulu, thinking that his heel work was just beginning, Beyer decided to have photographs taken – five poses, one hundred copies of each – one with the figure-four leg lock on Lord Blears, a move Blears personally had taught Beyer, and four others with horror-movie facial distortions, shaved head, and menacing postures with outstretched arms. He originally had planned to use the photos to promote himself in Oregon, before Strongbow called and his plans for the spring of 1962 changed from Portland to Los Angeles. Beyer brought the photos with him to L.A., convinced the booker would want them for program publicity or newspaper promotions.

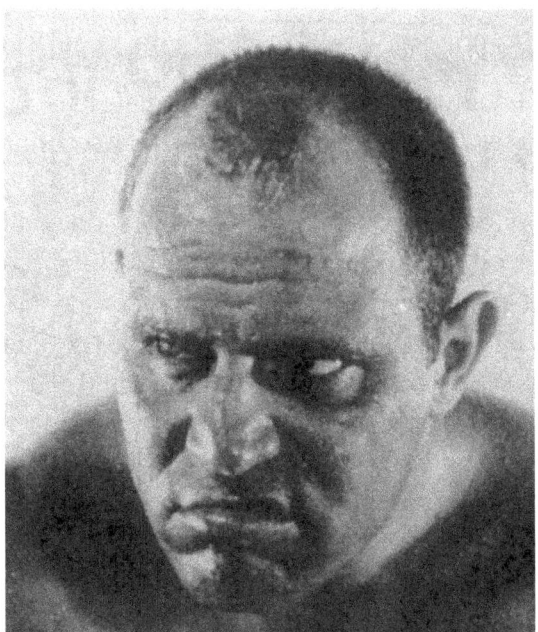

Early 1960s photo of Beyer as a heel.

At 5 feet 10 inches and 230 pounds, Beyer, now thirty-one years old, had a body made for wrestling. With bold, broad facial features, flattened nose, and gap-toothed grin, his short but stocky, well-built, low center of gravity physique worked to his advantage in the ring and, with his deceptive speed, locomotive strength, and ability to work inside and outside the ring, he was able to out-maneuver most opponents. But most opponents loved working with him because he knew how to wrestle. Many of the marquee names in professional wrestling did not have a true wrestling athletic background, but their sheer size, gimmick, or ring personality made good draws at the box office. Beyer was one of the few who possessed the skills and maneuverability that made a good show even better, and opponents enjoyed grappling with him because the performance had pace, reminiscent of a technically sound Broadway production. Beyer understood that his constituency – promoters, fans, and other wrestlers –wanted to see good exhibitions and his athletic background of collegiate wrestling, football, and coaching experience plus his military training served him well. He had found his métier. He knew how to play to the crowd visually and verbally and enjoyed the immediate feedback, though he preferred the crowd's showering of boos to their occasional shower of booze. It came with the job. In the ring he was able to bring out the best in his opponents. He was all business. He thought the new heel image he created in Hawaii was going to be his signature persona and the photographs were going to support his identity for years to come in wrestling publications and regional promotions. Strongbow believed that, based on Blassie's experience and recommendation, Beyer would be a good fit for the upcoming wrestling cards he had scheduled for the territory, but he had a plan for the wrestler that was markedly different from Beyer's own ideas.

Beyer arrived at the L.A. commission office early in the afternoon to pick up his license. After telling the clerk his name, "Yes, Beyer, like Buyer - beware," the officious clerk feigned a half smile while Beyer drummed his fingers on the counter, waiting for the document to be retrieved. The clerk came back to him, empty-handed, and curtly lisped: "Mr. Beyer, your name is not on the license list." Surprised and a bit incredulous, Beyer asked to see the list since there must have been an error in spelling or some other plausible explanation. When he did not find his name in the listings, his anger began to perk; a legitimately angry professional wrestler is pure energy just shy of a Kansas tornado. But Beyer kept his composure, for the moment, asked the primping clerk for the telephone, and called the promoter's office. Getting Jules Strongbow on the phone, Beyer said: "You guys must not want me in here. I'm at the commission office and my name isn't on the list for a license." Strongbow responded quickly: "Well, you're not in here as Dick Beyer." "What the hell have you got me wrestling under?" Beyer shot back. Strongbow said: "We're going to put a mask on you and call you The Destroyer." "I don't even have a mask!" "Well, when you get to San Diego for your first match, Vic Christy will have one for you." Now, in a combustible mix of disbelief, fatigue, and rising rage, Beyer hammered the phone back on the cradle with a passing "I'm not doing this!" Beyer was given the license under the new working name Strongbow had for him by the cowering clerk and bolted the office for the hotel. Pacing the room, he told his wife: "Willy, they're putting a mask on me…I haven't worn a mask since fifth grade Halloween; this is a big mistake; five hundred perfectly good photographs shot to hell." "The Destroyer," he yelled to her, "a damn appropriate name for what I'm feeling right now."

Promoters and match makers in professional wrestling could make or break any wrestler in the business. They controlled the wrestling world which was divided into territories and championships – the WWA or World Wrestling Alliance championship was recognized in Los Angeles territory, Hawaii and the Far East; the New York territory had its own champion, St. Louis region had the National Wrestling Alliance championship and Minneapolis had the American Wrestling Association champion. Other regions had area-specific crowns or state championships. Each territory was headed by a promoter or match maker who brought in the talent and rotated the 'boys' as they were known among the different cities and towns in the territory to draw attention, heighten the popularity of specific wrestlers, and build business. A wrestler might lose in one city and a promotion set up as a 'grudge match' in another city in the territory so that fan interest centered on the second chance to see whether the outcome would result in revenge or another defeat.

Strongbow and promoter Cal Eaton had built a reputable showcase environment in the Los Angeles area. Wrestlers enjoyed working the L.A. territory since the fan base was usually strong, television coverage was gaining popularity, and the money was very good. In addition, wrestlers were paired with some of the biggest names in the industry, helping them to rise to another level of awareness with the wrestling-hungry public and with that awareness, gain stability, and work.

MASKED DECISIONS

The routine in the L.A. territory was to work Pasadena on Monday, Long Beach, Tuesday, the Olympic Auditorium in Los Angeles on Wednesday, Bakersfield, Thursday, San Diego on Friday and San Bernardino, Saturday. Occasionally, Las Vegas was added to the circuit. With this rotation, wrestlers typically hunkered down in a hotel or an apartment in L.A. for an extended period of time and worked the circuit, often travelling city to city, week after week, with the wrestlers who were filling the card at the next stop; same company, different dance partners. A travelling fraternity guarded closely by those who pledged.

The weekend schedule called for Dick Beyer as the masked Destroyer to wrestle in San Diego on Friday, April 27, the day after he arrived in California and in San Bernardino the following night. Beyer rented a car and mapped out a route to San Diego, feeling less apprehensive about finding the location of the arena on time than the prospect of using a mask. The San Diego promoter, Hardy Kruskamp, wanted a masked man for that particular evening's card to face Seymour Koenig, a handsome body builder turned wrestler who, with Samson (Canadian Samuel Burke) had won the International Television Tag Team championship in the late 1950s. Kruskamp's desire for a hooded heel prompted Strongbow to alter Beyer's image – and plan. Strongbow knew a little something about image; standing 6'3" and weighing more than 300 pounds, the former wrestler had a television show that previewed upcoming matches. The show was sponsored by a diet specialty company and each week on the show Strongbow stepped on the scale and announced he had lost another pound. The camera never focused on the measurement and no one really knew if he had lost or gained. Still, it was a convincing television promotion. Strongbow knew Beyer had shaved his head and was working the heel side of the business in recent weeks. His L.A. talent pool was loaded and another bald heel was not something he wanted or needed, but he had longed to develop something more mysterious – a solid heel wrestler whose identity was unknown. Beyer's reputation for sound technical wrestling had spread industry-wide and it gave Strongbow the talent he sought for a masked man.

It took Beyer less time than expected to get to San Diego but more time than it should have to find the arena, frustrated by wrong turns and poor verbal directions that contributed to his elevated blood pressure and his temper. Stepping out of the car and grabbing his gear bag, Beyer made quick, long strides following signs to the arena back entrance, still believing he had a chance to wrestle under his own name, convinced Kruskamp would change his mind, but once he arrived inside the venue, he was informed he would indeed go 'under the hood.'

In the dressing room, he barely nodded to the other wrestlers and didn't say a word. Beyer was clearly irritated. Since he didn't have a mask, or accept the circumstances in which he found himself, he finally made his feelings known to Kruskamp in earshot of the other wrestlers in the dressing room. His frustration, anger, and repulsion at having to wear a hood, and in effect deny his own existence, an identity he worked hard to cultivate, born from years of football and wrestling struggles and drawn from the integrity and dreams of his father, poured out in a cathartic moment.

Vic Christy, a veteran wrestler and prankster, walked into the room during Beyer's outburst. The two had worked as part of a three-man team in Honolulu a few months earlier. Christy was instructed by Strongbow to bring a mask to the arena for Beyer; knowing it was Beyer's first west coast swing, the jokester brought a mask that was itself, a joke. Seeing Beyer emote, Christy had second thoughts about giving him the mask, but it was too late. Beyer had always prided himself on looking his best when he entered the ring on the side of either good or evil, with shined white boots, well-fitted trunks, and, in tribute to his alma mater, a Syracuse University warm-up jacket. When Kruskamp said "Give Dick the mask you brought him," Christy slowly reached into his gym bag and apologetically handed it to Beyer.

"This is how you repay a friend?" Beyer said in a Caesar-to-Brutus manner. He was referencing a televised interview the two had given in Hawaii and a phone book incident that almost cost Christy his reputation. The disguise looked like a moldy potato sack; it was dark, old, musty, made of wool and burlap; it slipped down over Beyer's head, covered his whole upper torso, the front and back tied together under the crotch. The entire apparatus was tight, scratchy, mephitic, and scattered with moth holes. It had two very small eye slits, no nose or mouth ventilation, and limited the movement of his head to only full upper body turns. When he breathed, the smell made him sick. In the mirror, he looked hideous, like a cartooned vegetable bag growing human limbs. "I ain't wearing this!" Beyer's muffled voice was heard as he pointed at Kruskamp, "I can't breathe, can't see, can't do a bloody thing with it, and I never worked under a hood before." It was everything he abhorred. A baby face his first six years turned heel, Beyer worked under his own proud name and was not into gimmickry or gags. Dick Beyer was a wrestler, a damned good one, and that is how he made his name, not with accoutrements. It wasn't his style, it wasn't his way, and it wasn't him.

Hardy Kruskamp was beside himself. The promoter and former wrestler who with Billy Varga had years earlier won a television tag team title, never expected to see the enraged reaction Beyer displayed toward wearing a mask, and as time approached for the opening bell, he was concerned that he would not have a semi-main match. Hardy allowed Beyer the time to vent and didn't interrupt him. When he thought Beyer had cooled down, he approached him in an almost avuncular manner, put his arm around the broad shouldered wrestler, and in calm tones told him he understood his plight and, given the professional he knew him to be, asked that he give the mask one try so that the evening's card fulfilled fan expectations. Since his real name was not to be disclosed, there was no risk of public embarrassment. After a considerably lengthy pause of stares and silence -- Beyer begrudgingly agreed to do it.

The 673 paid patrons dotted throughout the cavernous San Diego Coliseum saw Johnny Walker defeat Mario La Pantero and Enrique Torres take Ox Anderson in one-fall preliminaries. In the main event, Billy Varga won two of three falls from Primo Carnera, the former heavyweight boxing champion of the world, now in the twilight of his second career as a wrestler. But the semiwindup event played out as Kruskamp imagined – a classic study in contrast. Muscular and handsome New Yorker Seymour Koenig against the challenger – "Making his West Coast debut, a masked man of mystery, The Destroyer." A few less-than-enthusiastic claps and several muted boos were heard. Initially, the crowd appeared disinterested. As a match, it was a good but not great contest; The Destroyer, occasionally unable to see where his opponent was standing and moving clumsily about the ring in the mask-suit, eventually won two of three falls. Throughout the match, the indignant Beyer maintained his sense of mission to create an aura of intrigue while battling poor vision as the mask moved about his face and head during close-up action, scraped and irritated when it changed position around his nose and cheeks, and made him nauseous as the sweaty stench from the mask rose in intensity. Despite the inherent obstacles associated with the mask, Beyer as The Destroyer gave the Coliseum's crowd something to remember. As a pure wrestler, his speed, agility, and artistry in technique and body holds were evident as was his sense of timing and connection. He didn't look or feel the part, but a new prototype of wrestler emerged during the undercard that night, and the fans sensed it.

Immediately after announced as the winner, with sounds of THE DESTROYER still echoing off the walls, Beyer shifted the mask around his face to give his eyes room to see, found the side of the ring to make his exit, walked slowly to the ropes, lifted the middle rope up and moved his body angularly through the ropes and down the steps. He was not aware of the many in the crowd that had stood up without a sound, in awe of what they had just seen, and watched him leave the ring. He walked heavily up the crowd-parted walkway and quickly slipped into the locker room. Once inside, in full view of the other wrestlers, he tore off the mask, pointed to Hardy Kruskamp and said: "Hardy, you guys had your joke. Go back and tell Strongbow and the office that you just saw the first - and last - of The Destroyer." Kruskamp, looking panicked and shaken, replied "No, no, you've got to work for at least another four weeks. We've booked you that far ahead." Beyer, irritated, aggravated, and a bit constipated, realized he could do little to change the schedule - not if he wanted to work, and get paid, in the territory. He looked over at Kruskamp, acknowledging the inevitable, and said to him "Well, after four weeks, I'm taking it off; *four more weeks as The Destroyer.*"

Watching the exchange between Beyer and Kruskamp was Ox Anderson, the Salt Lake City wrestler who had performed in the preliminaries and who knew Beyer from matches they wrestled in Texas. He thought Beyer distinguished himself under difficult circumstances in the evening's bout and, as a colleague, wanted to help out this new guy in the territory. Anderson walked over to his locker, opened up a duffle bag, and pulled out what initially looked to Beyer like a woman's white swimming cap. "Here Dick, try this on" said Anderson, tossing the item to Beyer.

As he unfolded it, Beyer quickly realized that it wasn't a cap, but a mask. Unlike any mask he had ever seen...it was lighter, had generously cut holes around the eyes, nose and mouth, and was made from elastic material that seemed comfortable and stretched to conform to the head and face. Putting it over his head and down around his face, Beyer said to Anderson "Hey, this isn't bad. I can breathe...I can speak...I can see. Ox, what's this made from?" With a little hesitancy in his voice, Anderson replied "It's... made out of a ...woman's girdle." Beyer looked at Anderson -Anderson at Beyer- over several seconds neither reacted. Not wanting to know if the material was new, or used, or just not caring, Beyer asked Anderson if he could borrow and use it in San Bernardino where he was scheduled to wrestle the following night. Anderson agreed. Beyer, poking his fingers into the various holes, said "If she really wants it back, you'll have some big explaining to do."

With the unexpected mask now a prized possession, Beyer felt a modicum of relief. For him, the next month was not going to be as bitter under the hood, but it still wasn't the kind of wrestling he anticipated performing and it certainly was not something he planned to do beyond four weeks. He wanted to meet with Strongbow to redesign a schedule for Dick Beyer to be followed by a wake for the soon-to-be-deceased Destroyer. As it turned out, his match in San Bernardino the following night against Tom Zink resulted in a second win for The Destroyer. The mask Anderson had given him was much better; his sight and breathing significantly improved under the girdle mask and, as a result, so did The Destroyer's performance. The crowd again took notice of the masked man's mastery. On the drive back to the hotel in L.A., he wondered what decisions he would have to make to continue working in California, and continue his career, once he removed the mask for good in four weeks.

CHAPTER 2

IT WAS SUNDAY. Beyer had planned to return the mask to Ox Anderson but The Destroyer was scheduled to wrestle on the circuit all week, beginning with a match against trickster Vic Christy in Pasadena on Monday night. There was no way he was going to wear Christy's original mask. After calling Anderson to tell him he'd have his mask for him in the dressing room in Pasadena, Beyer asked his wife, a tall, dark-haired beauty, to accompany him downtown to find material to make his own mask. Leaving the care of their two-year old son in the hands of a friend in the hotel, Beyer promised Willy he would rent an apartment for the family as soon as they found a textile for a substitute mask. Beyer was confident that with the right fabric, he would have a mask in no time since Willy was a talented seamstress.

The couple took a short bus ride to south Broadway Street in the city and found F.W. Woolworth's Five and Dime Store. Beyer jumped off the bus, took his wife's hand to help her down, opened the door of the large department store and was immediately met by the aroma of hot dogs and freshly brewed coffee wafting from the busy lunch counter. The smells brought back memories of running a summer hot dog business and the valuable lesson from that business he applied to his sport. He walked briskly through the store with Willy trailing well behind. Remembering what Ox Anderson told him about the mask's construction, he tracked a beeline to the women's lingerie aisles. The store was unusually crowded for an April Sunday after Easter, and the lingerie department was full of women in their Sunday finest looking for bargains and necessities. As Beyer stepped politely around and through the gathering of women shoppers, his head scanning left and right, he came upon the mother lode he was searching for - girdles. Beyer looked at the sizes and types of girdles, pulled several from the display counter and held them up for close inspection - a proverbial bull in a lingerie shop. Spotting a man standing alone lifting underwear up to his face, a saleswoman came over to stop his foolish behavior and asked what size his wife wore; Beyer replied "Oh, they're not for her, they're for me." At that moment Willy arrived, still huffing from her hike through the store, smiled at the sales associate and breathlessly said to her husband "Did you find what you needed for your face?" The stunned employee, with her mouth agape and disbelief on her face, slowly and aimlessly walked away.

With Willy by his side and the employee safely out of sight, Beyer began to put the undergarments upside down over his head. He was a veritable Goldilocks in girdles. Some girdles didn't stretch enough and were too tight, others stretched beyond their limits and fell out of shape. As he placed one after another over his shaved head, he asked Willy "How does this one look?" In time, he determined the girdle that was most comfortably fitting. Women wearing silk stockings used girdles with garters that hung down from the underwear to hold up the stockings and the garment simultaneously gave them the tuck they desired around their hips. Sizes ranged from small, medium, large to short, medium and tall. Beyer stood there and tried on just about every size in every style and found that he took a small-tall. Willy worked with him like a magician's sidekick, pulling the garter belts up around his head, trying to see if she could finish off the top by sewing the two sides together. The stretchy nature of the material combined with the slightly tighter fit convinced Beyer that he had found the right underwear for his mask. Oblivious to his surroundings for some time, Beyer did not sense the scores of fixed eyes, horrified faces, and muted sounds of the women in and near the lingerie department as he put one girdle after another on his head, ably assisted by the lovely woman with him. The store was bustling with activity, yet the lingerie department was silent and motionless; people stood like mannequins in frozen positions. One woman had her hand over her daughter's eyes. Two older women wearing fox boas, black gloves and small hats with face nets, were seen mouthing "Well, I never!" A small boy, no more than four years old, having seen Beyer put girdles over his head, picked up a brassiere, placed it on his head, and holding the straps under his chin ran around the aisle yelling "I'm Batman," with his mother giving chase, as the bra cups slid down to cover both his ears, giving him the appearance of a mutated character from nearby Disneyland. Having tried on countless foundations, Beyer settled on his mask material and sizes and walked to the checkout counter with a dozen girdles in his hands and a peculiar smile on his face. Those still in the lingerie department stood immobile.

Willy stopped in the fabric department and purchased some bias binding in different colors, red, green and blue, to sew the ends and accent the white mask. She figured that after cutting holes for the eyes, nose and mouth, she'd sew around the holes with the colored bias material and add a stripe starting from the lower back end of the mask near the neck, moving up the back of the head and down the front, similar to a stripe on a football helmet, connecting to the eye, nose and mouth holes, thus giving the mask a finished, even look. Happy with their shopping, the couple boarded a bus back to the hotel. Willy busied making a few new masks while Beyer went searching for an apartment. By the end of the day, both were successful and delighted with each other's work.

As he stood in the mirror and tried on one of the new masks Willy had sewn, Beyer noticed that the distortion and exaggeration of his facial features from the elasticity in the material made him look more fierce and mean. His brows were visible shadowing his steely blue eyes that radiated out from the mask holes, his nose, broken several times, looked flat but less distinguishable, and his mouth ventilation was large enough so that anyone could see and hear what he had to say. The vertical stripe at the top of the mask was in perfect linear coordination with the gap between his two front upper teeth. Even with the changes and especially the new openness to the mask, recognition of Dick Beyer was nearly impossible. His true identity was not ascertainable upon casual observation. The new disguise was at least ego-syntonic. If he had to wrestle under a mask, he was going to make the spectacle a sensational display of world-class wrestling. All this and Beyer's own over-the-top facial expressions helped him regain some confidence as a heel whose appearance was important to him; he wasn't wrestling as Dick Beyer, but he was wrestling as a character he now had exerted some control over, and was about to re-enter the ring with his shined white shoes, colored trunks, and color-coordinated mask, if only for four more weeks as The Destroyer.

In 1873 Paris, the first ever masked wrestler entered the ring to continue a sport that had begun more than 3000 years earlier. He was known as 'Le Catcheur Masque'-the Masked Wrestler. The annals of modern history will point to April, 1962, as the genesis of arguably the greatest unintentional wrestler ever to wear a mask.

CHAPTER 3

BUFFALO NEW YORK. 1930. Given a city of grain storage and flour mills, engine building and steel manufacturing, residents proudly proclaimed Buffalo a 'lunch bucket town' and a step-sister to the honeymoon attraction, Niagara Falls, twenty miles to the northwest. Still, the city was well-positioned as an important intersection for the migration of products around the country via its mature rail and water ways.[1] Due in part to its diversified industrial base, Buffalo felt insulated from business downturns echoed in other cities. All was about to dramatically change. Just months earlier, the Great Depression had cast its first ominous shadow; families were straining and resources diminishing in cities like Buffalo and throughout the country. Many families and lives collapsed under the weight of the economic calamity; those that survived were forever changed and humbled. For most, it was the promise of life and the hope found in new days that, together with hard work and prayer, contributed to the sustenance of family life across the Niagara Frontier.

Against this backdrop, each day for Ford Assembly Plant worker Dewey Beyer and his wife, Celia, was a new struggle in making what they had stretch for their growing family and Celia's elderly parents residing with them. On July 11, Celia had given birth to a son, Richard John, or Dick as they preferred to call him; it was a bittersweet moment for the Beyer family, celebrating their new arrival while recalling the birth years earlier of their first son and the tragic loss of that baby soon after. Dewey, a former minor league baseball pitcher, prepared to introduce his new boy to a world of opportunity with responsibility, just as he had done with daughters Jean and Dorothy, but the current distress in and forecast for the country, posed many uncertainties. Within two years, Dewey and Celia welcomed a third daughter, Shirley, to complete their quartet. Dewey, his wife, three daughters, one son, and two elderly in-laws occupied a small, two-bedroom, one bath home at 86 Manhattan Avenue, located off Amherst Street on the northeast side of Buffalo. It was a tight-knit, blue collar community, filled with first and second-generation immigrants, mostly German and Irish, where one could sit on the front porches of the simple single family and double-block clapboard homes and watch kids play in the streets and neighbors walk to and from the bus stop on trips to downtown Buffalo and nearby communities. In the neighborhood everyone knew everyone; everyone helped everyone. While money, food, and jobs were in short supply, Dewey and Celia Beyer were abundantly blessed with love and overarching determination to create an environment of values to carry forward each of the children, every day.

When Dick and his sister Shirley were toddlers, their father built and finished an area in the front of their home's non-insulated attic to serve as an apartment for Grandma and Grandpa. Dewey and Celia occupied the back bedroom, Jean and Dorothy had the other and young Dick and little Shirley opened up day beds in the dining room that every night doubled as their shared sleeping quarters. Dinner was always at 6:00 pm – sharp - and everyone sat down together at the round table for the evening meal. Meat and dessert were infrequent and limited, but everyone got their fill on potatoes and whatever vegetables were grown in the garden. Dewey was an active father in his children's lives; despite the daily anxiety and worry over job cuts and working hot, grueling hours in the assembly plant, he always made time for his children. He fixed up an old Model T Ford and took his kids to the parks in the summer and sledding in the winter; for the kids, it was like travelling around the world. On Sundays, Celia made fudge from the sugar and chocolate she had left over and on those evenings, before preparing for school and work, the family gathered around the radio and listened to shows like The Shadow, Jack Benny,

The Lone Ranger, Burns and Allen, Your Hit Parade and The Green Hornet. Every Sunday, they attended church and the kids went to Sunday school.

Church was both a galvanizing force and stabilizing factor in the lives of many especially during the 1930s. Taber Lutheran Church, the house of worship the Beyer family attended, held many dinners for its congregation, partly to raise money, mostly to feed the hungry and to enable members to socialize, learn what resources were available, what jobs were open, and who was in need of special assistance. It was a place for the spiritual and for lifting spirits. The adult groups wrote and performed plays and comedies; members participated in the Christmas pageant and organized softball teams for adults and kids. As a youngster, Dick took part in many of the church activities and, following his family's example, an interest in helping people. He witnessed how people gained strength from their spirituality – from living a good and giving life and, from that, how it was possible to help others even when little was available. The experiences nurtured his soul and his values which, later in life, were to play a key role.

The Beyer family was unable to afford day camps or other special programs for Dick and his sisters so his parents and grandparents engaged them in home activities ranging from board games and cards to playing ping pong on the dining room table. Creativity, improvisation, and making the best of what they had were things that stuck with the young boy and his sisters. The girls learned to knit, sew, cook and bake; young Dick watched carefully as his father and grandfather fixed things around the house and worked with tools. He learned early the meaning of self-reliance. His father always insisted that before he left the house, he was to kiss his mother…and he did…every time, no matter what age he turned. The family had little, but the kids did not realize how poor they were; to them it was the best place to be.

MASKED DECISIONS

Dorothy, Jean, Shirley and Dick were always very close.

Manhattan Avenue was no more than two blocks long and dead-ended just beyond the Acme Builders and Supply building, at an area called the quarry. This was an operating rock quarry from which crushed stone was strip-mined, steam shovel-loaded onto trucks, hauled out and transported for use in construction. The older, obsolete section, separated by four railroad tracks from the active newer quarry, had large, flat areas of dirt and grass cleared for football and baseball fields used by the workers from Acme Supply and on which the Bennett High School football team practiced during the fall. To the kids in Beyer's neighborhood, the quarry was heaven on the avenue. When the Acme workers and high school football players were not on the fields, the neighborhood kids descended upon them like an ant colony. The quarry also contained two water holes, one larger than the other. In the large one, the kids swam during the summer months; the small, shallow one was used for ice skating. During the winter, every kid's last name was 'Zamboni'. The kids were religious in their preparations for the ice rink – shoveling snow and meticulously smoothing the ice surface for skating with their mitten covered hands. Almost any time of year, the kids played games like kick the can, red light/green light, hide and seek; as they grew older, the games turned into sports like baseball, hockey, swimming, football; sometimes four or more different sports were played simultaneously at the quarry and many spilled out onto Manhattan Avenue for the tougher kids to take advantage of the harder surfaces. Getting up a game was never a problem; between house number 70 and number 128, there were 33 households. Within them, 50 kids lived on the Beyer side of the street and 30 on the odd numbered side. Beyer, always first out on the street, endlessly played with the kids and competed, any game, any time, any number of players. The Manhattan Avenue neighborhood was a safe place to grow up but all families had a rule – *when the street lights come on, be home before the light hits the ground.*

A precocious young boy, Beyer not only loved the grit of competition but also took on any dare or challenge. He was pugnacious when provoked. Jimmy Carroll Jr., a neighborhood elder (Beyer's term for anyone four or more years older than he), once bragged to those assembled in the quarry that he was the toughest kid around, and to prove it, told young Dick to punch him in the stomach as hard as he could. Beyer, much younger than Carroll, took on the challenge, stretched his arm back and, with all the force he could muster, hit him about as hard as Carroll had ever been hit; the surprised Carroll, not wanting to show any pain to the others, grabbed young Beyer and tossed him into the bushes, deflecting attention, for the moment, from his midsection discomfort. Undeterred, Beyer got up and without any hesitation - or warning - again hit Carroll in the solar plexus. As those around him laughed uncontrollably, Carroll, now with embarrassment added to his throbbing abdomen, picked Beyer up off the ground in a swinging motion, dumped him back into the bushes, and walked home holding his stomach as Beyer looked on from his bushy perch. Beyer enjoyed telling his friends he got his athletic start in a 'bush league.'

Don Newer, another elder, told the short, fat six-year old Beyer that he was too young and small to play football in the streets with the bigger, rougher kids. It was a game they played hard and Beyer wanted in. He relentlessly kept at Newer and the others, taunting and pressing the older kids. To appease him, Newer allowed Beyer to play center on both teams so that he would be occupied on every play yet not be in the running or passing lanes to the side. It wasn't long before Beyer was jumping and burrowing into the fray of bodies stacking up and pushing back and forth as though in the middle of a rugby scrum, pulling at the ball as the others pulled at him. After everyone untangled and eventually got up on their feet, there was young Beyer at the bottom, often with the ball tucked tightly against his chest, yelling out "big gain" and ready to go the next down and distance. The physical nature of the sport was sugar to him.

Buffalo's Public School #61 on Leroy Avenue was in walking distance from Manhattan Avenue; it was where Dick Beyer, his sisters, and most of their friends attended school. Mornings on his way he often caught a glimpse of his mother waiving to him as she left to catch a bus downtown for her work as an office secretary. Each year started – and ended - like the year before. Beyer's sisters worked hard and earned good grades; Dick struggled making the grade. His parents and older sisters tried to help him with his studies and though he appreciated their interest, he felt frustrated and angry. For him, learning was a ballroom dance – one step forward, one to the side and one back. At times he fretted he would never get out of grammar school. *I'll still be in eighth grade…and have a son in first.* It wasn't that he was a difficult student – he just found being a student difficult.

To help his family during tough times, young Dick Beyer persuaded a friend to give him his paper route delivering the Courier Express newspaper daily and Sundays, 70 papers during the week and 212 on Sundays. The Sunday paper was always thicker, heavier and more voluminous, so at times he enlisted the help of his sisters – he sat in the wagon folding the papers, Jean pulled the wagon and Dorothy took the paper to the porches. "Hey, it's my route" was his explanation for the curious division of labor. There was something about the routine and regimentation of delivering daily papers on time that appealed to him and he developed an awareness of every family in each house including names, number of kids, and relationship to others in the neighborhood. He became the community census taker. He also knew which kids were hungry and often brought some candy he had purchased with his own money for them. With his wagon, he walked his beat as though on military maneuvers, regardless of Buffalo's snowy, dark winters, hot sticky summers, or wet windy springs and falls, and became well known for his reliability. When the weather became too harsh to be out alone, he and his sisters packed the papers into the back of their father's car and were driven around the neighborhood to deliver the news. The money he earned was put into the family fund from which he was given a few cents each week for his work; he often gave his allowance to his sisters to help them buy little things they wanted or needed. Beyer adored his sisters, had enormous respect for all the families, and developed a sense of timeliness, dependability, and sensitivity.

On a cold Sunday afternoon in early December, 1941, Beyer was in one of his favorite places, the candy store, not far from his Manhattan Avenue neighborhood, when he heard the owner and a customer talking about an attack at Pearl Harbor in Hawaii. The words and tone of the conversation frightened him; he could not understand why the country of Japan sent airplanes to bomb the American ships anchored at the shore. He ran home, darting for cover under store awnings, occasionally glancing at the skies to see if any Japanese planes were flying over Buffalo. In the aftermath, he held the Japanese in contempt.

MASKED DECISIONS

For Beyer, Japan was to be a source of anger, resentment and curiosity for years to come.

As the country mobilized its resources for battle, Dick Beyer found respite from the sobering news and his school stumbles, in sports. A twelve-year old on the swim team, his school won the 1942 City Championship. Defeating an opponent, playing by the rules, raising a hand in victory, it was magic to Beyer. What made that championship very special was that his school did not have a pool of its own; his team had to walk an hour to practice on Saturday mornings at School #63 through two quarries and over several sets of railroad tracks, often in ice and deep snow, as school swimming took place in the winter in Buffalo. It was not the only championship he tasted that year.

In the summer, Beyer successfully tried out for a city Midget League baseball team, sponsored by Slim's Texas Red Hots, a popular hot dog stand at the corner of Ferry and Niagara Streets on the west side of Buffalo. Practices were held in Delaware Park, to the city's north, a two-mile bike ride from Manhattan Avenue. The park, a beautiful expanse of trees, lakes, meadows, fields and walking lanes, partially intruded upon for the 1901 Pan American Exposition, was developed by Frederick Law Olmsted, the architect of New York City's Central Park. After several hours of practice, Beyer and the boys rode another two miles to Slim's for a free hot dog, walked to 'Bare Ass' Beach, took off their clothes (thus the apt name) and swam in the Erie Canal near Niagara Street before pedaling home. This became Beyer's daily summer routine – the short, fat kid worked himself into good physical condition.

Given his rookie season, Beyer played well that summer, as did his teammates, and his Slim's Texas Redhots baseball club won the division and moved on to play in the league championship game at Offermann Stadium, the hometown Buffalo Bisons' minor league ballpark, situated at the corner of Michigan Avenue and East Ferry Street. It was a venue Beyer knew well. He had seen many games there with his dad, a baseball lover; Offermann, home to popular left fielder Ollie Carnegie, was always a special occasion for young Beyer; six cents to ride the trolley to the stadium and back, twenty-eight cents for bleacher admission, five cents for a bag of peanuts – to experience baseball with his dad was worth far more.

Beyer could not contain his exuberance with the knowledge that his team was to play seven innings for the league championship at Offermann before a regularly scheduled Bisons' game. He arrived at the stadium early, sat in the dugout with the hometown players he admired, and watched the big guys take batting and field practice before his game was to begin. On this day, no life was better than his. Dewey Beyer, Celia and the three girls watched every inning from the bleachers; every so often, Dewey excused himself for the restroom, telling his family something was making his eyes tear up; Celia knew the truth; it wasn't what was in his eyes but on the diamond.

From the field, Beyer looked up far into the stands and at the crowd, absorbing the atmosphere, chilled by the excitement generated by the game and environment. In the end, winning the league championship, as thrilling as it was, did not compare to the feeling of being on that stage and performing to the best of his twelve-year old ability. At that moment, having won two championships in two different sports in the same year, Dick Beyer decided that on the battlefield of competition was where he wanted to be. He had contracted a chronic case of irreversible athlete syndrome.

The day bed and the dining room were no longer appropriate for the maturing young man. With the help of his father, Dick Beyer moved a mattress, desk, his clothes and personal items up to the back portion of the attic, behind his grandparents' small apartment, leaving Shirley the dining room to herself. The attic was not finished – hot in the summer, freezing in the winter, but he now had his own space. The daily routine of navigating the back stairs had one unique advantage – in that stairway lie his mother's freshly baked cookies cooling on the tin. On his way to bed each night, a few cookies were pocketed with no one the wiser...his mother's wink in the mornings told him otherwise.

Over the remaining weekends of the summer of '42, Beyer and his father played on the church-sponsored softball teams. Dewey Beyer always managed to hit a shot over the third base side no matter how the opposing team tried to defend him; his son outwardly put up a fuss whenever Dewey walked to the plate but secretly he pulled for his dad and admired his ability even as his father aged. Young Beyer's team was coached by Chet McMahon, a brick layer, who lived at the corner of Leroy and Marigold Streets, across from a Methodist church. McMahon owned a flat-bed truck that no matter how dusty it was, the kids piled in and rode home from games. On those trips, Beyer became increasingly aware of the Methodist church and the sign in front of the worship house noting its sponsorship of a Boy Scout troop. A cub scout for three years, Beyer had thoughts of moving up to the 'big leagues' but was reluctant, until Lloyd Hahn, an Eagle Scout and Manhattan Avenue neighbor, suggested he visit the troop. He instantly took to it, convinced that at least he would learn things that he was unable to learn in school.

Boy Scout Troop #69, which met Tuesday evenings in the basement of the Methodist church, had a reputation as one of the most active and well-managed troops in the Buffalo area; Ed Haynes, a giant of a man even to adults, was Scout Master; Hahn served as assistant Scout Master. Haynes' dedication to the scouting program and to his troop was inspiring to Beyer, noting that Haynes took his only two-week vacation each year to run the two week Boy Scout camp. The way he worked with the boys impressed Beyer; the example set was motivational. The Buffalo Boy Scout Council operated three camps – Scout Haven, a summer lakeside camp, Schoellkopf, a 3-day winter and summer camp and Toad Hollow, another 3-day all seasons camp. That November, Beyer prepared for his first weekend scouting camp at Toad Hollow. He had never before been away from home and looked forward to the experience; it would have to wait. When he arrived at Lloyd Hahn's house, having packed his clothes and supplies in a duffle bag, bundled up and trudged the windy, slushy street, he was informed by Hahn that the weekend trip was cancelled due to snow…too much snow. It was the only time during Beyer's scouting years that a camping trip was cancelled; he attended every winter and summer camp-out from then on, earning badges along the way – Tenderfoot, Second Class, First Class, merit badges, Star Scout and Life Scout. Scouting developed into more than badges and bunking; Beyer was learning in a way new to him and he enjoyed it. More importantly, with his new knowledge, Beyer discovered an ability to enable others as he had been…in a direct, constructive way.

Returning to School #61 to complete his eighth grade year worried Beyer. He was concerned about his poor grades and the high school he would be forced to attend as a result. In October 1943, the first term report cards were issued - Beyer failed 4 of 5 subjects. At home, Beyer nervously paced the kitchen anxious over his father's reaction, not that he feared punishment but a fate much worse - he feared disappointing him. After reviewing the report card, his father placed it on the table, looked over at his contrite son and said to him "You are spending too much time on that one subject." Dick Beyer looked up at this father, both smiled. With a new relaxed approach given to him by his father's perspective, and with the love and support of his mother and sisters, Dick re-committed to the eighth grade, employing the new learning skills he acquired through scouting, and by the final report issued in June 1944, he had passed all his subjects. Relieved, Beyer's decision to attend Seneca Vocational High School surprised his family, and in truth, surprised him. His cousin, Don Metz, had attended Seneca High and landed a good job with the telephone company; at that time, the telephone and power companies hired graduates from Seneca; since Beyer did not expect to go on to college, he thought Seneca gave him at least a fighting chance to get a job.

His affection for sports in full bloom, the newly minted eighth grade graduate developed an affinity for the physicality in football. He was built bigger and stockier than most boys his age and his size was well suited to the gridiron. Having played a lot of football at the quarry, it had become his first love, to the chagrin of his father, who wanted him to play baseball. To appease his father, young Beyer started a neighborhood baseball team known as The Manhattans that, without enough boys to field a full contingent, included his sister Dorothy and her friend Carol Shevlin. Other teams laughed at the sight of Beyer's mixed team - until they played them. The girls were often faster than many of the boys. Unlike others his age, Beyer was inclusive of not only gender but of those who had lesser skills. The Manhattans were a rag-tag bunch that gave more talented teams a run for their reputations. But football occupied Beyer's mind. Football to him was more than a sport - it was an obsession, an obsession that was to provide an unexpected opening through an unforeseen door.

At the start of his freshman year at Seneca High, on encouragement from friends, Dick Beyer tried out for baseball. He didn't make the team. He did, however, make the track team as a shot putter, and used the sport to help build his physique for his real passion. To play football in the Buffalo Public School system, boys had to provide permission slips signed by a parent; an excited Dick Beyer ran into the house and presented the slip to his mother for signature; with an expression on her face only mothers knew well, she said to her son "Go talk to your father." Beyer half-expected his mother's reaction to his desire to play football, but he was hell-bent to play and prove to her that he would not sustain serious injury. His father - caught between a son's desire and a mother's nightmare- slowly reviewed the permission slip before signing it, and as he did told his son "Be careful, for your mother's sake." Onto the outside back near the bottom of the weathered leather helmet, Beyer carved three barely detectable letters – MOM – that every time he suited up reminded him of his promise.

On the first day of football practice, an enthusiastic Dick Beyer eagerly arrived to show he was the next great Seneca High School quarterback. The coaches assembled the boys on the field and put them through routine calisthenics, stretching and running exercises, throwing and catching. Afterwards, head coach Les Boehmer brought the boys to the center of the field and said: "Receivers go over to the left, linemen to the right, backs stay here." The coach took a look at the bulky freshman Beyer and said "You, over there with the linemen." Beyer was in disbelief. All the time he spent honing his passing skills and leadership abilities wasted. A freshman, he dare not try to persuade the coach to put him in with the backs. He trotted over to where the linemen were stationed but silently vowed before long to win a role as quarterback.

Academically and athletically, Beyer's first two years at Seneca High, to use football analogy, were third and long; his grades marginal and his playing time limited. During his freshman year, he was relegated to the 'chain gang,' a group of boys that moved the yard markers and first down chain after every play. In the classroom, as he learned of Hiroshima and Nagasaki, his long-held hatred of the Japanese was mollified and replaced by a limitless hunger to understand. Current events were of interest, but did nothing to improve his overall grade standings. With the war having ended in June prior to his sophomore year, he figured the euphoria and optimism from its conclusion would carry over to the field; he didn't play a down his sophomore year. The head coach told him to watch the linemen on both teams in order to gain the knowledge to play in the trenches. Beyer didn't want to play on the line as he harbored dreams of starring at quarterback. He observed the line play in each game and, by the end of his sophomore year, knew the nuances to play any of the line positions. Beyer absorbed the football technicalities with ease. He seemed a football prodigy to some, but Beyer believed his skills from scouting were actually helping him learn. Undeniable was the convergence of his work and study that culminated in his ascension that year to Eagle Scout status. Dick Beyer, historically a poor learner, had achieved the highest order in scouting at age fifteen, and with it a fresh outlook. With his build now at 5' 10" and 210 pounds, he recognized his dream of quarterbacking the team was fading, so he gave all he had as a lineman during summer practices. The coaches took note of his exceptional diagnostic ability, speed and power. Beyer, a junior, had developed into a formidable force.

In the fall of 1946, the coaches projected Beyer to be a threat on the field. From the opening kickoff, he didn't disappoint. Dick Beyer started his first game for Seneca High in September against Riverside at All High Stadium, just a stone's throw from his Manhattan Avenue home. On a clear evening with his parents, siblings, and friends in the stands, Beyer played both ways – offensive guard and defensive nose guard; he never left the field. He was to start and play both ends of the field for the remainder of his high school football career. Beyer became the anchor on both the offensive and defensive lines, plugging holes to confound opposing runners and pushing back defenders to make way for his offensive backfield. Dick Beyer flourished as a football player, and soon the league, press, and fans were aware of the rock from the quarry.

The recognition Beyer received in the newspapers and on the streets validated his decision to play football, but he appreciated more the fact that so many people associated him with positive things like scouting and helping his community. For a maturing young man, and one who represented his family, those attributes were important to him. He parlayed his accolades for a job with the post office, delivering mail during winter breaks from school; the money helped his family and helped him buy an old 1937 Ford that his dad fixed to working order. Beyer drove the car to work and school. On his way to the post office on a slippery frosty morning, Beyer's car slid over a snow bank at the corner of Fillmore Avenue and Main Street striking the side of Hall's Bakery. Beyer was uninjured; the same could not be said of the car. The damages were extensive, and repairs would take months. Beyer called his father. The car was towed home and with it, Beyer's pride.

Dick Beyer never took himself too seriously, and kept all the attention in balance. He stayed true to his values, his beliefs, and his core character shaped by the strong example set by his parents and influential others. His sisters loved the brother he had become, and the brother he had always been. In the summer before his senior year, he asked his sister Dorothy to go to the church festival with him. Dorothy was touched by his request since she knew he could have asked, and taken, any girl in the neighborhood. As they strolled around the grounds of the festival, many people stopped Beyer to tell him how solid he was in a particular game or to thank him for his work with their young son in the scouts. Dorothy was so proud to be with him. In an endearing gesture, Beyer, holding his sister's hand, approached others and said "Hi, I'm Dorothy Beyer's brother." For both, it was an affirming experience – siblings and friends for life.

Beyer's senior year of high school did not progress in the manner he sought. He had worked hard during the summer, kept in top physical condition, and looked forward to capping his career with multiple victories. It was a good, but not stellar, season. As a result of his on-field talent and accomplishments, Beyer received scholarship offers to play football at Canisius College in Buffalo, St. Bonaventure in Olean, Niagara University, and Idaho University. Beyer was quite surprised to receive one offer, let alone four, given his earlier grades. *Maybe college isn't out of the picture* he thought to himself. He had a decision to make. The Buffalo School System allowed students to return and play athletics for a fifth year, provided the student passed three required academic subjects. Knowing he had several scholarships in hand to some very fine schools, Beyer nonetheless chose to go back to Seneca for a fifth year, in hopes of improving his grades, his chances for additional scholarship opportunities, and a shot at winning the Harvard Cup - the symbol of high school football supremacy in the city of Buffalo school system.

In the summer run-up to his fifth year at Seneca High, Beyer completed training at the National Aquatic School in New Jersey with honors in swimming, rowing, canoeing, and life-saving skills. He fulfilled his commitments to Scout Troop #69 by working the summer camps as a life guard and took advantage of the camps by running, hiking, swimming and conditioning his body to a level he had never before achieved.

That fifth and final year, Beyer displayed a more focused resolve toward his academic work. He attended East High School in the mornings, where algebra, geometry, physics and general science were taught – all required. Long hours were put into these courses and to the others he took in the afternoon at Seneca High. The learning skills he adopted from scouting were brought into the classroom with alacrity. Dick Beyer desired to become a student athlete – equal parts of each. He knew it was his last best hope for achieving something big.

On the field, Beyer demonstrated just how much he benefitted from the extra year – he was more mature, bigger, stronger, faster, and he played with more confidence. At guard, he excelled in every game that year.

During practice midseason, two Syracuse University alumni from Buffalo who helped recruit for the school, Charlie Stiemke, a lawyer and Fred Machemer Sr., a policeman, drove over for a look at Joe Karl, one of the better tight ends on the team. The line coach spoke with the two scouts and, having learned their intentions, told the two men "You might want to talk with Dick Beyer - he's our team's best college prospect." Beyer was unaware of the coach's comments; after evaluating Karl, the two scouts met up with Beyer, asked a few questions, watched him work out, and departed. Beyer didn't know what to make of the encounter; having spent so little time with them, he thought his chances had been dashed.

In the next to last game of Beyer's high school career, Seneca's quarterback, Don Fuerst, broke his leg in the contest. Head coach Boehmer decided to go with the athletic Beyer at quarterback for the final game of the season. In the sports section of the newspaper the following day, the headline read *'Beyer Moves to QB at Seneca.'* After five years, Dick Beyer was to have his moment in the backfield.

As fate would have it, his last football game was against Bennett High

School, the school nearest his home, the school his sisters Dorothy and Shirley attended, and the school whose football team practiced in the quarry as a young Dick Beyer watched from the curb on Manhattan Avenue. Bennett High students Dorothy and Shirley Beyer cheered for their team during the first half, and walked over to the Seneca side to cheer on their brother in the second half. Beyer made a fine showing at quarterback that cold day in 1948, but no championship was in store for Seneca High or Dick Beyer. However, his accomplishments at guard during the season were acknowledged by the football press and Beyer not only was selected to the 1948 Courier Express Newspaper All High Eleven grid team, he also was selected the *league's outstanding lineman and captain of the All High squad*. The newspaper ran a special section on the All High team, with caricatures drawn of each player; for Beyer, it portrayed him wrestling an opponent to the ground while he smiled at the camera. It was an uncanny portrait of things to come.

Buffalo Courier Express 1948 All-High Eleven captain

◄ MASKED DECISIONS

The eighteen-year old Beyer had one more decision to make before he graduated high school. Though offered scholarships from the same four colleges, he also heard from two additional schools – Penn State and Syracuse.

﹥﹥﹥

It took about fifteen minutes to drive from Manhattan Avenue to the Central Terminal in downtown Buffalo, just off the busy commercial section of Broadway on the east side of the city. Dewey Beyer was anxious to get his son there early so he wouldn't miss his train. As Beyer and his father sat waiting for the rail liner to arrive, they talked about sports, family, and the things they did together over the years. Beyer was close to his dad, always had been, but knew this hour was a turning point. Dick Beyer made a decision that was to alter the course of his life. Unsure of the ultimate outcome, he mentally steeled himself just as the call came over the speaker "All aboard for Syracuse and points east."

1 Lansky, Lewis, "Buffalo and the Great Depression, 1929-1933," in Milton Plesur, ed., *An American Historian: Essays to Honor Selig Adler* (Buffalo, NY: State University of New York at Buffalo, 1980), 205.

CHAPTER 4

CONNECTING TRAVELERS FROM Chicago and New York City with the western region of New York State, it was designed to be a masterpiece, and the Central Terminal building its most iconic structure. Constructed in the heavily populated Polish community two miles east of center city by the New York Central Railroad in 1929, the Buffalo Central Terminal rail station on Paderewski Drive consisted of a majestic concourse, a seventeen-story office tower, a five-story baggage building, two-story mail building, a power station that provided heat and electricity to the complex, a passenger car service building, an ice house, a coach shop and the train concourse designed to accommodate two hundred trains per day and thirty-two hundred passengers per hour. Buffalo was a major rail hub in the 1920s, second only to Chicago, and the Central Terminal had been projected to be the city's crown jewel – prior to the Great Depression.

The breathtaking expanse had its epicenter in the Great Hall of the grand pedestrian concourse bookended by two six-story domes accented with geometric light fixtures at their apexes, looming Roman arched leaded glass windows, balconies on the east and west sides offering dramatic internal vistas, a soaring terra cotta and Guastavino tile ceiling that arched down kissing polished white marble wall panels, and a gleaming terrazzo floor with its linear and curving designs in four shades of pink, red, and beige marble; it was cathedral-like in scale. The ticket windows featured bronze grillwork with symmetrical patterns; travelers gazed in awe as they moved about the gold trimmed shops, news stand, offices, restaurants and service facilities without the noise and crowded conditions found in most rail stations – a deliberate design gift from the architects. During the early

MASKED DECISIONS

1940s, this station was at its busiest with seemingly endless soldiers and sailors arriving and departing through its walkways. Located near the main entrance, just beneath the eastern balcony, was a promotional item for the Buffalo Museum of Science – a large taxidermic bison nicknamed Stuffy, whose tuffs of fur were plucked and taken as good luck charms by many servicemen as they made their way to the terminal departure areas for theatres of war. A plaster casting, bronze painted bison replaced Stuffy when the bison began to show wear. The refrain "meet me at the buffalo" was familiar to all who moved through this hallowed terminus.

At the center of the hall stood a fourteen foot tall, four-sided, gold clock tower encircled by a central information desk and notions counter. Glancing up at the clock upon hearing the call for departure to Syracuse and connections east, Dick Beyer motioned to his father, grabbed his suitcase, and the two made their way through the Train Concourse archway, across the enclosed bridge, down a ramp and onto the passenger boarding platform. The warmth of the late August sun rendered the boarding area uncomfortable in contrast to the coolness of the main building, but the nineteen-year old had no complaints, he was on his way to college and to find his destiny.

Boarding a train in the same concourse that dispatched the 5th Avenue Special, Interstate Express, Midnight Special, Commodore Vanderbilt, Chicago Express and trains loaded with servicemen humbled young Beyer. He felt a loose yet conscious connection to those brave members of the armed forces who went to war, and with those who left Buffalo for work and lives in other cities, that departed from this very station. He couldn't help but believe that his future, like the futures of those who preceded him, was to begin when the train whistle blew. How ironic, he thought, that this new beginning in 1949 was to be launched with the sound of a whistle, like the start of a football game, the game that provided him a full athletic scholarship to Syracuse University - and his shot at the big time.

Beyer composed himself, stepped up into the gleaming silver coach, found a place for his suit case and an empty window seat, and settled in for the more than three hour ride to central New York State. His father abruptly left the train for a few moments and headed back to the main concourse. When he returned to the coach, he handed his son a book he had just purchased for him – a dollar dictionary – and said: "Son, whatever you put into your head nobody can take away from you." Inside the front cover a small inscription written by his father, *It's your decision.* Dick Beyer thought to himself that his father, a man who never graduated from grammar school, was the smartest man he knew; he thanked his dad and hugged him – with a hug only a father and son could understand, one that conveys mutual respect and love – just as the final call for departure was announced. His father walked off the train and stood along the boarding platform, looking proud as he gave one firm wave of his right hand to his son looking back at him from the window. The whistle blew. Dick Beyer realized the game of his life was underway.

Dewey Beyer – a son's inspiration

MASKED DECISIONS

The train shuffled off toward the east, moving down the line at varying speeds, stopping at stations in Batavia, Rochester, and smaller towns in the western and Finger Lakes regions to drop off or pick up more passengers. On the ride, Beyer figured out why other forms of transportation, especially automobile, were gaining strength while the railroad was losing it…multiple stops, mechanical problems, the screeching of metal on metal, the monotonous sound of the clacking track. "I'm glad I'm not working on the railroad" he mumbled. With the changing landscape moving past his window at a steady clip, he thought how lucky he was… to have had the good workout and game successes before the two Syracuse scouts, Charlie Steimke and Fred Machemer Sr., arrived at practice that fateful day; to be going to Syracuse; to be playing at a school close enough for his family to see him. He had already come a long way on his journey…he was proud of the way he matured emotionally and the way he developed physically. He was confident without arrogance. No longer the little fat kid from Manhattan Avenue, Beyer stood five feet ten inches tall and had morphed into a solid hulk of a man. The summer had been busy and full of activities. He worked hard at Toad Hollow and Shoellkopf summer scout camp, ran the hills to get in shape, and pulled double duty as lifeguard and water front director, earning enough money to help with incidental college expenses.

As he closed his eyes, surrendering to the motion and rhythm of the train, his mind took him on an abbreviated stroll through his life; he recalled the sacrifices his parents made for him, the support of his grandparents, the love his family gave that continuously nurtured him. He remembered things large and small that people did for him that impacted his life and brought him to this place in time. Lost for the moment in a dream-like retrospective, Beyer was quickly ushered back to reality by an elderly man's articulate voice aimed in his direction. "Was that your father seeing you off? He seems an honorable gentleman. Where are you going, young man?" Beyer slowly opened and fixed his eyes on the older questioner seated across and to the left. The man, dressed in a dark suit, holding his hat and newspaper in his lap, was not someone he knew, but out of respect Beyer sat up, straightened his necktie, and replied: "Syracuse University, sir." "College!" he nodded knowingly. "Let me give you a piece of advice – find what you really enjoy doing, engage others in your work, and find a way to get paid for it" the stranger said to Beyer before lifting his newspaper and returning to his reading. Beyer sat gazing at the man for a few seconds more, absorbing the comment he just heard. He wanted to give the man a worthy reply but his mind was chewing on the advice. *I enjoy sports and helping people but how can I do both and earn money?*

The train pulled into the Syracuse station late in the afternoon. Beyer was hungry and sore but ready to get a good start on his future in this city and its university. He stepped from the train following the elderly advice-giving man who, as passengers briskly walked past him, made one more turn toward Beyer, raised his folded newspaper and waived it in an emphatic pointing manner in Beyer's direction before disappearing from sight. Beyer understood the non-verbal message and thought about the advice as he proceeded to the assigned waiting area in the station where he was to be met. In a few minutes, a tall, slender, bespectacled man approached him. "Dick Beyer?" Beyer replied: "That's me." The man said, "I'm Les Dye." Beyer replied: "Coach Dye thanks for meeting me." A former NFL player and the new Syracuse freshman football coach, Les Dye personally greeted each new player recruited to his alma mater. In the early 1940s, after graduating from Syracuse, Dye played end in the National Football League for the Washington Redskins with quarterback Slingin' Sammy Baugh. Beyer heard Dye was a respectable, stand-up guy and was quickly at ease in Dye's company. Dye and Beyer walked a short distance to the parking lot where Dye's car was located. Approaching the car, Beyer noticed someone sitting in the front passenger side with his large right arm hanging out the window. At first he felt a flush of intimidation and a sense of inferiority; this was no longer high school - this was college level where the teammates and opponents are much larger, tougher and faster. "Dick Beyer, meet your teammate Tony Vergara" said Dye, gesturing to each. Beyer greeted Vergara with "Tony, I'm Dick." Tony Vergara was another freshman recruited by Syracuse whom Dye earlier had picked up at the bus terminal; as he stepped out of the car to shake hands, Beyer noticed that Vergara was shorter and lighter than he. Beyer vowed to himself that he would not be intimidated by anyone, no matter how large – real or perceived – ever again.

Syracuse was a smaller city than Beyer's hometown but it had similarities to Buffalo –situated near a lake and snow - a lot of snow. Beyer believed his experience playing in Buffalo winters to be an advantage. Unlike his hometown with its flat terrain, Syracuse was hilly, and on an incline to the northeast of the city stood the respected university. Dye drove Beyer and his teammate past venerable 30,000 seat concrete Archbold Stadium where Beyer said to Vergara "We are gonna make names for ourselves there, Tony." Vergara looked at Beyer and responded quickly with "Yeh, we'll carve them into the bleachers next to Bambi and Roxanne!" Beyer and Vergara laughed. Listening without commenting, Dye tightly turned down the street and drove up and through the back of the campus, parking in front of 301 Euclid, known as the Frosh House, two blocks off campus. Their new home was this university dorm with its twenty rooms of football teammates. Dye helped the boys remove their bags from the trunk, led them into the dorm, introduced them to their dorm proctor, Eddie Card, a former professional baseball pitcher who was working on his master's in education, some dorm staff, a few players and, after providing them a schedule of practices, departed for home. Beyer and Vergara were offered some fruit and milk from the kitchen and given a quick tour of the building by Card before settling in.

Beyer, suitcase in hand, navigated the steps to the second floor room and introduced himself to his roommates Bill Studeman and Gene Balish. As always, he wanted to make a good first impression; he conducted himself well; the three new roommates connected. The room looked crowded and congested but sufficient to accommodate the three athletes, three beds, desks, a table, an old record player and even older 78 rpm records, assorted clothes, books and personal items, and it offered more heat and cooling abilities than his old makeshift room in the attic of his parents' home. However he did feel a bit melancholy as he unpacked and thought of his mother's freshly baked cookies cooling on the attic steps. No free cookies were on the steps to his dorm room, he had to earn meal tickets.

Syracuse football garnered national attention in the early 1900's under Hall of Fame coach Frank O'Neill, but the team's fortunes faded in the decades that followed. In the fall of 1949, 44 new players were recruited by West Virginia native and incoming head coach Floyd Burdette Schwartzwalder, known as Ben, a credentialed high school and small college coach; Schwartzwalder also was a military veteran, who during World War II earned a Silver Star, Bronze Star and Purple Heart as a paratrooper with the 82nd Airborne, landing in Normandy and behind enemy lines. To be one of the 44 new scholarship recruits to train under this new head coach was a high privilege for Beyer. With new surroundings, new coaches, new friends and a renewed attitude, Beyer had no doubt that his next four years were going to be extraordinary years during which his football career was to surge, and his future open.

Freshman football at Syracuse was not a varsity sport; a freshman schedule was followed, playing against freshman teams from schools such as Colgate, Army and neighboring Cornell. Early practices consisted of drills and conditioning; while in the best shape of his young career, Beyer was always near the back of the pack during laps around the field. He realized that his speed was not in the same gear box as his teammates. Beyer practiced hard every day, played guard on the offensive line, and learned much from his initial college football experience and even more from the teachings of coach Dye. He respected Dye, not only as coach, but also as a mentor. Dye had poor vision and wore very thick eyeglasses; after practice and a shower,

MASKED DECISIONS

Dye placed his hands on the shower walls and used them to guide his way back to his locker area; his NFL career most likely would have been extended had better lenses existed at that time. The players never heard him complain or utter any frustration. He was first class all the way. Dye taught Beyer to recognize limitations and find ways to adapt to or overcome them, and Beyer took copious mental notes. Beyer's grades during his freshman year were not Dean's List caliber, but what he learned on the field and from Dye made him mentally tougher and prepared for what lie ahead. It wasn't long into his freshman year, as Beyer contemplated his father's advice and that of the elderly man from the train that he settled on a major – physical education and a teaching career. It seemed to be the right choice as it combined the things he loved to do with enabling others – perfect symmetry. He had his future picked out and couldn't wait to get there right after college.

Beyer (far right) in leather helmet as Syracuse freshman

On the varsity side, Coach Schwartzwalder began to sculpt a profile of, and create a mission for, Syracuse football that heretofore was unseen. Coach Ben was every bit a drillmaster that his five-foot eight inch stature belied. His formula included a blend of hard charging physical contact, military-precision strategy, a relentless, punishing, ground attack, and adherence to conditioning. The 'Freshmen 44', having completed their inaugural season, soon found out that Syracuse football meant commitment and giving more – much more – than they had ever given before.

The Frosh House was often in disarray, but rarely dissolute. In it, freshmen experienced college life at its best, and at times not its best, but always to the fullest. Most everyone got along well, jawboning and playing jokes on each other. Beyer loved to roughhouse, getting into a three-point stance, and going low as he tackled the guys and held them down. He was competitive in sports and life in a by-the-rules way. Dick and three dorm mates were playing pinochle on a windy and cold October evening when someone placed a sheet of paper on the card table; Yips Yaple, a freshman football player and one of the four card players, turned over the sheet and noticed it was the answer key to an upcoming exam in freshman history. Yips stood up and shouted to those in the room: "The answers to Friday's history exam are here…anyone want to see them?" Beyer was first to invoke a "Hell No" – brought out by his strong values; cheating was never on his agenda. Then, in unison, the room resounded with an emphatic "HELL NO" and the four card players went on with their game, the answer key sat nearby, face down. The untouched answer list was still on the table when it was tossed into the trash by dorm proctor Eddie Card at 2:00 am. Card was an easy going almost taciturn proctor who tried to get the dorm athletes to play cards less, study more, keep the residence cleaner, return lobby furniture taken for their dorm rooms, all to practically no avail – the guys liked Eddie but didn't always follow his directives; nothing personal against Eddie, though he felt slighted and a little disrespected by their actions.

MASKED DECISIONS

A few days before Christmas vacation, the freshmen at Frosh House were anxious to get home; most were in unpleasant moods since papers and projects were due before they were allowed to leave. It had been snowing heavily most of the week, adding cabin fever to the list of diagnoses. Around midnight, a ruckus was heard, low and distant initially then building into a crescendo of male yells. Nearly twenty of the jocks, including Beyer, poured down the fire escapes, stairways, the roof and porches, landed in the yard wearing nothing but tee shirts, undershorts, or pajamas and hooted and howled like a pack of unleashed crazed animals. Two sides started to throw snow balls at the other, venting frustration and stress as they did. Lost in combat for a few minutes, both sides failed to recognize that several members of the fraternity across the street had joined in the battle, attacking all the freshman players. The fraternity soon realized it had made a strategic error in waging war on the half-clothed freshmen. The two dueling sides of freshmen joined forces and retaliated against the aggressors. It only took a few snowball throws and a five-to-twenty disadvantage to convince the invading fraternity to return to their dorm and turn off the lights. As the freshmen started back into the Frosh House exhausted and frozen but exhilarated by their victory, several well developed snow missiles came from out of nowhere and hit members walking up the steps. The projectiles kept coming in a steady stream, pelting most of the participants from the evening's extemporaneous fight. Puzzled and mystified, the freshmen looked around for the source; they didn't have to look far. On the landing of the fire escape stood Eddie Card, house proctor and former baseball pitcher, armed with an arsenal of firm snowballs, firing fastballs and hitting many of the half-naked freshmen causing a stinging and chilling after-effect; Card looked deliriously happy, exacting his payment due from the guys who hadn't given him much respect. As their frigid butts were drilled by precision throws, the players scampered, making beelines for any cover they could find, but heard Card gleefully shout: "I don't get mad…I get even!"

For the trip back to Buffalo for Christmas, Beyer had his repaired 1937 four-door Ford sedan that his father drove to Syracuse for him weeks earlier. Five other football players from Western New York squeezed into the small car. They had clothes in laundry bags wired to the roof and duffle bags tied to the trunk and door handles. It looked like a motorized family of gypsies. With no heater, the six were bundled up in knit hats and football jackets as they made their way through the snowy two-lane roads west. Before they reached the Finger Lakes region of New York, two squad cars with sirens and lights flashing pulled them over. As officers drew their guns, the six were instructed to get out slowly, walk to the hood of the car, and stand spread-eagle with hands on the hood. It was a frightening experience, as they were frisked and watched their bags emptied by the police officers. After all bags were inspected, one of the officers said "Sorry boys, there was a Brinks robbery in Boston and you all looked suspicious." Beyer glanced at the bags tied to the car and his passengers with knit caps pulled low over their faces and said "I guess we do."

Near the end of his first year at Syracuse, Beyer had a chance encounter and weighed an unexpected invitation to another facet of college life. On his way to class on the first floor in the Hall of Languages, Beyer was stopped in the hallway by an old friend, Bill Kliber, a former elementary school classmate, now a student at Syracuse; the two former neighbors from Manhattan Avenue hadn't seen each other in several years. Kliber said "Dick, it's been a long time since we walked to school together but it looks like you've been doing more than walking" as he eyed Beyer's developed physique. Beyer responded "I have Bill…football, scouting, swimming, running…and that was just this morning…seriously I have been busy." After the two friends spent several minutes of catch-up exchanges, Kliber said "Dick, with your background and interests, you should look into pledging with Phi Gamma Delta…have you given a fraternity any thought?" "A fraternity…Bill, I can't even spell fraternity let alone join one, what's so good about Phi Gamma Delta?" "This brotherhood is special, Dick, lots of values, the guys are great and it can make a big difference in your life." "I don't know, Bill, my lunch pail is full with classes, football, and I need to get a summer job too, but I'll consider it, OK?" The two Buffalo boys shook hands, parted ways, and headed for their respective classes. It didn't take long for Beyer to recognize the importance a strong fraternity played. Months later, the Phi Gamma Delta house welcomed a new pledge. Beyer could not foresee, nor anticipate the enormous significance, this serendipitous encounter with Bill Kliber, and resulting fraternity pledge, would have on his athletic career… and the course of his life.

Toward the latter part of June, 1950, the Beyer clan got together for a happy occasion as eldest daughter Jean married Frank Martinke in Buffalo. It was a festive event for Dewey and Celia; Jean's sisters served in the wedding party. Beyer was home from his freshman year at Syracuse and everyone inquired about his adaptation to college life away from Buffalo. Before Jean departed for her honeymoon she grabbed her brother's hand, pulled him aside, and said "You have been the best brother to the three of us…I may be the first to marry but you will always be close to my heart." They embraced as Dick whispered "Now that you're leaving, can you convince Dorothy to take the attic so I can have your room?" The two chuckled as they did when they were kids delivering Sunday papers.

The following day, the nation steeled its collective nerves upon news of an outbreak of war, this time in Korea. On college campuses around the country that fall, mandatory meetings were held, and male students were given several options in response to the nation's military needs: option #1 – sign up for Reserve Officers' Training Corps; option #2 – enlist in the National Guard; option #3 – join the Army Reserves; option #4 – enlist for active duty or await the draft. Many students who attended the meetings at SU were in ROTC or in the Guard in their home state; they knew what to expect. Others, including Dick Beyer, were confused and unsure. To wear a service uniform for his country Beyer considered a high honor, but he had trouble coming to grips with the choices and the impact of each on his prospective teaching career. He phoned his dad for counsel. "Try to make your best decisions during the most uncertain times" said his father. Beyer knew the final choice was his and his alone; he did his homework on each alternative and, in the end, chose the Army Reserves. He knew of the required weekly meetings, six year commitment, and annual two-week summer camps, but he trusted and believed that the decision was the right one that would prepare him to serve abroad when needed. He later discovered that the two-week summer training camps held at Camp Drum in upstate New York were to be supervised by head coach Ben Schwartzwalder, an Officer in the Reserves. Other football players at Syracuse chose the same option in order to learn and work under the tutelage of their head coach. As it turned out, Beyer had made a pretty wise decision, militarily and athletically.

At the start of varsity football practice his sophomore season, 1950, Beyer was moved from offensive guard to outside offensive tackle on an unbalanced line, which was to become the signature formation for Syracuse under Schwartzwalder. The coaches asserted that Beyer was better suited to the position as it gave his broad but tight body frame more room and time to maneuver. Beyer labored but adjusted to his new role on the offensive line and that September, he started his first varsity football game at home against Rutgers University. His mother, dad, and three sisters travelled by car from Buffalo to Syracuse to make their support known to everyone seated nearby in their section of Archbold Stadium. As Beyer stretched and worked out on the field before the game, he spotted his family in the stands and recalled their support as a young boy playing baseball and football; now a collegian, Beyer thought how some things changed yet some things remained the same, and he was grateful.

Syracuse, especially the offensive line, played exceptionally well that day, controlled the line of scrimmage and dominated the contest. Late in the game, with Syracuse leading 42-12, Orangemen quarterback

MASKED DECISIONS

Bernie Custis called '721 rollout cutback' – Custis was to roll to his left and then turn quickly to the right; Beyer's job, and that of his line mates, was to make the initial block a 'poor' block, so as to allow defenders to penetrate the line, then as the quarterback rolled back to the right, the linemen were to cut down the defenders. Beyer made a good cross-body block on his man, but the Rutgers' tackle fell on him and dislocated Beyer's right shoulder. He never started again that season until the next to last game against Colgate. In that game, taped up like a mummy and wearing a cast, Beyer gave all he had, but pain arose every time he hit the dirt. A bad block late in the Colgate game put Beyer on the bench. The five-win, five-loss record was a step in the right direction for Syracuse football, although Coach Ben fumed that the season should have been better. The team's offensive line drew notice from coaches and observers alike that season. Beyer was showing progress, other linemen were exceeding expectations. The center on that line was another of the 'Freshman 44' named Jim Ringo. Schwartzwalder and his wife, Reggie, were in Phillipsburg, New Jersey early in 1949 making home visits to prospective recruits, when Ringo and his best friend Joe Szombathy, recent graduates of Phillipsburg High, decided to attend college together and, after meeting the coach, signed with Schwartzwalder and Syracuse. It was a decision both never regretted. Ringo's talent was evident early. Beyer, Ringo, Szombathy, Vergara and others developed close relationships – as friends and as a team. To a man, they believed they had something special to showcase in their remaining two years at Syracuse.

Phi Gamma Delta housed thirty male fraternity brothers and was known as the 'Attic Dorm,' because all the brothers slept in the 'attic' with the windows opened year round. After a snow storm, it was not uncommon to find a fraternity brother, who had slept near a window, covered with several inches of snow. Once awakened, the brothers handed him a shovel to remove the snow from the room. Despite its icy reputation, Phi Gamma Delta was one of the more efficiently run and meticulously clean fraternity houses on campus. The house was well-organized, with elected officers and a house committee that exercised oversight of all internal activities. Dick Beyer knew, after pledging before fraternity 'father' and wrestling team captain Howie Tice, Phi Gamma Delta was the right fit for him; it had an upstanding reputation, a multi-faceted brotherhood that included several football teammates, his old neighbor Bill Kliber, and a good mission centered on service, morality and excellence, and it knew how to have fun. He was glad to be out of the Frosh House and into a new environment interacting with peers, upperclassmen and war veterans, but before he was fully accepted, there was a price he had to pay called 'Hell Week.' During this tradition, pledges were to gain access to the house only through the basement back door that led up to the game room, dining room and lodge meeting room. To be admitted upstairs, pledges were instructed to kneel at the bottom step and to recite loudly "Oh hallowed and noble brothers of Phi Gamma Delta, kneeling at the portals of this sanctuary of brotherhood and good fellowship, this unworthy pledge offers supplication for admittance to these revered halls, not as one worthy of such consideration but rather as one who seeks to follow the favor and protection of the great white star of Phi Gamma Delta." Often, during the pledge's recitation from the basement steps, upperclassmen yelled down "We can't hear you," and the pledge was forced to start over. Pledges also were instructed to wear a coat hanger around their necks with an onion affixed to it just at mouth level. When a fraternity brother asked "What do you have to say?" the pledge had to reply "I'm always wrong, I'm never right in fact I think I'll take a bite." At times, they were forced to eat the entire onion. This part of Hell Week Beyer found amusing since he enjoyed the give and take, had memorized the pledge and, unbeknownst to the brothers, loved onions. For him, Hell Week wasn't such a fiery matter.

His roommates at Phi Gamma Delta were three athletes whom Beyer referred to as 'The Italian Connection.' Enzo Marinelli played football and wrestled, Nick Caivano was a football player and an artist, and John Donati was a quarterback. Though football was the common denominator, the four shared other interests, helped one another with academic and social pursuits, and ribbed each other often. Beyer maintained his reputation as a rough-houser, pushing the limits of man-to-man battles with lower and upperclassmen, but always within the rules of warfare. The camaraderie within the fraternity exceeded Beyer's expectations. Returning to the campus from breaks, the three Italians always brought back plenty of homemade Italian food to share among the four; Beyer's contribution to these feasts was his mother's famous cookies. Just after the Christmas break of 1950, as Beyer sat back from his fill of meatballs and pasta before heading to the game room, an event was about to unfold that was to serve as prelude for a most unlikely journey.

It was a blustery, cold, winter night in January 1951. Dick Beyer, Ed 'Yips' Yaple, and several football players were deeply engrossed in a game of pinochle in the game room of the fraternity house. Howie Tice, Beyer's fraternity father and wrestling captain, had just returned from wrestling practice; he entered the room and spotted the guys playing cards. Tice walked to their table, stood near Beyer, and asked in a matter-of-fact manner "Guess who's going to be our next heavy-weight wrestler?" Knowing there were six football players and six wrestlers residing in the house, Beyer, without looking up, answered: "Probably Bill Skyinskus, he's listed as the heavyweight." Tice narrowed his gaze and responded slowly but directly to Beyer "Bill Skye, your heavyweight fraternity brother, blew out his knee tonight at practice.....YOU - are - our - new - heavyweight." Yaple, sitting next to Beyer, repeated Tice's words in a whisper. Dick Beyer, unlike his cards, was flushed. He wasn't certain he heard Tice correctly; as he sat motionless in the now hushed room, he ran it back in his head, like rewinding a tape recorder, and after several moments of disbelief replied, "You have got to be joking...I never wrestled before!" Beyer looked up and fixed his eyes squarely into Howie Tice's gaze, searching for some assurance that this little comment of his was a gag, but none was forthcoming; meanwhile the room erupted into a cacophony of yells and positive affirmations from the guys; Beyer, still transfixed, heard the sounds of 'you can do it' 'you'll be great' 'way to go, Dick' and other exclamations in the background, but was unable to move.

Enzo Marinelli, one of the Italian Connection, got up from the card table saying "Game to be continued" and proceeded to move the table out of the way, while Tice motioned to the other brothers for the furniture to be moved to the outer corners of the room. In a matter of seconds, the game room, and its wall to wall carpeting, was transformed into a makeshift wrestling arena. Beyer hesitantly got up from his chair, the last to do so, shaking his head slowly left to right, still in doubt, looking at the fraternity brothers as they grouped in a circle around him and Tice, whistling and calling, as if they all were about to engage in a street gang fight.

Over the course of several hours, Dick Beyer was literally brought to his knees. Lee Martin, Tom McDougle, Okie Harris, Tice, and Marinelli each took turns with Beyer demonstrating, drilling him, and re-demonstrating on the referee's position for an up and down wrestler and also tossing in several moves from both positions. Martin, McDougle, and Harris were lightweight wrestlers while Tice was a middleweight and Marinelli a light heavyweight; Beyer was learning maneuvers from different weight classes and from different skill sets. It was basic wrestling 101that evolved into a semi-master class. Beyer was in an unfamiliar environment, challenged to do things he had never done before as his athletic background was in team sports. By the end of the evening, Beyer was sore, his nose reddened from having been pushed around the rug and into the floor, his knees brush-burned from the carpeting, and he barely stood straight from the physical punishment. Beyer said to his brothers, "Thanks for a wonderful evening of improvisational dance and humiliation" As the guys left the game room to return to their dorm rooms, they joked with Beyer, but each had favorable things to say and encouraged him to give it all he had and make the best of this unexpected opportunity. Beyer wasn't so sure he had what was needed to be successful. It was an opportunity he wished hadn't knocked. That night, he slept uneasily and asked himself *should I bail out or go all in?* He wrestled with the idea of wrestling.

The following afternoon, Beyer, in shorts, a sweatshirt and sneakers, walked to the wrestling gym. The decision was his. He had no idea what to expect of the experience, or himself. Joe McDaniel, the Syracuse wrestling coach, met him as he entered the practice area off the locker room and said: "Beyer, I hear from Tice that you're a good roughhouse wrestler in the fraternity; I'm glad you're here; if nothing else, this will help keep you in good football condition." Beyer shrugged, replying "Coach, I never wrestled before, but I'm game to try; I need a lot of work from what I learned last night." McDaniel, not one to wait to determine a man's talent, decided to administer a quick litmus test on Beyer. Eyeing big Pete George, one of his more experienced wrestlers, McDaniel said: "Beyer, how about trying to bring down that big guy standing in the middle of the mat…he's a beginner like you." Unaware of the grappler's three years' experience, Beyer agreed; he shook hands with George, took a stance, and for the next several minutes, to the complete shock of everyone in the gym, Beyer gave George a working over that none soon forgot. Only timing and a sudden move enabled George to gain the upper hand over the raw talent of Beyer. Coach McDaniel, with eyes wide open and mouth to match, proclaimed to the team "Meet our new heavyweight" as an out-of-breath, panting, bent over Dick Beyer, hands on his hips, raised his hand to acknowledge his new teammates and, after informed of the 'rookie experience' laughed and waited for the next practice routine to be given by McDaniel. Pete George took McDaniel aside, out of hearing range of the team, and told him "Beyer wrestles like a pro – I mean rough. If he learns a few holds, he'll be unstoppable."

Most of Beyer's try-out session mirrored the previous evening's impromptu lesson, but with more intensity. He was roughed up, pushed around, held down, unable to extricate from various holds, and as he told his friends "pinned more times than a baby's diaper." But he persevered, and with it came a rise in his determination. He looked around the room and knew that he could take on all of the guys in a straight-up bull rush like in football, but he had to learn finesse and the finer points and techniques of the sport of wrestling. He had to be patient; he had to first be a student, then an athlete.

Practices, meetings, more practices; for hours in his dorm room Beyer studied the ancient Greco-Roman style, he asked questions, improvised on the mat, and each week improved over the previous one. His development was noticeable; he began to think more on his feet. He built a reservoir of techniques, probing the weaknesses of opponents, exploiting their faults, using his newly acquired skill set to maneuver around opponents with speed, agility and above all, with an edge to his wrestling and his attitude. By the time the wrestling season opened, Dick Beyer was a collegiate grappler, confident and more aggressive than ever before in his athletic career. He looked every bit the heavyweight contender with his hulking, muscular frame, close-cropped hair and gap-toothed mouth. He was ready for his debut match. It arrived. Beyer was pinned in five minutes.

Beyer accepted the loss in what would become typical Beyer bravado. In retrospect, he did go up against the heavyweight from Lehigh who had won the 1950 NCAA heavyweight wrestling championship. Beyer told everyone, "It took the champ five minutes to pin me...I gave him four minutes and fifty-nine seconds of sheer doubt." But there was no doubt in Beyer's mind; he enjoyed the independent, competitive nature of his new sport, uplifted by his decision to gut it out. He was thankful he inherited his father's stubborn German pertinacity. He learned from his coach the things he could have done to improve his chances in his first match, and eagerly looked to his next encounter. Coach McDaniel, pleased with the progress of his new heavyweight, discerned in Beyer a certain quality he had never seen before in his wrestling career.

Prior to the next scheduled match in Cortland, the Syracuse wrestlers met after practice and, to make the outcome more interesting, agreed to put up twenty-five cents each for the guy who posted the quickest pin. Beyer entered his match, only the second of his young career, posted the fastest pin and won the money, $1.75. He bought a round of Coca Cola's for his bankers on their way back to campus.

By the end of the wrestling regular season, Beyer managed to work himself into an intercollegiate post-season tournament and on to the Niagara AAU tournament in his hometown of Buffalo. The rookie heavyweight surprised many as he moved through the preliminaries to the finals of the heavyweight division where he lost to University of Buffalo wrestler Don Beitleman 5 to 3. Though Beyer was twice taken down by bear hugs, the match with the experienced Beitleman was closer than expected. Watching the final match, Ed Don George took notice of Beyer's aggressive yet unrefined abilities and made written entries of his observations into a black notebook. George, a former professional wrestling champion, was the promoter for the Buffalo territory in professional wrestling, and scouted tournaments for new talent. He had come to sign Beitleman to a professional wrestling contract after the finals, but his interest in young Beyer had been piqued by Beyer's unanticipated strong performance. George, after obtaining Beitleman's signature, walked over to Beyer who had showered and dressed, introduced himself and said "If you're interested in turning pro in a few years, watch as much wrestling as you can. You might have a shot at a career." Beyer, with a smile, looked at George and replied "I just started wrestling this year; I'm more of a football player." As George turned to make his way out of the locker room, he paused and said "If wrestling is something you enjoy, the crowd will sense it. For a beginner, I think you have what it takes in this business but no need to decide now." He departed the room leaving Beyer alone to finish packing. Beyer didn't give much thought to George's parting comment; his future was football. As he put on his Syracuse jacket and looked into the mirror on the wall, he posed for a moment, folding his arms across his chest, and with youthful optimism told himself "I do have what it takes," before tripping over his duffle bag and nearly falling to the floor as he exited.

CHAPTER 5

THE BEYER HOMESTEAD never looked so good, especially after having lived in a house full of rambunctious athletes for nearly a year. Arriving home from the wrestling tournament late that evening, Beyer, warmly welcomed by his parents and two sisters, devoured a home cooked meal, brought them up to speed on his wrestling and school activities, went upstairs to the attic and fell asleep for what to him seemed like a semester.

Mid-morning the following day, Beyer awoke, pulled a t-shirt over his head and boxers up his legs, poured some coffee, and finding his dad in the dining room, quickly dismissed any notion of a career in professional wrestling. "It was a nice gesture by Mr. George to tell me I showed promise, but a career…out of the question," he told his father as the two sat waiting for Celia's pancake breakfast. "Besides, I still have a chance to play pro football."

His sisters came down the steps and huddled around him, and he began to regale them with tales from SU. They convulsed with laughter as Beyer told them of the 'Short Legs Club' he, Tony Vergara, and Danny Reimer founded for guys with inseams under twenty-nine inches; the club's membership included Tony's brother Al, the Italian Connection's Marinelli, and the Dobrowalski brothers. Beyer explained they formed the unofficial club, comprised of football players under six feet tall, as nothing more than a lark "but some asked to join, thinking it was for people who loved seafood." Returning for a moment to the topic of wrestling, Beyer said his membership in the 'Short Legs Club' probably disqualified him from making it in that business. "At five-ten, I'm pretty average height." His father assessed his situation and said to him, "Look, you just completed your sophomore year of college, you enrolled in the Army Reserves, you played varsity football, wrestled for the first time ever, and you have at least two years to go before starting a teaching career." "You're right, dad, anything can happen between now and then;" his dad replied, "… and it usually does; you don't have to decide anything until it becomes necessary, and when you do, it's *your* decision." The pancakes were stacked high on Beyer's plate like a winner's poker chips – and gone as quickly as a bet on a bad hand.

That summer preceding his junior year, Beyer worked the weekends at scout camp, helped his father with fix-up projects, kept in shape, and landed a weekday job courtesy of Syracuse scout, now personal friend, Fred Machemer Sr., whose father worked at Kendell Roadway in Buffalo. Machemer knew Beyer was a special individual the moment he saw him work out at Seneca High years earlier, and looked out for him even when Beyer did not seek his help. He told Beyer to meet him at the union hall to obtain a union card to work labor jobs at Kendell. Beyer appreciated Machemer's guidance and filled out the paperwork for his card. On his first day of work, he manned a cement mixer, loading 80 pound bags of lime into it. After a few instructions, he got into a routine, but shortly after his shift began, three large union workers approached his work area and surrounded him without saying a word. For a moment, Beyer thought he had done something wrong; he then thought he might be in for some roughhousing, as the union probably had its own version of 'Hell Week.' He looked at each of the men, dropped his shovel, and steadied his nerves for an attack from any position. One of the burly three demanded to see his union card; Beyer obliged. All three men looked it over, looked at Beyer, handed it back, and walked away. He was never approached by anyone again for the duration of his time with Kendell. "I might have ended up in a different short legs club," he told Machemer and thanked him for getting him the job.

Two weeks before school was to be back in session, Beyer's first Army

Reserves camp commenced. He had departed Buffalo, bags packed and anxious to get on with this new experience. Camp Drum was located near Watertown, in New York State's North Country. In the early 1900s, Brigadier General Frederick Dent Grant, son of former President Ulysses S. Grant, arrived with thousands of men and found Pine Plains to be suitable for army training purposes. Later known as Pine Camp, it served as a training site for General George Patton's 4th Armored Division and, after the war, renamed for the commander of the First Army during World War II, Lieutenant General Hugh Drum. By now, Beyer was used to barracks-style living but the early wake-up calls, marches, drills, military strategy and tactics were new, and taxing. He wasn't alone. Others from Beyer's football team had also joined the Reserve unit under Officer Schwartzwalder and found the going demanding. One by-product especially for those on the football team was improved physical conditioning; Schwartzwalder put them through grinding fitness and strengthening work that prepared them for the upcoming football season.

School and football got underway and Beyer was back, uncomfortably, on the bench, not due to poor practice or play, but because Bob Fleck, the 6'2", 256 pound sophomore future All American, was moved to Beyer's offensive tackle position. Beyer wasn't happy with the move. He worked hard to become a starter; after practice, he asked to see Schwartzwalder: "Coach, Fleck is good and can start at almost any position…but my play is better than it was, you know it and the coaches know it." Schwartzwalder replied, "You have improved, Beyer, no doubt about it, and when you have improved *enough* to start with Fleck, Ringo, and the rest, I will let you know." Beyer got the message, and never said another word to the head coach during his third season.

In the fourth game against Illinois, Bob Fleck was injured and Beyer finished the game; though Syracuse lost 41 to 20, Beyer performed well, controlled his part of the line, displayed tact, physical aggressiveness, and attitude. Ringo, Fleck and others got headlines that year, but Beyer's quiet play attracted the attention of the coaches; they were convinced he was peaking at the right time. Before the season had ended, Syracuse lost to Penn State, Cornell, and Dartmouth but won five games to those four losses, scoring 180 points and giving up 147. It was marginal improvement over the previous year's 5-5 record however it was the first winning season for the Orangemen since 1942. Schwartzwalder, in language full of meaning and emotion, told the team after the last game that he expected significant progress to be made by each player during the off-season, and to arrive at the start of the 1952 campaign ready for combat; from the first practice they were going to send a message throughout the country that Syracuse football was serious football.

As the 1951 football campaign drew to a close, wrestling season began; Beyer sprang effortlessly from offensive tackle to junior heavyweight. He knew he was to wrestle in every match and was excited; for him no 'benching' in this sport. The physical development from summer Reserves camp, football workouts, and his own conditioning made Beyer a strong, bull-shouldered wrestler. He studied, learned techniques from Coach McDaniel, practiced and practiced more. His determination was incontrovertible; he not only looked and acted differently, he believed he was every bit a champion heavyweight.

Beyer won his first match, then his second. He wound up winning six matches with no defeats – a tie with Army's Al Paulekas was all that stood in his way of a perfect regular season. The University's *Daily Orange*, the *Buffalo-Courier Express*, Syracuse papers and other upstate publications printed article upon article about the young wrestling star, as he gained a solid reputation in the collegiate and amateur wrestling community, having only taken up the sport a mere fourteen months earlier, and he moved into the post-season tournament rounds with high expectations. In one *Buffalo-Courier Express* article published March 13, 1952, Beyer's wrestling coach Joe McDaniel, a former three-time NCAA and four-time AAU champion from Oklahoma A & M said of Beyer, "That heavyweight is the greatest surprise I have ever had in wrestling. He's tough, he loves the sport, he has learned faster than anyone I have ever seen…and he's good."

With success, Beyer's self-confidence in the sport rose to new altitudes; *I might be short on height but I'm tall on ability* he often described himself. He looked forward to the Eastern Intercollegiate wrestling tournament. On the basis of his regular season record, Beyer was seeded second in the heavyweight division behind the previous year's Eastern and National Intercollegiate heavyweight champion Brad Glass of Princeton. He and Glass knocked off early opponents in rapid order to reach the finals. Glass and Beyer squared off in the heavyweight final like two gladiators in the Coliseum, each fighting for high stakes. The wrestlers charged each other hard, daring the other to make one fatal move. It was a classic irresistible force against an immovable object. In what Beyer would later refer to as a "hell of a fight", Beyer lost to Glass by a narrow 4-3 verdict, in a bout that was tied until the last remaining half-minute. Glass retained his heavyweight title, Beyer was runner-up in that tournament; with unfinished business, Beyer decided to enter the Niagara AAU tournament, the same one in which he had lost to Beitleman the previous year. This time, the outcome was much different. Beyer won the Niagara AAU district heavyweight championship in Buffalo, defeating Walter Ferguson of the University of Buffalo, and qualified for the National Amateur Athletic Union wrestling championships at host site Cornell University.

In the qualifying round, Beyer, fresh from his first heavyweight championship, scored an upset by defeating Robert Maldegen, a member of the 1948 Olympic wrestling team; in the next round he pinned Ken Cox of Bethlehem, Pennsylvania in three minutes, thirty-seconds to move to the semi-final rounds. There, he faced Dick Clark, a football and wrestling star from Cornell University now an Army serviceman stationed in Utica. Beyer knew Clark well – he had worked out with Clark at Syracuse University the previous summer; Beyer had helped

Clark to get in shape. Perhaps he did too good a job – Clark beat Beyer, who ended up in third place in the National AAU tournament.

Disappointed but not disillusioned, Beyer took stock of the success from his second year in wrestling, and was garnering the kind of attention from the media that his more popular football teammates usually received. He discovered that he enjoyed talking it up to reporters and fans; he had a natural gift for speaking extemporaneously and heightening the hyperbole – a talent he was to employ more fully in years to come.

Almost overnight, Dick Beyer, a founding member of the 'Short Legs Club,' had become a big man on campus. He read about it, but he did not allow himself to act upon it, preferring to stay true to who he was, a regular guy, and not get caught up in the temporary rush of celebrity. While his notable football teammates were widely and rightfully being written about for their prominent performances, Beyer had been slowly building a body of work that, like a freight train, had ambled up the mountainside, but with full steam unleashed momentum coming down. Moreover, students and faculty recognized Beyer's achievements and told him they admired his down-to- earth approachability, and his preparations in athletics and academics. Those comments made him feel better than anything he read in the papers. His grades improved, especially in math and science, and having earned a mostly B and C report, his cumulative was sufficient to retain his scholarship.

School was out, it was June, and Beyer was ready to enjoy the summer. With his senior year upon him, he knew he had but a few weeks to get in some fun before conditioning himself as per Schwartzwalder's directive, and to parlay that conditioning into a successful final year of football and wrestling, followed by graduation and a teaching career.

Beyer set goals for himself that summer, but they placed second to the goal of helping his father at home. There were things Dewey wanted to get done during the year – wallpaper and paint the house – but his long hours at the plant left only evenings and weekends; at times, those winter weekends were occupied with wallpapering someone else's home, as Dewey picked up extra money for his family's needs. The younger Beyer was aware of how hard his dad worked; he idolized his father and wanted to do everything possible to lessen his burden. Beyer knew his dad would be tired from a full day of work, and he prepared everything in advance so that they were able to get right to the tasks after dinner each night. Beyer thought of it as a way to thank his father for all the times he played catch, and for all the things his dad did for him as a kid; for Dewey, he just enjoyed his son's company.

Beyer's two-week Army Reserves camp that summer was the equivalent of three years' preseason football practices. Schwartzwalder paced the men through military training during the day and conditioning training most of the evening. The drills were tough, exhausting, the muscles in the legs and backs of the men burned from the constant repetition and exercises to which they were exposed. To be sure, there was no discussion of football; the Reserves camp focused on military readiness and conditioning. It was the most physically challenging two weeks the football players, and most of the others, had ever experienced. Some of Beyer's teammates quietly complained after each night's workout that Schwartzwalder was a madman hell bent on getting even with the guys for last year's underachieving season. Some felt he had taken it personally and was taking it out on them. It wasn't until those players arrived at fall practice that everything fell into place; the same guys who bitched about Schwartzwalder at Camp Drum were the same guys in superb conditioning from the start, and they thanked the head coach for it.

That fall, the Syracuse Orangemen assembled for practice for the 1952 football campaign, Beyer's last as a player, the team looking sharper with more confidence and in better condition than any team in school history. During field laps, Beyer found himself not in his familiar position at the rear of the pack, but in the leading group, running like a gazelle, albeit a large barrel-chested, muscular, gap-toothed gazelle. The team was physically solid and mentally sound; it absorbed the year's playbook and strategies in record time and practiced with precise movements and timing. Beyer was in particularly good spirits and his practices demonstrated just how far he had matured. Even Schwartzwalder said to him, "Beyer, I think wrestling has helped you improve for football; you're better on your feet and your lateral movement is exceptional." Beyer replied, "Coach, you're right. All I need to do is put on that orange helmet and wear wrestling trunks on the line – I will pin every defensive opponent we face!" Beyer had the entire squad and coaching staff laughing uncontrollably. It was a fall practice season like none other – light hearted moments sprinkled among hard charging, physically demanding play and spectacular field choreography by the skilled players.

The coaches had a dilemma - where to play Beyer. He had improved to such a degree that a starting position was warranted, but where? At offensive outside right tackle was two year starter Bob Fleck; the inside tackle position was held by 6'3" junior Les McClelland; left end, Carl Karilivacz, a 6'senior starter; left guard was 6' junior Sam Johnson; Jim Ringo played center at 6'1"; Danny Reimer, 5'10", held right guard and was a two year starter, and Joe Szombathy, 6'1" was at right end. Schwartzwalder did not want to over-think the line and possibly diminish its effectiveness, and struggled to find the best possible combination for the offensive unit.

It was new line coach Rocco Pirro, a Solvay, New York native ,who came to Syracuse in the offseason having coached and played in the college and professional ranks, who informed Schwartzwalder that Beyer's blocking technique on both his left and right side was equally strong. Beyer's movement on the line was sharp and fast, prompting Pirro to practice Beyer at guard rather than tackle. Pirro put Beyer through arduous drills and practice situations in the guard position and found no weaknesses when Beyer blocked to the left or right. Pirro also noted that Ringo's nagging sore ankle limited him from pulling and going full out after snapping the ball. Beyer's skill was necessary in the running schemes the coaches wanted to deploy, and having a guard to go strong blocking left or right, was the key selling point Pirro made to Schwartzwalder. Beyer explained to coach Pirro that after injuring his right shoulder his sophomore year of football, he engaged conditioning and strengthening exercises that were beneficial to both shoulders, not just the affected one. He had learned to use both shoulders effectively, largely in wrestling practices, so that both were dominant. In a coaches meeting, Pirro said to Schwartzwalder: "Coach, Reimer can give us good offensive play, no doubt about it, but with Beyer we have speed and strength going left and right, and there is something to be said about his ability to help Ringo – he has it all where we need it… at the guard position." The head coach gave thought to the suggestion. Once Schwartzwalder was convinced he had his lineup to execute the detailed offensive schemes, and help cover for Ringo's sore ankle, he announced it to the team. Beyer was to start at right guard, replacing Dan Reimer, whose skills were transferable to defense as well as for special and substitute situations on the offensive side. Captains were to be selected for each game. The team was ready. The season was on.

SYRACUSE UNIVERSITY VARSITY SQUAD, left to right: Front Row—Don Ronan, Nick Rahal, Joe Perry, Pete Lessard, Dick Beyer, Bill Skyinskus, Joe Szombathy, Ed Yople, Carl Karilivacs, Avatus Stone, Mark Hoffman. Second Row—Joe Orzehowski, Paul Slick, Mike Skop, Neil Brenneman, Bob Leberman, Sam Johnson, Jim George, Bill Wetzel, Les McClelland, Herb Steigler, Jim Ringo, Ed Dobrowolski, Dan Reimer. Third Row—Bill Moll, Jack Westcott, Ed Smith, Joe Dominik, Bob Fleck, Dan Althouse, Pat Stark, Al Vergara, Bruce Yancey, Ray Perkins, Mickey Rich, Art Troilo. Top Row—Bill Claus, Bob Dobrowolski, Tony Vergara, Dino Hadjis, Paul Kernaklian, Bill Sprague, Joe Coppadona, Paul Reimer, Sam Alexander, Bob Trees, Mike Jaso, Nick Voelger.

First Syracuse squad to earn a bowl berth

◄ MASKED DECISIONS

The Syracuse Orangemen opened their 1952 schedule with a home night game at Archbold Stadium against Bolling Field Air Base. Bolling was loaded with All American and All Conference players who had transferred from other colleges prior to enlisting in the Guard or Reserves before the Korean Conflict spread. At quarterback was Al Dorow from Michigan State, Dorne Dibble from the Big 10 was a receiver, Maryland's Elmer Wingate played defensive end and Joe Dudeck played defensive nose guard. On the first offensive play for Syracuse, Dudeck lined up directly in front of Beyer, and on the snap, drove into Beyer, hitting him in the face harder than Beyer had ever been hit before. The newer, rubber-plastic helmets provided more protection over the head than the old leather helmets, but just like the old ones, they did not protect the face. The hit knocked Beyer back and drew blood from his nose and mouth. Beyer was angry, at himself. He forgot what he had learned on film about Dudeck; the blow to the head stirred his recollections and he wanted retribution. In the huddle, Beyer asked quarterback Pat Stark to call '238, 2 series, 3 back through the 8 hole' a run play designed for the fullback. Beyer told Ringo and McClelland he had the guy over him. The play was called; Beyer hit Dudeck like a hurricane, blowing him back 10 yards from the line of scrimmage. As Dudeck lay on the ground with Beyer next to him, he turned slowly and said "That's the way to hit, Dick." For the rest of the game, Beyer's play against Bolling Field Air Base was everything the coaches wanted from a strong pulling guard; he worked seamlessly with Ringo who always played intelligently, blocking Ringo's defender while Ringo blocked down on the tackle or linebacker. The offensive line worked in sync like a precision military unit. It was a close contest but Syracuse dropped its opener 13 to 12.

They atoned for the loss the following week at home with a win against Boston University 34 to 21, and again on the road with a 27-0 drubbing of Temple, as Beyer continued to excel on the offensive line. Cornell was next. The Orangemen dominated the contest and Beyer had a memorable day, throwing a key block that paved the way for one of their halfbacks to take off on a long run for a touchdown; Syracuse won 26 to 6. As good as they were that week, the following week they were just awful against eventual national champion Michigan State. The game, played in East Lansing, Michigan, was radio broadcasted back to Buffalo; Beyer's family tuned in. The play of the Orangemen was terrible and the team was losing badly. As interest waned and family members meandered to different parts of the house, someone in the Beyer household turned off the radio. A half-hour later, the telephone rang; Beyer's sister, Shirley, picked up – the voice on the other end said something about her brother scoring a touchdown; Shirley dropped the telephone and yelled at the top of her lungs "Dick scored a touchdown!" Everyone ran back into the parlor to press their ears next to the speakers. They later learned that on a play called '2-20 roll out pass', quarterback Pat Stark dropped back to throw, but was hit as he released; the ball popped in the air, remained seemingly suspended for a time, before it floated back down, and was caught by Beyer behind the line of scrimmage. While the newspapers reported that Beyer 'lumbered 35 yards for the score', Beyer said he "sprinted to the goal line for Syracuse's only touchdown of the game." Syracuse lost 48 to 7. Their record stood at 3 wins and 2 losses with 4 games remaining on the schedule, and in Beyer's collegiate career.

Schwartzwalder was not in a pleasant mood on the trip back to Syracuse. He was beside himself. The team he and his coaches had assembled was better than their current record indicated, and he was not about to let the season get away. Before practice, he told them a few stories from his war experiences, not about himself, but about his buddies and fellow paratroopers, men who sacrificed for others and for a common goal. The inspirational stories impressed the young football players, many of whom were in the Reserves or Guard. The team met privately, without coaches, and each player stood up and pledged stronger effort to get them to a better place. When they arrived on the practice field, Schwartzwalder put them through hell.

In billiards terms, Syracuse ran the table. The Orangemen beat Holy Cross, 20 to 19, in the last thirty seconds of the game with a Pat Stark to Don Ronan touchdown pass; the win removed Holy Cross from the ranks of the unbeaten. Next, they took on a tough Penn State team. During the tight struggle, several Syracuse players were injured, including backs Bob Leberman and Mark Hoffman. Midway through the close contest, Syracuse blocked a punt, and took over near midfield. Before running onto the field with a depleted offensive squad, quarterback Pat Stark looked at Schwartzwalder and said, "Coach, what play do you want to run?" Schwartzwalder responded "Just sneak it." Stark ran out into the huddle and called a quarterback sneak; for a moment, the offensive players looked at each other, then they smiled; they knew exactly what to do next; they were ready to surprise the enemy. Stark barked out the signals, the offensive line surged ahead. Beyer and his linemates exploded on their targets as if practicing on the blocking sleds. The Penn State defensive line was rocked off the line of scrimmage, a gaping hole created in the defense. Ringo pushed ahead with such force that all Stark had to do was run behind him – and run he did, 50 yards for a Syracuse touchdown. The Orangemen won 25 to 7. National publications began to pick up on the story of Syracuse as they prepared to play the final home game of their season. With his family in Archbold Stadium, Beyer's team beat Colgate 20 -14, to set up a tug of war the following week against Fordham with the chance to win the eastern college championship Lambert Trophy on the line.

The final regular season game in the college careers of Jim Ringo, Joe Szombathy, Tony Vergara, Dick Beyer and others was played on the road against Fordham University. To a man, the team was confident, and believed no team, no way, was going to impede their journey. Syracuse beat Fordham; their record stood at 7 wins, 2 losses.

There was no word from the NCAA for several days; the wait was excruciatingly painful and agonizingly cruel for Syracuse players and fans. When notice came, it was official; Syracuse University had been awarded the Lambert trophy for eastern college supremacy, the first in school history, and had earned their first ever bowl berth - the Orange Bowl in Florida on New Year's Day- against the Alabama Crimson Tide.

The announcement spread like wild fire through the campus and down through the city; students and fans were unable to contain their joy and themselves; spontaneous parades formed on campus, and before long joined and extended into downtown Syracuse, growing so dense they required police escort. It was the biggest thing in some time to hit the central New York region, and everyone wanted to be in on the history and celebration. Everyone, except Schwartzwalder; he called a team meeting as the festivities were still in progress. The players assembled; Beyer took a seat in the front row, agreeing with Ringo that their coach probably wanted to set objectives for practices and travel arrangements to Florida, the detail man never let up. The meeting left Beyer in disbelief. Coach Schwartzwalder announced that Dick Beyer had been selected co-captain of the Syracuse football team, and shared the captaincy with Joe Szombathy. Both stood up and faced the team and coaches for well-deserved recognition. As the applause died down, Beyer began to return to his chair but was stopped by his head coach. "Wait a minute Beyer, there is one more thing I have to say," Schwartzwalder barked with a stern look. Beyer cringed. Dick Beyer was also acknowledged as the 'most improved player' on the Syracuse squad. Beyer was in shock; he heard the cheers from teammates and watched his hand shake the hand of his head coach, but it all seemed slow-motion surreal. Co-captain and most improved player. Nothing will ever top this moment in his athletic career, he told his family and friends.

The Syracuse Orangemen football team had only five weeks to prepare for its first ever post- season appearance, fittingly, in the Orange Bowl. Their opponent, the Alabama Crimson Tide, was coming off a stellar season of 10 wins and 2 losses, and was heavily favored. Syracuse did not have much of a scouting report on Alabama, and only half of the expected game films were delivered. Giving no excuses, the Syracuse squad entered preparations. Beyer knew it was to be his last game in a Syracuse uniform and possibly his last as a football player. As a kid he had dreamed of playing a football game on Thanksgiving Day like the turkey day games he had seen at All High Stadium or heard on the radio; as he grew older he desperately wanted to play professionally. Neither had come to pass, so Beyer approached the New Year's game as if it were a professional game on Thanksgiving. The co-captain and his team charged out onto the field.

The 1953 Orange Bowl Game in Miami was televised, for the first time to a nationwide audience, by the CBS network. The contest was broadcast in black and white, but in Syracuse, all they saw was black and blue. A 15 yard, Pat Stark to Joe Szombathy touchdown pass, brought the Orangemen to within one point of Alabama in the first quarter, but the extra point attempt failed. That missed extra point played on the minds of the Syracuse players for the balance of the contest. Midway through the second quarter, Beyer sprained his ankle and sat on the bench for the rest of the game; it was the first time all season Beyer was out of the offensive lineup. He watched helplessly from the sidelines. As the sellout crowd of 66,000 looked on, the Crimson Tide, with a split T and a Notre Dame attack, rose to 586 yards of total offense on big plays including a 50 yard touchdown pass to Corky Tharp from Clell Hobson, an 80 yard punt return by Cecil Ingram, and a 60 yard interception return by Buster Hill. Bobby Luna and Tommy Lewis each scored a pair of touchdowns and Alabama's backup quarterback, Bart Starr, threw a 22 yard strike to Joe Cummings. With a defense that played better than anticipated, the Crimson Tide won easily 61-6. The final score set a record for most points in the Classic with ten other records equaled or felled.

The first bowl appearance by a Syracuse football team ended, dismally. There were no excuses, no places to hide, no one to blame but themselves. Humbled, the football team returned to Syracuse on January 2, 1953 and held a meeting shortly after their arrival to assess their performance and put it into perspective. It was Beyer's last team meeting as co-captain, and he wasn't going to leave until he had his say. Beyer was direct; he told the underclassmen not to tolerate defeat but learn from the exposure and make better things happen as a result of it. As Beyer continued with his commentary, Coach Ben Schwartzwalder sat silently and listened from the corner of the room. The head coach was pleasantly surprised, not only by the passion with which Beyer delivered his message, but by his accurate and detailed assessments and observations of the team's play. He sounded more like a seasoned coach than a three-year varsity player. Schwartzwalder would not soon forget.

Beyer's senior year of wrestling was to begin on January 4 but his ankle was taped, still swollen and painful from the sprain he sustained in the Orange Bowl debacle. Hardly able to walk, he asked several players, who had incurred a similar injury, for advice on a quick cure. Several told him Novocain injections helped to relieve pain before games. On the morning of his first scheduled wrestling match, Beyer limped to the campus hospital, was treated with Novocain and a basket tape procedure that covered his ankle all the way to the calf of his leg, and returned to his room to rest it up. Some mail had arrived while he had attended to his injury; Beyer opened the two letters and sat back in stunned amazement. The letters, both from professional football organizations, expressed interest in his services. Mixed emotions churned as he reflected on his boyhood goal of playing professional football, but that goal seemed implausible and unrealistic in recent years. His superior guard play as a senior opened the eyes of many and, as it were, at least two professional teams. The euphoria he thought he would feel when such a day arrived was somehow lacking; it felt as though a former girlfriend had returned to him after a fling with other guys. As he searched for answers and direction, it became clear; wrestling had stolen his heart from his first crush. During the last three years, his love of football remained steady, but his passion for wrestling intensified. Still, he was happy to be invited by two teams to try-out for a position in professional football, but for now he needed to prepare for his evening's match.

The best word to describe Beyer's senior year of wrestling was articulated by his wrestling coach "stellar." Several weeks into his final undergraduate season, Beyer stood undefeated and untied. One of those matches nearly got out of control, and provided Beyer with a mantra he used for the rest of the season. During his match with Penn State heavyweight Hud Samson, as the two were locked up in the center of the mat, Beyer heard Samson's coach tell him, "Take him down, take him down, he's a bum." Beyer was incensed by the remarks; the more he heard the coach call him a 'bum' the more he controlled the match. Beyer won. As the referee held up Beyer's hand declaring him the winner, Beyer looked over to the opposing coach and mouthed, "This bum will never go down."

In late February after wrestling practice, Beyer was summoned to the coaches' offices. No reason given. Beyer, curious and slightly nervous, hadn't missed any practices, was doing well academically and nothing seemed askew. To be told to go to those offices was never a very good thing. He entered the office suite and saw Coach McDaniel, head football coach Schwartzwalder, several assistant coaches, and a few athletic department employees standing in the room. Beyer was asked to take a seat; his pulse began to race; this was not a typical athletic department meeting. The coaches sat down, but Schwartzwalder remained standing. He looked around the room, giving time to allow quiet to descend, and let his eyes land on Beyer. "Dick, we called you here today to discuss something very important. Stand up here with me." Dutifully and respectfully, Beyer arose and stood as instructed. He had no idea what was about to unfold. Schwartzwalder said "Dick, the university coaches in a vote have chosen you athlete of the year at Syracuse University, congratulations." The room erupted into applause. After an initial reaction of relief and a deep exhale, his worried look was replaced by joy and smiles. He never saw this coming, not even a clue he was under consideration for such an honor.

The surprise nearly knocked him over and for several minutes he was unable to speak, let alone comprehend the enormity of the recognition. Among all the excellent athletes at Syracuse University, in all the sports in which the school participated that year, Dick Beyer rose above the many to be the one; he captured not only the attention of the athletic department, but the distinguished award it bestowed. In a few weeks, he and Schwartzwalder were to board a train for New York City to attend a dinner, in Beyer's honor, given by the Syracuse Alumni Club of New York.

That evening, alone in his room in Phi Gamma Delta house, Beyer cried. Not tears of sadness, but of validation. Football team co-captain and most improved player, now this. All those years of work – as a young boy to high school to college – were worth this one defining moment. His family was overjoyed for him; his friends could not be happier. Yet as he sat silently in his catharsis, he allowed himself to believe that, through this honor, he was 'paying back' his father, and Fred Machemer, for their steadfast belief in his ability and potential.

Beyer never lost a regular season match during that year – a perfect record as a senior.

When he arrived at the National NCAA wrestling tournament in March, he was surprised to find the name of Penn State's Hud Samson, whose coach Beyer had 'bummed out', not on the heavyweight list, but in the 191 pound division. He had been looking forward to his rematch with Samson, but it was not to be, and he was interested to learn why Samson had chosen to move to the 191 pound class. It finally dawned on him; it was a smart move; Samson wrestled well as a heavyweight, and with that experience probably believed he'd do even better in a lower weight class. Beyer had never considered that strategic move - not that he had anything against it –he just never gave it much thought as he faced off against others in his class during the regular season. Tournament rounds, however, were very different, he learned, and Beyer usually found himself matched up against guys much bigger than he; this tournament proved to be no exception. His first round match was with big Ed Husmann from Nebraska. Beyer lost 6 to 5. At the end of the meet, Samson had emerged national champion in the 191 pound division.

Beyer mentally kicked himself all the way home. Had he done exactly what Samson had and dropped to a lower division, he very well might have won it all. Instead, an opponent with more weight and size overpowered him; that was always the risk in the heavyweight class. For Beyer, a lesson learned the hard way, but one he was not to forget. Beyer was one implacable grappler, unable to draw solace from his perfect regular season, and his college wrestling career had come to a sudden imperfect conclusion.

The train to New York City seemed to fly down the tracks, rather than chug the six hours that typically elapsed from Syracuse to Grand Central Terminal. Beyer marveled at how jovial and relaxed Coach Schwartzwalder appeared during the trip; the coach incessantly diagrammed football strategy with X's and O's, followed by an in depth lecture to Beyer, peppered by language that only Schwartzwalder could make sound biblical. Beyer actually believed his coach enjoyed the excursion more than he, and let him take the conversation wherever he wanted. Before their arrival in Manhattan, Schwartzwalder put down his pad, and told Beyer he was proud of the way he handled himself the last few years and reiterated his belief that wrestling made him a better football player. "The old coach thinks that was a good decision" he told his young graduating senior; Schwartzwalder often liked to refer to himself in the third person. The coach spoke at length about the 'athlete of the year' award, telling Beyer only one athlete is chosen each year at the school and "You should be very proud of your accomplishments." Schwartzwalder turned toward the train window as the afternoon sun bathed the interior of the car, and let his comments ramble about someday riding a train to New York City… a great honor for the school… and other disconnected phrases. Beyer was unable to decipher his coach's musings, and before he had a chance to ask for clarification, the train had stopped, and it was time to get to the restaurant.

Of the April 7th event and Beyer's recognition, the Syracuse *Daily Orange* wrote - 'Dick Beyer, a guy with an unbeatable will to win, is Syracuse's Athlete of the year of the 1952-53 athletic campaign. Beyer was chosen by a group composed of all Syracuse university coaches. The honor is annually bestowed on the leading hill athlete. Among the earlier men who have won are football star Bernie Custis, boxers Marty Crandall and George Kartalian, and runner Dick Church." The article progressed to note Beyer's football and wrestling achievements and commented that it was fitting that Beyer receive the award " for if the coaches had to choose another athlete on the hill who displayed more fight, enthusiasm, and eagerness to learn, it would be very hard to overlook the Buffalo N.Y. senior.'

Syracuse University 1952-53 Athlete of the Year

MASKED DECISIONS

A humbled and appreciative Dick Beyer stood at the dais of Manhattan's Brass Rail restaurant in front of the Syracuse Alumni Club of New York, thanked his coaches, parents, family and teammates for their support, and told those in attendance "For a guy who struggled to get good grades but who loved sports all his life, I guess I have come far by some standards. But this I say, you've only heard the beginning of Dick Beyer."

On the return trip to Syracuse, Beyer sensed a different tone in Schwartzwalder's discourse, as if treated no longer like a student, but a friend. The interchange was frank, more conversational and personal; Beyer liked it. However, never one to stop thinking football, the coach resumed his whistle-stop composition in modern football strategy, but somewhere between Albany and Binghamton, Schwartzwalder ceased football ideology, adjusted his glasses, and asked Beyer when he thought he'd land a teaching job. Beyer said "Well, first I'm going back to Buffalo and think about my options of playing pro football." The look on Schwartzwalder's face, a look most players had seen all too often, the one with his glasses near the end of his nose as he peered over them, convinced Beyer that, in reality, neither one truly believed those options would prove fruitful. Schwartzwalder motioned out the window to the railroad crossroads and told Beyer the crossroads represented his young life at that point in time, and said the choice needed to be based on the available information and made with his head, not his heart. It was advice he had heard before from others whom he also admired. Then the coach said something to Beyer that changed the outcome of the game; he asked Beyer to consider attending graduate school at Syracuse to obtain his master's degree to improve his teaching opportunities down the line. As Beyer began contemplating the suggestion, the coach offered something more immediate; "How about joining my coaching staff?" In addition to his improved play and understanding of Schwartzwalder's complex schemes, Beyer's pep talk with the underclassmen after the Orange Bowl impressed his coach who, when the need for a freshman team coach was identified, thought of his co-captain. The offer got even sweeter – if Beyer were to serve as house proctor to incoming freshmen, the costs for graduate school tuition, room and board would be waived.

In June of 1953, Dick Beyer graduated Syracuse University with a bachelor's degree in physical education and a minor in mathematics. He was one of eight men selected to Phi Kappa Alpha, the senior men's honorary society.

CHAPTER 6

WAS I DREAMING? Did I accomplish all those things? The questions were rhetorical, the reality indisputable, as Dick Beyer reflected back on achievements in his studies, football and wrestling, the Lambert championship, team co-captain, the Orange Bowl, 'athlete of the year', honorary society and graduation from Syracuse University. Twenty percent of his life had been spent in Syracuse; he had much to show for it, and potentially more to add after the out-of-the-blue offer from Ben Schwartzwalder. He pondered on his walk back to Phi Gamma Delta house after seeing off several of his friends headed for home, how he managed to get into so many right places at the right times; perhaps it was luck, or luck in making choices, but whatever it was he prayed for it to continue.

With his stuff loaded into every square inch of the back seat and trunk of his father's car, and right before he and his dad hit the road for Buffalo, Beyer ran to see Doctor Shaw, the department head of physical education, to determine the requirements for completing his master's degree over two semesters; not knowing whether Schwartzwalder's offer extended beyond the first year, Beyer hedged his bet so that the post-graduate degree was in hand should coaching the freshman team be only for a one year term. The work load, from what Doc Shaw showed him, looked to be heavy, and given his coaching and proctor responsibilities with incoming freshmen, time would be an issue.

The summer of 1953 started off well. Beyer attended the wedding of his sister Dorothy to Roger Stoessel; what made it extra special was that his mother was able to attend, despite a series of strokes she experienced in recent years. Her presence made for a wonderful family celebration. Days later, Beyer received a letter from Syracuse University informing him of his selection as house proctor to twenty-four incoming freshmen football players to be housed on campus, not the Frosh House. With this confirmation, Beyer gave consideration to the kind of living environment he would establish for the freshmen, but he already knew the first two rules he'd postulate – respect and responsibility for their own actions. If scouting and the Army Reserves taught him anything, it was respect for the chain of command, to always be prepared, and to conduct oneself in a straight-forward manner; they would be the cornerstones for those under his watch.

In Buffalo, summers were the best part of the year. The flat terrain allowed the breezes from the west, cooled by the waters of Lake Erie, to flow uninterruptedly across the Niagara Frontier, often gently, sometimes boldly, but always as a refreshing zephyr. Beyer never got enough of the outdoors in summer. As a kid, every day was an out-the-door to play sports day, until the street lamps came on. Even now, as a new college graduate, he appreciated the moderate summer conditions, especially since he rejoined Kendell Roadway that summer, spreading hot asphalt on Buffalo's roads. Those westerly breezes felt like frosty kisses from a snow angel.

As was his summer custom after work and helping at home, Dick Beyer drove down to Point Breeze on Old Lake Shore Road, near Angola, south of Buffalo, and to Dim's hot dog stand. Angelo Dominico, or Dim as he was known to the regulars, and his wife Eleanor, owned the popular little eatery that had become a destination for people going to the nearby beaches, or those travelling up to Niagara Falls or over to Crystal Beach amusement park in Fort Erie, Canada. Dim's hot dog stand was a magnet for families and for singles looking to be not so single, if only for a brief time. Its location near the lake was ideal; even when the wind shifted and the pungent odor of sulfur, generated from the Bethlehem Steel Plant in Lackawanna, wafted over the stand, it was just another sign of summer to the faithful. The stand usually was crowded when Beyer arrived in the evening. One night in mid-June, Beyer was talking with some friends at the stand and noticed Dim and his wife moving faster than usual, taking orders and hurriedly preparing the sandwiches and sides. Beyer said, "Looks like you need some help, Dim." The owner raised his head beaded with perspiration and shot back "You want to work?" Beyer took up the challenge by leaping over the counter simultaneously yelling "Where do I start?"

Beyer was given a crash course by Dim in short-order cooking, beverage and counter service. In a matter of minutes, Beyer was employed, cooking, pouring, serving, waiting, cleaning, and he found himself enjoying every minute of it. He took to the hard work and weekend schedule – Friday nights from 9:00 pm to 4:00 am; Saturday nights from 6:00 pm to 4:00 am, Sundays from noon till 6:00 pm. It was very different from the asphalt job he had weekdays with Kendell, but the interaction with the paying public was energizing, and the glances from the girls hanging out at the stand didn't hurt either.

Beyer learned the 'sizzle' at Dim's

MASKED DECISIONS

On one particularly balmy July evening, a young woman named Wilma Thomson walked up to the counter. She had come to Dim's with some friends, having been to the beach earlier in the day. It had been quite some time since Dick first met Wilma; she lived in the same neighborhood as he, on Thatcher Street, just off Kensington Avenue, but their paths rarely crossed during their formative years. He knew of her through school talk and from neighborhood crowds, and had seen her around town before, but not this way. Wilma had developed into an attractive brunette, employed as a supervising draftsman, managing several male employees, designing power lines for the Niagara Mohawk Power Corporation. Seeing her was electric for Beyer, and prompted him to make the first move; he offered to buy Wilma a beer at Sneekie Pete's, a bar across the street from Dim's. She said to him, "Do you buy every girl a drink?" "Only the pretty ones" he answered. Wilma looked at him and with a demure smile said, "Do I fall into that category?" to which he replied "You're the only one in that category." As Beyer worked the food stand, the two struck up a dialogue, talking about growing up in Buffalo, school, sports, mutual friends, anything and everything… the evening flew by. After cleaning up and helping close the stand, Dick headed over to Sneekie Pete's to meet Wilma for a beer. When he arrived, he noticed she was sitting with eight of her friends, so he bought a tray of ten beers for a dollar and personally delivered them to the table. Her friends were impressed by his thoughtfulness, Wilma by his pursuit. At the end of the night, Dick had her home and work telephone numbers – Wilma had a smile on her face.

Beyer dated Wilma Thomson, whom he playfully called Willy, several times during that summer and found himself liking her very much, but unsure she felt the same. By the end of the summer, it was probably best he didn't know, since he needed to shove off to Army Reserves camp and on to Syracuse for his initial year of coaching and graduate school.

The weather at Camp Drum that year was brutally hot. The drills and conditioning seemed more mentally challenging than before. Beyer held the perspective that, if he could get through camp, he could handle twenty-four freshmen. Each night, after all military business was completed, Beyer looked forward to spending a few minutes alone with Ben Schwartzwalder; unlike previous years, Schwartzwalder set aside time late in the evening to discuss football strategy with his new freshmen line coach. Those nights sitting with the head coach, learning football from the inside, getting to know the man, enabled Beyer to forge a different relationship with Coach Ben, not quite father- son or peer to peer but more like an apprentice learning the craft from the master. By the time camp concluded, Beyer was prepared to meet his new challenges head on, this time without a helmet.

Twenty-four freshmen football players arrived for fall practice to showcase their talents, looking to become Syracuse seniors of 1957, but that was four years away and many unknowns in between. For some, freshman football would be their last. As they sipped their first taste of college life, they discovered the 'night and day' comparison of collegiate athletics to high school sports. Some were not able to effectively compete, while others showed strong potential and promise. One such young man – one of the few black players on the freshman team – came from Manhasset High School on Long Island with multiple credentials and a headstrong attitude to match. His name was Jim Brown. A thirteen- letter star in football, basketball, baseball, lacrosse and track, Brown had chosen Syracuse primarily at the behest of a benefactor, who had played lacrosse at the college years earlier. Despite scholarship offers from numerous other schools, Brown selected Syracuse, with expenses to be paid by a group of Long Island businessmen, who were aware of Brown's limited means but enormous potential. Beyer became aware of Brown's strong running ability during coaches meetings, however Beyer's main focus was the offensive line and to prepare them to block for any halfback or fullback.

Football practices were conducted in the same manner as when Beyer played. Though this was freshman football, it was still Syracuse football, just as intense as varsity with identical expectations – toughness, discipline, and winning. Beyer felt comfortable as the rookie assistant coach. Working under coach and former freshman mentor, Les Dye, Beyer had the experience and knowledge needed to help mold the offensive line into a cohesive fighting unit. More importantly, he had the interactional skills with the younger players that were important to communicating vital information from the coaches' level and for sustaining morale.

From the opening whistle, he put in hours upon hours with the offensive line, both on the field and in the dorm, driving them to strive for positive improvements and results in their play, and in their relationships with the coaches, and each other.

Rumors about Brown swirled around the team; he became known not only for his ability but for his irritability. Without question the fastest player on the freshman team, Brown, nonetheless, sat out most of the season for various reasons. During one practice, Brown was sullen and brooding, showing no interest in exercises and warm-ups. It was Beyer who headed up the exercise regimen that day and, having observed Brown and several others not participating, said "If you can't or won't do them, then you all might as well go home." When head coach Dye agreed with and affirmed Beyer's decision, Brown walked off the field, returning not to his room but to Long Island. He told his benefactor and others he was fed up with the difficult atmosphere at the college, and confided to some that he had few friends on campus and felt distanced from teammates and coaches. Beyer was uneasy with the episode. For him, there was no hidden motivation behind his actions, racial or otherwise, he just wanted to get the players' attention, nor did he intend to deprive the team of any asset, yet he believed he was tested as a rookie coach and needed to take a stand for his respectability and for the betterment of the team's morale. Brown returned to the team several days later, after it was determined that his anger and resentment were caused by unrelated incidents; it wouldn't be the last time Brown threatened to quit. The coaching staff was becoming aggravated by Brown's demeanor and sour attitude. They all recognized his unbridled ability, but without self-discipline, he was not going to rise to the level required by head coach Schwartzwalder. The coaches wanted to help Brown prepare for a much harder time to come.

As a graduate student, Beyer's school experience changed; he had learned how to learn. He picked up quickly on his graduate curriculum and earned excellent marks. The load was, indeed, heavy, as Doc Shaw had warned, but Beyer was up for the challenge. His study habits, like his values, guided him well, and he was convinced he would complete his master's degree in the one year time frame he had set while balancing his *in loco parentis* responsibilities with the freshmen in the dorm.

The dorm was actually a Quonset hut that housed the twenty-four student athletes and proctor Beyer. It was a one-floor, lightweight structure, built from corrugated galvanized iron, with a semicircular cross section. These hut structures had been used in the military for temporary, mobile housing, and gained popularity on some college campuses for the same use after the war, when the government began selling them off. Beyer often had wondered why Brown was not in the hut with the other freshman players, but it was none of his concern, though later he found out that Brown had earned a different scholarship, funded by the alumni on Long Island, that allowed him to stay at Sky Top, a more comfortable freshman living center. In Beyer's mind, whatever Brown earned he was entitled to and hoped the troubled young man, who ran more powerfully than anyone he had ever seen, would eventually earn a spot on the varsity roster. Beyer served as proctor, father, mother, uncle, brother, and occasionally as therapist to his student athletes. Perhaps his age, but more likely his personality, made students feel at ease and able to communicate with him on almost anything. Beyer was only a few years removed from his own freshman year, and recalled what it was like and the difficulties typically encountered. He had empathy for his charges, to a point; he also held them accountable and kept a close eye on activities within his jurisdiction. He ran a tight hut. The players respected and appreciated him.

Early January, 1954, after returning to the campus from Christmas break, Dick Beyer went to see Joe McDaniel to ask for his assessment of the wrestling team's prospects for the new season. Not wanting to lose touch with McDaniel, a coach he highly respected, Beyer also wanted to stay close to the sport he had come to love. To his utter amazement, McDaniel said, "Dick, you developed into a great technical wrestler; since the football season is over, would you consider helping out with the wrestling team?" Beyer didn't need to think about it. "When do I start?" he quickly replied. The two shook hands. Over the next few months, Beyer worked closely with McDaniel and the wrestlers; he assessed their skill level, observed their technique, and provided remedial training. He was in his element. He also found he missed the thrill of head to head competition that only the sport of wrestling provided; he acknowledged his addiction to McDaniel as both recognized what Beyer needed to do next – enter the district AAU meet.

Beyer had read about the national tournament, scheduled for the spring in San Diego, California. Winners in each weight class of that tournament were guaranteed a trip to Japan for a wrestling exhibition. Beyer wanted in; he had an unquenched thirst to experience the country that, as a kid during the war, had frightened him, and which he despised. To get there, he first needed to win the district meet in Buffalo. One thing was going to be different this time around – Beyer had trimmed down sufficiently to wrestle in the 191 pound division rather than as heavyweight.

Despite his relative success in previous years, the Niagara AAU district championships, for Beyer, were considered dubious. College wrestlers had grappled in NCAA sanctioned tournaments during the season and knew each other's relative strengths and weaknesses through experience. For amateurs out of college, little was known about a collegiate opponent; they had to rely on the advice of others, who had seen the wrestler, or go into the match blindly. Beyer was one year removed from the college wrestling scene and not as familiar with opponents, but with McDaniel's guidance, he prepared well for his graduate student debut in a lower weight class.

Frigid weather gripped the Buffalo region that March, but the grad student was on fire. Since he had won this tournament in the heavyweight division, he relied on his experience and technical know-how to help him through the preliminary rounds. For this meet, he found he had another source of strength – his mother. Celia Beyer had never before seen her son wrestle, but her stable health and the tournament's location made it easier to attend; she was accompanied by her husband who sat next to her and explained the art and the science of their son's sport.

Beyer was at his best in the early rounds. Age of the opponents made no difference as the tournament was based on weight class, and in an early match, he locked up with a high school student. Beyer made it look easy; his mother hardly looked. She later confessed she was pulling for the high school student who had to wrestle the 'stronger older guy.' Beyer laughed; "What about me, the stronger older guy?" His mother always held a soft spot for any underdog. Beyer had an easy time reaching the finals in his weight class and his opponent in the championship round was a freshman from Cornell named George (Tim) Woodin. The Cornell student had size and ambition, but Beyer's determination was too much to stop. He handily beat the freshman to claim the championship in the 191 pound weight class. In the center of the circle, as the referee raised his hand declaring him the champion, Beyer was magnanimous in victory. He told the young Woodin how well he had wrestled, and expressed confidence he had a future in the sport. Celia Beyer stood proudly and applauded, a few tears flowed down her cheeks as she watched her son accept the trophy.

MASKED DECISIONS

The victory qualified Beyer for the next phase - the national AAU championships in San Diego, California.

Beyer had one problem – no money for the trip to San Diego. There were no sources from which to borrow, certainly not his cash-strapped family, no friends or relatives to ask and repay with money to be earned in the near term. He seemed stuck. Fred Machemer heard of Beyer's dilemma one evening while playing poker with several Syracuse alumni. Machemer knew how important this trip was to Beyer and wanted to help the young man, whose character he admired. During the card game, he asked the others to pitch in to help out the former college sports star and ambassador for Syracuse University; by the end of the night, Machemer had collected $500 for Beyer, more than enough to cover all expenses. All Beyer could do the moment Machemer handed him the money was hug him.

It was sunny and in the low 70s when Beyer, Coach McDaniel and Ed Rooney, a good middleweight underclassman from Syracuse, landed in San Diego, quite a contrast from the cold, blustery conditions Beyer experienced a few weeks earlier during the Niagara championships. He arrived comfortable and full of confidence for the AAU tournament. The event was hosted at the San Diego Naval Base where the participants and coaches shared quarters. Beyer tossed his luggage into his barracks then walked over to the wrestling venue to inspect the arena and learn the identity of his opponents for the opening matches. He met a few old friends, swapped stories of wrestling matches, and told them of his new job as assistant football coach. Beyer was naturally extroverted and his likeable personality helped him develop good relationships. When he returned to the barracks, he got down to business and prepared for his matches in the 191 pound weight class.

Beyer approached the early rounds like a 'do or die' mission, knowing that one slip up or miscue could cost him his chance at a championship, and Japan. His weight was only 14 pounds under his normal carrying weight of 205, but it made a difference in the way he moved; he was faster, more agile, and more in control.

Outfitted in his traditional black singlet with an orange 'S' on the chest, Beyer's speed and technical abilities were in full force from the opening match; he glided past his first three opponents and into the advanced rounds. There, he encountered Knobby Newbauer from San Francisco; he didn't know much about Newbauer, but Beyer took no chances. Beyer and Newbauer wrestled intensely, matching each other's speed, moves and counters. By a razor-thin margin, Beyer earned a decision over Newbauer, and vaulted into the finals; his opponent was Dale Thomas, a two-time Olympian and former champion in the weight class. Beyer was ready; it seemed that this was to be his year. Beyer bore down on Thomas in the final and would not yield any ground. Thomas gave him all he had, but Beyer was still standing, still in it to win. Just past mid-match, to the surprise of everyone, Thomas pinned Beyer. The Syracuse grad was in good control when Thomas made a move that caught Beyer off guard. It was a tough loss; his strategy to win in the lower weight class foiled.

In the end, Thomas repeated as champion in the 191 pound division, Beyer earned second place and Newbauer came in third. Standing on the ceremony platform before the second place medal and ribbon were placed around his neck, as Thomas stood to his left and Newbauer to the left of Thomas, Beyer played back the sequence of moves that left him vulnerable to the loss and off the plane to Japan. The disappointment was evident on his face; to him a second place finish in the National AAU championship was like playing second string; in addition, he lost a golden opportunity to travel to Tokyo, but more tragically he felt as though he let his family and supporters down. What he didn't realize was the excitement he had generated by his performances and the respect he had gained throughout the amateur wrestling community. It was not the number of wins, but the *way* he wrestled, that was truly remarkable, and because of it, his life would never be the same.

◄ MASKED DECISIONS

Returning to Syracuse from the west coast, Beyer was warmly received by fans and supporters of Syracuse wrestling who acknowledged his outstanding runner-up performance in the National AAU Senior Wrestling tournament. Beyer appreciated the recognition, but thought that people made too big a deal over a second place finish; he was largely unaware of the favorable press his performances generated or of how his success was vicarious success for the university and the city. In addition, everyone so loved the way he conducted himself in victory or defeat. Beyer was just being Beyer, but that was what most observers respected, the genuineness of his character. He didn't feel or act like a hero, yet to countless fans, he had a cape tucked under his shirt.

Over the last half term of graduate school, Beyer studied extensively; he rarely came up for air and pushed hard to be sure he completed his self-imposed one year program. After all the lectures, papers and research, while exhausting all his energy, he knew he had his master's degree well in hand and graduation was still a few weeks away. What a relief to realize a goal and with it, the credentials to secure a good teaching job. But he didn't have to look for one, one found him. Days before graduation, Beyer was contacted by Dansville High School, a Genesee county school located 45 miles south of Rochester, New York, in regard to a vacancy on their staff. He drove to meet the superintendent and for an interview; it could not have gone better. Beyer's academic and athletic credentials impressed the school, which offered him a position as athletic director and high school football coach, with teaching assignments, and compensation at $4500 a year. The job was perfect and he nearly accepted it on the spot, but chose to mull it over; the superintendent gave him a week to review the offer and call back with his decision.

Beyer knew he wanted to take it, there was no reason not to take it, and he was just about to call the school to tell them he would take it when the phone rang. "Dick, this is Ed Don George, the promoter in Buffalo, how are you?" Beyer hadn't spoken with George since his sophomore year loss to Don Beitleman at his first Niagara AAU tournament. George took the lead in the conversation; aware that Beyer had graduated, he asked if he had a job. When Beyer explained the offer under consideration, George surprised him by telling him he had followed his amateur wrestling career and had received very favorable reports from friends who had seen him wrestle in the AAU championships in San Diego. George said to Beyer "If you're ready to turn pro, I can make you an offer and get you into the business." Frozen, Beyer barely made a sound; the words were vaguely familiar, having heard something similar from George three years earlier, but Beyer had outright dismissed the notion of a pro career at that time. He asked George to repeat. George chuckled, told Beyer he understood how he probably felt at that moment, and laid out the deal that included $250 a week and weekly gross receipts over that amount split 50-50. Beyer did the math; the prospect of $13,000 a year plus 50% draw of anything over $250 a week made his throat dry and tighten; it was too good not to consider. His buddy, Jim Ringo, had signed an offer to play professional football for the Green Bay Packers for $4500 a season, the same amount on the table from Dansville High School. Another decision stood in front of Dick Beyer. In hand was the offer he was schooled for and the job he wanted after college; on the phone was an offer fraught with uncertainty, but an opportunity to do something with the sport he loved. With Schwartzwalder's 'railroad crossroads' analogy fresh in mind, Dick Beyer made a decision, switched off the main line and onto the unknown and unplanned track to professional wrestling.

The first phone call to Dansville High School lasted mere minutes, the second, to his parents, a bit longer. His dad, excited for his son, asked the 'are you sure about this' question several times until convinced his son had made the decision with a clear head and that he had a back-up plan should he and his wrestling career get thrown out of the ring. Beyer had already put things into motion before his call to his parents; he had secured permission from Schwartzwalder to work only the early part of preseason camp, and return full-time for the following year's campaign, and he told his parents he would apply for teaching jobs if wrestling were to end too soon. Privately skeptical, they nonetheless acquiesced.

In June of 1954, Dick Beyer earned a Master's Degree from his alma mater in Physical Education and Administration. He also earned permanent teacher certification in New York. Packing a resume that included a bachelor's degree, a master's degree, and a stellar amateur athletic profile, Beyer entered professional wrestling school.

Ed Don George intuitively recognized Beyer possessed enormous wrestling talent for the pro variety. He had seen his quickness, speed, strength, agility and temperament, but Beyer needed to learn the nuances of the professional circuit – a very different form and variation of the ancient art. George knew what he was talking about. With collegiate wrestling experience at St. Bonaventure University and the University of Michigan, George later wrestled to a fourth place finish in the 1928 Amsterdam Olympics; he entered the pro ranks, became a top draw in the 1930s, and held the National Wrestling Alliance world heavyweight title. During World War II, he taught hand-to-hand combat to naval cadets, was discharged with the rank of Commander, and eventually became the wrestling promoter for the Buffalo territory.

George met with Beyer in downtown Buffalo in the early summer of 1954 to outline his thoughts for moving Beyer forward into the pro ranks. It was George who suggested that, instead of jumping into the business, Beyer first go to Columbus, Ohio to work with promoter Al Haft, who had a reputation for developing young wrestlers. Though not a big city, Columbus was one of the largest wrestling territories in the country, was home to several big name wrestlers, and had a good television base that extended south and east. Ohio was a place to get a solid foundation. Beyer agreed to go. Upon his departure for Columbus, George told Beyer "Watch the other wrestlers and learn from them…pick out something good from every wrestler and make it your own, your way."

Al Haft had worked the wrestling business from both sides; prior to World War I, he wrestled under the name 'Young Gotch' before moving to the promotional and developmental end. As his success grew, so did his interests; he raised prize cattle and won numerous blue ribbons by showing his horses and steers. Haft also owned a small motel on Route 40, about 8 miles east of Columbus, where some of the wrestlers stayed; young Dick Beyer arrived in a beat-up old Ford, checked into the motel, and was told to meet Haft at the gym that afternoon.

On the 4th floor of 261 South High Street in downtown Columbus, one flight up from his office, hidden from public view, Haft's gym was a noisy, sweaty, buzz saw, wrestler-making factory. Haft didn't employ trainers, instead he used the crop of wrestlers, both local and travelling, to work with each other and with new talent to teach the trade and develop technique. Like George, he could spot a good wrestler, as he could a prized steer or horse, and was fond of grapplers who had amateur experience. At almost any time, day or night, wrestlers could be found in his gym working and re-working routines, since Haft expected the best from them, and they had to deliver if they wanted to remain in the territory. Once a prospect was physically honed and knew leverage and mechanics, Haft often worked with the wrestler to develop a gimmick or teach how to create tension with the crowd. It was wrestling's version of finishing school.

Haft arranged for Beyer to meet and train with big Eddie Albers who, like Beyer, had an amateur wrestling background but, unlike Beyer, stood 6'5" and weighed more than 300 pounds, an imposing figure in, near, and out of the ring. In Haft's vision, the two presented an interesting juxtaposition of size and speed but he had an ulterior motive -he wanted Albers to lose weight. Before their initial workout, Haft whispered in Beyer's ear that if he could work Albers down to

270 pounds, Albers would be his opponent in his professional wrestling debut on one of Dayton's Saturday live television shows. The challenge appealed to Beyer. Haft liked Beyer from the moment he met him and it was coincidental that Haft's wife hailed from Buffalo. He perceived Beyer to be a smart, thinking man's wrestler, and recognized what Ed Don George said about him – a new kind of talent. Albers and Beyer worked together for weeks, twice a day in Haft's gym and every evening at the YMCA, perfected their moves and learned each other's favorite holds; they got along famously in and out of the squared circle.

From Albers and other wrestlers who trained in the gym at that time, Beyer learned the finer skills of holds, aerials, falls, and how to interact with an opponent in the ring. His mentors included former NCAA champion Dick Hutton, Big Ten champions Bill Miller from Ohio State and Joe Scarpella out of Iowa, Buddy Rogers, Don Eagle, Ray Stevens, George Marcacotis, Eddie Gossett, Fred Atkins, Ike Ekins, Ray 'Thunder' Stern, Leon Graham, Whitey Whittler, Nick Roberts, Whitey Walberg and Irish Mike Clancy. Listening to them was like listening to a wrestling Ph.D. dissertation; they demonstrated the why and how of the professional ranks.

When Beyer and Albers had the opportunity to work the main ring at the gym, other wrestlers who came by to pick up bout money, or get in a light workout, stopped to watch and offered suggestions to the young likeable guy from Buffalo. One of the first veterans to instruct Beyer in the ring was Dick Hutton. A champion from Oklahoma, Hutton lived in the trailer park owned by Al Haft known as Haft's Acre. He was generous with his time and advice, and taught Beyer how to take a stance, move with the opponent, deflect blows and react with timing. Ray Stevens, a young veteran, was more direct with Beyer, telling him "You're not an amateur any more…look like a professional…stand up and look taller." The gym had floor to ceiling mirrors that gave the grapplers almost a 360 degree view as they worked on standing holds like the head lock, double wrist lock, hammer lock, bear hug, full nelson and others. It was good advice from Stevens for the 5'10" Beyer. When he believed Beyer had 'learned the ropes', Al Haft offered some final advice. He told Beyer that in amateur wrestling there are two opponents on the mat; in professional wrestling there are two camps in the ring – the two opponents and their respective fans. Fans of professional wrestling 'participate' in every hold; they feel the movement and punishment, it's what gives them the excitement. Haft told Beyer to move slowly from one hold to another so that his opponent had time to 'sell' it to the crowd, to allow the fans to experience the pain or react to what they observed. Haft sat Beyer down at a table in his office and taught him the wrestling code, known as 'Kayfabe.' The word had its origins in the old travelling carnival days of wrestling but came to mean keeping the secrets of professional wrestling at all times. Breaking Kayfabe was not something promoters took lightly as it undermined the business. Beyer was instructed, perhaps more like mandated, to stay in character, whether baby face or heel, whenever an outsider was in his presence, singularly, or in the presence of more wrestlers. The business, he soon learned, was full of esoteric values. This course in human psychology Beyer never studied in college.

Days prior to his professional debut, Beyer put in additional work in the ring and picked up some last minute suggestions from veterans and fellow rookies who had made him feel welcomed in Columbus. One wrestler, whose company Beyer enjoyed, was Brooklyn-born Italian Lenny Montana, one of the funniest guys Beyer had ever met. Montana's practical jokes and slap-stick routines kept the gym alive and the wrestlers doubled-over with laughter. Another wrestler whose company Beyer wished he had kept more of was Mary Ann Kostecki, known as Penny Banner, a beautiful eighteen-year old blonde from St. Louis making her pro wrestling debut that summer in Columbus. Beyer told the guys he wished he could teach her his favorite hold – the double lip lock; he occasionally caught a peek of Banner training with other women wrestlers, but he never got further than hello and

MASKED DECISIONS

friendship during their time in Columbus as both were preparing for the start of their careers.

On a clear, cool, Dayton, Ohio evening the 23rd of October, 1954, Dick Beyer laced up his boots for the first time as a professional wrestler. In the dressing room of Dayton's WLWD television studio prior to the first undercard, Albers, wrestling his fourth pro bout, didn't say much, and neither did Beyer, but both were acutely aware of the need to give a strong performance. Beyer put on his college letter jacket, walked into the studio and entered the ring nonchalantly, polar opposite of what he was feeling; this was what he trained for, where he wanted to be. After Albers' introduction, the bow-tied ring announcer mono-toned into the microphone "Making his professional wrestling debut, from Syracuse, Schoolboy Dick Beyer." A light smattering of applause was heard in the studio audience. While it bothered him a bit to use Syracuse rather than Buffalo, the college reference made sense with Haft's suggestion to use the 'schoolboy' moniker as a way to underscore his rookie baby face image. Beyer raised his clenched right fist, scanned the crowd right to left, jumped lightly, and loosened his arms in front of his chest forming an 'x' as they crossed. In white trunks and white boots, he looked like the prototypical rookie good guy. Unlike most rookies, Beyer stepped to the center of the ring and, together with Albers, performed a technically sound and well-crafted bout, as the two former amateur stars used all of their favorite holds and high spots during the first ten minutes of the match that rendered a fast paced, exciting display for television and in-studio fans. That the match ended in a draw was immaterial, the theatre was what mattered. They had practiced and rehearsed enough the previous three weeks to fill an hour on the card, but gave forty-five minutes worth of good televised wrestling sufficient to impress the crowd and Al Haft, who gave them the nod to remain in the territory.

Fresh from his opening night, Beyer called his parents, Ed George, McDaniel, and Machemer to tell them he had wrestled well and was staying in Columbus. Excited and eager for more, a strong sense of belonging coursed through his system. He knew he had made the right decision; Dansville and other high schools would have to wait – Dick Beyer was a professional wrestler and working to become a star. Mostly, he wanted to work every night, but that wasn't to be the case in this territory. Two or three nights a week was all he was able to get with the talent pool around him. Given the opportunities, he didn't miss a single one on the circuit; he travelled to Huntington, West Virginia, Lexington, Kentucky and Dayton, Ohio from his hotel room outside Columbus, and gave his all.

Beyer was training at Haft's gym one afternoon when Whitey Whittler stopped by and, seeing a small crowd of wrestlers around Beyer, challenged him in the practice ring. Beyer recalled a warning he had received weeks earlier from another wrestler that, if ever challenged by a veteran in practice, his reputation and future could be on the line. Whittler tossed his shoes out of the ring and got on his hands and knees, the down position in amateur wrestling, and said to Beyer, "Pin me." As the crowd gathered, Beyer bent over the prone Whittler and outwardly tried his best to overtake the veteran, but after a few minutes, declared he was unsuccessful in the challenge. Whittler got up, put on his shoes and said, "I just wanted to see how tough you were." Beyer knew he had done himself, and Whittler, a favor by not pushing the matter; he could have easily taken Whittler down, but that would not have proven anything. As it was, the outcome engendered more respect for Beyer from the wrestlers, including Whittler, who eventually became a friend. The schoolboy had indeed learned well.

Time seemed to drop off the calendar during Beyer's inaugural term in the business but it wasn't all work and no play. The 'boys' knew how to relax, have fun, and have more fun. Once a headline match and an undercard were crafted for a city in the territory, those wrestlers scheduled for that card often drove to the city together. The stories related to these trips became legendary and the stuff of locker room banter in every territory in the country. Beyer's outgoing manner and personality attracted wrestling colleagues to him like metal filings to a magnet; he drove in the company of many different wrestlers, and soon experienced several classic pranks courtesy of his new friend, Lenny Montana.

Beyer, Montana, and another veteran wrestler were slated for matches in Lexington, Kentucky when they were asked by Haft to pick up another rookie wrestler on the way. Montana's eyes grew wide and he told the two of his plan to carry out his famous 'hitch hiker' rib. Before they were to pick up the other rookie, they drove several miles down the road from the pick-up point, where Montana got out and waited along the roadside. Beyer and the other wrestler went back and, at the appointed time, picked up the rookie, who sat in the front passenger seat, and they started their journey. Beyer, the driver, spotted a man hitch hiking and asked his passengers whether they should offer the man a ride. Hearing no objections, Beyer pulled over; the hitch hiker got in the back seat next to the other in on the gag. The hitch hiker looked at the guys in the car and commented how big and strong they looked, asked if they were wrestlers, asked if the matches were fake, asked if the guys really got hurt and on and on, incessantly. The rookie grew more than agitated by the onslaught of questions. When the hitch hiker became 'angry' at not getting answers, he pulled out a gun, told Beyer to stop the car, and all to hand over their wallets. Shaken and terrified, the rookie did what he was instructed…and within a few minutes the hitch hiker told him he'd been had…the gun was a toy…all howled…although the rookie was more guarded from that moment forward.

One evening prior to a match between Montana and Frankie Talaber in Huntington, West Virginia, Beyer saw Montana peer out from the dressing room and spot a large number of female fans at ringside; Montana folded a hand towel into a tight cylindrical shape and placed the towel down the front of his dark wrestling tights and shorts. When Beyer asked what he was doing, Montana replied, "You'll see Dick." At one point during the match, when Talaber had Montana on his back, Montana did a 'high bridge' maneuver which positioned his crotch at the apex of the 'bridge' thus accentuating his large male 'appendage' for the crowd to see. Talaber stood up and, with a raging fist, punched Montana squarely on the bulge; the ladies sitting near the ring let out a collective 'ouch' while the men, almost in unison, brought one leg over the other. Beyer, Montana and Talaber cried laughing during the drive back to Columbus but Montana had the last laugh telling Beyer "I told you what you'd see!"

Beyer was booked to wrestle in Kentucky late in the fall of 1954 and rode to the venue with Ike Ekins and Irish Mike Clancy in Clancy's brand new Cadillac. Ekins always travelled with a pet raccoon and used it as part of his gimmick; he tied the raccoon to the ring turnbuckle and forced his opponent into the corner toward the raccoon where the animal took a swipe or bite – the fans always got a rise out of the bit. After the undercard matches and just before the main event that featured Don Eagle and Stu Gibson, the promoter asked Ekins, Clancy and Beyer to stick around in case any trouble broke out after the main match; the wrestlers put their bags and the raccoon in the car, and waited in the dressing room. Once the match was over, Clancy, Beyer and Ekins rushed out the back door and got into the car – but to their horror the raccoon had evacuated whatever was in its system all over the front and back seats of Clancy's new Cadillac. The Irishman was enraged and shouted "I'll kill that coon!" The three reached into their duffle bags, withdrew towels and cleaned up the seats, but it was a very odiferous 150 mile ride back to Columbus, and Clancy fumed all the way.

Back in Columbus, Beyer told the hilarious story to Eddie Graham, Nick Roberts, and Whitey Whittler. Two days later, on a Saturday night after their Columbus television matches, Whittler invited the other three on a spare-of-the-moment hunting trip. Beyer drove his Ford and his hunting buddies to a lodge owned by friends of Whittler, a twenty-five minute drive into a densely wooded area east of Columbus. Once inside the lodge, Whittler's buddies met the guides and noticed the lodge was full of hanging animal skins – the skins were of raccoon and it gave the three a rather uneasy feeling. After assurances from Whittler about the place and the owners, the three wrestlers were given hunting jackets with large back pockets in which to place the animals after they had been shot. The wrestlers had a better idea for the large pockets, and each put six cans of beer in them for the trip through the dark woods. A very unusual outing ensued; the four wrestlers drank beer and made various animal noises, not the typical decorum for most hunting trips, but the hunting guides didn't seem to care. One told the wrestlers "We listen to the dogs; when their barking sound changes, we know the coon is up a tree; that's when we go in." He stopped and said "That's when you wrestlers go to work; we'll shine a light up the tree and shoot it; your job is to get the coon before the dogs get it." The four out-wrestled the dogs all night and returned to the lodge with six dead raccoons and twenty-four empty cans of beer. As they walked to Beyer's car, Whittler grabbed one of the dead raccoons and tossed it into the trunk. "It's not for me, it's for Ekins." They each knew what Whittler had in mind, and held their stomachs from laughter as they drove home, knowing what was to come.

The four drove back early that morning to Haft's motel where Beyer and Ekins had rooms. Every night, Ekins tied his raccoon to the tree located outside his motel room. Under cover of darkness just before dawn, Whittler skulked slowly up to the tree, untied the raccoon, replaced it with the dead raccoon from the hunting trip, and took the live raccoon back with him to his trailer park. It was Beyer's job to watch for Ekins as he got up to feed his raccoon. Ekins awoke at his usual time, stepped outside to the tree, and as Beyer peered out from his motel window, heard Ekins let out a loud, foul expletive followed by "I'll kill that Clancy" believing Clancy had done the deed as he had promised after the soiling incident involving his new Cadillac. Beyer immediately phoned Clancy, explained what had happened, and told him to get out of his home before Ekins got there to cause trouble. As Ekins drove off, Beyer called Whittler, who scooted back to the motel and replaced the dead raccoon with the live one. When Ekins returned from his unsuccessful trip to find Clancy, he was shocked to see the raccoon on his leash playing in the grass as if nothing had happened. Looking around to see if anyone was observing, he pulled down on his shirt as if to straighten it out, pointed to the animal, shouted "That's better" and strutted back into his room. Beyer laughed for hours.

It had been five months since his professional career began and Dick Beyer was still not getting the work, or the pay, he had sought. As a small fish in a large talent pool, he worked a typical rookie schedule and picked up a few extra matches in Akron, Springfield and Cleveland, but desperately wanted more work and learning opportunities; a rookie rut had set in. In the gym during practice, Al Haft mentioned to the wrestlers that Ken Marshall, the promoter from Bowling Green, Kentucky, was in town looking for young baby face talent to work with his heels, Tor Morgan and Jules Larance, six nights a week; wrestlers interested in working Kentucky were instructed to meet with Marshall that afternoon. Beyer was first in line. Though Marshall liked his look and desire, he did not promise Beyer much more money, but did offer the six nights a week schedule. Beyer looked at it as an opportunity to work more and to learn more as he worked; he took it. Marshall also chose Leon Graham as the other baby face. Together, Beyer and Graham made their way down to the Kentucky territory and a schedule that included Evansville, Indiana on Mondays, Bowling Green Tuesdays, Glasgow, Kentucky on Wednesdays, Hopkinsville, Kentucky Thursdays, Paducah, Kentucky Fridays and Somerset, Kentucky on Saturdays.

Beyer's first week in Kentucky consisted of singles matches; the second week, two thirty-minute singles matches and a tag team match; the third week, two one-hour singles matches. Wrestling almost every night of the week in singles, tag teams, special bouts, didn't matter to Beyer – work mattered. In Bowling Green the promoters not only booked Tuesday wrestling matches but other kinds of shows during the week. One Sunday, short staffed, they asked Beyer to work the concession stand during a performance by a new singer named Fats Domino. Beyer worked the stand and met the young, upstart performer, who from the stage introduced Beyer and plugged his match the following Tuesday evening. Beyer yelled back: "Thanks, Mr. Domino."

Apart from the physicality of the business, Beyer learned more about its psychology, how to wrestle in front of different types of crowds and create reactions. He watched how baby faces and heels cranked up the crowds with verbal and physical behaviors and listened to the promoters describe scenarios for 'drawing heat.' He learned well. He also wished he had a crystal ball during a meeting with the promoter. On a night prior to a match in Somerset, Kentucky, Ken Marshall walked into the dressing room with his brother and co-promoter, Joe. Ken told Beyer he appreciated how hard he worked and, that night, offered Beyer a choice - earn $25.00 or 10% of the house. Up to this point, Beyer earned $20.00 a night; he looked at the 500-seat auditorium, the proposed card for the evening, and believed a sellout was imminent. With the price of a ticket at $1.00, a sellout was $500 and 10% of that was a $50.00 payday. Not even Lou Thesz and Buddy Rogers, both big-name heavyweights in the business, were earning 10% of the gate. He jumped at the percentage. Prior to match time, a heavy rain storm rumbled through the city – the match drew 60 people. As Marshall figured out Beyer's take of 10% of $60.00, he counted into Beyer's hand "One dollar, two dollars, three dollars, four dollars, five dollars, six big dollars." With each count, Marshall tried not to smile while Beyer winced. Money in hand, Beyer looked at Marshall, who was in full convulsions of laughter, and said "This is both the biggest learning experience and the biggest mistake of my career."

Before the end of his term in the Kentucky territory, Beyer found a photographer in Lexington, posed in his white trunks and boots and paid for new baby face photographs. Once the photos were in his possession, he hand-wrote letters to all 50 promoters in the country, included one of the photos in each envelope, and asked each promoter to consider bringing in 'this young, good-looking wrestling prospect.' The response was overwhelming…zero. Not a single promoter in the U.S. replied to his letter. No one knew Dick Beyer, or wanted to know him, he concluded. The rookie was deflated.

On his way to a match in Evansville, Indiana, Beyer was feeling low about his fledgling career. He didn't realize that his speed had crept over the posted limit and soon a police car's red flashing light was visible in his rearview mirror. Beyer pulled over quickly. The officer asked for identification and promptly processed a ticket. Beyer, short on cash after his recent $6.00 payout, asked the officer if he could return to the courthouse in one week to pay the fine. Initially reluctant, the officer changed his mind and afforded Beyer the extra time, telling him to report to the courthouse at 2:00 pm Monday. The following week, Beyer drove to the courthouse to settle his traffic infraction. When he arrived at the courthouse prior to his appointed time, he was taken aback – there, in the lobby, were 26 people and the officer who had stopped him. Beyer said to the policeman "You must have been busy that day" to which the officer replied "They're not here to see me, they're here to see you." The officer, having recognized Beyer's name when he stopped him, tipped off several people in town that the wrestler would be back on Monday afternoon. "If you sign all the autographs, I'll let you go without a fine." Beyer got busy signing every piece of paper and wrestling program thrust under his nose; 26 autographs and a sore right hand later, Beyer was free to go. From those people who had seen him perform on local television or in person, he heard positive comments about his wrestling and Beyer began to rebound from his funk. He experienced his first real taste of celebrity, and it tasted sweet. Even better, they liked his style of wrestling.

One of his final matches in Kentucky in early 1955 was a tag team match with Johnny Gilbert as his partner. Gilbert, a baby face from

MASKED DECISIONS

Chicago, was brought in by Marshall for a series of matches. Beyer wanted to leave a good impression with the fans and promoter – he didn't realize he was to leave a greater impression on Gilbert. As the two were preparing to walk down to the ring for their match, Beyer said to Gilbert, "Can you jump over the top rope?" Gilbert replied "Sure." On their way into the ring, Beyer grabbed hold of the top rope and in one quick sideways thrust of his powerful legs, sailed over the rope and landed in the ring on his feet with his hands at his side. Gilbert grabbed the rope and began his leap – but his foot caught the rope and instead of gliding he tumbled into the ring. Gilbert quickly recovered from his embarrassing entrance and stood in the corner awaiting the introductions. The ring announcer, after introducing Beyer, said: "Teaming with Beyer, a television star from Chicago, Johnny Gilbert." Beyer overheard a fan in the front row say "Big TV star, he can't even get into the ring." That comment bothered Beyer, since it was he who suggested the jump entrance. He wanted to make good. Beyer enabled Gilbert to a solid match – giving Gilbert a number of opportunities to showcase his repertoire on their opponents. Gilbert, impressed with Beyer's speed and maneuvers, made notes of what he observed and returned to Chicago to brief the promoter of his experiences in the Kentucky territory.

CHAPTER 7

ON THE DRIVE from Kentucky to Buffalo in the spring of 1955, Beyer's mind wandered to Army Reserves' camp, coaching football, women, but was predominantly saturated with wrestling, specifically, how to get established in a territory and work longer stretches. So engrossed was he in his thoughts, Beyer hadn't noticed he had travelled north to Cincinnati and Dayton, east through Columbus, northeast to Cleveland, and was near the New York State border. Away since October, it felt much longer; perhaps what made it that way was his self-described lukewarm start in the business. He hadn't made the money or the name for himself he thought he'd have by now, and while confident in his skill set, he was less confident in future bookings. Columbus was good training and Kentucky was good work but *what's next?* Put bluntly, he was struggling. The wrestling business was a nomad existence – he was aware of that before he signed with Ed Don George – and while he wanted to be known, and accessible, to promoters in territories further west and south, he knew his Army commitment and work with Syracuse football limited his travel and stay options to the east. Besides, not a single promoter answered any of his 50 letters. He was troubled with today, and fretted about his tomorrow.

The young rookie sought out the advice of his mentor, Ed Don George, immediately after his return to Buffalo. George put it into perspective and told Beyer to be more patient during the first year of his career and to "learn, give good shows, meet the people in the business who can help make things happen." George said that other wrestlers were often the best sources for getting into new territories, since they wanted to work with good talent to make the events interesting and generate revenue at the ticket window. "Forget about the 50 promoters…" George said, "…and impress your first 50 opponents." Sage advice not lost on the rookie. George created some work for his protégé around Buffalo that summer. Schoolboy Dick Beyer worked a few outdoor wrestling shows, facing off against the talented Tony Verdi, Firpo Zbysko, and fellow Buffalonian Donn Lewin. The matches were not well paying but helped establish the name Dick Beyer, professional wrestler, in his home town. Attending the matches were his family and friends who hadn't seen Beyer wrestle since his collegiate days. They enjoyed cheering on their favorite son and followed his matches in the newspapers. In Buffalo, Beyer became a personality, though a minor variety.

George booked Beyer anywhere that would take him- into north and central New York - Watertown, Rochester and Syracuse; he performed in mostly run-down joints with low level talent. Rookie baby faces were cheap labor but Beyer chalked it up to experience; he never lost trust in George. During his tag team match in Rochester that summer, a brawl broke out in the stands; although Beyer and the wrestlers were not involved, his name appeared in the newspapers as part of the card that performed that evening; not exactly the publicity he had sought. George also booked him into Albany, New York for a match with Sandor Kovacs; the Hungarian-born Canadian wrestler had developed a good reputation, especially in Hawaii. Kovacs liked what he saw in the baby face Beyer; Beyer responded by giving Kovacs a good, clean match, one of his best as a rookie wrestler to date, that ended in a thirty minute draw. Within weeks of that match, Beyer received an unexpected letter from Al Karasick, the promoter in Hawaii, inviting him to work in Hawaii for 3 months beginning late January 1956; like Haft, Karasick was fond of technical wrestlers who had amateur experience, and it was Kovacs who had tipped off Karasick that Beyer was the kind of wrestler he liked. Ed Don George was right. Beyer was thrilled; Hawaii in the winter, compliments of a Hungarian Canadian– *koszonom, Kovacs Sandor.*

With little work and little money that summer, Beyer needed to generate income; his weekday summer job with Kendell Roadway, fortunately, was still his thanks to his work record and his friend Fred Machemer Sr., but Beyer wanted to fill his dance card. He and former high school classmate Bill Ziegler, both playing on a softball team sponsored by Salvatore's tavern on Delevan Avenue, came up with an idea. They approached Dim with the proposal – to rent the hot dog stand from him, manage it, and split the profits equally. Dim liked and trusted Beyer and since his main source of revenue was his grocery store, Dim agreed to the deal, and the two young softball teammates became working managers at the popular seasonal eatery.

The summer weekends at Dim's were events unto themselves; it was as though all of Buffalo went there to order the charcoaled hot dogs, hamburgers and Italian sausage. The hands-down favorite was the sausage, as Beyer and Ziegler cooked more than 450 pounds every weekend. Hot dogs were a quarter; hamburgers thirty cents; sausage was thirty-five cents, however most ordered a 'double' for seventy cents that included an Italian roll cut in half with two sausages cooked, sliced, and flattened onto the roll.

After a long, hot work week at Kendell, Beyer drove home, cleaned up, and raced to the hot dog stand for his weekend work. He enjoyed cooking the meats and working the crowd as he did, melding the two to create a show. He poked into the dogs, hamburgers and sausages with a long fork to allow the inside of the meats to get up to temperature, and let the outsides tan well over the coals, partially blackened as most preferred. He moved the meats around the grill as grease dripped into the coals creating spurts of hissing with rising streams of smoke, lightly toasted the buns, then finally, and ceremoniously, married the meat with the appropriate roll, all while talking with customers and telling stories.

Beyer began to take notice of a peculiar phenomenon that occurred on Friday nights. Many of his Catholic friends arrived after 9:00 pm and waited till midnight before ordering a sandwich, to satisfy the Church directive of no meat on Fridays. Given this observation, Beyer began to cook more meats before midnight, filling the atmosphere with a pungent, charcoal broiled flavor, creating mouth-watering interest and fanning the flames of hunger in his Catholic customers, who began ordering early- not one but multiple sandwiches, then devouring them at the stroke of midnight. It was a successful marketing tactic. The hot dog stand took in $1500 each month that summer. Beyond the revenue it earned for the partners, Beyer realized that it was the way he cooked and the sizzle of the meat that often created interest and demand, a metaphor he would carry forward to the business of wrestling.

Beyer dated Willy Thomson several times that summer, but he told her up front that he did not want to move their relationship to the next level because of his travels to Syracuse, potential for matches in other territories, and his new commitment to Hawaii in January. He did not deny that there was something special about her; he just didn't want to commit to something steady at this point for fear of disappointing her. For her part, Willy was in no hurry. She was busy with her career at the power company, and enjoyed after-hours activities with her two sisters (Georgia and Norma) and her brother (George). When she and Beyer were together, it was fun, and comfortable, and she had no illusions of anything additional blossoming from their relationship. Beyer treated her like a lady; she appreciated and acknowledged his manners and deportment; his aggressiveness as a wrestler/athlete never interfered while the two dated. Beyer knew how to relate with women, having been taught well by his mother and sisters.

After his fifth summer Army Reserves camp at Fort Drum, Beyer quickly drove to Syracuse for football with the freshmen line, and scouting duties for the varsity. When he arrived on campus, he was summoned to Coach Schwartzwalder's office. The last time this happened was when he was informed of his selection as Syracuse University Athlete of the Year, so Beyer approached this order in a matter-of-fact manner. Syracuse University Chancellor William Tolly had read the story of the brawl that broke out during the wrestling matches in Rochester earlier that summer; the story linked Beyer's name to the coaching staff at Syracuse. Fearing untoward public relations, the Chancellor told Schwartzwalder that Beyer could not wrestle professionally and simultaneously coach on staff. The reasons were outlined to Beyer. He listened as Schwartzwalder said "We can't have you on the coaching staff this year." He told Coach Ben "Then I guess I won't be coaching this year" and walked out the door and off the campus. Players reacted with shock and anger; coaches, even the stoic Schwartzwalder, believed that Beyer was given a raw deal. Syracuse football felt different that season – as did Beyer.

It bothered him that a newspaper article ignited a fire that lead to his dismissal as a coach. Beyer had always believed he could juggle both, having convinced Schwartzwalder of it a year earlier. That a meaningless fight where he happened to be wrestling would prompt this action was the last thing he imagined. He described the entire sequence of events to his father at their home in Buffalo after he arrived late that night, and still could not believe it came to such an abrupt halt. Feeling bewildered, he looked at his father and remarked, "I guess I should look into a part-time teaching slot for a few months." His father reached up onto the china cabinet in the dining room and handed a letter to his son that had arrived a few days earlier. "You might want to read this now," his father told him. Beyer took out the letter from the opened envelope and began reading – his dejected face soon took on a look of utter glee. Beyer was invited to the Chicago territory to work from October to December; Johnny Gilbert had spoken highly of the rookie he worked with in Kentucky to Chicago promoter, Fred Kohler, who sent an inquiry letter to Beyer's Buffalo home. "I'm not down for the count yet, Dad" was his comment while giving his father a big happy hug. He made preparations to get to Chicago the first week of October, to work there until late December, return to Buffalo for a few weeks, then pack again for a tour in Hawaii. 'Go west young man' was a prescriptive he'd happily fulfill.

The chill in the October air was crisp, and the buildings with names like Wrigley, Marshall Field, Montgomery Ward, Sears and Roebuck, Morrison, and Soldier Field made it clear he had arrived in Chicago. Steering his 1955 black four-door Ford - with 2000 odometer miles and twin spotlights on the driver and passenger doors – a law enforcement demonstrator car he bought through his father, Beyer could feel the tailpipe thumping as he navigated the busy, congested streets looking for a spot to pull over and fix the tailpipe, and to find a restaurant for some dinner before going to the Chateau Hotel, where he would hole up during his time in the Windy City. Excitement and hope had been restored in his soul. He knew the next few months were important for landing additional work, given the successes he experienced from matches with Sandor Kovacs and Johnny Gilbert. The first thing he was going to do, once he got to the hotel, was to call Johnny Gilbert and thank him for putting in the word that brought about this trip to Illinois. Beyer always showed his gratitude and loyalty to anyone who helped him in any way; that was the way he was brought up. After dinner, he wound his way through the north side, up North Broadway Street to where the Chateau Hotel was located. He checked in, unpacked, called Gilbert, called the promoter Fred Kohler to find out what time he wanted to meet with him the next day, then fell asleep, still dressed in his shirt, pants, coat and shoes.

The Chicago territory had emerged as a top wrestling venue under Kohler's leadership. A no-nonsense type, Kohler knew the region and what it took to be successful. The son of a Chicago bar owner, he had taken over the wrestling business at its lowest point, and developed it into a powerhouse that included television broadcasts, seen as far away as New York; wrestlers knew that working for Kohler translated into working other territories, provided they did what Kohler wanted them to do. Kohler's formula was to get the talent to work hard each night. Beyer's meeting with Kohler was brief. Every meeting with

Kohler was that way. There would be no time to develop in this territory, no mentor; all wrestlers were instructed by Kohler – work your ass off at every match and give the fans their money's worth. Kohler watched Beyer practice in the ring and told others he was "good talent." He saw the amateur background and foundation Beyer brought to the business, a generous set of holds and moves, foot speed, adaptability, and a workable baby face style. Beyer knew what he had to do.

The talent pool in the Chicago territory read like a wrestlers' 'Who's Who' manifest. Dick 'The Bruiser' Afflis, Reggie 'Crusher' Lisowski, Bearcat Wright, Angelo Poffo, The Mighty Atlas, Gypsy Joe, Hans Schmidt and others, making big names and big money. Kohler put Beyer to work on the circuit from Chicago to Indianapolis to Milwaukee, matched against the likes of Pat Bartu, Jon Arjon, Maurice Robeere, Duke Demitri, Bronko Lubich, The Sheik of Arraby, Tony Ross, Art Bull, Benito Gardini, and an old partner Johnny Gilbert – sans rope jump entrance. The experience was good, and tougher than anticipated. Many nights Beyer returned to his hotel room bruised and battered as the veterans and up-and-comers took turns punishing the rookie baby face with devastating tosses and body blows. Beyer returned fire and made his matches more than memorable, displaying his abundant energy in combination with strong holds and moves that were fast becoming staples in his repertoire – dropkicks, flying head scissors and awesome speed.

One night in Michigan, Beyer got his first dose of reality, the Chicago way. He was on the undercard of the main event that pitted Hans Schmidt against Bearcat Wright in Benton Harbor, located in Southwest Lower Michigan, on the state's Lake Michigan shoreline. It was a frigid, blustery and snowy night, and Beyer had completed his match earlier in the evening, having turned in a crowd-pleasing performance. Schmidt, who was actually Canadian Guy Larose, but renamed by a Boston promoter because he looked German, was preparing in the dressing room when word came that Wright was not able to get to the arena due to impassable roads. The 6'4" 250 pound Schmidt, angered by the worsening conditions, became livid. After a brief discussion with event personnel, the announcer entered the ring and informed the crowd that Wright was unable to attend; following the announcement, he asked the fans - based on wrestlers they had seen in the earlier matches - to choose a worthy opponent for the hated heel, Hans Schmidt. The 'Schoolboy' was their man.

Beyer didn't mind pulling overtime; he was delighted the crowd chose him over the others on the undercard to go against Schmidt in the main event – the first of his career. Schmidt didn't see it that way. To him, it was not a headline event to take on a no-name rookie; his anger and frustration had boiled into rage, and he took it directly into the ring and poured it all over Beyer. For forty-five minutes, Schmidt, eliciting jeers and stoking the anti-German passions left over from the war, dusted the floor with the baby face, using the rookie as a tackling dummy and punching bag, severely inflicting pain and punishment the likes of which Beyer had never experienced. No contest. 'Schoolboy' was savagely pummeled by the class bully. Days later, Beyer told others that, in retrospect, Schmidt could have ended the match in five minutes, but it appeared he wanted to take it out on the rookie. Still sore, Beyer was given a few days off the schedule – and he needed every one of them.

During his respite, Beyer took a flight back to Buffalo to attend the wedding of his younger sister Shirley to fiancé Steve Clergy; Beyer kidded his sister about marrying a 'Clergy' and the rhyming of her name, now Shirley Clergy. The family was happy to have him in Buffalo, if only for a few days, before he was to return to the Midwest and resume his education in the business.

On Chicago's North Side, not far from hallowed Wrigley Field, the Chateau Hotel served an eclectic clientele. People from varying walks of life lived or loitered in the hotel, which made Beyer's stay there interesting and, at times, disconcerting. He was surprised to learn that Dick 'Bruiser' Afflis called the Chateau Hotel home whenever he worked Chicago, and the two wrestlers soon befriended each other. Gypsy Joe and his wife lived nearby and became travelling companions of Beyer for out-of-town matches. Afflis, a gravel-throated, cigar chomping, beer swigging Chicago favorite, convinced Beyer to go with him every morning and work out with the guys at Marigold Gardens, a wrestling hall resurrected by Kohler that formerly attracted musical floor shows - and unsavory mob members - as a night club in the 1920s, and later became a premier boxing venue for several years. The routine was to get up early, head for the Marigold and a workout, then stop for breakfast at a little nearby bar; breakfast consisted of V8 juice mixed with beer. Some nights, Afflis and Beyer drove to Calumet City where Afflis' girlfriend worked… and where Beyer learned much more about life on the road.

For three months, Beyer wrestled with the best talent in the territory, splitting wins and losses, and building a solid respectable reputation. With Dim's hot dog stand as a mental template, he put 'sizzle' into each performance. He was getting noticed. Some Sundays, he walked the roughly half-mile to Wrigley Field to catch a Bears football game from the press box, on invitation by Jack Brickhouse, the play-by-play broadcaster for WGN radio and television, who also broadcasted televised pro wrestling from Marigold Gardens on Saturday nights. Beyer enjoyed his relationship with Brickhouse, whom he regarded as a celebrity, having heard him on television the year before during the World Series as 'Brick', moonlighting for NBC, described the famous over-the-shoulder center field catch by Willie Mays that preserved a game one win for the eventual Series' Champion New York Giants. Sunday, November 6, the Bears hosted the Green Bay Packers at Wrigley. Beyer went to see his former college football teammate, Jim Ringo, play for the Packers and, after the game, the two met up in the locker room for the first time since graduation from Syracuse. Beyer needled his college friend about his team's loss to the Bears and told Ringo a funny story that occurred days before the game. Returning from an out of town match, Beyer, Reggie Lisowski, Benito Gardini, and two female wrestlers decided to stop at a nightclub owned by friends of Gardini, located on 55th Street on Chicago's South Side. Beyer drove his black Ford, with Crusher Lisowski and Shirley Strimple in the back seat and with Gardini and the other female wrestler in the front, next to Beyer.

When they left the club around midnight and climbed back into the car, one of the females remarked "Dick, your car looks like a squad car." They laughed and drove to the Eastside Parkway, to a connector to the North Side of the city. At a stoplight, Beyer noticed someone following them in the car behind and, in one impulsive move, slammed his car into reverse to get a closer look at the followers; he stopped, suddenly, as he realized the car behind them was, in fact, a police car! An officer stepped out, and asked for Beyer's driver's license – things went from uncomfortable to panic when Beyer remembered he had left his license in the hotel room. The officer instructed Beyer to follow him to the precinct house; the three men in the car went inside with the officer. After thirty minutes of explanations, the officers, wrestling fans as it turned out, accepted their story and were ready to let them go when Benito Gardini, "The Little Flower" as he was known in the ring, thought it would be fun to play a rib on the girls in the car; after cuing the officers in on the joke, he went outside and told the girls that all five had to stay overnight at the station. The two girls became incensed. Once inside the station, the Captain told Shirley Strimple he observed her kissing Lisowski in the back seat and asked her if he was her husband. Shirley tipped her head to one side, looked at the Captain and said, "Didn't I see you at a party last Saturday night, and was that woman you were with your wife?" The Captain hastily replied "You can all go." Shirley smirked and was convinced she got everyone off the hook with her clever retort; she never knew the true story, and the three men were afraid to level with her. Ringo laughed hard and said to Beyer "You'll probably have a lot more happen to you before you leave Chicago." It was a prophetic remark.

As the year wound down and his time in Chicago drew short, Beyer went to Fred Kohler's office to thank him for taking a chance on a rookie baby face, and to see if Kohler was interested in bringing him back to the territory in the near future. Listening to Beyer's words of appreciation, Kohler, a man not given to sentimentality, took a magazine off his desk and threw it at Beyer. The stunned wrestler caught the magazine against his chest and thought the promoter was angry with him for stopping by his office. A brief awkward moment ensued, followed by Kohler yelling "Look at that!" Beyer held up the publication – *Wrestling Life Magazine* – and there, on the cover, was Dick Beyer, Rookie of the Year for 1955. "Is this real?" Beyer repeated a number of times. He dove into the article like a hungry scavenger and read: 'This year's selection stands head and shoulders above the freshman crop of professional wrestlers.' The article outlined his collegiate wrestling and football achievements and noted a good 'accounting' against named wrestlers during his first year. The article concluded 'In November 1955, via the WGN-TV Chicago network, Dick met one of professional wrestling's great young heavyweight stars, Angelo Poffo. The match, one of the most thrilling ever staged in the Windy City, ended in a draw. Overnight Beyer was skyrocketed to national ranking and established as a serious threat to present heavyweight title holders Lou Thesz and Verne Gagne.' Beyer walked out of the office still reading the publication, his feet never touching the ground.

As a result of his accomplishments and reputation in the territory, Beyer began to field requests for personal appearances and promotions. He found it difficult to turn down any request that involved children, and it wasn't long before he immersed himself in a kids' program. The Uptown-Chicago Lions Club, with help from Beyer and *Wrestling Life Magazine*, posed a unique challenge to 24 boys, ranging from 9 to 14 years of age, at the Lions' youth center on Chicago's North Side. Beyer provided group instruction in proper warm-up, calisthenics, and amateur wrestling holds; afterwards, the boys participated in warm-ups and paired off to engage in a three-minute wrestling match, all under Beyer's supervision. The result of the experiment proved that wrestling was a good activity as it involved exercising most every muscle in the body; it lent support to the promotion of stronger bodies and healthier minds among children. At the conclusion of the evening's program, all participants were given an autographed photo of Dick Beyer and a copy of *Wrestling Life Magazine* that contained the article on the rookie of the year. It was an enjoyable experience for Beyer, who returned to the center on many occasions to help out and promote its programs; the experience also stamped an indelible mark on his consciousness that was to drive him back to helping kids learn in many ways.

Packing his car for his return to Buffalo, Beyer was briefly interrupted by Gypsy Joe, who had stopped to say goodbye and good luck to his new friend and newly crowned rookie of the year. Joe shook hands with Beyer and said "You came into Chicago a clean cut college kid, and leaving for Hawaii a well-educated professional wrestler." Beyer liked the association of those words – well educated professional wrestler – and filed the concept away for future reference.

The sands of Waikiki looked better in person than in any photo or postcard he had ever seen. It was mid-January, 1956, and for the next 16 weeks Beyer was to be on the island working – on his career, and on his tan. The deal from Karasick was good – paid airfare and a guarantee of $150.00 a week for a weekly match at the Civic Auditorium in Honolulu, and the potential for other matches on the outer islands. For the Rookie of the Year in professional wrestling, things were beginning to look up. With help from the office of promoter Karasick, Beyer secured an apartment at the Waikiki Ebb Tide, at the corner of Kalakaua and Liliokolani, across the street from Kuhio Beach in Waikiki. With apologies to John Milton, Paradise Found.

Pro wrestling promotions had existed on the islands prior to the early

1940s. They attracted more attention after World War II, as the multicultural influences emerged in the wrestling business, with Japanese in the heel roles, American wrestlers often as overbearing and self-centered, and the Polynesians as warriors. There were exceptions to these stereotypes. Karasick liked wrestlers who had skills, not just bulk, size, or a gimmick, and he knew that the fans in Hawaii also appreciated technical ability from their wrestlers. Judging by what he heard from Sandor Kovacs and others, Beyer would not only perform well but, more importantly, be accepted by the fan base. The American baby face with rookie accolades was placed in the mix to keep wrestling fresh and attractive in post-war Hawaii.

Before he settled into a routine in Honolulu, Beyer knew there was one place he had to visit. The place beckoned him. The anxious, confused feeling he experienced as an eleven-year old, when he first heard about the attack while standing in a candy store in Buffalo, never really left him. He had to see Pearl Harbor.

The site moved him more than anything he had experienced emotionally to date. As he stood, silently, near the USS Arizona memorial, with its single U.S. flag flying above, the feelings rushed back. He recalled the news accounts of the attack, and quietly thanked those who died in defense of the American Navy and its Hawaiian hosts. In his mind's eye he saw the planes, the bombs, the explosions, the ships, the dead. He thought about his fear of the Japanese, and his hatred toward them, only to realize that those emotions from a different time had given way to a level of acceptance. What he felt that day had more to do with curiosity and understanding than revenge. The pull of Japan was undeniable, of wanting to know the people and culture, but he was unable to determine its origin or why it was so. Had he won the AAU tournament in San Diego in 1954 and travelled to Japan, the draw of the Far East might have ended. In this hallowed harbor, where cultures clashed during a difficult time in history, he thought it probably would be the closest he'd ever come to fulfilling the dream. He kept his sunglasses on though it was a cloudy day, his eyes moist, his heart heavy, as he absorbed the Pearl into his soul.

During the first several weeks, Beyer saw action in singles and tag team matches, meeting Doug Dawkins, Sandor Kovacs, Hans Snabble, old friend Don Beitleman, and working with Al Lolotai against Lord Blears and Gene Kiniski. Wrestling once a week was not what Beyer had in mind, but in the location he found himself, it was acceptable. Since he had more free time, he decided to register with the school district, and put his name on the substitute teacher list for local high schools. With his master's degree and teaching credentials in the States, he was certain he would get calls in short order. Weeks went by and no calls. *Were these people related to the 50 wrestling promoters in the States*, he sarcastically wondered.

One morning, Beyer awoke to his ringing phone; it was a call for work at McKinley High School. He agreed to the assignment and dashed out the apartment door, arriving at the school for instructions and with minutes to go before change of class. Finding the classroom, he noticed the students were not in their seats, but on the lawn outside the classroom window. He went outside, told them who he was, and instructed them to go inside the classroom; all but three husky football players heeded the call. Beyer, new to Hawaii and the school system, said to the three "Do you speak and understand English?" Two of them got up and walked inside while the third remained on the grass. Beyer knew a test when he saw one; he had been challenged by tougher people in the practice ring in Columbus. He walked deliberately to the remaining holdout, grabbed him by his belt buckle, and tug-boated him into the classroom and into a seat, telling him "Don't move until I tell you!" Seconds of silence ticked before the bell rang, and when the entire class got up to leave, Beyer, using his best imitation Dick 'The Bruiser' gravel-voice, shouted "Sit down!" He got their attention. He decided to take attendance and upon completion said "Now you can leave." The class stood up in unison- Beyer again yelled "Sit down." Every student dropped back into their chairs as if pulled down by a gravitational super-force, failing to see that Beyer was pointing only to the dissident student from the lawn. "You don't move until I tell you, and I didn't tell you" he said sternly.

Beyer apologized to the rest of the class and excused them. For what probably felt like an eternity to the remaining student, Beyer verbally tore into him and then gave a pep talk about student responsibility and the role of teachers in the classroom. As he dismissed the boy, Beyer noticed that the next class had already gathered outside the door; there were no hallways in Hawaiian schools, only covered walkways, and the students at the door stood frozen, not knowing if they were next on the sub's list. In the faculty cafeteria over lunch, teachers asked Beyer what he did to that boy, as they observed his behavior in subsequent classrooms to be above par. "Just a little belt tightening" he replied. The next morning, and for several weeks, Beyer received calls to substitute from a number of schools– word travelled fast. At Kaimuki High School, Beyer was interviewed for the school newspaper, The Bulldog, for an article entitled 'Brawn Plus Brains Too – Wrestler Subs A Day As Teacher,' in which he was quoted as saying he liked substitute teaching in order to remain in education – "It's what I wanted to do after college." The article described his wrestling experience in Hawaii, and the toughness he brought to the ring. So many offers poured in that Beyer could have worked five days a week as a substitute, but he chose assignments when he wanted to work and spent time working out, officiating the school's basketball games, and relaxing at the beach.

Wally Tsutsumi, a well-respected island resident, was the Hawaii Judo champion in the early 1950s who later became a pro wrestling referee. He trained every evening at the Honolulu Army-Navy YMCA where he met Beyer. The two formed a friendship. Tsutsumi was a Fifth Grade Black Belt. Watching him train, Beyer thought that the discipline could help him in wrestling, or maybe with another difficult student, so he asked Wally to instruct him in the martial art. Over weeks, Beyer learned the basic techniques of judo and how to wrestle with a judo jacket – a skill that came in handy for a match and a fateful introduction.

Beyer fell in love with Waikiki. He couldn't get enough of the beach, ocean and sunsets that he came to cherish every day. It was crystal clear to him why Kovacs, Bietleman, Blears and Kiniski chose to live there. Deep in his heart, he knew this place was nirvana to him. He bought a surfboard and tried self-teaching – spending more time under the board than on it. In exchange for wrestling tickets, a beach boy named Junior Kahili, whom Beyer befriended on the beach, taught him everything about surfing – from how to prepare the board, to avoiding body oil before surfing, where to go and when to stand. As with most sports, Beyer was a fast learner and soon was hanging ten with the best of them, surfing some of Hawaii's better waves.

Wrestling talent from Japan frequently rotated through Hawaii, and some of the wrestlers developed strong followings and support from the Japanese living on Waikiki. When Karasick decided to stage a judo jacket match, Kokichi Endo was in town with several of his Japanese partners. Endo was a judo expert turned wrestler who on the islands had a good fan base of native Hawaiians and expatriate Japanese. Karasick knew that Beyer was learning judo and working toward his black belt with referee Wally Tsutsumi; not wanting to pit one Japanese wrestler against another, he envisioned these two on the card – a skilled Japanese judo tactician against a rookie American grappler new to judo.

The hype for the Endo/Beyer judo jacket match, and the rest of the card, drew a good though not quite sellout crowd to the Civic Auditorium. Karasick had both wrestlers outfitted in judo jackets, tossing each other around the ring and landing an array of punishing blows. It wasn't traditional judo, nor was it meant to be, but the melding of judo and pro wrestling maneuvers proved to be entertaining for those in attendance. During a tie-up near one corner of the ring, Endo attempted to pull his arm out of Beyer's grasp and retake control when he accidentally head butted Beyer above his left eye, causing a bleeding gash. The cut was deep enough to require medical attention, ending the match a draw.

In the dressing room, Beyer was treated by house medical staff and instructed to allow a few days for the gash to heal before returning to the ring. Endo felt badly about what had happened to the rookie, and insisted that Beyer join him and his friends as his guest for dinner after the matches. Beyer accepted and was thinking steak – Endo had other ethnic ideas. They drove to a tiny, obscure Japanese restaurant in downtown Honolulu, where they met up with Oki Shikina, who had refereed their match, and where Endo introduced Beyer to their training partner, a seasoned champion wrestler and founder of Japan Pro Wrestling Alliance, Rikidozan. The quiet wrestler and current king of pro wrestling in Japan had watched the Endo/Beyer match from ringside and liked what he saw of the rookie American. The three Asians introduced the young twenty-five year old American to sushi and sashimi. Rikidozan, a former sumo wrestler of Korean heritage, sat next to Beyer and examined the wound close-up from his vantage point; Beyer said to him "Are you a doctor, too?" Through Shikina as interpreter, Rikidozan replied "No, a patient like you." The two bonded closely that evening; Rikidozan told Beyer how much he appreciated his wrestling acumen. They bid goodnight offering respectful bows, and expressing mutual desire to work the ring with one another. Beyer left the restaurant never dreaming that the next time he was to be in Rikidozan's company his world would be forever changed.

It was a successful trip, Beyer concluded. With only a few weeks remaining on the island, he took stock of his performances, his opponents, and the connections he established, convinced that he had done well; no argument from Karasick or other wrestlers – Kiniski and Kovacs told him he had a good future to look forward to, and even Blears had enjoyed his company. Lord James 'Tally-ho' Blears, who with Kiniski held the NWA Hawaii tag team title, lived with his wife

◄ MASKED DECISIONS

in an apartment overlooking the beach; Beyer got to know Blears, and loved the view from his home. It was only twelve years earlier that Blears, serving in the English merchant marines as a radio operator, was taken prisoner by the Japanese, after their ship was torpedoed by an enemy submarine. While he escaped his captivity and was eventually rescued at sea, he witnessed the torture and killing of others who were aboard his ship. Everyone on the island respected Blears, and Beyer was no exception. It was an honor to know him.

Beyer became comfortable in his own skin during his time in Waikiki, and his long range outlook improved. No longer harboring nagging doubts about his prospects in the business, Beyer learned that the more he connected the dots, the more opportunities came his way. The equation was getting resolved. He believed he had earned the right of passage to more matches in the States, and he was certain, beyond a doubt, he would again see Diamond Head and the waves of Waikiki. With his future coming into focus, he let himself be himself. Even his sense of humor developed a kind of comedic timing exceeded only by the likes of Jack Benny, Sid Caesar, and Jackie Gleason. On the beach one morning for a walk, Beyer came upon Sandor Kovacs, Gene Kiniski and their wives, sitting on blankets playing a board game; the four players were in need of a piece of string for the game, and Kiniski said to Beyer "Do you have a piece of string on you Dick?" Beyer loosened his swim trunks, looked down inside, turned to the four on the blanket, replied "No" and resumed his walk. The four could be heard laughing hysterically for hundreds of yards along the beach.

Beyer's phone rang one afternoon around 3:00 pm; it was a familiar voice with a surprising request. Ben Schwartzwalder apologized for "calling so late" – it was 9:00 pm on the east coast- "but we gotta have you back." The head coach told Beyer that the Chancellor had relented and allowed Beyer to coach while wrestling professionally. "Holy cow, I never expected to hear that," Beyer replied. But Beyer, astute as he was inquisitive, got to the bottom and uncovered the real reason behind the call– when Beyer proctored the freshman hall, he made sure everyone studied and went to class; during the time he was away, twelve freshman student athletes dropped out. Schwartzwalder believed Beyer had a positive influence in keeping the boys in school, and convinced the Chancellor to accept Beyer's return to resolve the problem. For Beyer, it was good feeling wanted, and even better feeling vindicated. When the conversation with the coach ended, he sat back with a smile on his face, knowing he had made a difference and was about to do it again. But another phone call that evening, this time from his dad, brought a premature sunset to his Hawaiian high.

The letter from the United States Army stated that, if Beyer did not report to the Army Reserve meetings (having not attended any since January), he would immediately be drafted into active duty. Sand between his toes didn't slow Beyer from calling Karasick on the run to offer a brief explanation for his sudden departure to Buffalo, where in June, 1956, he reported for his physical examination. The examining officer informed Beyer that, due to his age, there was an outside chance he might not be drafted. With only three weeks before his 26th birthday, Beyer agonizingly waited to hear the outcome. No draft notice came. Camp Drum was a little less ominous that summer. Beyer, appreciative for the opportunity to remain in the U.S., took it all in stride and prepared for his return to freshman proctor duties and those as assistant football coach.

Beyer's instincts as a coach came to life and matured during his second year on the coaching staff. Having played four years in the Schwartzwalder system, he had insights into how the coaches wanted players developed, but he began to reveal a true coaching sense and sensibility that could not be taught. In addition, he and Les Dye formed a close, working relationship to such a degree they seemed to be in sync on just about every aspect of the team's play. In the fall of 1956, the freshman squad travelled to West Point for their annual game. It was very cold and exceedingly windy on the field of play, located adjacent to the Cadet parade grounds, with flat open land around much of the venue. Midway through the second half, the Plebes backed up the Orangemen to their own goal line. On fourth down, the Syracuse freshman punter, Tom Gilbert, punted the ball from deep within his end zone into the air, and into what appeared to be an updraft, as the ball lifted off and sailed up and out, with a hang time that, to the Plebes, felt like forever; the ball eventually returned to earth, then bounced another fifty yards, stopping after travelling the length of two football fields. It was the longest, and strangest, punt Beyer had ever seen. Before the end of the game, the wind became even more of a factor. The goal post on the left end of the field blew down. In the fourth quarter, with Army driving downfield toward that end, the referee came over to Les Dye and Beyer and asked if they would allow Army to kick the extra point on the other end should they score. In unison, Dye and Beyer told the referee "They won't score." They didn't. Dye briefed Schwartzwalder on the details of the game when he returned to the Syracuse campus, but saved most of his higher praise for the work of his assistant coach.

The 1956 Syracuse University varsity football season was to be the last for Jim Brown. The recalcitrant running back, now a senior, had displayed impressive offensive and defensive prowess his junior year, and led the team to a 5-3 record. With a talented corps of players around him that included Jim Ridlon and Dick Lasse, Brown developed into a force unseen in college gridiron history. Schwartzwalder knew he had a good team…and a star. That season, in addition to his freshman line duties, Beyer helped Roy Simmons scout the opposition for the varsity. The program came together well – Syracuse finished the season at 7 wins, 1 loss, winning the Lambert trophy as best team in the East, on Jim Brown's record 986 rushing yards and All America honors. Syracuse received an invitation to play Texas Christian University in the Cotton Bowl in Dallas, on New Year's Day.

To prepare for their first Cotton Bowl appearance, the Syracuse football team and coaches flew to Norman, Oklahoma and the campus of Oklahoma University, a four hour drive from Dallas; the invitation was extended by OU coach Bud Wilkinson, a former Syracuse coach whom Schwartzwalder held in high regard. Ben kept practice consistent with the practices he held during the regular season- hard hitting and intense -the varsity in orange and their 'opponent' (the practice team) in green; Beyer coached the practice team or 'greenies' as they were known, during these sessions. The evening after the second practice, Beyer received a phone call from Leroy McGuirk, the wrestling promoter in Oklahoma City, asking him if he was interested in wrestling on the local card the following evening. Without having Schwartzwalder's blessing in advance, Beyer was reluctant to accept McGuirk's offer, so he told him he'd call back. Beyer went to his head coach and explained the matter, expecting him to provide reasons to decline. Instead, Schwartzwalder told Beyer not only was it Oklahoma OK, he would see to it that the entire team accompanied Beyer to the match! The following evening, in the auditorium in Oklahoma City, the Syracuse football team cheered on their assistant coach and professional wrestler. Coincidentally, Beyer's opponent that night wore green wrestling tights and assumed the crowd was supporting him by their 'Go Greenie' yells, not knowing that it was a term of endearment for Beyer, and the name used for Beyer's practice squad. One of the most vocal Beyer supporters sitting among the football players that night was number 44, Jim Brown, returning the support he had been given from a wrestler-coach.

The following day, to thank Beyer for wrestling on such short notice, McGuirk called Houston territory owner Morris Sigel and pitched a match for Beyer in Dallas. Before Beyer boarded the bus to Texas, he received word he was booked to wrestle Duke Keomuka, NWA Texas tag team and heavyweight title holder, and one of the feared heels in the territory. Beyer put up a good fight against Keomuka in Dallas, and once again had the support of the Syracuse football squad prior to the Cotton Bowl game on New Year's Day, 1957.

TCU had not recorded a bowl victory in its previous six post-season appearances, while Syracuse lost in its only bowl berth three years earlier to Alabama, Beyer's senior year – one of them was about to claim their first win. The 68,000 fans in attendance and a television audience saw a close Cotton Bowl contest, and a stellar performance by Jim Brown, who scored 3 touchdowns, racked up 132 rushing yards, kicked the extra points, and was named MVP. One of Brown's extra point conversions was blocked by TCU's Chico Mendoza, and the Orange lost by a single point, 28 to 27. It was a hard loss for the team and its head coach, evidenced by the chew marks on Schwartzwalder's cigar, but the play of Brown and his colleagues put Syracuse in the national spotlight, and helped the university to recruit higher caliber talent that would lead the football program to its greatest athletic achievement.

CHAPTER 8

DICK BEYER CAPITALIZED on his 'Schoolboy' wrestling persona in the Buffalo and Toronto territories when he returned to the region from the previous year's football campaign. For each match he entered the ring cloaked in his Syracuse University warm-up jacket and always white trunks and boots, projecting the image of a clean-cut, hard-working, intelligent Syracuse University graduate and promising fans a good show. In early 1957, his wrestling career finally was showing improvement – he was getting work, averaging eight matches a month. Also improving was his relationship with Wilma Thomson. They dated on and off, more on by mid-year, still with no commitments – each was free to date others if they wanted. Willy attended many of his local undercards, attracting attention as 'Schoolboy's girl' – she liked it, but didn't tell Beyer. In singles matches, Beyer met great wrestlers that included former Columbus instructor Dick Hutton, Steve Stanlee, Hardboiled Haggerty, Pat O'Connor, Carlos Moreno among others, and teamed with Billy Red Lyons, Ilio DiPaolo, Mighty Ursus and Tim Geohagan. Dick Beyer had developed into a steady undercard performer, no more, no less.

At home for the summer, Beyer decided to buy a boat kit from Sears and assemble the vessel with some help from family; fishing the waters around Buffalo relaxed him. His brother-in-law, Frank Martinke, married to Beyer's sister Jean, lived only a few doors down the street and offered his garage for the construction. Beyer and Martinke worked several months on the project, completing it around Labor Day weekend. They named the boat 'Tudor Time' after Tudor Beer, the cheapest beer available and the one they consumed heavily during those summer evenings.

MASKED DECISIONS

At the conclusion of his late-year routine - summer Army Reserves' camp and the 1957 Syracuse football season- Beyer was invited to the Tennessee territory by southeast promoters Nick Gulas and Roy Welch, members of the National Wrestling Alliance (as were many of Beyer's promoter bosses) in which promoters exchanged wrestling talent while backing a unified NWA heavyweight champion; each territory claimed and promoted its own champion outside the heavyweight class, and several territories boasted 'World Tag Team' champions simultaneously. Gulas and Welch told Beyer they'd give him opportunities to work undercard and main events with big name talent; the offer was appealing to Beyer as a way to move up to better venues and better pay. He departed Buffalo late December looking forward to celebrating 1958 in Nashville.

The Tennessee territory was another robust wrestling region whose live arena shows and televised events were supported by avid fans. It was commonplace for fans and 'arena rats' (girls who courted the wrestlers) to gather at the venues well before the opening matches and to linger long after the main event for autograph hunting, or for a brief glimpse of their favorites as they exited the building. While the territory was vast, the best attendance was found in Nashville, Memphis, Chattanooga, Birmingham Alabama, and Louisville Kentucky and the talent that drew included Ray Stevens, Joe and Jean Corsica, Tex Riley, Len Rossi, the Welsh, Green, and the Fargo Brothers. In this territory, the main event men did not receive more money; everyone was paid the same. Despite Gulas' reputation for not easily parting with a dollar bill, the wrestlers knew that by building interest and intrigue with grudge matches and rematches, they'd boost their take and prolong their engagement; during one extended stint, Beyer and the Corsica Brothers, working a program (feud) together, went from $25.00 a week to $125.00 a week as the town 'stayed up' and bought into the program for six months.

One of the first big name wrestlers Beyer faced in the southeast was Freddie Blassie, owner of several regional championships and by far one of the most hated villains in the ring. A former boxer and World War II Navy veteran, Blassie gained fame in the business with his outlandish behaviors that incited opponents, infuriated fans, and swelled box office cash registers. In his first match with Blassie, Beyer, looking to impress the veteran, absorbed numerous blows in the ring; at one point in the bout, Blassie grabbed Beyer's arm and threw him into the corner; Beyer made the toss across the ring look more forceful; he hit his head hard on the corner post, fell out of the ring onto his back, writhing in pain and moaning as the crowd stood up to get a closer look. In no time, Blassie jumped out of the ring near his opponent, put Beyer in a low head lock, and whispered to him, "You dumb shit, why are you taking such crazy punishment?" Blassie won the match, and afterwards told Beyer over dinner at the Gerst House that he appreciated the bruising he sustained for the good of the show "but never fly like that again." Beyer replied, "OK, I won't; but I want a main event sometime down the line." "We'll see…We'll see."

The two wrestlers stayed at the 200-room Maxwell House Hotel in Nashville, home to the territorial wrestling office on the first floor. Directly across the street was a strip joint, whose girls also roomed at the Maxwell. Blassie was fond of playing jokes on just about everyone, including the girls, most of whom he knew quite well. One evening after a match, Beyer and Blassie walked over to the hall to watch the girls perform; Blassie had in his pocket a small container of hot mustard spray that when contacted with skin caused a burning sensation. Blassie got close enough to one of the girls and sprayed her back 'business end' as she walked to the stage to perform; in a few moments, the girl was moving her bottom twice as fast as any other girl on stage. Blassie and Beyer were in hysterics. When the manager found out about the prank, he barred Blassie and Beyer from the establishment. Around the territory, Beyer faced Blassie in singles matches and later worked as his tag team partner in two matches against the Corsica Brothers. Blassie observed how the young wrestler created and sold mayhem in singles and team shows. The baby face from Buffalo registered well with the veteran.

The Alabama region was next up; Beyer made his first trip to Birmingham with twenty-year old Ray Stevens, a fellow graduate of Al Haft's school of wrestling who was marketed as the Southern Junior Heavyweight Champion. The 'blond bomber' heel had garnered reviews in the business as a yeoman worker with a good finishing move called 'bombs away' in which Stevens jumped from the top of the turnbuckle, ending up with his knee on the throat of his opponent. When the tag team and former Columbus colleagues arrived at the arena in Birmingham, Stevens said to Beyer, "This town has a lot of arena rats." Stevens, bleached blonde with an altar boy face, knew his way around, and into, the hearts of the ladies. As they entered the building, they saw several pairs of girls lined up along the walkway. "I told you," said Stevens to Beyer, "Wait till later." After the matches, the two walked from the dressing room down the stairs to the lobby, and paraded past a bevy of attractive young women, all indicating availability for the evening. Toward the end of the queue, Stevens stopped and spoke with two women who were not as well presented, well dressed, or well-endowed as others they had past; Beyer was stunned when Stevens turned to him and said, "Dick, meet our dates for the evening." Late that night, after dinner and some nightclubbing, Beyer asked Stevens, "Ray, why did we pick up the ugly sisters?" Stevens looked at Beyer, like a teacher about to impart valuable knowledge to a student and with both hands on Beyer's shoulders replied "Next week, when we return to Birmingham, every woman will know they have a chance to go out with us." In every hotel and city that summer, Beyer reflected on his relationship with Willy Thomson, in contrast to the one-night dates from the arenas. Despite the occasional companionship, life on the road was lonely; many nights, all he had were his thoughts, and from all the reflection that summer came a decision he'd act upon when he got back to Buffalo.

The Tuesday night matches held at the Hippodrome, on West End

Avenue in Nashville, were crowd-inciting spectacles that often mixed singles, team, and feature attractions with 'Rassle Royals' that involved a ring full of wrestlers battling for themselves. Beyer participated in one 'Royal' with Tex Riley, Len Rossi, Mike and Doc Gallagher, Jean Corsica and Al Smith. Akin to square dancing in its choreography, the battle gave Beyer an opportunity to display his speed and arsenal against a backdrop of differing wrestling styles. He was impressive. On July 1, Beyer again was paired with Ray Stevens in a tag team match scheduled as the first of a double main event against Mighty Lobo and old nemesis, Hans Schmidt. Told of the opponents beforehand, Beyer's eyes widened and he took Stevens aside telling him, "This will be a receipt night" (gaining justified revenge), still haunted by the memories of the pounding his body endured three years earlier in his first match with Schmidt on a snowy Michigan night.

Stevens started the match with Schmidt, giving his opponent a few good and unexpected body blows that staggered the big man. Stevens tagged Beyer, standing just outside the ropes, to take his place in the ring; Beyer couldn't get in there fast enough; he grabbed Schmidt's arm, swung under it, and connected a hard open kick to his chest that, had it been a football, would have travelled fifty yards. The surprised Schmidt, now reeling from the powerful thrust of Beyer's leg, tied him up in the corner and breathlessly said, "What are you doing?" Beyer said to Schmidt "This is a Benton Harbor receipt." The balance of the bout was nothing short of sweet revenge; Schmidt got a heavy, exhausting dose of comeuppance and lost more than a match – he lost the mental edge over Beyer. Four years in the business qualified Schoolboy Beyer to cash in an IOU, and it paid out with dividends.

Prior to leaving the territory, one match with a legend both inspired and motivated Beyer; it occurred in Birmingham, Alabama, when Beyer and tag team partner, Len Rossi, defeated Brother Frank Jares and Gorgeous George. It was the first meeting between Beyer and the nationally popular 'Toast of the Coast' as George was known; everything Beyer had heard about 'The Human Orchid' – his flamboyant androgyny, peroxide blonde hair, strutting gait, girly cowardice, feminine costumes, and perfume- spraying valet, was even more outrageous in person, but he saw how effective George's behaviors and accessories were in drawing heat, and enveloping the match in loud, jeering fan reaction. With the crowd into every move, hold and throw, it reminded Beyer of his football playing days at Syracuse, and it was exciting just to be in the ring with this master showman and entertainer. Beyer learned a valuable lesson in how to be a great heel from the match, and from George, who was complimentary toward the young baby face and his work. Beyer departed the Nashville territory with good press, good relations with the wrestlers, and good feelings about the direction his career was heading.

Beyer looked forward to attending Army Reserves' camp that summer with greater anticipation…it was to be his last. After eight years in the military reserves unit, he had fulfilled his obligation and was honorably discharged with the rank of sergeant in late summer 1958. He was proud of his service, comfortable in the knowledge that he had prepared well for active duty and was ready to serve had he been called. As he drove out for the last time from Camp Drum to Syracuse, he reflected, with a sense of belonging, on those who fought in Korea and in World War II, and the men and women in uniform with whom he was privileged to serve. He looked upon his eight years in the reserves much like a second-stringer on a team – he had been ready to defend his country if needed and was fully supportive of those who had been on the field. Now, it was his time to move on.

That fall, the freshman team was alive with an infusion of good talent led by a gifted back from nearby Elmira named Ernie Davis. Davis, recruited by Schwartzwalder with an assist by Jim Brown, was a high school All American and regional player of the year with such potential that he was offered scholarships to more than 50 schools; he wanted to stay close to home. Schwartzwalder told Davis he would give him Brown's number 44 jersey if he were to come to 'the hill'– to Davis that beat going to Notre Dame or UCLA; Davis became an Orangeman. On the field, Davis picked up where Brown left off. Beyer pushed the offensive line hard to open holes for the newcomer; Davis' freshman team recorded the University's first undefeated season; the varsity finished with a surprising 8-1 record, ranked 9th in the Associated Press year-end poll. Syracuse was invited to play Oklahoma in the 1959 Orange Bowl in Miami – the site of their first bowl appearance – captained by Beyer in 1953.

As was his custom, Ben Schwartzwalder flew the entire team, not just the travelling squad, this time to North Carolina to scrimmage and prepare on the campus of North Carolina State University. It was their reward for a good season. When they arrived, the atmosphere was not what the players anticipated; they were greeted by snow on the ground, regimented training and dorm room quarters; in addition, the head coach hit the team with twice a day practices that had them exhausted. Players wondered when the 'reward' for a bowl berth would begin. Once again, Beyer was given the responsibilities of serving as the opposing coach during scrimmages; he assembled his 'greenies' (redshirts, third and fourth stringers), lashed into them, fired them up, ordered them not to let up on the varsity players, to prepare them for the real Oklahoma team. For much of the week, the green team beat the stuffing out of the starting players. Coach Ben was infuriated by how poorly his starters were playing. In the meantime, Beyer was making believers out of young practice squad players like linemen Gene Grabowsky, John Brown and Leon Cholokis, and backs Dick Easterly, Dave Sarette and Jimmy Wright. They, along with other 'greenies,' rose to his challenge, pushed back the advances of the starters, and essentially took control during the week's practices. Beyer, under the assumed identity of Oklahoma's head coach Bud Wilkerson, had beaten Schwartzwalder's varsity team so badly Ben stopped scrimmages before making final game preparations.

January 1, 1959, more than 75,000 fans entered the turnstiles at

Orange Bowl Stadium anticipating a contest of speed versus power; speed and big plays won– the Orangemen lost to the Sooners 21 to 6. The Syracuse players, and coaches, never seemed to be in the same playbook, let alone on the same page; the team was sluggish and inconsistent. Syracuse and Schwartzwalder took damning criticism from the press and alumni for the loss, but Coach Ben deflected the faultfinding, and told his staff and players he was proud of the '58 team, and thanked them for a good season. He later told Beyer and other assistants the experience for the players prepared them for a tougher challenge ahead.

A quiet but significant change had occurred while Beyer was working in the Tennessee territory and months before he returned to Buffalo from Syracuse and the Orange Bowl - and it was not a welcome change. Ed Don George, having decided to leave the area, sold the Buffalo/Cleveland territory to Pedro Martinez, an old-school promoter and former pro wrestler. Martinez wasted no time booking events from Cleveland to Syracuse, banking on his success as the promoter of the New York territory in the early 1950s. His daughter, Ethel, was married to wrestler Ilio DiPaolo, whom Beyer had come to know and respect from the Buffalo and Toronto circuits. With Martinez in charge, Beyer knew he'd have to start from scratch.

Before Beyer asked for a meeting with Martinez, he met with Willy and, acting upon the decision he made in the south while on the road, he asked her to marry him. She accepted. The excited couple began to make plans for their future. Martinez proved to be more difficult. He said to Beyer early in their initial meeting "You are too small to make it in this business." When he told Willy of Martinez' comment, she said, "Aren't you glad I didn't say that when you proposed?" She instinctively knew how to depressurize him. Beyer never before was told by any promoter he was too small; at 5'10" and 215 pounds, while not a big man, there were shorter guys – Ray Stevens for one – getting headline events. Beyer asked Martinez "How about my success in Tennessee?" Martinez leaned over the desk toward Beyer and said, "Success in the business isn't just how good you wrestle, it's how well you draw money…and I think you're too small to draw money." The debate was over before Beyer could mount a strong rebuttal. Beyer left the office angry, upset with the prospect of toiling on undercards for years to come with the new promoter.

Dick Beyer and Willy Thomson were married in Buffalo, February 1959, amid snow showers and a temperature of twenty-one degrees. For two people from the same neighborhood who barely knew each other, who were reacquainted at a hot dog stand, whose relationship paralleled his mercurial wrestling career- it was an improbable union. Yet the wrestler and the power company supervisor were ready to face new chapters together, starting with their honeymoon – to Cuba.

Ed Don George, after leaving Buffalo, took up wrestling promotions in the late 1950s for the casinos in Havana. A host of high-end casino-hotels had developed out of the influx of American commercial interests that poured into Cuba, and in what emerged as a sexy, tropical city full of night life dancing, song, and nocturnal seductions, outside of any governmental restrictions. Wrestling became a good diversion, and kept the wealthy tourist-gamblers in town longer. George knew talent and he knew Beyer would be a great addition to the cards he was putting together in Havana for the tourists and locals in February. The city, like its bongos, was drumming for action, and all along the Malecon excitement reverberated. George asked Beyer to come to Havana for a few matches with expenses for two fully covered. What a perfect wedding present and at just the right time. The newlyweds couldn't wait to get to the warm Caribbean. They drove first from Buffalo to New Jersey, so that Beyer could introduce his bride to his college buddies, the Italian Connection, whom they met for dinner, then drove two days until they reached Florida. Beyer called Florida promoter Milo Steinborn to see if he had an opening on a card during the few days he and Willy were scheduled to be in town before flying to Havana. Steinborn was an astute promoter, who years earlier had purchased the Orlando rights from promoter

MASKED DECISIONS

Cowboy Luttrall for a thousand dollars, and made wrestling into a popular attraction. Fortunately for Beyer, Steinborn had one vacancy on the card; the 'Schoolboy' put on a magical show at the American Legion Arena for the residents of Central Florida before he and his wife took off for Cuba.

The Hotel Nacional De Cuba, built near the end of the San Lazaro cove, on the Taganana hill in western Cuba, was expansive, elegant, and reigned in the center of Vedado, the heart of Havana, in proximity to the business district dominated by large American corporations, and underworld entities, that viewed Cuba as limitless, fertile ground and a conduit to other Caribbean and South American markets. With its palm tree lined drive up to the main entrance and construction of eclectic architectural designs topped by twin red-capped turrets, the eight-story hotel featured lush gardens, heavy wood-beam ceilings, mosaic tile arches, a magnificent lobby reminiscent of a Catalan monastery, and panoramic views of the sea and city. It played host to the famous and infamous including Winston Churchill, Ernest Hemingway, Meyer Lansky, Frank Sinatra…and the Beyers of Buffalo. Willy was thrilled to be in Cuba; Beyer to be in Cuba wrestling; both to be warm. They took the first day to look around, snap photographs, and acclimate to the culture and conditions. The rich, flavor-full aromas of coffee and lush tobaccos gliding on gentle samba-infused breezes hovered at every corner. Havana both relaxed and excited the senses. The buildings were taller than they envisioned, the people, friendlier than expected, and the views from everywhere were breathtaking. The newlyweds perceived Havana as an adult playground – a blend of Las Vegas and Miami elements– with Willy remarking "Let's enjoy it now; it will be over before we know it."

A few weeks earlier, President Batista, on the heels of a revolution, fled the country which came under the control of a young lawyer-rebel, Fidel Castro, and his followers. While no one knew for certain what to expect from the change, there were indications that the promises Castro was making of restoring the Cuban constitution and holding free elections, may not come to fruition as articulated. A pervasive sense of uneasiness settled over some Cubans and Americans living on the island in the weeks before Beyer and his wife arrived, and a political and societal 'perfect storm' was brewing.

After a wonderful dinner at their hotel on their first evening in Havana, as they shared champagne in the quiet of the gloaming, Dick and Willy were suddenly interrupted by a soft knock on their hotel door; it was Ed Don George, an unexpected visitor who had stealthily rushed over to see them. He quickly entered the room, closed the door behind him, and spoke in hushed tones as if to lessen the chances of someone overhearing his remarks. "Dick, you have to leave town, tonight" said an anxious George. Beyer had never seen his friend and mentor behave in such a nervous, edgy manner. "It's not safe here now – I was told today the matches are cancelled and there could be trouble with the casinos. I made arrangements for you to leave on a flight in a few hours, but you must not look like you are in a hurry or panic." Beyer was incredulous; their luggage wasn't fully unpacked, the bed hadn't been turned down, it was their honeymoon, it was dusk, and they were being told to go home amid potential danger to their lives. George turned off the lights, parted the curtains in Beyer's room, and pointed outward; looking west toward center city, on the rooftops of the same buildings that Beyer and his bride had photographed that day, they now saw men taking up positions, with rifles. George gave final instructions and left, noiselessly, down the back stairs, while Dick and Willy sat on the bed in disbelief. They slept little, and nervously, that night, occasionally jostled by the sound of crackling gunfire off in the distance. At the appointed early hour, Beyer and Willy made their way down to the lobby, checked out without incident, walked with luggage in hand toward the north end of the driveway to a waiting vehicle, and slowly entered. They drove away from the hotel as two men watched from the hotel lobby entrance. En route to the airport, they had no way of knowing whether they would arrive or be diverted. Terrified, they sat motionless, without conversation from the unknown and uncommunicative driver. With tickets, security, and a plan arranged by George, Beyer and Willy unassumingly walked through the airport procedures and boarded an early morning flight back to the United States. Willy's prophecy had been eerily fulfilled.

"How was the match?" Willy asked, as Beyer returned home nights from undercards in the Buffalo and Toronto territories. "Another day at the factory," was Beyer's reply. To him, it was work, he gave his all each night, the money was a cut above minimum, but he wasn't moving up to main events anytime soon. It was a frustrating time for Beyer. Fans appreciated his work ethic yet he was unable to get the top spot on any card. Nevertheless, in each match he worked as though he was the headliner.

Pedro Martinez in Buffalo, and Frank Tunney in Toronto, scheduled Beyer for a few rare shoots (unplanned events), many works (planned outcomes), singles and tag team matches. Among his many opponents, Beyer met Fred Atkins, Lenny Montana, Bill Miller, Ed Albers (now Ed Miller) from his Columbus days and Reggie Lisowski, Gypsy Joe, and Mighty Atlas from his time in Chicago. His old buddies told him he had matured sufficiently to garner headline matches, and were surprised the promoters hadn't given him the opportunity. Even new opponents like Baron Gattoni, Fritz Von Erich, Chief Chewacki, and tag partners Ilio DiPaolo, Bob Leipler, Bobby Brown, Man Mountain Montana, and Bobo Brazil agreed with the assessment of Beyer's potential.

Beyer's home matches were staged in War Memorial Auditorium, located near the former Erie Canal, between Lower Terrace and Lake Street, in downtown Buffalo, home of the minor league Buffalo Bisons hockey team since 1940, and the venue for circuses, auto shows, roller skating, and other events, including a memorable 1957 visit by a young heartthrob, Elvis Pressley. Many a night, unbeknownst to his son, Dewey Beyer sat in the 15,000 seat arena thanks to a co-worker from the Ford plant, who moonlighted at 'the Aud' and allowed the wrestler's father access through a back door so he could see his son perform. On other nights, Beyer bought his dad a ticket near ringside. Opponents and partners loved working with Beyer; it was the local promoter who had problems with him and Beyer wanted, and needed, to confront the issue, and him, head on.

In July, Beyer asked Pedro Martinez for another meeting. This time, he was not going to take 'too small' for an answer. Beyer knew that while working a hometown main event was a wrestler's dream, for various reasons it also was a promoter's nightmare; many promoters did not like using local talent in main events, fearing the headliner might not 'go over' well for rematches, his reputation too well-known to locals, and other considerations – this operating tenet of the wrestling business was about to be challenged by a local baby face.

"I want to wrestle a main event" Beyer emphatically stated to Martinez, before the two sat down in their chairs. Martinez had figured out the reason Beyer wanted to meet him and, without a blink, replied, "Put your money where your mouth is." Beyer asked him to explain. Martinez said, "If you think you can draw money, buy the house!" He furthered his comments by telling Beyer he would test his drawing power - in Cleveland - against a worthwhile opponent – top villain Fritz Von Erich – and if the test proved successful, Beyer stood to earn main event bookings in Buffalo. "But you have to guarantee that you and Fritz can draw six thousand dollars – that's the average house – so give me a check for half that, as insurance, and I will book the match for three weeks from this Thursday."

Beyer never heard of such a business quid pro quo in his five years in wrestling; neither did any of his wrestling colleagues whom he sought out for advice on the matter. It was a first for all of them. Flashing through his mind was that evening in Somerset, Kentucky, when he took the percentage of the house over a guarantee, and ended up with six dollars for his evening's work – What if another rain storm keeps fans away? Wanting to prove he was ready and able to produce big, Beyer decided to call Martinez and agree to the terms. "OK, Pedro, you will have my three thousand dollars." Next, Beyer wondered where he was going to get three thousand dollars. His bank accounts contained far less than he needed, his family and friends were not in position to help to that extent. He went to a bank and pleaded for a personal loan that, under normal circumstances, would have been difficult to obtain, but known as he was in town, and with a few items to claim as collateral, he secured the money. He took the certified check to Martinez, handed it to him saying, "I expect to get that back from you the night of the match when you see how much we bring in." Beyer left the office and began silent prayer…Please, God, let me get that money back.

The card, set for August 13, 1959 in Cleveland, was full of wrestlers Beyer got to know over the years. The opening match was Mighty Atlas against Roy McClarty; the second bout put Ilio DiPaolo and Stan Lisowski in the ring; the third was Chief Don Eagle and Baron Gattoni; the fourth bout was a midget tag team match of Pee Wee James and Sky Low Low wrestling Little Beaver and Dandy Andy Moore; this was followed by another tag team match with 'brothers' Ed and Dan Miller against Guy and Joe Brunetti. And in the main event, 2 out of 3 falls to a finish, Fritz Von Erich and 'Schoolboy' Dick Beyer.

For three weeks prior to the match, Von Erich and Beyer promoted the event on Cleveland television during the broadcasts of studio wrestling; the promotions were full of insults hurled at Beyer from Von Erich, and from Beyer at Von Erich, with predictions of winning outcomes from both wrestlers, accented by loud over-the-top descriptions of what each had planned for the other in the ring. They crossed their fingers and shook hands before the match in hopes their marketing plan would achieve the $6000 needed as the average take. The night of the match, they took in $12,000. After the main event, Pedro Martinez walked into the dressing room and handed Beyer his original check of $3000. Putting it into his pocket, Beyer said to Martinez "I can do even better; give us a return match in two weeks." Martinez looked at both wrestlers, nodded affirmatively, and walked out without another word said. Beyer never again put money up front.

The rematch drew more fans and more money – close to $17,000 – almost three times the average house. The experiment, beyond any doubt, convinced the promoter that Beyer was a draw, and proved that Beyer was not afraid to invest in himself and take risks; more importantly, it proved to Beyer he was ready to springboard from the undercards, and to take his rightful place as a marquee name in the main events.

CHAPTER 9

THEIR SMALL, DRAFTY apartment above a garage in Woodlawn, near Lake Erie, south of the city of Buffalo, was to be vacant for several months while the couple took up residence near Syracuse during football season. Willy and Dick had travelled to central New York earlier in the summer to find a place that offered a short commute for Beyer to Archbold Stadium. They found and rented a cottage at Skaneateles Lake, a thirty minute drive to Syracuse; the cottage, quaint and charming, had just enough room and was inexpensive, which allowed the couple to retain their apartment in Western New York and move back after the football season.

Settling into the lakeside cottage, Dick and Willy Beyer were in good spirits. They talked about the upcoming football campaign, the main events and undercards Dick had wrestled in the Buffalo and Toronto territories, families, Willy's ideas and her desire to do more drawing and oil paintings; situated as they were on a quiet lake, she anticipated opportunities to further develop her hobbies.

With newfound enthusiasm in headline events for Dick Beyer, Pedro Martinez worked around Beyer's coaching and scouting routine to schedule him into matches through December in Rochester, Erie, Syracuse, Buffalo and Cleveland opposing Doc Gallagher, Mighty Atlas, Tom Bradley, Mike Valentino, Lee Henning and teaming with good friends Ilio DiPaolo, Bobo Brazil and Roy McClarty. The 'good guy' wrestler had become a favorite on the upstate circuit, a local hero by any wrestling fan's definition. On the streets of Buffalo, Rochester, Syracuse, and in promotions wherever he wrestled, the 'Schoolboy' identity was systematically and deliberately replaced by the more mature 'Syracuse mat star and coach.' Beyer was respected by everyone for the way he worked; he brought a glint of celebrity to a blue collar region, and the people were proud to call him one of their own.

Just as things were on the rise, Beyer's life-long hero, tragically, was brought down. From a garage roof on which he had been working, Dewey Beyer accidentally fell, resulting in a compound fracture of his leg. Hospitalized, his leg in a cast, the outcomes, over time, did not materialize, and the leg had to be amputated. Beyer drove home often to visit his dad, donate blood, and spend whatever time he had during the autumn of 1959, balancing his football duties with his overwhelming desire to be with his father. His dad whispered to him to remain strong for his family and never stop learning; it reminded Beyer of the day he departed Buffalo for Syracuse by train and the dollar dictionary his dad purchased for him inscribed with 'It's your decision.' Beyer wanted so desperately to make a decision that would help his father, but there were none to make. Infectious hepatitis developed weeks after the amputation. In October, Dewey Beyer died.

The loss of his father, his only true role model, was a devastating void he wasn't sure he'd overcome. But the love from his mother, sisters, and his bride kept him emotionally afloat, enabled him to grieve and, in time, to accept the reality. Beyer dedicated the upcoming football season to his dad, and made a quiet promise to himself – to never stop learning from everything and everyone and to blaze a trail that was to be somehow, someway, unique.

Ben Schwartzwalder held several meetings with his assistant coaches prior and during pre-season workouts and scrimmages. He laid out his plans for the '59 campaign and instructed his lieutenants to work the boys hard, to stay on them for every mistake so that they understood what they did wrong and corrected it on the spot – he wanted his players to leave all the mistakes on the practice field.

For the players, the practice routine was the same as it was since

Schwartzwalder first arrived; suit up, run out from the Archbold dressing facilities, make a right turn, down a slight slope and across a road that circumnavigated the stadium, go down another slope and onto Hendrick's field. Hendrick's practice field was large, about the size of two football fields with tennis courts on the west end; on the east end concrete bleachers lined the field on which people sat for lacrosse games and freshman football games. It had been nicely greened and landscaped by the university's school of forestry. In the spring, the football team occupied one field, and the lacrosse team the other; when the day's football practice was nearly over, those who also played lacrosse ran to the opposite field to begin practice in that sport, under head coach Roy Simmons, who also coached the defensive backfield for football. Simmons made sure the two-sport players got in both practices; when Jim Brown played, Brown moved seamlessly from football to lacrosse, others found it more difficult. Varsity football practices were brutal; beginning with the rope climb and moving into drills and specialty routines, to the players it felt more like military boot camp – and in a way it was – a carryover from Schwartzwalder's service years, but it was his way of getting the boys prepared. Though practices were typically harsh the previous few years, those of the summer and fall of 1959 were exponentially tougher.

By mid-season, the Syracuse Orangemen football team was undefeated. There were a few testy moments in early season games with Kansas, Maryland, Navy and Holy Cross, but overall, Syracuse dominated opponents, outscoring them by a combined 138 to 33. The players showcased their enormous talent, turning in superb performances offensively and defensively; the coaches were monitoring every detail under the ever-close watch of their head coach. Players and coaches were firing on all pistons.

Dick Beyer was engrossed with the offensive line, green team, and scouting duties with Roy Simmons. Intense as football was, he carved out the time to wrestle – he needed it. It became routine for Simmons, the lead scout, defensive coach, boxing and lacrosse coach, to work Beyer's corner, even though in pro wrestling there was no need for a corner man as in boxing. But Simmy loved to be close to the action and support his friend. The weekly schedule and plan called for Simmons and Beyer to leave Syracuse on Fridays, scout the team they were to play the following week on Saturdays, return and present their scouting report to the coaches and team on Sundays. Roy Simmons was a master scout and tactician; he dissected every upcoming opponent's offensive and defensive schemes and evaluated every player; by the end of each scouted game, Beyer and Simmons had enough material to closely predict the team's behaviors. Every Sunday, Simmy stood in front of the entire team and precisely diagnosed the opposing team's strengths and weaknesses, calling attention to the Orangemen's potential problems offensively and defensively and how the game plan needed to be constructed. His analyses were spot on, but he always held something back to motivate the team, leaving the impression that the next opponent was better than any team on record.

In the days leading up to a mid-season game against West Virginia, Beyer was informed by Martinez that he was scheduled to wrestle Friday night in Buffalo, the day before the game against West Virginia. Simmons said to Beyer, "Great, we can drive to Buffalo on Friday afternoon; after you wrestle we'll drive to Erie and watch the Friday night fights on TV. Saturday morning we will go into Pittsburgh, scout their game and head back to Syracuse." At times, it was obvious that Simmons enjoyed those wrestling weekends more than his wrestling colleague. Simmons knew a lot about pro and amateur boxing and discussed it in detail with Beyer who learned a great deal about the sport and incorporated boxing footwork techniques into his wrestling repertoire. The student never stopped learning. Reporting back to the team on Sunday, Simmons outlined details of what he and Beyer observed at Pittsburgh in that team's performance against Texas Christian. Led by quarterback Ivan Tonsic and junior end Mike Ditka, Pittsburgh held at breakeven for the season with 3 wins and 3 losses, but they were fighters, especially Ditka, whom Simmons labeled "A head hunter - don't turn your back on that guy." Syracuse frustrated Ditka and his team all day, registering a 35-0 thumping of Pittsburgh, one week after defeating West Virginia 44-0. The Orangemen went on to beat Penn State, Colgate and Boston University, racking up points, yardage, and accolades to become the number one ranked college football team in the nation, with one regular season game remaining - a showdown with UCLA.

In the Los Angeles Coliseum, on a sunny day with temps in the low 80s, Syracuse kicked off in its quest to register the university's first undefeated season. The Orangemen never looked back, as the team built a 21-8 halftime lead, held the threat of UCLA's talented thrower Billy Kilmer in check, and finished with a 36-8 score, completing their amazing regular season 10 wins no losses, ranked first in the country. Only a date with Texas in the Cotton Bowl on New Year's Day stood in their path to full recognition as national champions in college football.

A crowd of more than 10,000 ecstatic people cheered the Orangemen at the Clarence Hancock Airport when they returned home from their west coast triumph. The city of Syracuse was madly in love with its college football team, and many across the country were feeling the same about the Orangemen. Beyer was pleased to be a contributor to the larger success of the team, and while very happy for players and coaches, he sensed a gap in his own level of satisfaction. At home over dinner, Beyer told Willy everything he was feeling. He poured out his emotions; he was proud of the season but saddened that he could not share it with his father. "I guess I picked a good year to dedicate to dad," he said misty-eyed to his wife. "He would be so happy for you, Dick," she reassured him. Beyer later told her the experience had given him a new way of looking at his career; seeing the team get national attention made him realize being a local celebrity is fine, but the larger spotlight was drawing him in. The vow he made to himself after his father's passing, to be unique, was increasing in intensity.

MASKED DECISIONS

The Syracuse football program- as he saw it- paralleled his wrestling career and his life– a slow start, building over years, and eventually achieving enormous success. He wondered aloud when his big break might come, but there was little time for self-pity or examination; he needed to help the team prepare for the biggest game in the school's history.

Schwartzwalder gave his team a week off to catch up on school work and get away from the football frenzy. He, too, learned lessons from previous trips to bowl games, and he was not about to let anything distract him, or his charges, from the most important mission of their university lives. A few days of practice in Syracuse were followed by an early departure to Houston, where the team was set to practice twice daily for ten days before travelling to Dallas to meet Texas in the Cotton Bowl.

Hearing the news of the Cotton Bowl matchup, Morris Sigel called Beyer and offered him several matches while he was to be in Texas. He remembered Beyer from his Texas debut in 1956, prior to the last Cotton Bowl appearance by the Jim Brown-led Orangemen; he liked what he saw in the young 'Schoolboy'. Sigel built Houston into the largest wrestling territory in the country, and had a hand in developing some of the finest wrestlers in the business. With Syracuse flying to Dallas to play Texas in the Cotton Bowl, Sigel smelled action, and wanted the Syracuse coach on the card to draw off the interest brewing in the football game and he, with help from Dallas promoter Ed McLemore, put together three matches for Beyer – one in Houston, a rematch with Duke Keomuka, and two in Dallas, wrestling Jimmy Hines and Texas State Heavyweight champion Nick Kozak for the Texas belt.

The Syracuse team and coaches sequestered, practiced, and worked on their game plan at the University of Houston's football facilities; Beyer put in extra time helping to ready the big offensive line. He, too, liked what he saw. When the mid-week practice was over, he took a cab and arrived early at the Houston wrestling venue, City Auditorium, on the evening of his bout with Keomuka. In the dressing room he exchanged stories with Danny McShane, former heavyweight champion Pepper Gomez, Ox Anderson out of Salt Lake City, and current champion Pat O'Connor. It was an exciting evening of wrestling action for Houston area fans. After the match, Beyer sat with Keomuka and reminisced about their first encounter in 1956; Keomuka told Beyer he had been very worried about that match since it appeared Beyer didn't understand what they were to do once in the ring, as Beyer must have entered his dressing room at least six times before their match to discuss the holds and maneuvers to perform. "I thought you were gonna kill me with your stupidity" Keomuka yelled. Beyer howled; it was all a joke on Keomuka and everyone wrestling that night had been in on the rib. Keomuka said to Beyer "I didn't know it was a rib until we hooked up in the ring and you put on some great moves."

When the Syracuse football team arrived in Dallas, Beyer stopped by a newsstand and picked up a copy of *Rasslin'*, promoter McLemore's wrestling publication; the headline with an accompanying photo shouted 'Syracuse Mat Star And Coach Dick Beyer Returns Tonight' with a sub heading 'Mat Whiz Is Coach of Great Line of Cotton Bowl Bound Syracuse.' He hastily opened the program to read the promotional copy: 'As an athlete a wrestler is superior to all others. And a man who is dedicated to wrestling soon realizes this. Such a super wrestler is handsome Dick Beyer, a man with a Master's degree who has contributed a lot to the sports world. Dick Beyer wrestles in our semifinal tonight taking on rugged "bear baiting" Jimmy (Bad Boy) Hines…the Alabama roughhouser, a lineman himself in his football days, says he'll trim the visiting celebrity when they tangle.' With mention of Beyer's previous champion opponents, college mat success, and football experience, the article concluded: 'Ranked as Number One in the nation this year's Syracuse team can boast of the best line possibly in the history of the sport – at least statistically. It is a thumping herd of heavyweights who really respond to Beyer's commands. Needless to say, Dick Beyer is a most popular man.' Beyer murmured, "Handsome? Yes, but hardly popular, certainly not in Texas this week." He and Hines eventually locked up in the ring, and exceeded all expectations for a great North/South match. Afterwards, interest began to swell in the bout with Kozak for the Texas belt, just as Sigel and McLemore had predicted. It was to be the battle between Syracuse and Texas before the football contest between Syracuse and Texas.

The Kozak match, last of the three scheduled for Beyer, was pumped up in the *Dallas Morning News* with the line- 'Beyer, an assistant Syracuse football coach, will attempt to win the Texas heavyweight wrestling championship Tuesday night at the Sportatorium and will be on the sideline Friday in the hope of helping direct Syracuse to win over Texas in the Cotton Bowl.' Beyer laughingly thought *could it be any more subtle*. That night, before the matches got underway in the Sportatorium, Beyer introduced himself to several wrestlers he had not previously met - Prince Neff Maiava, Mad Maurice Vachon, and Tosh Togo (Harold Sakata a Hawaiian of Japanese descent). In the dressing room the Samoan, the Canadian, and the Japanese swapped stories with Beyer, and encouraged him to continue working hard and look for opportunities to work with them down the road. He liked what he heard. Beyer was building a solid network within the wrestling community, and believed that his big break was drawing nearer. He dressed, warmed up, and took the long walk to the ring. Big D was in Big D.

In what had become an odd tradition, Ben Schwartzwalder took the entire squad to the match to support the team's assistant coach, to relax the players with a night out, and the head coach even led the cheers during Beyer's bout – unusual behavior for the basically reserved Schwartzwalder. The largely partisan crowd witnessed a good struggle that ended in a draw, with the Texas heavyweight title belt remaining on Kozak. "It's the only title staying in Texas" Beyer shouted as he left the ring, to the frenzied delight of the football team.

Game day, January 1, 1960; a sold-out Cotton Bowl crowd and millions watching on television anticipated a battle. What unfolded was a war fought on multiple fronts. Syracuse, undefeated on the season, had never won a bowl game, and the heat was on the Orangemen to validate eastern football legitimacy. Failure this day meant #2 Mississippi, #3 LSU or #4 Texas would become national champions. What made the challenge burdensome was the questionable condition of Syracuse star Ernie Davis, who had injured his leg in practice before the championship game. Beyer looked at the faces of the players as they listened to their head coach before leaving for the field; he didn't see anxiety or panic or doubt; he saw determination, confidence, and a quiet coolness, emotions in control, a distinctive difference from previous Syracuse bowl teams. Davis was in pain, but cleared to play; other players had butterflies; the coaches had done their best to prepare the team. Everyone wanted to do well for their respected head coach. The moment was at hand.

From the sidelines, Beyer had an unobstructed view of football history. Syracuse won the coin toss, and the Orangemen returned the opening kickoff to their 26 yard line. A loss of yardage on the first down run, and a penalty on the following play, forced the Orangemen back to the 13 yard line. A play was sent in from the coaches; Beyer barked out reminders and encouragement to the 'Sizeable Seven' offensive line. On second down and 26 yards to go, halfback Gerhard Schwedes took a pitch from the quarterback and ran to his left in an apparent run sweep, but he stopped near the hash marks and looked for open receivers downfield; the ball, thrown deep into the Texas secondary, was caught by Ernie Davis, who ran it to the end zone for a Syracuse quick-strike, 87 yards and a new Cotton Bowl record. Davis scored again on a one yard run halfway through the second quarter, and a two-point conversion made the score 15-0. What injury?

Texas was jolted…and angry. For much of the first half, Syracuse and Texas pounded on each other, but Texas took the hitting further, legally but sometimes questionably as Beyer saw it; the Orangemen were not getting any help from the officials, who seemed to be calling dubious infractions on Syracuse. Frustrations mounted late in the second quarter- for the Orangemen from perceived illegal hits, poor officiating, and alleged racial remarks by Texas players; for Texas from the score, the strong play of Syracuse, and the embarrassment of losing on Texas soil. The game ceased... and transitioned into a fight for survival, morphing into football's version of hand to hand combat that climaxed prior to the end of the first half.

Only feet from where Beyer stood, John Brown, a Syracuse tackle and one of the three black players on the team, took exception to a remark he claimed Texas tackle Larry Stephens made toward him, after a Syracuse fumble killed off a scoring drive. The two grabbed hold of each other, Brown swung at Stephens. Another Texas player jumped in at the very moment both benches emptied onto the field and headed toward the two combatants. Within seconds, without thinking, Beyer had run into the fray -the first responder to the potentially explosive scene – and, spotting the Texas player in front of him, he restrained Stephens from behind and pulled him away, averting more damaging consequences for the players, as teammates surged and tensions mounted, jets and sharks without music. The head coaches, assistants, officials, and security rushed to the area and ushered players off the field before the situation could escalate. It was a brief, but awful, sideshow to what was, to that point, an awesome display of speed, strength, and skill. Beyer's quick reaction helped quell a firestorm and restore order. The game continued into the second half without incident. The Syracuse lead was never in jeopardy, and when the final gun sounded, Syracuse, led by game MVP Ernie Davis, had a 23-14 win and the National Championship of college football.

Something unusual occurred in the Syracuse dressing room in the early minutes after the hard fought game. There was no shouting or jumping, few congratulatory exchanges, not even a 'we're number one' yell. What occurred was reflective thought under smoldering emotions. The players were physically and emotionally spent, with many harboring anger that surfaced quickly; some offered criticism of certain Texas players for poor sportsmanship while others, including coaches, had strong comments about the officiating. They needed to vent before they needed to celebrate. Soon, reserve back Dick Easterly stood up, looked around the room, and said emphatically "Hey, we WON the game, didn't we?" As the time ticked by and the team calmed, the Syracuse Orangemen basked in the warm glow of achievement, and realized what they had accomplished - a first for the university and for themselves - a national championship.

In the days that ensued, various news sources retold the game story and summary, but all agreed it was the best of the bowls that year, and perhaps the greatest Cotton Bowl of the modern era. The January 2, 1960 edition of the *Dallas Times Herald* – which reported on page four that Massachusetts Senator John Kennedy was to announce his bid for the presidency, challenging other democrats including Texan Lyndon Johnson - did not display on its front page a photo of the national champs, of MVP Ernie Davis or of either the Longhorns' two touchdowns, rather the photo was of the second quarter mob scene, with Dick Beyer holding back Larry Stephens, the caption 'The Good Old American Way,' and a full description of the event on page two. The photo, article, wrestling reference, and quotes attributed to Beyer prompted Syracuse sports information director Val Pinchback to say to Beyer "You're getting more press than the national champs!" It wasn't the kind of press Beyer wanted to generate; he did not want to be a distraction to the team's success, and although Pinchback was kidding, Beyer removed himself from the celebratory festivities in Dallas and took his wife to Las Vegas for a few days, before returning to Syracuse for the city and university welcome home events. He just felt better doing it that way – he said to Willy "I don't want them talking about me breaking up that fight, I want the attention back on the game and the team so they get all the credit they deserve."

MASKED DECISIONS

Beyer breaks up the on-field scuffle

The Syracuse Orangemen football team of 1959 captured the national championship, and was first in the nation in total offense, rushing, scoring, total defense, rushing defense and touchdowns; offensive linemen Roger Davis, Robert Yates and Fred Mautino earned All America honors; Ben Schwartzwalder was named Coach of the Year. It was a powerhouse of a program. The team made history, but one more historic achievement was around the corner…a sentinel event that would forever change the complexion of college football.

After the noisy celebrations of the football championship had quieted to distant echoes, the money and the matches improved on the circuits for Beyer. His reputation in wrestling, and for coaching the

Syracuse football team, created interest in him in territories beyond Buffalo as main event work landed, though not consistently, on the table. Martinez happily kept Beyer busy in Western New York, Central New York and Ohio tangling with the likes of Waldo Von Erich, Fred Atkins, Baron Gattoni, Bronko Lubich, Angelo Poffo, Billy 'Red' Lyons and others. Frank Tunney imported him to Toronto and Montreal for several headline matches, and it was during this time period that Beyer struck up a friendship with Charley Iwamoto, who wrestled under the name Mr. Moto, a name that had been used by other wrestlers of Japanese heritage. The two wrestlers just seemed to hit it off and became good friends almost immediately. Scheduled appearances in Pennsylvania and Tennessee, where Beyer teamed several times with Lester Welch against Mr. Moto and Tor Yamato, got his picture and a write-up in the papers; his input to the success of the Syracuse football program was always referenced in sports articles and wrestling promotions. Moto kidded his new friend often, telling him "You don't see Asians playing football, so leave wrestling to us."

Beyer often said to his wife "Wrestling life is a tough life, but in real life it's a good living." Beyer adored it – he was absorbed by it - so much that he wanted to expand his involvement in the business. With the blessing of Pedro Martinez, Beyer approached a television station in Buffalo and asked to work as a commentator on its broadcasts of arena bouts. He pitched the idea of an industry insider, a pro wrestler who knew the business and the players, the angles, and the programs, the strengths and weaknesses, competent to describe the intricacies of the matches. Beyer was confident; in college, he had given interviews to the press; in the pros, he regularly sold his matches on camera during studio television bouts in the weeks leading up to his event. He was good on the microphone. He knew how to enhance the heat for a heel, and draw support for a baby face; he was articulate, knowledgeable, had a great sense of humor and had no intentions of upstaging the match or the announcer.

WKBW-TV in Buffalo gave Beyer the sought-after opportunity. Beyer's job was promoted in the press as a dual role of wrestler and commentator for Saturday afternoon wrestling at Buffalo's Memorial Auditorium. After his own match, Beyer left of the ring, donned a robe or short jacket, sat down next to the television announcer, and began commentary on the subsequent bouts and individual wrestlers, sweat pouring from his forehead, chest and hands as he held his microphone. The television audience loved it, the attendees loved it, and Beyer really loved it. For many fans it was like having a family friend…someone on the inside who gave the 'real dope' on the wrestling world. They trusted what he had to say. Professional and provocative, Beyer's commentary was meant to educate the public, enhance the event, and at times, entice a wrestler into an on-air verbal tete-a-tete, that led to a follow up confrontation in the ring between Beyer and the wrestler. It was effective and helped drive attendance at the live matches. Beyer's voice was a mix of styles – deep, booming, gravely, timely inflection with a measured cadence. Anyone listening instantly recognized the wrestler was also intelligent and thoughtful. It was deliberate; Beyer was breathing life into the comment Gypsy Joe made about him "…a well-educated wrestler."

Beyer's diversification in the business didn't end with his additional duties behind the microphone. Having toiled in the Buffalo territory for several years, Beyer formed close friendships with other wrestlers stationed in Western New York, notably Ilio DiPaolo, Billy 'Red' Lyons, and Fritz Von Erich. The four wrestled against and teamed with each other numerous times locally, and on the road, and had formed a brotherhood that eventually became a social circle of girlfriends, wives, and families. Beyer even introduced his friend, Billy Red, to one of Willy's sisters, Norma. The two began a courtship.

The four wrestlers were acutely aware of attendance problems with the Rochester area matches; the imported talent to Buffalo sometimes skipped out of Rochester bouts, leaving only local talent to fill the card. Promotions were scarce. With little new to add, the matches had become stale, attendance was evaporating. Over drinks at DiPaolo's home one afternoon, the four discussed the situation in Rochester, questioning whether collectively they had the wherewithal to turn the wrestling fortunes around, and into a successful operation in that city. Questions dissolved into solutions; problems repositioned as opportunities. That week, Beyer, DiPaolo, Lyons and Von Erich approached Pedro Martinez – DiPaolo's father-in-law – and proposed buying the Rochester territory from him. They expected a struggle; instead, they got support. Martinez, who was focused on building Buffalo and Cleveland, told them he would sell the territory for $6000, and if they didn't like promoting, he'd buy it back for the same amount. The four were floored. Within a few days, they each had anted up $1500 to Martinez and became proud promoters of a wrestling territory.

For six months, Beyer and his pals labored to bring fresh wrestling matches and renewed excitement to the show in Rochester. They used studio wrestling bouts, which aired each Saturday afternoon from 4:30 pm to 5:30 pm over WROC-TV Channel 5, to stir ticket sales for their Wednesday night matches at Rochester Memorial Auditorium. Earl Wood and Dick Beyer worked the matches as announcer and commentator respectively for the studio bouts; Dick also provided color commentary during the matches on Wednesday nights. Fritz Von Erich was the territory heel, the villain who took on all comers; DiPaolo and Lyons worked as baby faces. Each called in IOUs from their friends in the wrestling community; the result - the town buzzed, stayed up for most of their term as promoters, and made money for the investors. The television station that aired the studio shows negotiated a sale to a new owner that did not have any interest in hosting or staging wrestling matches; the writing was on the wall; at different intervals, the four wrestlers approached Martinez who, true to his word, refunded each investment for the original amount. The four believed it was better to put the territory back into the hands of someone dedicated to full time promotions. They returned to full time wrestling.

Martinez moved fast to book interesting matches for the budding wrestling star, Dick Beyer. He set up several bouts with Baron Gattoni,

MASKED DECISIONS

a big, bearded, long-haired 300 pound mountain of a man, of Italian heritage, who grew up in Argentina; Gattoni, who once weightlifted 300 pounds with one hand, appeared ferocious-looking in the ring. Fans were largely unaware that this wrestling heel and physically punishing opponent played violin, loved classical music and spoke several languages. One of the Beyer/Gattoni matches was covered by *Ring Magazine* with a three-page spread and action photos that foretold of great things to come for the Buffalo grappler and football coach. More publicity for his matches came at lightning speed.

Ring Magazine covered a program that Martinez cooked up for Beyer, Angelo Poffo and his 'manager' Bronko Lubich. Poffo had gained fame as a champion and was memorialized in 'Ripley's Believe It Or Not' for completing 6033 consecutive sit-ups, setting a new record at the time. He and Hungarian-born Lubich - a Canadian wrestler and part-time cane-swinging cornerman – travelled to territories to wrestle as a team, and at times worked individually, while other times Poffo worked solo in the ring with Lubich patrolling the perimeter as manager. Weeks before the meeting between Poffo and Beyer, Poffo had been losing several matches but somehow managed to pull out wins with the help of Lubich and his cane – poking, prodding or hitting opponents just enough to distract them and give Poffo the time to position a win. This set up the match with local baby face, Dick Beyer. In the contest, Beyer had the upper hand and was close to pinning the wily Poffo when the sneaky Lubich, unseen by the referee but witnessed by thousands, caned Beyer over the head, giving Poffo the opportunity to escape the hold and pin his opponent to the loud objection of the crowd and a visibly outraged Beyer.

A week later at the matches, during a televised interview with Buffalo sportscaster Chuck Healy on WBEN –TV in which he discussed the surprise assault by Lubich, Beyer was presented with a cake by a member of his fan club in celebration of his first wedding anniversary; during the interview, on cue, Poffo and Lubich shoved their way on camera, berated the interviewer, took the cake and, in a rage,

Lubich smashed it on the floor of the auditorium yelling "This is what I think of you, the anniversary and Buffalo." In the midst of the uproar, as Beyer was restrained and the crowd shouted at Lubich, Beyer challenged Lubich to a match to resolve their dispute. The grudge match resulted in strong attendance numbers and, as fans had hoped, Beyer beat the hated Lubich, ending the match with a flying dropkick to gain retaliation; now he wanted to settle the score with Poffo. Martinez signed the match in the ring that evening, and scheduled it for the following week; attendance soared to nearly 8000. With Lubich seated in a chair near ringside, Beyer picked up Poffo and threw him into the lap of the tuxedoed sideman; as Beyer looked over the ropes at the heap of humanity on the floor, Lubich tried to use his cane on Beyer, resulting in the disqualification of Poffo for Lubich's interference. It was great theatre…and great box office returns.

Wrestling in Buffalo was proving to be a good financial decision for Beyer, so good that he decided to become a home owner and he purchased his first property, 85 acres and a 5 bedroom farmhouse, in Akron, a sleepy second-circle farming suburb of Buffalo, for $19,750. Willy didn't have to work, and was given the time to focus on her painting and other pursuits. It wasn't long before one of those pursuits was screaming, hungry, and needed changing – Willy gave birth, in September, to the couple's first child, a boy they named Kurt. Beyer's world had dramatically changed, in an inspiring way, and he began building additional supports for him and his family. He took some of his growing income and started a home construction business in Clarence Center, with his new brother-in-law, Billy Red Lyons, who had married Willy's sister Norma, and his other brother-in-law, Richard Breissinger, who was married to the girls' older sister Georgia. Only insiders, and a select few, knew the relationship between Beyer and Lyons; neither wanted future matches with each other dampened by fans' knowledge of their familial ties. Beyer was a proud parent, devoted husband, known wrestler, sports announcer, football coach, construction firm owner and teacher when he wanted to be. He was

◄ MASKED DECISIONS

playing a full hand and before long needed to decide which cards to hold and which to fold.

In autumn, 1961, he drove his young family to their rented cottage in Skaneateles Lake and returned to the sidelines as an assistant coach on the Syracuse football squad. Beyer detected a difference in his approach to the game – the work was still interesting and he enjoyed the coaches and players immensely; unlike previous years, he had other obligations to fulfill, and a young family he wanted to enjoy.

Beyer (far left) coached offensive line that enabled #44 Ernie Davis to the Heisman

The Orangemen were coming off a 7 win, 2 loss record in the 1960 campaign, for which junior Ernie Davis had earned his first All America honors. In this his senior year, Davis was given the keys to take the team further. He didn't disappoint. Davis never did…he was so loved and respected that even his father-son relationship with the head coach was not something other players objected to. The offensive line had a pivotal role to play for Davis, as it had during the championship season in 1959. Beyer worked grueling hours with the other coaches in preparations for each game.

The 1961 season proved to be grinding and arduous; Syracuse lost three close contests to Maryland, Penn State, and Notre Dame and won seven. But the brilliant performances of Ernie Davis once again boosted the recognition of Syracuse football; by season's end, Davis had eclipsed Jim Brown's collegiate rushing record, earned his second All America honor and more importantly became the first black player to win the coveted Heisman Trophy, symbolic of college football's best of the year. It was unprecedented for Syracuse, and for college football; Syracuse had its first Heisman winner, college football its first Heisman winner of color. Beyer caught up with the head coach soon after word spread of Davis' selection and asked the coach to recall the train ride in 1953 they took to New York City when Beyer was selected Syracuse 'athlete of the year.' Referring to Davis' Heisman, Beyer told the head coach "The train you were hoping to ride back to New York City has been here for three years…and it's the Elmira Express." Beyer and Schwartzwalder smiled and shook hands, but Beyer didn't let go; he held onto the coach's hand, having given this moment much thought, and told Schwartzwalder he was leaving the coaching staff. Beyer knew his time at Syracuse was over. A bittersweet meeting in Ben's office confirmed that Beyer had decided to move into wrestling year-round. Schwartzwalder said to him "Dick, yours is the strangest career I've ever seen but you've always done well…and you will continue to do well." Syracuse was in position to land one more bowl game, so Beyer stayed in town, and on the staff at Schwartzwalder's request, to hear the announcement and work one last game with his head coach and friend.

Syracuse, on strength of schedule, was invited to play in the Liberty Bowl in Philadelphia against the University of Miami in December. Young Kurt Beyer, too small to travel in the cold, stayed with family, allowing Willy to fly to Pennsylvania with her husband and watch him work his last game. The 100,000 seat Philadelphia Stadium was only 15% occupied for the game that was played in freezing twenty-two degree weather. To make themselves feel at home, Miami brought several artificial palm trees up from Florida and placed them near each end zone. The warm feelings they conjured up must have helped. Syracuse was down 14 points to Miami in the first half, but played a sound second half, as Davis ran and set up scoring drives that pushed the Orangemen into the lead and an eventual 15 to 14 win. Davis was voted MVP. He was later selected in the first round of the NFL draft, but no one realized they had witnessed the last game ever played by the talented and personable Ernie Davis.

Beyer and Willy returned to Skaneateles Lake to begin the process of packing up and moving back permanently to Buffalo. It was a very cold December day when they arrived at their cottage. As Dick opened the front door, he heard a noise, followed by the sound and the experience of water gushing out of the door, into his shoes, and out into the yard. It was later determined that, while away in Philadelphia, the electricity had gone off, and the water pipes, which ran in the ceiling of the cottage, had burst due to the extreme cold conditions inside. To Beyer, the scene inside the cottage looked like a miniature Niagara Falls in winter. While repairs were being made, and they packed for their trip home to Western New York, Beyer facetiously asked his wife "Should we wait for the Maid of the Mist and sail back to Buffalo?"

CHAPTER **10**

"I THINK IT'S time I move on." With those words, Dick Beyer articulated his thoughts to a surprised Pedro Martinez about where his wrestling career was, and where it wasn't. He'd been wrestling in his home town of Buffalo, the nearby city of Rochester, his adopted Syracuse, the western part of the territory in Ohio, and in Frank Tunney's Toronto and Montreal, for more than three years. Without question, he did better-than-average financially and became a known baby face, behind Ilio DiPaolo and Billy Red Lyons in Buffalo popularity, one of the most versatile and multi-talented in the business, and had been given a trophy as "the most popular wrestler" in Syracuse. He was a big fish in a relatively small pond; he wanted to test himself against larger fish in the open sea. Competitiveness, wanderlust, and a desire to fulfill a promise to his father and himself motivated him. Over several weeks, discussions with Willy - marathon sessions that stretched into the early morning hours - brought them to a conclusion that was as frightening as it was exciting. His wrestling buddies understood – Ilio, Billy Red and other Buffalo based talent agreed with his plan. He received support from his sisters, mother, and Willy's family – everyone acknowledged the inevitable. Knowing him the way they did, he was not going to be satisfied with the status quo. It was time to un-quo the status, and time to shuffle out of Buffalo.

The next question to be answered was – where? Most of the territories he previously had worked - Columbus, Kentucky, Chicago, Tennessee - had well-entrenched baby faces, and the probability of getting a call from a promoter in the west or southeast was remote. This time, he knew he had to do it on his own. It was a difficult decision. The allure and attraction of the tropical beaches of Waikiki was, to him, as strong as a rip current, but he hadn't heard from the Hawaiian promoter since the day he hastily gave him notice and departed for Buffalo- and an army physical - six years earlier. Beyer wasn't sure he'd be welcomed back, or if the promoter held grudges…if there was work available, or no vacancy on the circuit. He took a deep breath, then the initiative, and called Al Karasick in Honolulu. "Al, Dick Beyer in Buffalo… I'm calling to ask if you would consider having me back in Honolulu." "Who is this?" "Dick Beyer, Al…I wrestled for you six years ago…from Syracuse U…" "Syracuse who…?" Beyer didn't need to start another sentence once he heard the laughter through the telephone. Karasick liked Beyer, fond of the way he worked in 1956, even of his pinochle playing, and he told Beyer he'd dust off the welcome mat for the good tough baby face and rotate him in matches around the islands. "How about the same deal as last time…only give me more card games and more notice if you need to leave" "I'll stay the four months if you give me a little more money since I'm bringing my wife and son." "You'll need to beat me at pinochle to get more money," said Karasick. What Beyer didn't know was that negotiations were underway for Karasick to sell the territory to popular island wrestler Ed Francis.

A long, multiple stop, six time zone plane trip west across the continent and the pacific was followed by a short, one-stop cab ride from the airport to the hotel in downtown Honolulu, where Beyer and his family rested and relaxed several days before renting an apartment at the Waikiki Ebb Tide for the remainder of their Hawaiian tour. The promoter's office helped the family find an apartment in the same complex Beyer stayed during his initial trip; this one was larger - a two-story, L-shaped apartment near the complex's swimming pool. It was everything and more. Willy instantly loved the island. "Reminds me a little of Havana" she said holding back a smirk; "We'll be here longer, consider it a second try at our first honeymoon" her husband replied, pulling on his swim trunks, grabbing Kurt and jumping into the pool.

Beyer's first match on the island was scheduled with Maurice Vachon, the Canadian he met in the dressing room prior to the matches in Dallas in 1959, when Syracuse played Texas for the college football national championship. Vachon, who with his brother Paul won several team titles, competed in the 1948 Olympic Games, and wrestled to a gold medal in the 1950 British Empire Games in New Zealand; as a pro, he created a fan-hated heel identity as a wild, crazed grappler, accentuated by his relatively short 5'9" stature, bald head and long goatee. The match with the compact, menacing 225 pound Maurice Vachon was promoted as a stern test for Dick Beyer's return to the Civic Auditorium in Honolulu. The main event, held on January 3, 1962 and won by Beyer propelled him back into the pacific limelight. Before January had faded away, Beyer recorded wins against George Drake and Lou 'Shoulders' Newman, displaying the dynamic skills and speed that had earlier captured the attention and sentiment of Hawaiian wrestling fans. He developed a loyal following in a short time span. Everyone on the island was interested in Beyer, and none more so than Karasick. He knew when he had a winning hand, in pinochle and in wrestling, and before Ed Francis assumed control of the business, he played one more card that had a profound influence on Beyer's future.

Other than the Wednesday matches in Honolulu, and the Saturday matches at Pearl Harbor, Beyer spent most every day at the beach with his family. Willy used the time to perfect her water color painting; the former power company draftsman redirected her artistic talent toward landscapes, developing a portfolio of tropical scenes. When he wasn't making things from coconut shells, surfing, or teaching his son to swim, Beyer worked out in two different venues. One was Dean Higuchi's gym on Kalakaua Avenue; an accomplished body builder, Higuchi opened a gym in the late 1950s that became a popular training site for body builders and professional wrestlers. Beyer appreciated Higuchi's generosity and reciprocated by training the body builder for a pro wrestling career; during this time, Beyer also helped train Harry Fugiwara (later known as Mr. Fugi) a bouncer at the Bare Foot Bar in

Waikiki, and worked out with Sammy Steamboat. In addition, several nights a week at the Dojo of sensei Wally Tsutsumi, building on his accumulated learning, Beyer accelerated his training, and soon was awarded his black belt in judo. To him, the discipline and belt did not signify an end, but rather a beginning with deeper peace of mind, greater fitness and balance in his life. He was not the type to boast or show off his newly acquired craft, he merely incorporated his learning into his wrestling toolkit – and it made him a sharper opponent, a more scientific wrestler, and a virtuoso performer.

Karasick arranged for the current Worldwide Wrestling Alliance champion, Fred Blassie, out of the Los Angeles territory, to work a title match on the island. He spoke with Blassie, who took over the crown from Eduard Carpentier, and told him he had Dick Beyer in mind for the main event; Blassie told Karasick he worked Tennessee with Beyer in the late 1950s and was in full agreement with the opponent. A current heel title-holder challenged by a favorite local baby face was, for Karasick, a dynamic duel; it had all the elements of power, fury, speed, and suspense and was one of the last matches he booked before Ed Francis took charge of the NWA Hawaiian region.

In early 1962, a new vehicle was added to the way wrestling was promoted in Hawaii – a Saturday afternoon locker room interview and studio wrestling show on KHVH channel 4- during which wrestlers pitched their scheduled matches at the Civic Auditorium, on South King Street in Honolulu and predicted the type of mayhem fans could expect at the events. The territory ownership changed; Karasick originally wanted to sell the rights to Lord James Blears, however, the popular star desired only to serve in a book making role, but later Blears also agreed to do the on-camera interviewing for the show. It was the beginning of the extremely popular '50th State Wrestling' program on the Hawaiian islands and was to usher in a new era of professional wrestling that consistently sold out arenas and halls, with talent such as Neff Maiava, Curtis Iaukea, the Masked Executioner, and Nick Bockwinkel.

"I'm wrestling Fred Blassie for the belt," Beyer excitedly told Willy, after meeting with the promoter. Regardless of the outcome, he knew his term in Hawaii wasn't necessarily over come April. "We might be able to extend our time here with more matches." "If you're going to wrestle him for his belt, see if you can get his money clip and wallet too." Beyer gave his wife one of those 'bang…zoom' glares before they began talking about the possibility of a longer engagement than originally planned.

The Blassie-Beyer title match, whose undercard included John Brown and Lou Newman, George Drake and Ted Travis, tag partners Neff Maiava and Lord Blears against Maurice Vachon and the Masked Executioner, was heavily promoted in press and on the new studio television program; Beyer made several TV appearances prior to the January 24 bout. Other wrestlers told Beyer he was 'great on the stick.' His extemporaneous speaking experience from his commentator role in Rochester and Buffalo was more than evident. The fans responded by crowding into the 5000 seat Civic Auditorium to witness the card. Blassie and Beyer performed a rousing ritual in three falls – Beyer winning the first, Blassie the second. Blassie took continuous heat from the fans for his ring antics which Beyer made look all the more exaggerated with his 'by the rules' approach. Baby face Beyer clearly had the crowd in his corner, was the sentimental favorite throughout the evening, and late in the third fall attempted a flying tackle on Blassie that missed; he bounded out of the ring and onto the concrete surface. Unable to return inside the ring on time, Beyer was counted out by the referee, and the belt remained with Blassie. Expectedly, the crowd became hostile; at the referee and Blassie the fans booed and shouted as they exited the auditorium and poured into the streets. Blassie told Beyer in the dressing room "Good work… you have developed into one of the best baby faces around, and I've seen plenty."

Lord Blears was ripening into a triple threat as wrestler/booker/interviewer; a former champion and one of the most prolific tag partners of his era, Blears was offered by Francis the enviable duty of booking matches for talent that he liked and interviewing that talent on the studio television shows which were gaining in popularity on the islands. Though it was projected to take years, he slowly began curtailing his wrestling events to concentrate on the promotional activities in the territory. That spring, Beyer met with Blears over breakfast to talk about Buddy Rogers' signature hold, the figure-four leg lock. Of all the finishing moves he encountered, Beyer believed the figure-four held the most interest, visually and competitively, due to his own powerfully-built legs. He was aware that Blears knew the hold and told him that out of respect for those using it, he never employed the figure-four lock. Believing that Dick Hutton, a well-known figure-four mechanic, was retiring soon, Beyer asked Blears for his thoughts. "Use it, Dick... I don't use it, but add a little something to make it different from Rogers and Hutton - make it your own," Blears said, with appreciation in his voice for Beyer's respect and discipline. When breakfast was through, Blears and Beyer got on the floor in sitting positions facing each other and, for an hour, Beyer was given detailed instruction on how to apply the figure-four leg lock.

Weeks of wrestling bad guys as a popular good guy attraction, while profitable for the promoter, was good work for Beyer, and enjoyable, to a point. Promoters and wrestlers always viewed extended winning periods with trepidation, fearing fan boredom or 'too much of a good thing' syndrome that limited other programs and talent. Something had to change in order for the new promoter to feel comfortable moving forward with Beyer in the ring. Another ingredient was necessary to keep the soup flavorful. Television interviews from the locker room provided the backdrop to delivering a new message. Dick Beyer was changing. Interviews with him showed a more temperamental side; he was sounding off toward the established order, railing against the fan favorites and switching sides before their very eyes. A new heel emerged in the territory.

It felt different, a bit difficult at first, wearing the 'black hat' rather than riding the white horse, but Beyer performed the transmutation well. In no time, he was fully at ease in the role, much like an actor in a new play. Wrestlers observed and gave him high grades as a heel; fans noticed too…and voted with their feet…attendance climbed as fans now wanted to see bad-guy Beyer get his due from their favorite good guys.

Beyer took the role change as far as he was able. To add to the character's identity, he shaved his head, started to pose more menacingly in promotional photos, and on camera pledged his support to other heels in the territory. In April, Fred Blassie returned to the island for a limited engagement to face fan-friendly Neff Maiava; to spice up the match, Lord Blears was assigned to Maiava's corner and Beyer to Blassie's as corner manager. Though Beyer did not wrestle in the match, he proved he could fan fire for the main event with his newly developed outbursts, taking his 'well educated' background and twisting it into a putdown of the fans and wrestlers "You people – I went to Syracuse University, not some rinky dink school here in Hawaii; the eastern schools are where we educated ones come from," he said into the microphone to the boos and jeers of the crowd. It worked superbly. Seated ringside was Don Owen, the likeable promoter for the Portland territory and one of the few promoters held in high regard by virtually everyone in the industry. Owen, a man of indisputable integrity, was rumored to have helped Ed Francis buy the Hawaiian region from Karasick; he was in Honolulu on vacation, and stopped by to visit with Francis and see the matches. Owen had heard that Beyer was a good baby face, so seeing him generate heat as a heel gave him a change of perspective. He liked the way Beyer got under his skin. After the match, he met with Beyer and inquired about his plans after Hawaii. "I was hoping to stay here longer but right now I'm through in April," he told Owen, who replied, "How about coming to Portland at the end of your stay?" A tentative date was discussed and a handshake followed. Beyer met with Francis to inform him of his new plans. Later, Beyer told Willy, who was surprised but not upset by the news of moving on to Portland; she said "Well, it *is* work in-hand and that's what we wanted when we set sail from Buffalo; besides, it will be spring when we get there and it will be a nice change." "I will get us back here someday," he told his wife. "I will hold you to that, surfer boy" Willy replied.

Fred Blassie stayed in town long enough to catch Beyer's match. He thought Beyer's work as his corner manager during the Maiava match was great - seeing Beyer perform in his new heel image surpassed that. Before he headed back to Los Angeles, he called Jules Strongbow, the L.A. territory booker, and told Strongbow to consider Beyer for the Los Angeles circuit, "You need to see this guy… the best baby face in the country… and can draw heat, he is that good." Blassie had worked with many wrestlers across the country, and as current WWA champion in the L.A. region, he knew someone with Beyer's skills and showmanship was certain to enhance and extend his own career.

Beyer was excited with his new image and, anticipating much more heel work in Portland and beyond, he went to a downtown Honolulu photographer and ordered shots taken in five different heel poses, including one using the figure-four leg lock on Lord Blears, who agreed to the photo provided Beyer pick up the tab for lunch after the photoshoot. Beyer glared, intimidated, loomed, and worked his image for the camera to create horror-movie quality heel photos for future promotions; he ordered one hundred of each, five hundred in total; not afraid to invest in his future.

Ed Francis planned several three-man tag team matches for Beyer before he was to leave for Portland. Studio bouts and on-air question and answer sessions provided fans with previews and promises, driving the demand for seats that led to sellout crowds for the events. During one on-air interview Blears conducted that previewed the match that was to pit himself, Neff Maiava, and Maurice Vachon against Shoulders Newman, Beyer, and the Masked Executioner, Beyer saved the professional reputation of one of his team members – one who also had a reputation as the biggest practical joker and ribber in the business. Vic Christy, working as the Masked Executioner, was a journeyman wrestler out of California who, in the 1930s, wore a mask as the Silver Streak and later worked with his brother Ted as a successful tag team combo in the fifties. Within the business, Christy was the man to avoid- not in the ring, but in the real world; his practical jokes were hilarious and legendary. One classic was alleged to have been played on Lord Blears during the first visit to California by Tally-Ho. Blears met Christy in the booking office in San Francisco, where the two were obtaining instructions for scheduled matches. Blears made it known that he was interested in getting to the beach to work on his tan, so Christy, ostensibly offering to help the visiting Blears, drew him a map to the beach and told him he would meet him there the following day around ten in the morning. Christy arrived at the beach early to set up his rib. He spotted a young couple that had spread a blanket out on the sand with a picnic basket on top. Christy positioned himself near the couple's blanket as they ran into the water; seeing Blears up on a walkway overlooking the beach, he motioned for Blears to come down to where he was standing. As Blears arrived, Christy told him to relax on the blanket and help himself to some refreshments in the basket, while he jumped in the water for a few minutes. When Christy headed for the water's edge, he spotted the couple walking back to their blanket. He stood and watched as the couple, aghast at the sight of a large man on their blanket drinking and eating from their basket, yelled and carried on at the intruder to get off their property! Blears, duly flustered, abruptly rose from his prone position, picnic food still in his mouth, and pointed to Christy standing a few blanket bodies away; with the eyes of the couple on him, Christy said "I don't know who that guy is, but he has a lot of nerve" and proceeded to walk away. It was not known whether Blears was just horribly embarrassed or whether he mentally filed the episode away to use as justification for revenge at a later date. Given the circumstances that unfolded during the interview with the Masked Executioner, there was strong argument for the latter.

On the live television broadcast, the tag team wrestlers were seated, with Blears walking among the other five, asking questions concerning the scheduled three-man team match. Blears approached Christy, cloaked as the Masked Executioner, and asked him about his famous 'claw hold' - a one hand vice grip that the Executioner used to cripple opponents. During the Executioner's remarks, Blears began to ad-lib, and tossed a telephone book at him saying, "If your claw hold is so good, tear up that phone book." This bit was completely unexpected, and had caught everyone off guard, especially Christy. The mask hid his expression, but his eyes widened and his body froze. At that moment, Beyer the heel spoke up "Give me that book," he growled "That's the biggest insult in the world to the Executioner, throwing him that thin Honolulu book. You've got to be kidding!" As Beyer tossed the book off camera, he looked back directly into it and said "Give him that big thick L.A. phone book and he'll show you some action." The interview ended without further surprises. Off camera, Christy said to Beyer "Thanks Dick, you saved my life. I don't think I could have ripped it." Beyer never knew if Blears had used the phone book intentionally as payback from the San Francisco beach…and he never asked.

Willy answered the phone; it was Jules Strongbow calling for her husband. "Dick, Freddie tells me you're a hell of a baby face and a hell of a heel; how would like to work L.A.?" Beyer didn't reply; he paced the apartment while thinking fast on his feet – he knew L.A. was high-profile and great for building name recognition, *but what about my pledge to Don Owen?* Letting Owen down was not something he wanted to do. He looked at Willy, thought hard, and decided "OK Jules, I will be there late April." He hung up the phone, told his wife about the change of plans, and called Don Owen to explain. Owen was not pleased to hear what Beyer had to say, but he understood, always the consummate professional; Beyer promised him that as soon as he finished in L.A., he would drive up to Portland and work for him. This time, it was unbreakable. Beyer and his wife packed for their relocation to California, and the start of another adventure. "I'll bet Los Angeles looks just like Portland in the summer…or maybe Havana" to which she heard "To the moon, Willy."

CHAPTER **11**

"WHAT DID YOU ask Strongbow?" "For more weeks – that's what I asked him," Dick Beyer said to his wife, returning home after a late May match in Long Beach. She smiled, crossed her fingers on both hands, and nodded in agreement.

What a difference a month made. It was just eight weeks earlier, in April, after a four month tour in Hawaii, that Beyer was informed by L.A. match maker Jules Strongbow he was to wear a mask and perform as The Destroyer in San Diego in his first west coast appearance – an experience that nearly cost him his reputation, his opportunity to work the Los Angeles territory, and quite possibly his career. Dick Beyer wrestled as himself – baby face or heel – not as a cowardly chump hidden under a mask, he unequivocally told Hardy Kruskamp, the San Diego and Long Beach promoter. Putting on a mask so repulsed Beyer, he had visions of leaving the territory, getting out of the business entirely, and going back to teaching. Though he initially abhorred the notion of wearing a hood, he later recanted after Ox Anderson, a colleague he had met in Texas, showed him a more pragmatic alternative to the disgusting body-cloak Vic Christy loaned him for his 1962 west coast debut. But at that time, he had given the promoter and the match maker a drop-dead date…to wear the mask only four additional weeks to fulfill his obligation. After he and his wife found material in Woolworth's to fashion his own unique mask for The Destroyer, things began to change. The improved disguise prompted a new attitude. It didn't hurt that ever since he became The Destroyer, he hadn't lost a single match – twenty-eight consecutive wins - against some very good talent that included Johnny 'Rubber Man' Walker, Mario Milano, Vic Christy, Ox Anderson, Chief

MASKED DECISIONS

Crazy Horse, Art Michalik, Don Duffy, and Clyde Steeves. Before he departed Long Beach for the drive back to his apartment, Beyer met with Strongbow and told him that wearing his newly designed disguise made it more tolerable to work as a masked villain, and that he was open for more matches. "I am asking for more weeks as The Destroyer," he told the match maker; "Good, I will set them up, good choice" replied a very satisfied Strongbow, who returned to L.A. to inform promoter Cal Eaton of Beyer's decision.

Dick Beyer's income, drawn from the work as the masked Destroyer, tripled from his previous high. He, as the masked man, began to headline more main events around the Los Angeles circuit. Wrestling publications such as *Wrestling Revue*, *Wrestling World*, *Boxing Illustrated- Wrestling News*, and sports pages from regional newspapers printed column after column about the new outlaw in Dodge. There was no denying The Destroyer was electrifying Tinseltown. Fans flocked to southern California arenas to catch a look at the new wonder of the wrestling world, whose mysterious identity, shrouded in secrecy, was held close to the vest by business insiders.

Dick and Willy Beyer were on cloud ten. Life evolved from good to 'good God is this really happening?' The risks they took when they left Buffalo for Hawaii were reaping rewards. Only a select few friends and associates living near their apartment in North Hollywood knew of Beyer's alter ego and had pledged to keep the secret; to them, it was a privilege to be in-on-the-know. What surprised Beyer were the lengths a few fans went through to uncover his identity. One young fan, completely taken by the masked Destroyer, was California teenager Art Williams. A high school student, wrestling fanatic, and one who had become instantly infatuated with the Destroyer, Williams had spotted a car with a New York State license plate parked in the wrestlers' parking lot; he knew The Destroyer had attended Syracuse and there were rumors about him having played football, so Williams took down the license plate number and wrote to the New York State Department of Motor Vehicles in Albany, New York, and requested information on the vehicle. When he received a reply noting the name Richard Beyer, he traced the name back to Syracuse University and putting the pieces together, Williams identified the mysterious masked man. Despite all the trouble he went through, Williams only informed Beyer of what he learned, not friends or other wrestling fans. Beyer was impressed by the effort and hard work Williams put in, and reached out to the young fan to thank him for his discretion. In short order, Williams became a friend and another member of the wrestler's silent protective force.

Beyer found the Jekyll-Hyde existence easy to take; without the mask, he went shopping, dining, swimming and enjoyed other solo and family activities like that of any other ordinary citizen in L.A. He went fishing on his boat 'Tudor Time', which his father-in-law had towed with Beyer's car from Buffalo to California. Fishing and boating in the west coast waters eased the mind of the hoodless Beyer. No one recognized him. He often joked *this is how Clark Kent did it*. He always pulled the mask on after he arrived at the wrestling venue, and promptly removed it before leaving the arena and getting back into his car. It could not have been more perfect.

Wednesday night matches at the Olympic Auditorium, situated on the corner of South Grand Avenue and 18th Street in central Los Angeles were staples for years. The old structure, opened in the 1920s and used during the 1932 Olympic Games, was the home for major boxing, weightlifting, and wrestling events, with capacity for more than 7000 on the main floor and balcony, but with extra seats near ringside and standing room, that number skewed upward, and often did. The beige colored rectangular structure stood as a beacon for live action, its double-sided marquee dotted with the block letters of the gladiators scheduled to wage war inside; three sets of doors readied to open to the anxious public. The concrete interior, with a ceiling height of 50 feet, carried the noise generated by excited fans forever. The building shook and vibrated as fans, caught up in the action in the ring, jumped up and down on the rafters that clanged against the iron underpinnings. For Los Angeles wrestling fans, this was ground zero, the place they all had to be to witness the best in the business.

The Wednesday matches held at the venerable Olympic were aired live on KTLA-TV and hosted by Dick Lane, a Paramount Pictures actor, broadcast voice of roller derby and midget auto racing, and a former master of ceremonies with USO troupes during World War II. Lane, who often wore black-rimmed glasses, was known for saying that as an actor, he died so often he knew every rock and pebble in the San Joaquin Valley. But to L.A. wrestling fans, his voice and unique phrases like "Whoa Nellie" added legitimacy and urgency to the broadcasts. For many around Los Angeles, television was their first opportunity to see and hear the newest villain that had overtaken the town. Lane's interviews with The Destroyer from the Olympic salted the thirst of southern California wrestling lovers. Lane's questions often were answered in an angry, disgusted tone by The Destroyer coupled with "I don't do anything illegal, I can wrestle." On at least one occasion, Lane's glasses were ripped from his face and broken on camera by the masked man. Beyer, by now, had added new dimensions to the dastardly Destroyer's persona. All the years of observing other wrestlers, on the advice of his mentor Ed Don George, gave him the shades and hues, like a painter's color palette, to shape and mold his character's core. He was mean all right, mean, conceited, intolerant, and god-awful nasty, but the way he manifested these traits was cleverly conceived. During the undercard bouts, The Destroyer was usually spotted near the back of the arena watching the wrestlers in progress; fans knew he was observing and mentally recording the strengths and faults of prospective opponents, and they felt they were part of the surveillance cover – no longer spectators but participants. As the time approached for his matches, The Destroyer never merely hopped into the ring and started kicking, stomping and booting... he confidently and slowly walked down the aisle and up to the ring, looking at the crowd looking at him, in one move he leaped into the ring then strutted around, occasionally stopping and folding his arms across his chest in a defiant display of cockiness, looking outward and upward at the gathered throng, acting as if he owned the platform…at that point, he indeed owned the crowd.

With his signature mask, color-coordinated trunks and gleaming white boots, he didn't fit the mold of the all-too-familiar bad guy in a black outfit or with an unruly appearance – his was unique to the times. Mask, trunks, boots, bare-chested with taught arms and magnificent, muscular legs, The Destroyer was first an athlete. Beyer made certain that his athleticism remained in the forefront, and he dressed in a minimalist style to bring out the best in his physical attributes. As the mask obscured most normal facial expressions, The Destroyer, borrowing from Al Jolson, made full use of his eyes and mouth to signify and highlight his emotions – narrowing them for getting down to business, opening them wide to show surprise or outrage at an opponent's tactic or referee's call. However the skin-hugging mask, like white-face on a mime, lent itself to the creation of facial contortions Beyer wanted to exhibit, so that The Destroyer's mad and, at times, zombie-like looks were exaggerated. If he was to perform as a character and be successful, he was going full tilt. In and out of the ring, he was generally considered dirty by the fans – giving an opponent an illegal move while hiding it from the referee's view, followed by a spoiled-child tantrum and an argument with the referee when told to disengage from the banned maneuver. The Destroyer's behaviors, taken literally, were antithetical to the family values, Eagle-Scout ethics, and fair play rules Beyer learned early and exemplified often throughout his life, but he knew how the psychology worked in this business and he applied it exceptionally well. He was Sigmund Destroyer and the fans were on his couch.

In the ring, the introduction of The Destroyer was theatrical drama. Rather than state the hometown or territory – and inadvertently disclose a clue – The Destroyer's background, like that of most masked wrestlers, was never provided. Jimmy Lennon, the long-standing ring announcer at the Olympic, and uncle of the singing Lennon Sisters, often kept his intro short– "From parts unknown, The Destroyer." Beyer liked to play off that introduction and told other announcers on the circuit to do the same. After the brief introduction, The Destroyer often pulled the microphone from the announcer's hands and said, "Until you know who I am, you will introduce me as the *Intelligent, Sensational* Destroyer." The announcers refused to do it and The Destroyer, in turn, refused to wrestle until they did. A stand-off lasting several minutes often developed. Psychologically, it accelerated a tremendous amount of heat from the fans.

When the matches ended, The Destroyer got back on the microphone and bragged about his wrestling expertise, superior intellect, his clever ways, his college sports background, and his university undergraduate and graduate degrees, always careful never to mention the team or city. Adding to the mystique, The Destroyer put up five thousand dollars to any opponent successful in breaking his patented figure-four leg lock, and made it known that, should The Destroyer lose two of three pin falls without a disqualification, he would voluntarily unmask. He teased the crowd with what he had planned for the following week's opponent and the ring announcer intimated that if the opponent was able "We might learn who is underneath the mask at the next event." What Jules Strongbow originated, Beyer as The Destroyer refined. Though Dick Beyer had surrendered himself to anonymity, The Destroyer had indeed become an intelligent sensation.

Charley Iwamoto, wrestling as Mr. Moto, became one of Dick Beyer's closest friends while the two had worked in the east and closer during their 1962 tenure in Los Angeles. Not only did they wrestle each other on numerous occasions, they also travelled to and from local matches together, went fishing, played golf, and shared the driving to Las Vegas for televised wrestling promotions and matches. Strongbow was awed by just how good a performer Iwamoto as Mr. Moto was in the ring, and told Beyer that Charley was the Red Skelton of wrestling – he could make people laugh, cry, and then hate him all within seconds. Moto, like Beyer, made wrestlers of lesser talent look like champions.

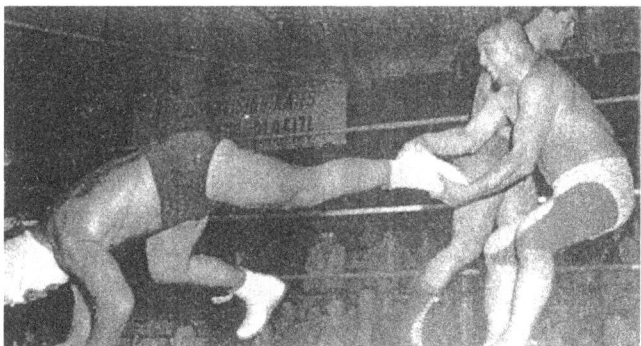

Mr. Moto and Morales had to gang up in an effort to overcome the Destroyer during their match, but it was to no avail as the Masked Man and his partner overcame their rivals in a thriller.

Destroyer and Mr. Moto were enemies in the ring, close friends outside it

Because of the overwhelming success of The Destroyer, Beyer now had to park blocks away from venues without secured parking and taxi to the arenas, so that fans could not trace his license plate number or follow his car. Iwamoto often joked about the changes Beyer complained of in his commute, telling him, "If you looked Japanese, you have more problems." Iwamoto, like many of the other 'Japanese' wrestlers of his era including Tosh Togo (Harold Sakata), and Tojo Yamamoto (Harold Watanabe) was not native Japanese but from Hawaii and a *'Nisei'* or second generation Japanese. He was a frequent guest at the Beyer dinner table and a welcomed visitor, especially for young Kurt, who referred to the goateed wrestler as 'Uncle Charley.' Married, with a home in south Los Angeles, the former sumo wrestler was the father of five sons, and confided in Beyer that he always wanted a daughter. "Maybe you already have one and don't know it," Beyer teased his good friend; "You sonnabitch" was an oft-said Charley-ism.

Iwamoto and Beyer had driven home early Monday morning from a weekend in Las Vegas when they were informed by the wrestling office that they both were scheduled to face Classy Freddie Blassie in late June; Mr. Moto was to wrestle Blassie on the 19th in Long Beach followed on the 20th with Blassie and The Destroyer, at the Olympic, a televised event.

Blassie was a familiar opponent for the judo chopping Mr. Moto who, with Blassie, had wrestled several highly entertaining and memorable matches; Beyer long held enormous respect for Blassie and was particularly indebted to him for calling Strongbow and recommending him for the L.A. territory. It was rumored that Blassie, who had lost the WWA belt to Asian icon Rikidozan in March, was itching to move back to Atlanta; Strongbow's call to Beyer confirmed it, but the televised match was set as the prelude to another Blassie-Destroyer showdown to follow.

Each week during broadcast interviews leading up to the scheduled event, Blassie was seen filing down his teeth, a gimmick he often employed, and told interviewer Dick Lane that he was going to bite through The Destroyer's mask and rip it off to expose his identity; for his part, The Destroyer laughed it off and adopted the position of an arrogant unbeatable. The program and angle played well – the crowd wanted to see the heel Blassie get the best of the monster heel The Destroyer. Close to 10,000 fans at the Olympic and untold numbers of television viewers watched as Blassie bit through The Destroyer's mask only to find another mask underneath; they grappled long and hard to a draw. "Every time I had him, Blassie rolled up under the ropes…that won't happen again" Destroyer told an interviewer. The next Blassie-Destroyer bout was scheduled for San Diego one month later. Blassie was never one to give in easily; wrestlers had to work hard with him to get the results desired. But even Beyer was surprised at how accommodating and cordial Blassie conducted himself in discussions before their match. Perhaps it was just a matter of being comfortable with the young man he first met in Tennessee and later in Hawaii, but Blassie was ebullient in his regard for Beyer's wrestling talent, especially as The Destroyer. Two days before their match, Blassie again wrestled Rikidozan and won back the WWA championship; this set up a title match with The Destroyer.

In San Diego, the city of Beyer's last amateur bout in the 1954 National AAU finals and his first masked match in a scratchy hood, Fred Blassie and The Destroyer fought a tough, pounding battle on

July 27, 1962; The Destroyer took two of three falls from Blassie and, surprising many, won the WWA World Wrestling Championship.

Blassie gave The Destroyer all he could handle and Beyer the breaks he needed

It was a gamble – heels like Blassie had held championship belts before, but this was the first time a masked heel had won a wrestling championship in the territory, and many believed the country. Would the fans' interest wane as a result? Was it a mistake to go in this untested and unchartered water? For Jules Strongbow, a lot of worry and strategy went into the decision, and the business weighed in the balance; he went with his hunch, but kept his moist index finger in the air to detect any shift in wind direction by the paying public.

World Champion; The Destroyer now had clout, fame, and opponents lining up for a shot at the crowned king of the World Wrestling Alliance. However, The Destroyer was not able to sit comfortably on his throne - a rematch was scheduled with Blassie at the Olympic in L.A. for August 15. Dick Lane's interviews with both wrestlers warned fans that this contest, a main event, was not going to be televised, and it was not going to be pretty. A capacity crowd of more than 10,000 filled the Olympic; hundreds of fans meandered outside the building to hear the results from those who attended. In what was penned as one of the roughest matches ever held at the arena, The Destroyer beat Blassie to retain his title. Blassie and Beyer talked at length afterward, each wishing the other warm regards and vowing to remain friends. Blassie left the territory for Georgia; Beyer went home to Willy.

Wrestling was as enjoyable and profitable as it was exhausting and punishing for Dick Beyer, but no objections. In his early thirties, he was young enough to withstand the physical torment inflicted on his body night after night. For those who at that time said wrestling was 'fake,' one look at the contusions, cuts, welts and assorted bone breaks and misalignments a wrestler took home, was all that was necessary to form a changed opinion of the true results of many contests. These were the occupational hazards of the men whose office was a hard-surfaced raised platform bordered on four sides by three ropes. Most nights at home, Willy applied cold compresses, heating pads and homemade remedies to her husband's aches, pains and joints. The couple viewed his work as a business and kept it all in perspective. "If you worked the assembly plant, I'd still be doing this for you every night" Willy often said to console her bruised warrior.

No one doubted that Dick Beyer had earned his promotion to the executive level in his industry and, as the recognized champion in the territory, The Destroyer was summoned against the better names, jobbers and talent circulating in southern California - Ricki Starr, Art 'Boom Boom' Michalik, Dick Hutton, Dick Garza, Ray 'Thunder' Stern and legendary NWA champ Lou Thesz. In singles matches, The Destroyer usually won; in tag team matches, The Destroyer almost always lost. Fans saw a great show whether he was an arrogant victor or contemptuous loser. Coupled with good partners that included Great Togo (Kazuo George Okamura), Hans Herman, Von Schober, The Preacher, Masked Marvel, and Ray Stevens, his best performances as a tag team partner came after being paired with Don Manoukian. An offensive guard with the Oakland Raiders in its debut year in the

AFL, Manoukian turned to wrestling for economic reasons and for staying power – at 5'7", wrestling opponents were closer in size than football linemen. He tasted success in the Pacific Northwest and Texas and eventually was imported to the L.A. territory by Strongbow who teamed him with The Destroyer. Manoukian heard of Dick Beyer on the circuit and in Hawaii but once they met, they clicked. Two college guys, former football players, and both with amateur wrestling experience, made the rounds in Los Angeles as a high-drawing heel combination – The Destroyer, a villainous masked braggart and Manoukian, a stocky, bouncing fireplug in the ring, but make no mistake – they wrestled. Jules Strongbow would later tell Beyer that he and Manoukian were the best tag team partners he ever saw.

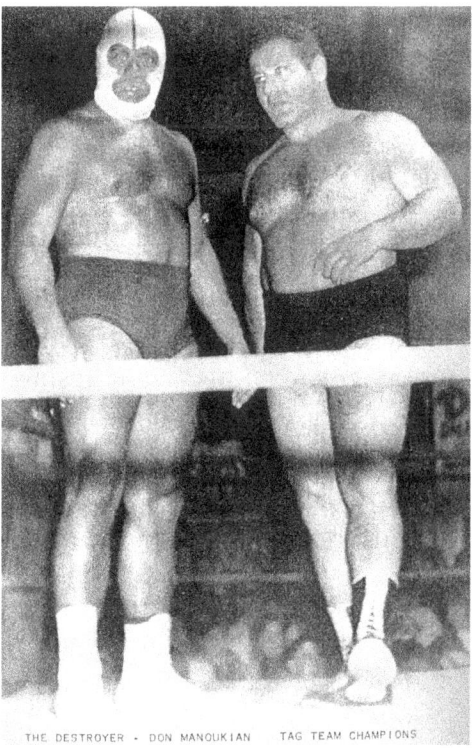

Jules Strongbow acknowledged that the team of The Destroyer and Manoukian was the best tag team he had ever seen.

MASKED DECISIONS

In October 1962, with the nation gripped in fear over missiles in Cuba, many in southern California and around the country turned to wrestling for entertainment and a brief emotional respite from real life stresses. For the first and last time, The Destroyer faced and beat Primo Carnera, the only man to hold world heavyweight boxing and world heavyweight wrestling championship titles. Some believed it to be Carnera's last match as a wrestler, but within the next fourteen months, The Destroyer would be the last wrestler to face two other prominent legends of the ring.

Gorgeous George, the outrageous, prissy, dyed-blonde re-creation of wrestler George Wagner, had been, for years, a wrestling, television and Hollywood celebrity the likes of which had never before been seen. Throughout the 1950s, few personalities rivaled him in shock value; he was the Human Orchid, The Toast of the Coast, The Sensation of the Nation with his gender-bending outfits, golden curly mane, perfume-spraying obsession and cheating tactics. During that decade, he ran neck-and-neck with Milton Berle as the most recognizable star on television, and made public appearances with Bing Crosby, Bob Hope and Jack Benny among others. But by the early 1960s, Wagner's excesses, particularly his drinking, had ruined his health and his life. Twice divorced, on the last leg of a showstopper career, his tavern business doing poorly, the Gorgeous One was broke and desperate. He remembered the young Dick Beyer he met in Alabama and knew his Destroyer was the new main attraction. One afternoon, Beyer asked the wrestling office for George's address; he wanted to stop by and reconnect with the legend.

Beyer drove up to the matches at Strelich Stadium in Bakersfield weekly, and on his way up that day, stopped by 'Gorgeous George Ringside' tavern on Sepulveda but was surprised, once inside, to find the place empty. The interior was decorated in homage to its founder – life size mannequins dressed in his lacy, frilly robes, photos of George and the celebrity elite filled the walls. Near the bar he met George and exchanged greetings. "Where is everybody?" Beyer asked. George told him "Customers don't arrive till the evening; Dick, can we talk?" Beyer had a match scheduled and had to get up to Bakersfield, but told George he would return after the match. Later that night, as promised, Beyer returned, stepped inside the two front doors, and again saw no customers or remnants of earlier activity. George poured him a beer and then said something that troubled Beyer. "Dick, I need a payday. We're not doing too good here and I'd like to wrestle you at the Olympic." George told Beyer an idea he had for a match – the two would wager their signature symbols, George's hair versus Destroyer's mask – if George wins, Destroyer is unmasked; if Destroyer wins, George's hair is shaved off in the ring. "George, you're not in shape." "I'll get in shape; I'll work out and be ready." Beyer sensed the desperation in George's voice and tacitly agreed to the concept. "You're gonna have to shave your head." George acknowledged the outcome, telling Beyer he would have his two hairdressers at the arena ready with clippers, and asked Beyer to talk with Jules Strongbow and convince him of the match's worthiness. Beyer looked around the empty room again, looked at George, and reached out to shake his hand. He was glad he consented to work with George, now convinced the former headline entertainer was in financial distress.

Jules Strongbow was not interested; he saw no reason to put a match together for two wrestlers moving in opposite directions, and he was no fan of George. Beyer pleaded with him "Give the guy a break; he was once a biggest name in the game." Reluctantly, Strongbow agreed, but only to a Wednesday night match despite Beyer's argument for a special Friday night card. "It won't draw" said Strongbow. Both wrestlers participated in pre-match publicity interviews – George with his two hairdressers and The Destroyer displaying a photo of an old bald man telling the audience, "This is what George will look like when I'm done with him."

MASKED DECISIONS

On November 7, 1962, 'The Hair Versus The Mask' headlined the Olympic in Los Angeles. *Referee Magazine* gave half its front cover to the match exclaiming –'Cal Eaton Presents All Star Mat Attraction With Gorgeous (Curls) George vs. The (Masked) Destroyer'…and under two photos of George it read "The stakes will be mighty high when George comes out of retirement to battle the Destroyer. If he loses, the Gorgeous One will have his curls shaved off right in the ring. If he wins, the fans will finally learn just who the Destroyer is, as he will remove his mask."

More than 7000 fans purchased tickets for the event; the start of the match, but not the ending, was televised, and Beyer told Strongbow, "The crowd would have been bigger if we had a Friday night match!" In many publications, the event was described as a 'savage' bout; the fans, into the match all the way, got their money's worth. Pain and punishment were visible on the faces of the foes and both sold it well. Though George won the first fall, the second and third went to The Destroyer, finishing George with his lethal figure-four leg lock. In the very building where George made his L.A. debut in 1947, he lay sprawled on the canvas in agony. The Destroyer loomed over him in dark victory. The noise from the crowd was deafening as the defeated darling of wrestling past, gasping for breath, sat on a metal chair in the middle of the ring, his two hairdressers shaving his golden locks and placing them in a plastic container. George remained seated, a towel around his shoulders, his eyes closed, clearly exhausted. Standing nearby, The Destroyer, arms raised in triumph, initially voiced his pleasure, but stopped short and just quietly watched. No more words or victorious histrionics. The crowd changed too; what was to be a humiliating experience for the vanquished wrestler turned into something else. Many became sorry for and sympathetic toward George, and a few cries of "Let him go" echoed in the hall. The Destroyer left the ring, returned to the dressing room, changed, and departed the Olympic. Beyer was not in a celebratory mood. He felt badly for the once-proud performer.

The famous 'Hair vs Mask' was the finale for Gorgeous George

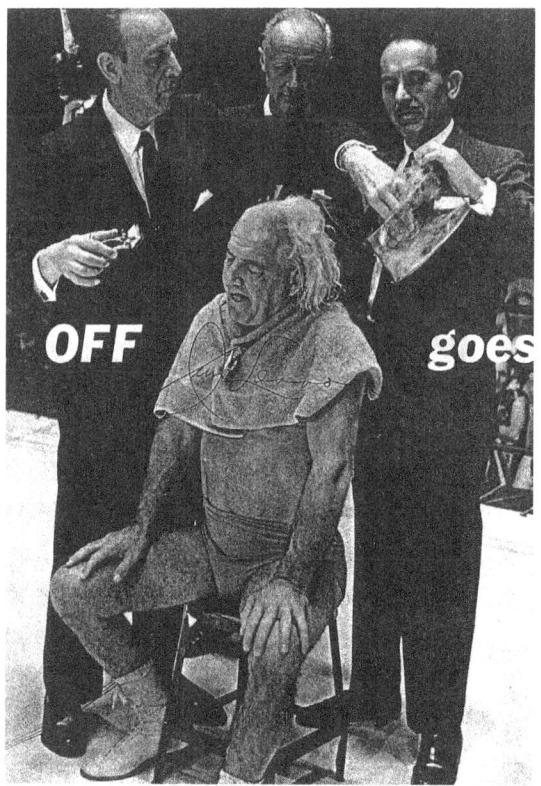

MASKED DECISIONS

While not a sellout, the match was successful; as a result Hardy Kruskamp wanted to stage a rematch in Long Beach. Beyer thought twice, but agreed to one more 'for old time's sake' and to help a colleague in need. The match had to be scheduled into December since George needed time for his hair to grow sufficiently for the rematch. The payout was less than the previous match, the outcome, identical. Gone again was the hair, and gone from the ring, for the final time, was Gorgeous George. He never wrestled again and, a year later at age forty-eight, he was dead.

Expecting the couple's second child, Willy remained busy at home looking after her young son's development and her husband's career, sewing Destroyer masks for the ring and for sale; ads placed in wrestling magazines were generating interest for Destroyer masks and Destroyer cigarette lighters all over the country. Fortunately, the apartment they rented had an extra bedroom that they used to store mask and lighter inventory, but only for a short time since it was to become a nursery in several months. California's scenic coastal and mountain areas offered Willy plenty of vistas to capture on canvas when she found the few times to pursue her painting passion. As a family, the Beyers were just like television's The Flintstones – it was where the only other Wilma he ever heard of existed, Beyer told his friends.

For most of late 1962 and early 1963, as television viewers were getting accustomed to a new late night entertainment team of Carson and McMahon, The Destroyer teamed with Don Manoukian in tag team matches, winning some-losing others, but the popular duo succeeded in laying claim to the International TV Tag Team title when they beat Abe Jacobs and Haystack Calhoun. The Destroyer now held two titles simultaneously; not bad for a regular guy from Buffalo. During their tag match at the Olympic, The Destroyer was set to perform a 'monkey flip' on Calhoun, the bushy-bearded, bib-overall wearing goliath who, on his six foot plus frame, weighed somewhere between 450 and 600 pounds. The Destroyer had Calhoun in a corner; there, he used the ropes to climb the man-mountain and placed his feet on his opponent's hips and his arms around Calhoun's head. In one move, The Destroyer fell backwards onto his back, bringing the gargantuan foe down toward him, but with one thrust of his piston-like legs, The Destroyer pushed Calhoun up and over, causing the opponent to flip over and land sharply and loudly on his back. Calhoun let out the most painful, agonizing, scream that sounded like a wounded moose; Beyer quickly covered him for the win. After the match, Beyer was interviewed for television and when he returned to the dressing room, Calhoun was nowhere to be found; Beyer was concerned that he may have caused Calhoun harm during the monkey flip maneuver, and started to believe Calhoun might plan a 'receipt' for a subsequent match, scheduled the following night in Bakersfield.

Beyer drove into the parking lot at Strelich Stadium in Bakersfield and spotted Calhoun's car near the back door entrance. *He's gonna really give it to me tonight,* he was convinced. As with many wrestling nights, this one started with a card game among the combatants. Beyer entered by way of the back door and proceeded directly to the dressing room where he smelled the aroma of cigars and observed the game already in progress, Calhoun seated at the table. Eyeing Beyer, Calhoun yelled "Beyer, get over here." Walking toward the enormous grappler, trying to figure out how to apologize to him for inadvertently causing pain, Beyer heard Calhoun say "Dick, I been seein' a chiropractor for weeks, but that flip last night did the trick and got my back in place…thanks." Beyer stood there – unable to respond – shaking his head affirmatively as if to say 'sure, no problem at all' when all he was feeling was complete relief that Haystack was not going to make the match a real pounding headache that night.

Calhoun, whom Beyer later labeled the most difficult foe he faced in the ring, wasn't the only behemoth he tangled with to draw considerable attention, and crowds, to the wrestling arenas and halls. Piquing the curiosity of wrestling fans in the States was a force of nature from Japan – a 6'11" 330 pound monolith, named Shohei Baba.

A baseball pitcher for the Yomiuri Giants and teammate of the popular Sadaharu Oh, Baba turned wrestler after injuries forced him to consider other work options. He was recruited by the father of 'Purofesshonaru Resuringu' (Japanese professional wrestling or *puroresu*) the now highly acclaimed Rikidozan, who trained Baba and another talented Japanese wrestler, Kanji (Antonio) Inoki. Baba was brought to the Los Angeles territory for a series of singles and tag team matches, having only begun wrestling professionally two years earlier and after being sent by Rikidozan to train in Crystal Beach Ontario, Canada, with Fred Atkins. His skills were not fully developed, but he made up for it with size, athleticism, and Japanese aura.

It was a no-brainer for Strongbow to pit the massive Baba against the masked Destroyer, but he asked Beyer if he could put him over. "I can put over a broom," Beyer told Strongbow. To heighten the focus and drawing power, the two wrestled approximately 20 tag team matches around the Los Angeles circuit before working singles, but it was their three mano-a-mano matches at the Olympic that, not only fomented a close friendship, but created a plethora of publicity for the two wrestlers– moderately consumed in the States, overwhelmingly in Japan. The match maker and, in fact, the wrestlers, didn't know what to expect in the first match, so it came as a shock to see a full house, sold out, a $22,000 gate. Strongbow walked into Beyer's dressing room the night of the initial match and said, "We have to do something to bring this back." Beyer replied, "We're gonna make that big Japanese look like a million bucks; let me handle it." The other two events sold out in no time. During the final moments of their first match, Baba, having won the first fall, beat The Destroyer and was about to have his hand raised by the referee when the bell rang – time had run out and The Destroyer retained his belt. For the second match, there was to be no time limit; Baba, again, was defeating The Destroyer when, near the end of the third fall, The Destroyer hit the referee – an automatic disqualification; since a title match could not end on a disqualification, The Destroyer held onto his title. The third match was a 'no time limit and no disqualification' bout; this time Baba gave all he had but The Destroyer prevailed. At each of the

Baba/Destroyer main events, Japanese photographers and reporters, covering Baba's U.S. visit, filled the ringside press seats and crowded against the ring floor; they sent hold-by-hold descriptions of the bouts back home augmented by after-match commentary from both wrestlers. The Japanese people, having come to appreciate professional wrestling largely through the efforts of Rikidozan, his followers, and his Japan Pro Wrestling Alliance, were thrilled to read and see photos of his protégé, Baba, on the world stage doing battle with the enemy American of unknown identity. In Japan, these matches were considered an extension of a tradition that began after World War II, when the Japanese were searching for heroes to believe in. They saw Rikidozan wrestle Bobby Bruns, Lou Thesz and other Americans on early television and were hooked; now, Baba was fighting a mystery man from the United States. The combination of technical wrestling, size, speed, Motherland pride, and the mystique and awesome skill of a masked title holder, stirred the collective curiosity of the Japanese and whetted their appetite for professional wrestling in general, and Baba and The Destroyer in particular. Baba returned to his homeland a national hero. Beyer was unaware at the time of just how important his matches with Baba were, and were to be to his career.

Jules Strongbow swizzled all the wrestling talent he could attract around the L.A. territory to pair off with The Destroyer. Fans saw Don Leo Jonathan, Vic Christy, Roberto Duranton, Tex McKenzie and other names try in vain to bring down and unmask the hooded wonder. But Strongbow, looking ahead for fresh material and promotion ideas, was giving indications that the masked Destroyer was soon to be exposed. This was unsettling to Dick Beyer, who argued with the match maker several times over the matter. For Beyer, it was out of the question; for Strongbow, it was the logical answer. When Edouard Carpentier came to town to wrestle, the one-time champion told Beyer in the dressing room, "Don't ever take the mask off...The Destroyer is well known around the country." Other wrestling colleagues gave Beyer similar takes on what to do with the mask. Beyer and his wife discussed it at home, and arrived at the same conclusion – why take it off when it was working so well, not only for Beyer (and making money for the territory), but for other wrestlers who got on the card with him. For the time being, Beyer forestalled Strongbow's desire for an unmasking.

A young wrestler from Hawaii, Curtis Iaukea, was brought into the Los Angeles area in the spring of 1963. He and Beyer wrestled several matches and talked afterwards at length about Hawaii and how well wrestling was doing in the 50th state. The islands, a favorite topic for Beyer, held a magical spell over him that was never to be broken. Beyer had heard a story about Iaukea that involved Vic Christy; as usual, the storyline was incredibly funny, albeit at Iaukea's expense. The way Beyer was told, early on his first trip to the west coast, the rookie Iaukea was informed by the wrestling office that he was to be picked up the following day by Vic Christy and taken to the city he was to work. Christy was unexpectedly early, arriving at Iaukea's hotel sooner than scheduled, driving his newer convertible with the top down. Iaukea was impressed with the car, and pleased to be riding in the open air under very sunny skies. Christy drove 120 miles south to San Diego, 100 miles east to Yuma, Arizona, 120 miles north to Palm Springs, and similar mileage west, where they arrived with about fifteen minutes to spare before Iaukea was slotted to compete. Christy told the Hawaiian another wrestler on the card was to transport him back to his hotel after the matches, and Christy departed hastily. The entire trip took more than eight hours; Iaukea was sunburned from sitting all day in the convertible; he gingerly walked up to the arena door, dressed quickly, and waited for his entrance call; it didn't help that his opponent gave him a barrage of slap chops all evening that caused his sunburn to feel like a stinging inferno. When the matches ended, a most uncomfortable and exhausted Iaukea found his driver for the return trip. Iaukea got into the car and before he settled in for his overnight journey, he had arrived at the front entrance to his hotel. The arena he had just worked was only fifteen minutes from where he was picked up that morning by Christy.

VINCENT EVANS

Billed as 'the magazine for ring fans,' *Boxing Illustrated-Wrestling News*, in its March 1963 edition, printed an article on the young heavyweight boxing contender Cassius Clay, a top challenger for the title held by Sonny Liston. The same publication contained a summary of The Destroyer/Gorgeous George 'Hair vs. Mask' wrestling match with action photos and the humiliating haircut. The Destroyer was in fast and interesting company. The following month, *Wrestling Revue*, 'the magazine for mat fans,' featured The Destroyer on the cover, and a special section on his 'home life' complete with photos of Willy, Kurt and The Destroyer enjoying family time, eating, exercising, even one of The Destroyer kissing his wife…all while wearing the mask.

The Destroyer is a national phenomenon

MASKED DECISIONS

Wrestling World magazine wrote a multi-page story on The Destroyer, giving wrestling fans across the nation an inside view of the mystery man's thoughts and preparations for matches, as well as some history and rationale for wearing a mask. In the piece, The Destroyer was quoted as saying, "I wear the mask in California because I don't want to go into the movies. I figure with my looks and physique, those Hollywood producers would be hounding me to go into pictures." Referred to as the man with 'the million dollar legs' – *I am the male Betty Grable* he often quipped. Accompanying the article were a number of photographs of The Destroyer in action and one with a young lad, television star Jay North (who played Dennis the Menace). Perhaps it was coincidental, or a bizarre twist when Beyer was called a 'menace' in real life soon after the magazine article was published. It had to do with a different Ladd.

Ernie Ladd, a 6'9" 315 pound defensive back, played for the San Diego Chargers of the American Football League; a powerful, rangy, fierce competitor, his quickness earned him the nickname 'Big Cat.' During the off season, he began a love affair with wrestling, and desperately wanted to get on the circuit. Hardy Kruskamp, the San Diego promoter, took him under his wing, and one of Ladd's first matches was a tag event teamed with Freddie Blassie against Don Manoukian and The Destroyer held in San Diego, Ladd's backyard. Manoukian's and Destroyer's job was to put Ladd over, to make him appear a skilled, talented wrestler. The match was nothing if not a complete disaster; Manoukian and Destroyer gave Ladd plenty of opportunities, but he failed to make the most of them; Blassie covered for Ladd as much as he could during the match, but it was painfully obvious just how over his head Ladd was during this bout. In the dressing room after the match, Kruskamp was livid. "Beyer, you menace…you guys killed my star…you killed my star!" Kruskamp went ballistic on the heels for several minutes. It took Blassie's intervention to calm him down and assure him that Manoukian and Beyer tried their best to put him over. To his credit, Ladd went on to develop into one of the finest wrestlers in the business as well as an All Pro football player.

A few weeks later, Jules Strongbow called Beyer into his office. Given their recent arguments, Beyer armed himself to defend his position in maintaining the mask. Strongbow did not mince his words - he told Beyer that The Destroyer was to lose his WWA title in early May… before The Destroyer travels to Japan on a tour. Beyer was dumbfounded; it was the kind of 'bad news, good news' routine he had heard in jokes and on television. "I'm losing the title but going to Japan?" The matches with Shohei Baba had created an enormous reaction in Japan and intense interest in the masked villain, so much that Rikidozan wanted The Destroyer for a series of singles matches with himself, Great Togo, and Baba, in cities around Japan.

It was a remarkable evening as Beyer told his wife about the details of his conversation with Jules Strongbow that afternoon, and the opportunity given him to tour Japan at the invitation of Rikidozan. "Funny how a little dinner with Rikidozan in Hawaii a few years ago started this thing…and how the Baba matches cemented it," he said to a delighted Willy. "I'm thrilled for you…finally…you will see Japan," she told him. "Oh, yeah, before I go, I lose the belt but keep the mask." "A good trade; who wins the belt from you?" said Willy. "I forgot to ask." Beyer learned later an old friend was returning to town for a limited engagement – Classy Freddie Blassie.

Preparations began in earnest for a special card scheduled for the Olympic on Friday May 10, 1963. The event included Mr. Moto wrestling Bobby Duranton, Cowboy Dick Hutton against Don Leo Jonathan, Curtis Iaukea (taking a cab to the event) challenging Tex McKenzie, Don Manoukian grappling Ricki Starr, a tag team match featuring Bearcat Wright and a now more experienced Ernie Ladd taking on Art Michalik and Don Jardine, and the main event of Blassie and The Destroyer for the belt. The two friends and super heels were united for another headline bout that was to upset the status of wrestling in southern California. A packed house was privy to the change in champions as Blassie waged a tremendous comeback to overtake The Destroyer and overthrow his reign. Within nine days, Beyer was in a land that, a short time ago seemed so very far away.

To the casual observer, it was difficult to determine who was gawking more – The Destroyer at the Japanese sights or the Japanese at the sight of The Destroyer. The disguise hid his face but not his exuberance; all those years of youthful, war-shaped hate had evolved into mature wonder about this foreign land and its people; his dream was about to be realized. He honestly didn't know what to expect, but honored to be a guest in the country. Beyer knew he had to keep the mask on wherever he travelled in Japan, in order to put the character over on the Japanese people, who were seeing him for the first time in person, and because Rikidozan insisted on it. What he didn't realize was how big an attraction he had already become – his celebrity preceded him to the Orient, with his major matches against treasured Shohei Baba. He slowly began to appreciate his luminary status during his first day in Tokyo.

Onboard a Pan Am flight, Beyer arrived at Haneda airport, 30 miles south of Tokyo, wearing a gray suit, white shirt and black tie; before deplaning, he donned his white mask; Dick Beyer landed in Japan, but The Destroyer walked down the steps to the tarmac, and the masked wrestler remained in character for the eight day tour. With representatives of Rikidozan and wrestling colleagues Killer Kowalski, Frank Townsend, and Fred Atkins who were in town for another show, The Destroyer meandered around the famous Ginza, walked by the Tokyo Tower, strolled in Ueno Park, and observed students training at the Kodokan, the center for judo, trying to satisfy his peripatetic desires in one day. Wherever he went, press and photographers, as well as the curious and star-struck, followed him.

That evening, he was introduced to the public during a professional wrestling tournament that had been running seven weeks in the city – the Fifth World League Tournament. Prior to the start of the final match between Killer Kowalski and Rikidozan, the Japanese ring announcer intoned an introduction that ended with "*The De-stroy-yaa*." The masked man entered the ring to the loud roar of the crowd, popping flash bulbs, some clapping and hissing, and plenty of questioning eyes. The Destroyer walked over to Kowalski's corner and, unrehearsed and unplanned, Kowalski whispered to him, "Don't shake my hand…stand there and look at me." The two American wrestlers stood toe to toe staring at each other. The crowd sensed something in the making. Kowalski again whispered, "Now slap me as hard as you can." With a mighty wind-up of his right arm, The Destroyer landed a thunderous slap on Killer Kowalski, to the shock and surprise of the fans. Kowalski was an established heel figure, who wrestled often in Japan, and the sight of another American wrestler disrespecting his fellow countryman dropped the jaws of everyone in the arena. Kowalski gave him one more silent directive; The Destroyer turned his back on Kowalski and proceeded to Rikidozan's corner. Standing in front of the Japanese hero, both men with arms at their sides, fingers twitching like a showdown challenge in a Western movie, the intense scene culminated as The Destroyer extended his right arm and, with a slight bow, shook the hand of the Japanese wrestler. The crowd erupted wildly. This gesture by the masked American toward their Asian Idol Rikidozan earned enormous admiration from the Japanese for The Destroyer, even though he was rightly a villain. The symbolism was not lost on the Japanese; they appreciated the full measure of respect he displayed toward their hero and, in effect, toward them. When the tournament ended, The Destroyer was extensively interviewed by the press from all over Japan. After the media event, he and his colleagues were invited to the Takarazuka Theater where they were entertained with Kabuki plays, native dances and musical performances. It was red carpet treatment and the kind of overarching hospitality and graciousness usually reserved for dignitaries.

MASKED DECISIONS

The masked American wrestler made front page headlines in many newspapers across the country. The page one publicity fortified the promotional material that had been in place for weeks - in print and on television- announcing the televised grand match between The Destroyer and Japanese hero Rikidozan set for May 24 in Tokyo. The hype had built up to a palpable crescendo and frenzy for tickets, information, and ways to experience the blockbuster event.

For most of the previous decade, with television only beginning to surface, the cost of privately owning a television set far exceeded the typical Japanese worker's financial wherewithal. Nippon Television, or NTV, as part of a marketing strategy to increase exposure and viewership, decided to place television sets in public venues including train stations, parks, department store windows and other high traffic locations. Soon, bars, restaurants and other accessible businesses followed suit, and the street television phenomenon was birthed in Japan, attracting large crowds around strategically positioned small black and white flickering cathode ray television sets, excited to see the new medium and broadcasts of professional boxing and wrestling and imported American programming.[2] In 1959, the wedding of Japan's Crown Prince Akihito and commoner Michiko Shoda spurred many Japanese to purchase television sets in order to watch the royal ceremonies. By the end of that year, there were approximately two million sets in distribution. Wrestling, both sumo and the professional variety, had become fodder for early broadcasts, and word of the Rikidozan/Destroyer match in 1963 contributed to a new wave of interest in both televised wrestling and private set ownership. But perhaps the single most important factor to further the demand for television sets was the anticipation of the world-wide broadcast of the upcoming Summer Olympic Games, to be held for the first time in Tokyo in 1964. Japan was originally granted the rights to the 1940 summer games, but those rights were retracted from Tokyo by the International Olympic Committee, due to the outbreak of the second Sino-Japanese war. For the Japanese people, national pride was at stake.

Rikidozan was a clever wrestler, controlling businessman, and cunning individual. Born Kim Sin-nak in Japanese-occupied North Korea in 1924, he became the adopted son of Nagasaki farming family Momota, and took on both a Japanese name, Mitsuhiro Momota, and a Japanese birthplace, to avoid long-standing discrimination of Koreans by Japanese; it worked limitedly and not without pain. After his family disowned him at age 13, he travelled to Tokyo to train as a sumo, and was given the *shikona* (sumo wrestler ring name) of Rikidozan, which translates into 'rugged mountain road,' suggesting the 800 mile route he took from Nagasaki to Tokyo to study sumo. While he achieved some success and fame, he abruptly left sumo in 1950, claiming it was for financial reasons, but sources said discrimination and a dispute with an official over a call may have played a role in his decision. He would hide his Korean heritage forever.

For a year he worked as a laborer and studied karate during his off time, conditioning his body and honing his self-defense skills. When an American pro-wrestling show came through town, he and some *judoka* (students of judo) decided to get into the business. He got his first break in Tokyo, 1951, wrestling American Bobby Bruns to a draw. A year later, he landed in Hawaii and trained extensively, before heading to the U.S and a 13 month, 260+ match tour, his first win on U.S. soil pinning Ike Ekins, Beyer's raccoon-carrying buddy from his Columbus training.

In the summer of 1953, with money borrowed from a friend associated with the *yakuza* (Japanese underworld), Rikidozan founded the Japan Pro Wrestling Alliance (JWA); early shows featured Rikidozan against primary foe Masahiko Kimura, one of the original *judoka* who entered the business with him two years earlier. Over the next several years, at home and abroad, Rikidozan faced many high profile wrestlers, developing into a national figure and hero to postwar Japan. He was the first Japanese heavyweight champion. Subsequently, either directly or indirectly, all wrestling titles in

MASKED DECISIONS

Japan – like roads to Rome – connected to Rikidozan. With success came opportunities, which he transformed into real estate, night clubs, hotels and other business ventures; he was building an entirely different Japanese empire. But his empire came with attachments –business associations with the Japanese underworld that would prove costly in the end. As money rolled in, his eccentricities rolled out. It was rumored that he slept with a briefcase full of American currency under his futon. He did not like anyone to cast a shadow on him, or onto his own shadow, and sat with others in a way where he controlled the dispersion of light. Shortly after meeting Beyer for the first time in Hawaii in 1956, he and Koukichi Endo won the NWA World tag team title, eventually developing a warm friendship with NWA title holder Lou Thesz. Rikidozan and Thesz staged a dramatic match in 1957 at Korakuen Stadium in Tokyo before 30,000 fans and a huge television audience that ended in a draw, and less than a year later, they again met in Los Angeles, where Rikidozan won a seldom used title, NWA International Heavyweight Champion, that was to be successfully defended for the next five years. In March 1962, Rikidozan beat Freddie Blassie to become the first Asian to win the WWA world heavyweight championship, only to lose it back to Blassie four months later. Blassie, in turn, lost the title to The Destroyer two days after reclaiming it. Rikidozan never forgot the generosity of spirit of Lou Thesz, the only American he publicly respected, and challenged those he trained to adopt the personal attributes Thesz espoused.

Rikidozan scheduled the first of his two matches with The Destroyer for Osaka, Japan's second largest city and center for commerce. The Destroyer arrived in Osaka from Tokyo by train and was met by scores of press and Japanese who ogled at the masked visitor. Newspaper accounts of their initial match told of a heated battle as Rikidozan absorbed the best of The Destroyer's attack; both wrestlers punished one another all evening with physical artillery; in the end, the sold-out arena witnessed the American masked man apply his figure-four leg lock to beat the Japanese champion wrestler. Fans and ordinary citizens spread the account of the match, and interest in the rematch spiked throughout the country. Before leaving Osaka, Beyer was given some time to see the city. As he walked along Osaka's many rivers and canals, up through the north and south sides of the city, there were times he just could not contain himself...*I am in Japan* he said often to no one in particular. He visited Osaka Castle, a 16th century structure and a signature of Japanese architecture in the city; he was photographed near one of the castle's cannons used by the Tokugawa shoguns. Many of the photographs of the masked Destroyer made their way into newspapers, magazines and television reports, resulting in a burgeoning quest for more details from rank and file Japanese on this stranger whose real identity was such a secret.

The Destroyer's next stop was Nagoya, the site of his match with Japanese favorite Great Togo. Kazuo George Okamura – the Great Togo – was another veteran wrestler working as Japanese – few knew he was actually from Oregon. With Tosh Togo (Hawaiian-born Japanese Harold Sakata) they wrestled for some time as the Togo Brothers and won the NWA Canadian Open Tag Team Championship in 1954. Both went on to solo careers that, for Okamura, included a stint as manager for Giant Baba. When Baba wrestled The Destroyer in L.A., it was Great Togo who managed him and his affairs while in the States. Regarding their three matches, Baba asked Beyer how much he was paid for the series – "About forty-five hundred dollars" Beyer told him, to which Baba replied, "Seventy-five dollar for Baba." Beyer never asked Baba if he ever pursued the matter to determine whether Togo's financial compilations followed the Generally Accepted Accounting Principles.

Another capacity crowd of more than 13,000 fans booed and hollered at The Destroyer for using, in their rather vociferous opinion, dirty tactics to wear down, and eventually beat, Great Togo. But additionally, they marveled at his wrestling acumen, his speed, and riveting personality in the ring; it was another great performance by the shielded showman. Having dispatched with Togo, it was time to move on to Shibuya, and a reunion in the ring with Giant Baba.

Photographers were positioned everywhere The Destroyer was to be. On the train, Beyer (as The Destroyer) was invited by the engineer to take the controls of the massive locomotive. A photo of the masked man at the helm of the train was taken for a national magazine – Beyer told his friends he felt like a kid at Christmas with his first Lionel, only a larger version. After changing trains and arriving at Shibuya Station, the wrestler and his small entourage stepped out of the car. They walked briskly, while The Destroyer signed numerous autographs en route, and soon were at *Hachiko-guchi*, meaning the Hachiko exit. Turning to view the entrance to the station, Beyer noticed a statue of a dog, and inquired about its existence to one of the Japanese escorts.

A professor who taught at the University of Tokyo in the mid-1920s, took the train to and from work each day, and was greeted every night in front of the Shibuya train station by his dog, Hachiko. This routine, with its customary meeting place, continued for more than a year as the dog faithfully showed up each night to greet his master and the two walking home from there together.

One evening as the dog waited patiently, the professor never arrived; he had suffered a stroke at work, was hospitalized, and died. Though the dog was given away following his owner's death, he frequently escaped and ran to the train station to keep his vigil. Passengers, who had often seen the professor with his dog, were moved to see the dog maintaining his watch for his master every night. Many stopped to pet him and provide small eatables for the awaiting animal that continued his nightly mission and became a fixture at Shibuya Station for ten years. During that time, a former student of the professor, curious about the animal, followed the dog to his new home and learned the back story. He took such keen interest in the dog's breed and history that he wrote a set of articles, one of which appeared in Tokyo's largest newspaper that, almost overnight, put Hachiko in the national consciousness. His steadfast faithfulness to his departed master became symbolic of loyalty to many Japanese, and a legend was born. As with many legends, a bittersweet irony follows the story – Hachiko died on the very spot he long waited for his master's return. Beyer listened intently to the story while gazing at the statue and visualizing the sequence of events that unfolded where he stood. He, too, was touched. The story resonated unusually deeply for someone who, as tough as he was in a violent business, thought he knew a thing or two about being loyal.

It was a warm greeting Baba had for Destroyer-san. The two drank sake and enjoyed each other's company for several hours that afternoon. Beyer told Baba "It was your matches in L.A. that got me here" but Baba replied "It was your skill as a wrestler." Their friendship became stronger as their legendary ring personalities grew. Before the day was over, 11,000 fans were whipped into a rage as Baba fought valiantly but was beaten by a series of assaults inflicted by the disguised Destroyer. The American wrestler, as the Japanese press reported, stood three wins and no losses going into his final match of the tour. Could the American withstand the best the Japanese had to offer him in the ring...Would the father of Japanese wrestling be defeated again in his homeland, or teach the hooded heel something about the resilience of the Japanese people? The stage was set for the return of the wrestling titans, Rikidozan and The Destroyer, in Tokyo.

The promotions ended. No ticket was unsold. All seats were spoken for. Not even Godzilla was big enough to gain access. As those fortunate 16,000 ticket holders lined up in front of the Tokyo Municipal Stadium in Sendaguya to see the battle in person, 5000 others promenaded outside the arena just to take in the experience; millions of others crowded around black and white television screens in homes and businesses while large throngs huddled together along public plazas throughout Japan, peering and squinting to see the images on the tiny screen of their community television. No one, anywhere, was disappointed.

A bruising match ensued as The Destroyer unleashed his arsenal of bludgeoning tactics, defended and countered by the local warrior and presumptive favorite Rikidozan. The Asian hero took control early in the match after landing a series of karate chops to the face that caught the masked Destroyer off guard and resulted in the accidental loss of his upper right front tooth. Blood seeped from the mouth opening of his mask. Beyer realized he needed to be cautious since Rikidozan might have been looking for revenge from his first home loss to any foreign wrestler yet he needed to be on the offensive when given the opportunity. It came when, after leaving the ring, he returned and scored on a thunderous kick to Rikidozan's upper torso that left the imprint of his laces on the local favorite's chest. Beyer could hear his opponent mumble some American profanity and knew he had answered the challenge.

For sixty minutes, they dueled and slammed each other hard to the surface to the delight and appreciation of the crowd awed by the spectacle; no booing of the challenger was heard the entire evening. At one point, a forehead wound was sustained by the Asian whose blood was absorbed by the mask of The Destroyer during lock up and close action. Red was the common denominator for both wrestlers in the ring; as one wrestler was about to close and seal the victory, the other barely escaped the potentially winning maneuver, causing an ebb and flow of the emotional tide for those watching. Looking more like two street fighters locked in a do-or-die, the American and Japanese wrestlers, as time expired, settled for a draw. A rematch was announced and scheduled for December.

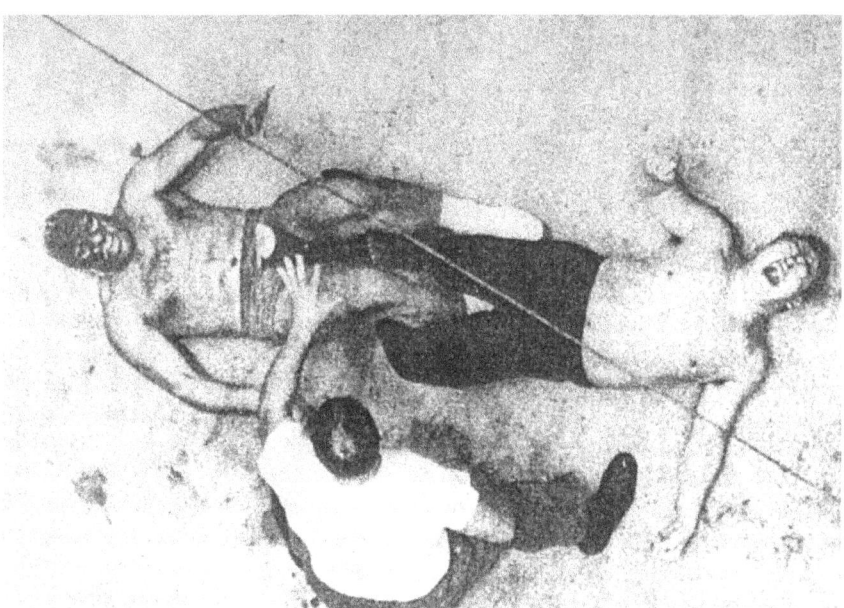

Destroyer vs. Rikidozan was seen by more than 70 million people

The match was the talk of the town, and the talk of the country. Though Rikidozan did nothing to lose his stature or reputation among fans and the public, the skills, mystique, and technical abilities of The Destroyer secured a foothold with the Japanese that was to advance their regard for him in years to follow. Newspapers wrote that The Destroyer was the only foreign wrestler to have toured Japan undefeated – an achievement, they noted, certain to draw the ire of Rikidozan and his countrymen focused on the mystery man's return engagement later in the year. Before he departed Japan, Beyer learned that, of the population of 100 million Japanese, the nationally televised match with Rikidozan drew 70 million people, an estimated 67.0 rating, and the largest viewing audience for any program in Japanese history. A bright new star had risen above the horizon in Japan.

2 Fox, Jeannette; "Japan", The Museum of Broadcast Communications; *Encyclopedia of Television 1st Edition*, Edited by Dr. Horace Newcomb; http://www.museum.tv/eotvsection.php?entrycode=japan; site accessed 3/19/2009.

CHAPTER **12**

THE JAPANESE HAVE an expression when one accomplishes something extraordinary– *Yatta*, which means 'I did it.' On the return flight to Los Angeles from Tokyo, Dick Beyer 'yatta, yatta'd' over and over in his mind, thrilled by the visit to the land he so longed to see, and satisfied with his performances against Great Togo, Giant Baba, and Rikidozan. He knew he had done well, judging by the size of the crowds, the inquisitiveness of the Japanese people, the reviews, the pay, and the remarks from Rikidozan. As he sat and gazed out the window that offered him a view of the Pacific from 30,000 feet, he played out the journey that brought him to the intersection of right time and right place and realized that, along the way, with a little luck, he had made some good choices and fateful decisions. Just as important, at this juncture, he believed he had the makings of something very special with the Japanese. Beyer was taken by Japan, and the hospitality of its people, more than he anticipated. At the same time, the Japanese were smitten by the masked American who, with an aura and skills unlike others they had seen, burst into their consciousness and left an impression that would not soon fade away. With an invitation from Rikidozan to return to wrestle in December, Beyer was certain that he lived up to the Asian champion's high standards, and looked forward to his return trip to re-experience the country and the people that had long held his interest and fascination.

It wasn't many weeks after settling back into his work and family routine in California when Beyer's wife Willy gave birth to their second child, this time a daughter. "Maybe it's due to a sake hangover or a strain of Asian flu, but we're naming the baby after you, Charley," Beyer told Charley Iwamoto. Out of deep respect for his friend, Beyer also bestowed upon Iwamoto, the father of five boys, the distinction of serving as the baby's godfather. It was a recognition that surprised and touched Iwamoto and one he happily accepted. Beyer and Willy played with the name and settled on a female derivative of Moto, naming the baby Mona Kris Beyer. Iwamoto was delighted by the name, honored by the title, and humbled by the sentiment.

Back in the ring, The Destroyer and his trusted tag partner, Don Manoukian, picked up where they left off before Destroyer's first tour of Japan. Aside from their individual matches, the combo faced Hutton and Torres, Blassie and Jonathan, Fox and McKenzie, and other teams, as fans continued to jam arenas and catch their matches on Wednesday night television. But their reign as International TV Tag Team champions came to an end on July 19, when they lost to the team of Bearcat Wright and Mr. Moto. "I thought you were my friend," Beyer jokingly said to Moto in the dressing room after the match, with Beyer's son Kurt waiting near his locker. "I am friend; that's why you still standing with son at side," Iwamoto said in fake broken English, sounding more like Tonto addressing the Long Ranger. It was not uncommon for three year-old Kurt to go to the matches with his father and watch the bouts near the ring or play in the dressing room with a staffer from the arena; he was comfortable among the giants who were his father's co-workers. He even had his own mask, copied after The Destroyer's that he wore at the matches. Like Destroyer, like son.

"It'll be a lumberjack match with Cortez winning and *you will* take off the mask," were the stinging and mind-numbing words Beyer heard from Jules Strongbow during a meeting held at the wrestling office in July. He listened to the match maker's reasons for creating the bout, projected to take place August 7 at the Olympic. Beyer tried to compute the short and long range benefits from the unmasking, but none made sense to him. He argued. He fought. He acknowledged his own fear, hesitation, and yes abject anger, when first directed by Strongbow to wear a mask however he contrasted his early skepticism with his complete transmigration to the hooded heel that lit a fire of new excitement in southern California wrestling. It was still working - in individual and tag team matches – people were buying tickets -The Destroyer commanded national and international wrestling press- and Beyer debated the merits of staying with a winning persona rather than de-legitimizing it. Given the strong gate attraction and payouts over the last year, largely due to the popularity of The Destroyer, Beyer had a most difficult time understanding the temerity of Strongbow to cast all that aside. At times Strongbow was vituperate. He had his mind made up and locked. For some unknown reason, The Destroyer was to come out from under the hood at this event, at this time, with this opponent.

After considerably tense exchanges, Beyer realized an impasse had been reached and told Strongbow he would honor his commitments to matches scheduled into early August, but left the meeting without agreement on the Cortez match. When he arrived home, after the kids were put to bed, he sat with Willy for the remainder of the evening and discussed the situation from every angle, and then he made a telephone call. It was a rainy evening in Los Angeles and Beyer's mood was reflective of it…stormy, overcast, and dark.

The following day, Beyer awoke from a restless sleep with ideas to fulfill his obligation to Strongbow and simultaneously protect the image of The Destroyer and his own reputation. Before the day was through, he had a plan, called Strongbow, and informed him The Destroyer and Cortez match was on – the masked man was going to be in the ring.

No one but Strongbow knew the rationale he used to conceive the match and configure the event; perhaps in his mind someone named Hercules endowed with near 'superhuman power' was needed to put over a two of three fall match in order to unmask The Destroyer and accomplish what other more prominent wrestling names were unable to do to this point. What was clear was the framework for the event - a lumberjack match, where other wrestlers, usually a group of both heels and baby faces not involved with the match, surround the ring in order to prevent the two wrestlers from escaping it and the consequences of the battle. Clearly, Strongbow wanted to hype the importance of the match by guarding the egress routes, thus confining the action to the ring and controlling the event and its outcome. Alfonso Carlos Chicharro, who began his career as Pepe Cortes in Spain in the 1950s, was a hulking, strongly built professional wrestler who took the name Hercules Cortez upon his wife's suggestion. The 6'3" 300 pounder gained credibility by wrestling the renowned Lou Thesz in New York City in 1962 and winning a championship belt. While not a scientific wrestler, his muscular chiseled physique and brawling style earned respect from wrestling insiders and interest from fans.

August 7, 1963 at the Olympic in Los Angeles, the main event featured a lumberjack match with Hercules Cortez against The Destroyer. The undercard having been delivered, the crowd noise swelled with anticipation as a band of eight wrestlers approached the apron of the ring and encircled the platform like armed guards flanking a maximum-security prison. The lumberjacks in position, the two headliners entered the ring, Hercules Cortez stoically through the ropes, The Destroyer with his customary jump-in over the top rope, an athletic maneuver few others could replicate.

Fans witnessed a tremendous conflict on the canvass with body slams and punishing hits put on by both heavyweights; at no time did any of the 'lumberjacks' enter the ring or assist either combatant as per the rules of engagement. For most of the hour-long struggle, no one knew for certain which of the wrestlers would emerge victorious. It all came down to a toss out of the ring by Cortez, who had grabbed the masked opponent and hurled him under the ropes and onto the concrete floor. The referee started a ten count – if The Destroyer was not back in the ring before the end of the count, the match would be over. While on the floor, Beyer peered through the left eye hole of The

Destroyer's mask and spotted the short aisle leading up to the doors on the street side – his plan was in place and about to be executed. The Destroyer slowly got up from the floor and, noticeably in pain, limped up the short aisle before any of the lumberjacks could get to him. The referee completed his count and declared Cortez the winner. The bell rang furiously. Fans saw a great show and were surprised by the loss, but none more so than Strongbow and Cortez, who were in on an unmasking deal, or so they thought. Strongbow entered the ring near Cortez and called for the microphone. As The Destroyer neared the door to the street, Strongbow announced "There goes The Destroyer- I didn't see his face but he looks like Dick Beyer." Fan noise made it impossible to decipher Strongbow's words which were clearly meant to destroy The Destroyer. Cortez appeared puzzled as pandemonium filled the ring and the match maker glared up the short aisle at the door.

The Destroyer lost a match but not the mask. Beyer was not going to allow it; he worked too hard over the last year to create the identity; he made money for the territory; he made a name for the wrestler; he had to take control to save the masked man; he carried out his responsibility for showing up, for wrestling, and for losing, but not even Strongbow was going to undo a story that was still being written. In one methodical moment, Beyer forever assumed authority over The Destroyer franchise. Don Manoukian, who had packed Beyer's clothes from the locker room after the lumberjack wrestlers exited for the ring, was waiting in the running car just outside the street side door. The telephone call Beyer made that rainy night in July was to Don Owen; The Destroyer was bound for Oregon.

Beyer was greeted warmly by Portland territory promoter Don Owen, the two having met in Hawaii prior to Beyer's decision to go to L.A. "You are true to your word, Dick," Owen said to Beyer with a handshake, in reference to Beyer's insistence he would join him in Portland once his Los Angeles time ended. "I appreciated your letting me out of our agreement so I could go to L.A. Don…and now I want to work for you here." The conditions for working in Portland were well known to the boys of wrestling; Owen paid exactly what was negotiated and never shorted any wrestler; that is what made him so respected among the wrestling showmen. Every name in the business wanted an opportunity to go through Portland and many big stars of the industry in fact did; George Wagner, before launching his international profile as Gorgeous George, was one of them. Owen's reputation for fairness and for creating a family environment for the wrestlers, contributed to the popularity of Pacific Northwest Wrestling, the northwest territory of the NWA, of which Don Owen was a founding member.

The story of what led to his phone call to Owen was retold by Beyer at their lunch meeting the day after he arrived from California. Owen never commented on the decisions made by Strongbow or Beyer, but told Beyer he was happy not only to have another strong heel in the territory but a masked one at that. Owen said he was going to give The Destroyer singles and tag team matches with the possibility of championships. It was a positive sign of things to come. Some talented wrestlers that included Abe Jacobs, Rocky Columbo, Andre Dapp, Billy White Wolf, Shag Thomas, Luther Lindsey, Tony Borne among others were in or due into the territory, raising Beyer's expectations for great shows.

Beyer and his family settled into a cozy, rented home on 82nd Avenue, on the north east side of Portland. Willy managed to organize the house in quick order and to get the children acclimated to their new surroundings. The family soon had several business insiders and neighbors as friends, making the atmosphere in Oregon comfortable and secure.

The Destroyer made his Pacific Northwest debut on August 9, 1963 against Abe Jacobs. Wrestling purists in Oregon caught wind of the enigmatic masked heel during his first few weeks in the territory; the lightning-quick moves and athletic artistry of The Destroyer brought fans out to the arenas and they left completely entertained and completely in awe. Without a loss in singles matches in his first four weeks, Owen decided to put The Destroyer with a tag partner who would be compatible with his style; chosen for the role was Art Michalik, nicknamed 'Boom Boom'. Like Beyer, Michalik was an 'athlete of the year' at Iowa's St. Ambrose College in 1948, chosen not only for his exceptional football prowess but for four undefeated years in collegiate wrestling. The 6'2" 230 pound Michalik played for the San Francisco 49ers and the Pittsburgh Steelers before entering pro wrestling.

Working the Portland territory involved more car travel than on the California circuit, but what made it worthwhile were the scenic mountain ranges and breathtaking views. The territory consisted of cities and towns in Oregon and Washington State; a typical week started in Portland at the Labor Temple on Monday with travel to Seattle on Tuesday, Walla Walla, Washington Wednesday, over to Spokane on Thursday, back to the Armory in Portland on Friday, and ending in Eugene on Saturday. Medford, near the California border and Salem, west of the Cascade Mountains, 50 miles south of Portland, were alternate stops on the route.

The tag duo of Destroyer and Michalik quickly developed into a formidable team, drawing rave reviews and roaring crowds, and by late September a match was set for the twosome with defending NWA Pacific Northwest tag title holders Shag Thomas and Luther Lindsay; due to an injury, Lindsay withdrew and Danny Hodge was substituted for the match. Shag Thomas was a strong member of the Owen stable of wrestlers in the Portland territory. At 5'6" and 250 pounds, Thomas, a former Ohio State football player, found a home and a good life in the Pacific Northwest. As a black athlete, Thomas labeled conditions in certain territories intolerable until he worked for Owen, who did not discriminate against any wrestler. Hodge was a star collegiate wrestling champion in Oklahoma, and a silver medalist in the 1956 Summer Olympics in Melbourne, Australia. He made his name as a main headliner in the Oklahoma territory under Leroy McGuirk, winning the NWA Junior World Heavyweight title in 1960. Hodge, at 5'10" 220 pounds with a boxing background, was a very strong and skilled wrestler, one of the toughest in the business, who needed no gimmick – he wrestled hard every night and opponents knew that they needed to bring their best into the ring. The main event for the title was held on September 25 in Salem where The Destroyer and Art Michalik beat Thomas and Hodge for the NWA Northwest Tag Team championship; a rapid rise in the beaver state for the Masked Man and 'Boom Boom.'

Michalik and Beyer travelled well together throughout the territory; their personalities interconnected, similar to the way Beyer meshed with Manoukian, and they discovered they had similar tastes in many things, especially food. The tag team partners departed early one Tuesday morning from Portland to wrestle in Seattle, Walla Walla, and Spokane. After the Thursday night match in Spokane, Beyer and Michalik pulled over to a 7-11 Store to pick up ingredients for a 'baloney blowout' – a wrestler term coined by Thesz for a baloney sandwich, and a six-pack of beer. Beyer kidded his friends that stopping at 7-11 Stores would assure they always remembered his birthday – July 11. About 100 miles out of Spokane on their way back to Portland Beyer stopped the car along the darkened highway for the two to heed nature's call. Down the road another hour or two, they pulled off the road again to buy refreshments, but Michalik could not locate his wallet in the car. Between them, they had earned nearly five hundred dollars from the matches, and Michalik was fearful he had lost his wallet containing his share. Without hesitation, Beyer made a U-turn and headed back to the 7-11 Store. On the way, he said to Michalik, "I wonder if it might be in the area where we pulled over to pee." Though now driving in the opposite direction, they scanned the roadway carefully, made another U-turn, and slowly drove along the shoulder of the road with Michalik seated on the fender, holding a spotlight aimed at the roadside. "This is like the needle in the haystack," Michalik said to Beyer…then yelled, "There's the needle!"

Beyer stopped the car as Michalik jumped off the fender and picked up his lost wallet with all the money accounted for. "Almost a very costly pee" he said to Beyer as he got back into the car for the protracted trip home, estimated at eight hours rather than the original five hour drive.

One of the most popular and established stars in the Northwest wrestling territory was Maurice Vachon. Beyer had met Vachon in Hawaii and, after they left the islands, both underwent life-changing metamorphosis. Returning to Portland, Vachon was given the name 'Mad Dog' by Owen for his mannerisms and temper tantrums in the ring, and it had thrust the Canadian into the spotlight. On November 21, 1963, Mad Dog Vachon defeated Nick Bockwinkel in Portland for his fourth NWA Pacific Northwest Heavyweight championship title. The following day, wrestling and titles were the furthest things from the minds of the wrestlers in Portland, and people around the country, as the body of the young U.S. President from Massachusetts was transported from Dallas back to Washington D.C. for burial ceremonies later in the week.

As an invited guest of Rikidozan, Beyer prepared for his second tour of Japan that was to take him away from his family for Thanksgiving and return him to Oregon the second week of December. Accompanying him on this two week trip was his good friend from Buffalo, Ilio DiPaolo; the *due amici* were to rendezvous in Japan with Killer Buddy Austin, a hated heel, who with Mike Sharpe defeated Rikidozan and Toyonobori for the All Asia Tag Team championship in 1962, for a rotation of individual, team and six-man matches with the Japanese force of Rikidozan, Great Togo, Toyonobori and Yoshimura.

In Japan, the bouts were promoted by Rikidozan's Japan Pro Wrestling Alliance as part of an ongoing series of matches stacking Japanese wrestlers against *gaijin* or foreigners. The Japanese were always cast as baby faces fighting the evil heels from other lands, but for Rikidozan, one role was very different – in June he had married former Japanese Airline stewardess Keiko Tanaka. Beyer brought gifts to present to the newly married couple.

It was a cold winter in Japan as the American wrestlers made their way from city to city by train and car to battle the Japanese in front of mostly sell-out crowds and large television audiences. Interest in *The De-stroy-yaa* intensified during this trip as more Japanese, having seen the masked American wrestle in May to the largest television audience in Japanese history, wondered about his life outside the ring in addition to his bold assertiveness and dramatic manner in the ring. An almost cult-like following sprung up within the Japanese wrestling fan domain, that had more to do with appreciating the hooded wrestler's technical skills and ring persona than with the typical hatred shown to *gaijin* heels. In knowing how to wrestle, Beyer fueled fan loyalty. Discussions with managers and event promoters indicated that some wanted The Destroyer to lose, but Beyer, in reference to his character told them, "No, I don't lose to anybody; if you want to beat me you go in the ring and try to beat me." He wrestled every match, never one to take a fall or give less than he was able. His code of conduct kept the matches 'honest' to where, aside from selling pain and punishment, a real contest emerged, thus assuring the fans a good show.

The Destroyer's scheduled three matches with Rikidozan were anticipated as 'get even' matches by the Japanese public, but when The Destroyer beat their national hero – again -before losing the second and working to a draw in the third, he became the first American wrestler to defeat Rikidozan more than once. It was another step up the ladder of respectability for The Destroyer in Japan. Similar to his first tour, Beyer was given specific instructions by Rikidozan to remain in the mask at all times. "I don't want you coming out on the streets without a mask; I pay you big money to come over here so you wear a mask," Beyer was told through Rikidozan's interpreter, known as Mr. Q. The king of wrestling in Japan was recognized for his discipline. He was also extremely volatile.

The last to wrestle Rikidozan; the matches made
Destroyer a household name in Japan

During the first week, Beyer caught up with Shohei Baba and told him he thought it odd that Baba was not part of the Japanese team that was to wrestle the Americans. Baba told Beyer that Rikidozan was not pleased with the new attention and focus given Baba by press and fans after his return from California and the matches with The Destroyer. Rikidozan, in effect, was jealous of Baba's newfound stardom; it was a shadow that cast negatively upon the master. In matches since those with The Destroyer, Baba was beaten badly in preliminary bouts by lesser talent. He knew he was being taught a lesson, and looked like a whipped puppy when Beyer saw him.

Rikidozan expected wrestling, and his wrestlers, to be tough, drawn from his sumo training. Baba told Beyer that Rikidozan often sat in the dressing room of the Japanese wrestlers under his tutelage and, using a whip-like stick, commanded the wrestlers do 1000 squats; if someone did something wrong, he upped it to 2000; at times it was 3000.

But his demands were not confined to Japanese. His expectations extended to anyone with whom he did business, and he demanded loyalty to his sponsors, Mitsubishi and Kirin. Rikidozan told Beyer he was only to drink Kirin beer, and no other, while in Japan.

Beyer and DiPaolo were in Tokyo on what was Thanksgiving Day in the States, and decided to celebrate by going to Nicola's Italian restaurant in the city. "Nothing says Thanksgiving like carving into chicken parmesan," Destroyer said to his Italian friend. After their meal and several beers – Kirin beer only - the two exited the building to hail a cab but were intrigued by the construction site out in front across from the restaurant. Upon questioning, they found out that an expressway was being built to Haneda airport to accommodate the traffic flow for the Olympic crowd expected in the summer of the following year. They noticed a group of Japanese workers huddled around a small fire on the cold, damp winter evening and each was taking a turn hitting an object with a sledgehammer. It seemed not one of the workers was able to break the object apart. Ilio DiPaolo, a large and extremely strong man, said to Beyer "I will be back," and walked across the street to the work site. DiPaolo motioned to the workers and one of them handed the sledgehammer to the wrestler; within two powerful arcing swings of the hammer, the object was completely shattered, the Japanese shouted something to the visitor with arms raised and apparent glee on the faces and in their voices, as the wrestler made his way back to the waiting Beyer - convulsing with laughter. "Now THAT is Thanksgiving," DiPaolo said to his fully spent friend.

Ten days later, on December 7, 1963, after several individual and team matches from Fukushima and Utsunomya to Osaka and Nagoya, the American and Japanese wrestlers arrived in Hamamatsu, 200 miles west of Tokyo and home of Hamamatsu Castle, built by the Shogun Ieyasu Tokugawa in 1570, and was the site of many historic strategic battles. Those who emerged as lords of the castle went on to claim important government positions, thus the structure's sobriquet 'the castle of success.' In the Hamamatsu City Gym, in the shadows of the ancient castle, another battle was to take place among six wrestlers in a ring, highlighting the enormous success of professional wrestling in Japan, while unknowingly serving as the last battleground for one of the warriors.

The six-man team match consisted of Americans Ilio DiPaolo, Buddy Austin, and The Destroyer against the homeland team of Yoshimura, Great Togo, and the father of Japanese pro wrestling, Rikidozan. Yoshimura was an excellent side-player and a former Japanese Junior Heavyweight champion before he received an invitation to join JWA by Rikidozan. As a team, the Japanese were very technical and savvy in their approach, while the Americans came out full of steam and power. One sensed the crowd's upsurge in intensity when Rikidozan and The Destroyer hooked up and locked in battle; both wrestlers gave impressive performances that included mind-boggling maneuvers, flying acrobatics and physical torture that made fans wince and moan. Ending in a sixty minute draw, the crowd nonetheless applauded as though their side had captured a title.

Later that night, Beyer and his two American colleagues were driven to a restaurant in Hamamatsu where a party, sponsored by and courtesy of Rikidozan, was held in honor of the visitors. The Americans arrived at the traditional Japanese restaurant, removed their shoes, and entered through the sliding doors, greeted as they did by several female servers and Rikidozan. The other Japanese wrestlers and Great Togo were already in the room. Once inside, the host clapped his hands twice and the servers scattered out of the room. Assisted by Mr. Q., his interpreter, Rikidozan instructed the Americans to be seated near the table. All others in the room – the Japanese wrestlers and even Great Togo – took kneeling positions along the edge of the room looking in toward the table. The feast lasted until midnight when all departed for the train station and their trek back into Tokyo. It was early morning when they boarded the train for what they hoped would be a short, pleasant trip. It felt more like a local bus going through the downtown streets during rush hour. Six hours later, around 7:00 am, the train pulled into the Tokyo station with three mood-ugly Americans. All three got to the hotel and went directly to bed.

Beyer and DiPaolo were scheduled to meet with Rikidozan early on the evening of December 8 just hours before boarding a 9:00 pm flight for their return to the States. They arrived at Rikidozan's Steakhouse, but only Mr. Q. was there waiting for them. He told Beyer and DiPaolo that Rikidozan had arranged a *sayonara* party for the visitors from America at a private banquet hall and would have Beyer's share of the payout ready for him. The two wrestlers were 'partied out' but went to the hall as instructed.

In raw, unrefined language, using the few English words he knew, Rikidozan said to Beyer "You son-a-bitch, you want girl…you want drink?" Beyer declined the former but welcomed the latter. After using the ceremonial warm moist cloth called *oshibori* to cleanse their hands, and with the Japanese version of bon appétit, '*Itadakimasu*'spoken by the host, all dined on miso soup and sushi that was served on wooden platters with a side bowl of dipping sauce, and drank sencha tea and Kirin beer for several hours in a formal yet relaxed atmosphere. DiPaolo excused himself early in order to tend to some business before heading to the airport to meet Beyer for the trip home.

More beverages were brought out including cases of Kirin, some Korean liquor, and endless cups of sake and after consuming a large quantity of each, Rikidozan via his interpreter said to the American, "You stay tonight, we go to cabaret." Beyer was honored by the invitation and though he wanted to stay, he knew he had promises to keep; still he was feeling ambivalent toward the offer. "Come on, we go to cabaret, *Kampai*!" he heard again from Mr. Q. He thought long and hard about the invitation as good feelings permeated the room and between the now chummier American and Japanese wrestling giants, but he wanted to keep his word to Don Owen to return for a scheduled match, and to see his family, having missed Thanksgiving with them. Beyer apologetically declined. Rikidozan reluctantly accepted, gave him his pay envelope, and the friends wished each other well as Beyer said, "*Gochiso sama deshita*" (a word of gratitude) and a final *sayonara*.

Beyer was driven to Haneda airport with seconds to spare before his plane was to depart. When he arrived at the gate, Ilio DiPaolo was standing in the doorway of the plane, claiming he didn't understand English as the stewardess attempted to close the door; it worked. Beyer and DiPaolo sat down as Beyer began to tell his friend of Rikidozan's offer to take him to a cabaret that night. "Did you want to stay?" asked DiPaolo. "I probably should have…but I have other commitments," he said. As they flew back on the late night flight, Beyer was conflicted with a sense of unease and wished he'd had one more day to spend in Tokyo with Rikidozan.

Hours later, the plane landed in Anchorage, Alaska; there, the two friends boarded separate flights, one bound for Buffalo, the other for Portland. They bid goodbye and promised to catch up again on Beyer's next trip home to Buffalo. Beyer landed in Portland and was greeted by Willy, who appeared disturbed and overwrought. Asking his wife "What's the matter, honey…" Willy showed him a newspaper with a headline above the story **Japanese Wrestler Rikidozan Stabbed in Nightclub.**

CHAPTER 13

MINUTES AFTER BEYER had departed the banquet hall for the airport, Rikidozan and his entourage drove to the New Latin Quarter, an upscale nightclub in the fashionable Akasaka District of Tokyo. Many observed him to be drunk and unruly as he made his way into the crowded night spot.

Near the men's room of the club, Rikidozan encountered a small time *yakuza* (member of organized crime group) named Katsushi Murata, who was aligned with a rival element of the Asian champion's underworld-connected friend, Nick 'Nicola' Zapetti, from whom he had borrowed money to establish the Japan Pro Wrestling Alliance. Stories had circulated that Murata's gang had been dumped from a business deal by Rikidozan in favor of rival groups, and that it was this matter that triggered the confrontation near the men's room that night. A brief but heated struggle erupted between the two; before being separated, Murata plunged a rusty blade into the abdomen of Rikidozan. Wounded and bleeding, the wrestling icon nevertheless threw Murata out of the nightclub. Reports were inconsistent from that point – some say Rikidozan continued to party at the club, while others indicated he sought medical assistance and was treated before being released to his 8th floor apartment dubbed 'the mansion' in a residential building he owned in Tokyo.

Beyer was staggered by the news. While he had wished he had more time to spend with Rikidozan that evening, he did not believe a circumstance like this could ever happen, not with the security around him, not to Rikidozan. In the immediate aftermath of the incident, Beyer had trouble concentrating on his work and ordinary daily routines. Several telephone calls he made to associates of Rikidozan in Tokyo implied the Asian was recovering at home. But on December 15, one week after the stabbing, thirty-nine year old Rikidozan was taken to Sannoh Hospital in Tokyo, where he later died from suspected peritonitis and indeterminate complications after surgery.

Thousands of mourners from across Japan attended the December 20 funeral of their beloved wrestling idol, television star, and business mogul. To many, he was more than a wrestler…he helped usher in the age of television in Japan; he was a national hero, who restored pride after the war to a nation humbled by defeat by standing up to foreign foes and beating them in a ringed microcosm, re-energizing a people in the process, but the viability of Japan Pro Wrestling now stood in doubt as the 'Father of Puroresu' was laid to rest.

It was a difficult Christmas for Beyer. Saddened by the reports about his colleague, he was overwhelmed by the rapid decline that led to his death. It felt surreal. It had only been a few weeks since he and the Asian wrestled; The Destroyer versus Rikidozan. Could anyone have predicted it would be Rikidozan's last match? Beyer had been with him up to one hour before the incident happened. He struggled with guilt. If only I had stayed one more night this would not have happened…If I accepted his invitation to the cabaret, I could have saved him…

Dazed by the sudden loss of a colleague whom he held in high esteem, Beyer was dealt a second and much harsher blow when informed his mother had suffered another in a series of strokes and was taken to the hospital. Beyer flew back to Buffalo to be with his mother for several days. He sat with her at bedside, walked the halls of the hospital with her, arm-in-arm, and gently told her how much she meant to him and how much he loved her. As he got back into the car of a friend who had driven him to visit his mother at Sisters of Charity Hospital, he said, "I think I just saw my mother for the last time." Celia Beyer quietly passed away a short time later.

Weeks of churning emotions and self-blame followed. Not even winning the NWA Northwest Heavyweight title from Maurice 'Mad Dog' Vachon could assuage his depression. While deeply grieving the loss of his mother, he was unable to escape night-sweat dreams of the circumstances surrounding Rikidozan. Beyer had heard what he believed were the warning bells during both tours of Japan, and never said a word. In rare moments during which he was accessible, he confided in Willy about what he had learned. He told her how in several of the Japanese towns they worked, the *yakuza* bought out the tickets, turned to business owners, and told them to buy a set number; they did. If they didn't, a window was found broken the following day or several lights were missing from the front of the store. He also heard that dangerous rivalries were brewing among competing factions of the underworld. Beyer's only previous knowledge about nefarious activities was with gangster movies set in the 1930s, so it was difficult to comprehend how they played out in reality and especially as they related to one so renowned and revered in his country as Rikidozan. He never asked him about nor informed him of what he had heard. "Maybe I should have said something," he told his wife; "What would it have done?" she asked him. "I don't know…it could have set off an alarm to be more careful, especially in public," he pondered. "Don't you think he thought he was invincible?" she asked; He replied, "In his mind, in his world, he was." "If he thought he was, whatever you might have said would not have mattered to him," Willy told her husband, trying to complete the circle of understanding and to move her husband to forgive himself. "If only I had stayed *that night…*"

On days off, Beyer took his boat into the waters around Portland, alternated among the Columbia, Willamette, Clackamas and Sandy rivers, dropped a line, and while fishing for salmon reflected on his relationship with Rikidozan. In time, he achieved a measure of inner peace that was bolstered by the unconditional love from Willy, Kurt and Kris. Solace came with one self-imposed condition – he must return to Japan and give back to the people and to those who helped advance his career. He felt he owed that in memory to his fallen friend.

Northwest wrestling fans were exposed to some wild, weird and wacky matches and experiences as The Destroyer and Art 'Boom Boom' Michalik won and lost the tag team title several times over. Having also lost the NWA Heavyweight title to popular stud Tony Borne, the masked heel took back that title in April. Don Owen continued to shuffle talent to face The Destroyer; he carded Paddy Barrett, Don Duffy, Ricky Hunter, Pierre Duranton, Paul Diamond, Danny O'Rourke, Val Velasco and Nick Bockwinkel who defeated The Destroyer for the NWA Northwest Heavyweight title. Bockwinkel, trained by his father Warren and the great Lou Thesz, was making a name as a solo performer in the business after teaming with his father in earlier years. The Bockwinkel/Destroyer matches were works of art, as both gave sound technical performances in addition to rousing displays of strength and movement. They also became friends and fishing buddies. Bockwinkel loved to tease Beyer. On one fishing trip to a local river, both were seated in Beyer's boat when Bockwinkel said "Are you coming over for dinner tonight?" to which Beyer replied "No." Minutes later, Bockwinkel asked again, "Are you coming over for dinner tonight?" and again Beyer replied, "No." This exchange continued for some time when after another 'no' response from Beyer, Bockwinkel said, "Good, I just wanted to make sure. I didn't want to see your ugly face anyway."

Owen later brought in Lou Thesz, one of the all-time great wrestling performers, who had figured prominently in several regional territories and in Japan. Hyped as a title match, both Thesz and The Destroyer won a fall before they collided in the middle of the ring and neither was able to get back on his feet within the count - the match ended in a draw, but Beyer learned a great deal in the short time he was with the legendary Thesz.

During one match in Seattle with Luther Lindsey, something occurred in the crowd and the fans got into a riot mode, swinging and punching at other fans and shouting nasty, threatening comments at the wrestlers. Beyer as The Destroyer was in the ring with Lindsey and both realized they needed to get out of there fast. Shag Thomas, Lindsey's tag partner, came out from the dressing room to the ring to help the heel Destroyer through the fight-filled aisle. The Destroyer put his arms in front of his face and the two pushed through the crowd; one fan grabbed the Destroyer's mask and held onto it, trying to force it up over Beyer's head. Beyer instinctively grabbed both of the fan's arms and when he did his elbows came down and away from his face, exposing it to another fan who threw a punch at The Destroyer that landed flush on his mouth. Beyer, bleeding, was able to return to the dressing room and attend to the injury that resulted in a lost front tooth, widening the gap between the upper teeth; Raging mad and looking to retaliate, Beyer was on his way back out to find the fan when discretion took over. It was an ugly episode that marred a good match but one in which Beyer learned to be more cautious; he realized how quickly things can happen and it taught him a deeper appreciation for what Rikidozan experienced that evening in the nightclub.

In early spring of 1964, Beyer received a most unexpected phone call. "Dick, this is Jules Strongbow." Beyer was completely shocked when he heard Strongbow's voice; the last time he heard it was the night he bolted from the Olympic during the Hercules Cotez match when Strongbow shouted his real name. He didn't know what to make of the phone call and hesitated several seconds before responding, thinking that he was going to hear about law suits and being drummed out of the business. He geared up for a verbal defense. What he heard next shocked him even more. "Dick, you have to come back and wrestle in L.A." "What? Why would you want me to come back there?" "Well, we… we made a mistake and we just need to have you back here wrestling in our territory. Besides, the fans are hollering for The Destroyer to come back." "See, I was a lot smarter than you thought!" Beyer said to hit home the arguments he put up when he and Strongbow disagreed about the unmasking and for his actions following the Cortez match. "You were, Dick. You made the right decision. The Destroyer will remain as The Destroyer, mask and all, and we will reinsert you into tag and singles matches for championships," Strongbow said to induce Beyer into returning before offering an apology for the way things had ended.

The phone call lasted several minutes - the decision took a few more. Life had developed nicely in the Pacific Northwest for the Beyer family; the environment was postcard picturesque, the work was steady, and Don Owen was every bit the gracious promoter that Beyer heard about. Beyer had been in Oregon ten months and that was a good long stretch for a territory like Portland, he reasoned. It was time. Beyer went to Don Owen later that week to discuss the offer. Owen gave Beyer his unconditional release and thanked him for his work and for living up to his promise.

To the sound on the car radio of British import The Beatles' *A Hard Day's Night*, Dick and Willy Beyer and their two children began their trek from Portland to Los Angeles for their second sojourn in the Southern California territory. "I *have* been working like a dog," he said to Willy. "But not a mad dog, only Vachon works that hard," Willy replied eliciting a smile from her husband. To outsiders, the Beyers sounded like George and Gracie or Desi and Lucy with their verbal serve and volley, but the two simply had complementary senses of humor. People enjoyed their company.

The Beyer family settled back into their California lifestyle with ease, as many of their friends rallied to welcome them back and help them re-establish a foothold in the community. What made it even better than before was having family in town. Billy Red Lyons, married to Willy's sister Norma, had recently moved his family to Los Angeles to work the territory; Billy told his brother-in-law about the housing complex in which they were located. The Beyers looked over the property and rented a home in the same complex, on Roscoe Boulevard in North Hollywood, between the San Diego Freeway and the Hollywood Freeway, further out in the San Fernando Valley from where they previously resided. Willy was thrilled to have her sister nearby. Dick as The Destroyer went back to work for the L.A. territory and Jules Strongbow, but this time he controlled The Destroyer in every situation in and out of the ring. That was fine with Strongbow, glad to have the masked man back on the circuit along with bigger crowds and big money.

Strongbow hyped the hooded Destroyer's encore to fans who had eagerly awaited word of his return; within two weeks The Destroyer wrestled 9 singles and 2 tag team matches, winning all. It was as if he had never left. With Manoukian out of the territory, Strongbow teamed him up with Antone 'Ripper' Leone, a wild, rib-playing, crew-cut heel; the tag team stormed through the L.A. territory wreaking havoc on duos such as Ernie Ladd and Paul Diamond, the Torres Brothers, Mr. Moto and Antonio Inoki (who also wrestled as Little Tokyo). The Destroyer later was paired with Hard Boiled Haggerty, real name Don Stansauk, an ex-professional football player who had won several tag team titles in other territories; one of his former tag partners was Beyer's friend from his training days, Lenny Montana. Haggerty was a solid champion heel with a distinctive handlebar moustache and a sneering arrogant manner. Together, Haggerty and The Destroyer created a heat-seeking heel combination that captured from the Torres Brothers the WWA World Tag Team title on July 30, 1964. It was the second title won by The Destroyer in eight days; the first came on July 22, but wasn't officially awarded until August 27. Only in L.A. could something so weird have stretched out over five weeks.

The championship match pitted The Destroyer against the current WWA World title holder and Beyer's Chicago pal, Dick 'the Bruiser' Afflis. The two friends had not seen each other since their Chateau Hotel and Marigold Gardens days in Chicago in 1955. They caught up for several minutes in the dressing room prior to going out to the ring. A crowd of more than 10,000 on a Wednesday evening at the Olympic saw both wrestlers claim victory in an unsettled decision. After Dick the Bruiser had left the ring during the match to engage Cowboy Bob Ellis, another contender for the title who was at ringside, Bruiser did not return to the ring within the allotted time, thus the referee awarded the match to The Destroyer. But it was reported that Bruiser had been disqualified, and no title can be lost on a DQ. The main event, which was not televised locally, caused a stir among the fans as to who rightly won and held the belt.

The wrestling press reported that the disputed matter was taken up at a meeting of the World Wide Wrestling Association on August 27 when after three ballots, it was decided that the World Championship belonged to The Destroyer. Reports circulated that among those who attended the meeting were members from New England and Mid-Atlantic States, Hawaii and Florida along with The Destroyer, Cowboy Bob Ellis, their attorneys, the Olympic's Cal Eaton, match maker Jules Strongbow, and Bruiser's attorney. After The Destroyer was awarded the title, Ellis' attorney argued that Cowboy Bob should be declared the champion because of his victories over both wrestlers however the WWA stated that those matches referenced by Ellis' attorney were not officially sanctioned as title matches. This 'legal drama' set the stage for a September title-defense thriller between Cowboy Bob Ellis and the WWA World Champion Destroyer.

It was a championship season for The Destroyer during which The Beyer and Lyons families prospered in the Southern California wrestling environment. Strongbow found new combinations for matches and stayed out from under the mask, allowing Beyer as The Destroyer – current WWA World Champion and WWA World Tag Champion- plenty of work opportunities and, in turn, he gave fans, who came out in droves to see the masked villain, unparalleled performances. The families often made their way to the arenas to see The Destroyer or Billy Red in action, but it was Kurt who saw more of his father's matches than anyone else. A bright four year-old, Kurt was his father's frequent travel companion to venues in the greater L.A. area. He hung out with his dad's work buddies in the dressing room, watched them play cards, and became close to many, referring to them as 'Uncle Billy Red,' 'Uncle Freddie,' 'Uncle Charlie.' The hulking wrestlers bought young Kurt chips, candy, and sodas as he sat well-mannered beside them, or on their laps, at the card table. During his father's matches, Kurt was allowed to sit ringside with the timekeeper, provided he didn't wander or attempt to climb into the ring – easier said than done, especially when the young boy saw his father getting pummeled in the ring by some stranger or worse, someone he knew and called 'Uncle.'

During the canicular days of 1964, a late August bout headlined The Destroyer matched against Mr. Moto at the Olympic. Kurt was situated ringside next to timekeeper Jerry Murdoch as the match got underway. Moto was wrestling in his typical Japanese style – bare foot and knee tights – while Destroyer worked in his usual white mask, trunks and white boots. The match evolved into a sweaty and bloody affair for Kurt's father whose mask, trunks and boots were stained red from the action in the ring with Moto. The wrestlers moved into the corner where Kurt was seated, near the bell and timekeeper. Moto had The Destroyer's mask turned around so that the holes were at the back of his head rather than the front, completely obscuring his opponent's vision, banging away at The Destroyer's body with vicious blows. The crowd was cranking up the volume and sitting on the edge of the seats. It did not look good for the masked man, or the masked dad, from Kurt's perspective. Timekeeper Jerry Murdoch looked over at a worried Kurt and said to him, "Your dad's in trouble, Kurt…what are you gonna do?" Murdoch wasn't trying to provoke the boy, but in an unthinking and unhesitating second, Kurt grabbed the hammer near the bell, leaned under the bottom rope of the ring and, as hard as he was able, hit the foot of his father's assailant with the bell hammer, breaking Moto's toe. The ring and ringside dissolved into something resembling a Keystone Cops comedy, as Moto jumped up and down on one foot all over the ring yelling unintelligible profanities at the top of his lungs, while The Destroyer bounced across the ring and into the ropes, looking like an out-of-control mouse in a maze, trying to understand what was happening, his mask on backwards and unable to see, as arena workers whisked away young Kurt from the ring and into the dressing room, the roaring crowd in disbelief of what had unfolded in front of them, all while Jerry Murdoch hit the bell repeatedly with the confiscated hammer that led to the chaos in the first place. Oh the humor and humanity of it all.

In the dressing room, Beyer was beside himself; angry, upset, disappointed feelings pulsed through his veins. When he regained control, he went to talk with his son who was seated at the card table…alone. "Kurt, I won't bring you to the matches anymore if you can't sit there and just watch…this is my work, my business, I am perfectly safe in the ring; Mr. Moto, Uncle Charlie, is your sister's godfather," he told him. Kurt sat there teary-eyed and with a quivering lower lip, not looking up at his father. To him, his dad was having a bad day at the office, and he just wanted to help him, after all, he *was* Kurt Destroyer.

In a few minutes, Iwamoto limped into the room with a bandaged foot, walked over to the seated Kurt, looked down at him and said, "You mad at me?" Arms folded across his chest, the young boy's bottom quivering lip protruded even more with a scowled, angry expression on his face as he looked down at the table rather than the speaker. "OK, pull my beard," Kurt heard Iwamoto say, as he pointed to his long, black goatee now directly in front of Kurt's face. Without peering up, Kurt lightly touched the goatee and gave it a gentle tug. Mr. Moto's eyes crossed, he muffled a scream, stammered backwards and hit the wall, fell forward over a chair and landed on the floor writhing in agony and yelling, ranting, rolling, holding his chin, and shouting "Get a doctor, I'm hurt" squinting in apparent pain. Then, the yelling stopped; slowly, he got up from the floor, looked over at Kurt's wide-eyed expression, and with his left eye gave him a wink. In that instant, Kurt got it; he understood. One little inside signal from his sister's godfather was all it took for the boy to comprehend his father's occupation. Never again was he worried when his father worked the ring.

The September 10 championship match with Cowboy Bob Ellis was promoted in the wrestling pages proclaiming Ellis the 'New King' of wrestling in the territory. An Olympic turn-away crowd of 10,400 took in a best-of-three fall match in which The Destroyer lost the heavyweight crown on a double pin by Ellis in the second fall. Strongbow and the Eaton family were happy with the attendance, and a rematch in San Diego was put in the works for November to be promoted by Hardy Kruskamp. In addition, The Destroyer and Hard Boiled Haggerty lost their tag team title in October in Long Beach to Fred Blassie and Mr. Moto. Their rematch was also scheduled for November in Long Beach. Without a title, Beyer as Destroyer continued to work the circuit, drumming interest in other matches and heavily promoting the rematches for the heavyweight and tag crowns on the televised studio shows. It was these televised promotions in the San Diego market that led to some on-camera follies for the masked wrestler, and had people talking and tuning in to a late night program with anticipation.

KOGO television channel 10 in San Diego was the setting for a Saturday afternoon studio wrestling program that spotlighted the big names of wrestling as they came through Southern California, with interviews and action segments promoting the bouts held at the Coliseum. Hardy Kruskamp made good use of the studio program to build interest and sell tickets, but it was the wrestlers themselves who spoke to the camera and told fans what they'd experience at the matches the following Friday. Beyer as The Destroyer was good at this bit. His experience rendered him a natural in front of the camera and on the microphone; his mystique, gravel-voice, articulation and conceited nature made for compelling television whether the viewer liked wrestling or not. He instantly developed a repartee with whomever he appeared on camera, and was quick with comments and replies, especially sarcastic or fun-poking exchanges that were not merely confined to his wrestling colleagues.

Channel 10 also carried on Saturday a late night talk show hosted by a former news anchor, who without writers and on a bare-bones budget, used his extemporaneous skills to open his show by talking about current events and his own life; the host's name was Regis Philbin. Having worked as a page for NBC in Los Angeles, among other jobs, after graduating from the University of Notre Dame and a stint in the Navy, Philbin landed a news position in San Diego in 1961 and later given a talk show to air live late on Saturday nights.

The studio wrestling shows were exhibitions for Beyer; he was able to project more of The Destroyer's personality using verbal taunts, elitist arrogance, and know-it-all behaviors. But he also displayed a wicked sense of humor through his jousting. Commercials that were shown during the wrestling program promoted the 'Regis Philbin Show' that was to air later in the evening. Kruskamp told Beyer the names of the guests that were scheduled for Philbin's show and, as the villain, The Destroyer put down everyone on camera with cutting comments – "Look at who Regis Philbin has on his show tonight…these people are all washed up…Regis needs to have me on the show…that will improve his ratings." Days later, Philbin mentioned on his program the comments attributed to the masked wrestler, derided The Destroyer for his boastfulness, and predicted he would lose his next match; in turn, on one of the Saturday afternoon studio shows, The Destroyer added to his commentary "…and by the way, to you Regis Philbin, you'll know you reached the top when you put me on your show." The ratings for the Philbin show rose as did the fan numbers for the San Diego matches. It didn't take many of these exchanges before representatives from Philbin's show contacted Beyer. A few weeks later, The Destroyer made a guest appearance on the live talk/variety program, 'The Regis Philbin Show.' Seated on stools in the middle of the stage, The Destroyer, in a dark suit, white shirt and tie, was interviewed by Regis Philbin; questions ranged from how he got started in the business to how he maintained his secret identity. The Destroyer answered all questions with typical verve. At one point during the interview, in response to a comment made by the host, The Destroyer said "Regis, with a face like yours, a mask would improve your looks," and pulled a white mask from his pocket and fitted it over Philbin's head until the facial holes were in their proper position. The studio audience reacted with applause and for thirty-five minutes, The Destroyer and Philbin conducted the straight forward interview, each in white Destroyer mask. It was instantly a classic… something usually reserved for 'Your Show of Shows' with Sid Caesar or the 'man in the street' interview segment on Steve Allen's 'Tonight Show' from the 1950s. The episode was the talk of the town, and became the first of several appearances The Destroyer made on the program.

Beyer as The Destroyer and Regis Philbin in mask on Philbin's early talk show

Beyer routinely drove to San Diego to wrestle in the Friday night matches; he'd stay over for the Saturday afternoon television studio program, and afterwards, drive to San Bernardino for their night matches. Whenever he was to appear on the Saturday night Philbin show, he flew from San Bernardino to San Diego on a small single engine Cessna, piloted by the wife of the owner of the little airport. It wasn't quite like the popular television program 'Sky King', Beyer told friends, "It was more like Scared King, and I didn't have Penny, but Pinky."

Through a mutual friend, Beyer became acquainted with Pinky, a veteran pilot of the southern California skies. A deal was struck between the two that was to help Beyer get to San Diego and back to San Bernardino the same evening.

On those weekends after the matches in San Bernardino, Beyer met Pinky and her Cessna on the grassy runway of the small airport, climbed aboard the plane, and sat in the co-pilot seat. It was a different experience flying from the cockpit. Pinky seemed to know everyone along the flight plan, as she called down to the control towers or others on her frequency. The flight generally took less than an hour, and during windy evenings, Beyer mentally counted every minute. After appearing on the Philbin show, Beyer met Pinky at the airstrip in San Diego for the return flight to San Bernardino, arriving later that night at the same grassy runway with green lights illuminating the landing area. On more than one bumpy occasion, Beyer, too, was green.

During one follow up appearance with Philbin, Destroyer introduced his 'private pilot' Pinky on the air – he wasn't lying since, for that night, she was. On another show, during the interview segment, popular actor and comedy genius Jerry Lewis, who stopped by the show whenever he landed in town, was in the control booth making the images of Philbin and The Destroyer appear upside-down on television screens; with cameras following, The Destroyer entered the control booth and loudly confronted Lewis, but was told beforehand not to hurt the star. As a guest on the show, The Destroyer made for unexpected and entertaining television.

In early November, The Destroyer with tag partner Hard Boiled Haggerty took back the WWA World Tag Title, defeating Freddie Blassie and Mr. Moto. In the dressing room before leaving town, 'Uncle Freddie' did what he often did to young Kurt Beyer – planted sloppy, wet kisses on his cheek. The boy objected to the ticklish affection to which Blassie told him "You're four years old kid, you gotta be kissed by everybody, but when you turn five you don't gotta be kissed by nobody." Kurt forgave Uncle Freddie and filed this piece of wisdom into his memory. Kurt had also forgiven 'Uncle Charlie' since the hammer on the toe incident, and Iwamoto had fully recovered and resumed traveling the circuit with the boy's father.

On November 13, The Destroyer defeated Cowboy Bob Ellis at the Coliseum in San Diego to again become the WWA World Heavyweight champion, his second term as title holder. The bloody bout, that drew thousands in San Diego, was refereed by Mike Mazurki, the actor/wrestler and ring referee whose 6'5" frame, deeply-etched and recognizable face, still commanded a presence. Mazurki, whom Beyer first met in L.A. in 1962, was a walking contradiction – while often cast as a low IQ, lowlife gang member in many films, he was a college educated, highly intelligent, articulate man who had many altruistic interests. He and Hardy Kruskamp helped organize bus trips in the fall to the Los Angeles Rams' home games played at the L.A. Coliseum; many wrestlers including Beyer joined them on these junkets, playing liar's poker on the bus and after the game regular poker at Kruskamp's home where the wives usually met up with them. Mazurki was good to his friends in many ways and as his movie and television career continued unabated, so did their loyalty to him.

After the death of Rikidozan, the Japan Pro Wrestling Alliance fell into disarray. Without its founder and leader, the JWA was listless. Toyonobori assumed the presidency of the organization and its main draw, Giant Baba, moved front and center as the headliner. Baba and Inoki worked tirelessly for months to keep pro wrestling breathing in Japan. They received support from their American counterparts and when asked to return to Japan, Beyer was quick to say yes. He as The Destroyer brought with him, on the December 1964 tour, the current WWA Heavyweight title; this was of keen interest to the officials at JWA. They wanted to promote a title bout in Japan for Toyonobori with an American. Prior to the scheduled December 4 title match, The Destroyer wrestled in tag team matches with Bill Dromo and Kurt Von Stroheim against Toyonobori, Baba, and Yoshimura who alternated with Koukichi Endo and Yoshimosato, in cities such as Osaka, Nagoya, and Kanagawa. These team matches helped hype the title bout held at the Tokyo Gym, in which Toyonobori defeated The Destroyer to capture what many would call the Japanese version of the WWA World Heavyweight title. The JWA was delighted to be able to proclaim Toyonobori heavyweight champion in Japan, and deeply appreciated Beyer's willingness to help in the way he did. With a heavyweight title, the JWA regained a share of the collective interest in wrestling in Japan. Beyer as The Destroyer returned to the States, still regarded as the WWA champion in Los Angeles, and continued to defend his title in southern California. Before the year ended, he and Haggerty lost the WWA World Tag Team title again, this time to Ed Carpentier and Cowboy Bob Ellis, and eventually dissolved their partnership; a new partner replaced Haggerty – one who knew the masked man quite well, Billy Red Lyons.

Lyons hadn't worked with his brother-in-law since their construction business in Buffalo, but just as they did when previously paired in the ring, the two kept their relationship to themselves and only business insiders were the wiser. The 6'2" 240 pound Canadian redhead won the Canadian Open Tag Team title with mutual friend Ilio DiPaolo in 1961, and had become a popular stalwart wrestler in Toronto and Buffalo, however, the lure of the west beckoned him and he moved his family to California to stake claim; as it turned out, it was a golden decision. But the big Canadian wasn't the biggest Canadian Beyer worked with during the early months of 1965. In February, at the

Olympic in Los Angeles, The Destroyer squared off against Victor, a 6'6"450 pound, Canadian black bear. Tuffy Truesdale owned and trained the bear that had wrestled both professionals and amateurs for several years around the country. Truesdale had wrestled professionally, but fared better wrestling alligators at carnivals and shows before his association with the bear. The match with The Destroyer was placed by Jules Strongbow on the undercard of the February 17 L.A. schedule. It wasn't much of a contest but it was entertaining and fascinating to watch man and animal go head to head. The Destroyer scored evenly with Victor until he hit the bear on the nose and pushed hard against its chest; after Truesdale jumped into the ring to complain, the referee disqualified The Destroyer for being too rough and, raising his paw, awarded the decision to Victor. The Destroyer never got the chance to put a bear hug on the bear, as he had predicted in the press, and left the ring raging and shouting.

Destroyer was disqualified for being too rough

The in-law tag team of Destroyer and Lyons worked the cities around the territory against Mr. Moto and Ken Hollis, Ernie Ladd and Paul Diamond, Dale Lewis and Billy White Wolf and other combinations,

MASKED DECISIONS

however it was a match in San Francisco that gave the Destroyer/Lyons team a short-lived boost when they beat the tandem of Ray Stevens and Don Manoukian for the San Francisco version of the AWA World Tag Team title. They held the tag title a short time, losing it the following month to the team of Ray Stevens and Pat Patterson. The Destroyer's third reign as WWA Los Angeles heavyweight champion also came to an end during a match in March with Pedro Morales; in front of a near-sellout Los Angeles crowd, the two were counted out of the ring in the early moments of the bout, each given a fall, before the Latino wrestler surged to overtake his masked opponent for the heavyweight title. Only Freddie Blassie had held the title more times than The Destroyer in southern California.

Their in-law relationship was an inside secret

In the spring of 1965, Beyer received an invitation to tour Japan at the behest of JWA and Baba. It was to become an annual event for The Destroyer, one that Beyer relished as a tribute to his friendship with Baba, to thank the Japanese people, and to honor the memory of Rikidozan. This particular tour took on a different vibe from previous trips to Japan; it felt more like the travels when he first trained in Columbus or those away games as a college athlete. On this trip Beyer was accompanied by his brother-in-law Billy Red Lyons, former tag partner Don Manoukian, Buffalo area strongman Jose Richardo Gattoni, known as Baron, and Toronto based Sweet Daddy Siki. Beyer knew each of the guys well; the group became more like brothers, making the trip fun and the matches more fun – for them and the Japanese fans. Siki, a Texan and former NWA Texas Heavyweight title holder became famous as a black throwback to 'Gorgeous George' complete with gauche costumes and bleached blonde hair. The fabulous five worked nearly eight weeks in Japan, visited cities large and small, performed in singles, tag team and three-man team matches. The Japanese lineup included Toyonobori, Baba, Yoshimura, and Yoshinosato. Of note was the June 3, 1965 tag team match against Baba and Toyonobori in which The Destroyer and Billy Lyons won the JWA Asian Tag Team title; it was the second tag title the in-laws earned that year and as the fortunes of wrestling go, they lost the title a month later in Shizuoka to the same Japanese duo. Among the Japanese people, respect rose for the American masked man who paid homage to their wrestling forefather and new wrestling heroes by travelling to their country every year; the respect was mutual.

◄ MASKED DECISIONS

Destroyer had risen to superstar status throughout Japan

⁌⁌⁌

Paul Boesch had wrestled professionally before he enlisted in the Army during World War II earning a purple heart, silver star, bronze star among other citations and awards; he returned to wrestling after the war, but a car accident forced him out of the ring and into a supportive role with Morris Sigel and his Houston wrestling operation. He became the radio voice of Houston wrestling and later its first television commentator when the show went live on the air. Boesch learned the ropes from Sigel and matchmaker Karl Sarpolis, helping them import star talent like Antonino Rocca, Duke Keomuka, Wild

Red Berry and others for their Friday night matches. Wrestling and Houston was a marriage made in heaven. Boesch developed a flawless reputation that was to grow and attract great talent to Texas.

The invitation from Boesch and Sigel to work the Houston circuit came at the right time for Beyer. He had returned from Japan and was near the end of the second go-round in Los Angeles; after a total of two and a half years in L.A., it was time to move the masked wrestler to another territory. That's just the way the business was, and he and Willy had accepted its consequences long ago. Beyer had positive feelings for Texas from his early wrestling years when, as a coach with Syracuse, he wrestled in Houston and Dallas whenever the team made bowl appearances. "I will be there mid-August," he told Boesch whereupon the Houston office set out to arrange a challenging schedule for their new masked heel.

Beyer swept into Houston with his car, boat, and boat trailer packed with clothes, toys, and assorted kid paraphernalia; Willy was sad to leave California, but another adventure awaited them in Texas, she told the kids. Upon the recommendation of a friend, the Beyers found an apartment complex on the north side of Houston and dropped anchor. Beyer was scheduled to begin wrestling the following evening, so time was of the essence to move in and get settled. It was August, it was hot, and it was humid. As things were being put away in the apartment, Beyer was unable to locate his work clothes. He panicked when after several minutes they could not locate masks or trunks. Willy, sweating and sticky from the work and weather, turned to her husband and said, "Look, for one night, just wear shorts and I'll paint your face white with colored lines around your eyes and mouth…" At that moment the boxed items were discovered, and Beyer looked over to Willy and replied, "They would have thought Marcel Marceau was a heavyweight wrestler."

The Texas loop was a Monday through Saturday journey – Fort Worth, Dallas, San Antonio, Corpus Christi, Houston and Beaumont with

MASKED DECISIONS

Waco an occasional stop – practically a horseshoe shaped route befitting the territory. Wrestling was legendary in Texas, and the fans were knowledgeable. If a grappler didn't perform to expectations or appeared lazy, he heard from the fans in multiple ways. The Destroyer jumped out of the corner from the very first match and gave the fans a Texas-sized helping of speed, skill and showmanship that got them interested early in the mystery man. Playing up his bad side, The Destroyer played to win against talented mat men like Ken Hollis, Fritz Von Erich, Antonio Inoki, Rito Romero, Killer Karl Kox, Torbellino Blanco, and the great Lou Thesz for the NWA title in a match that ended in a draw. As in L.A. and Portland, The Destroyer captured strong attention for his technical abilities and his stage presence, and the fans responded with heat, just the way The Destroyer liked it in steamy Houston.

Young Kurt Beyer celebrated his fifth birthday in September just the way he wanted – eating cake and watching The Destroyer in action in the ring. He loved wrestling, unfortunately, others his age and older didn't hold it in the same regard and teased him mercilessly; no matter, Kurt kept up his end of 'kayfabe' and never yielded to the temptation to 'spill the beans' and rat on the business. At home after the match, as he was about to be kissed by his mother, Kurt turned his head away and said to her, "Uncle Freddie told me when I'm five I don't gotta be kissed by nobody." Motherly affections rebuffed, Willy picked up the phone and gave an unexpectedly vitriolic earful to one Mr. Fred Blassie who, when Kurt was put on the phone, sheepishly said to him "Kurt, you *always* gotta be kissed by your mother." Blassie's ear hurt more that day than from any match in the ring.

The year wasn't three-quarters of the way through when Beyer got word that Billy Red Lyons was moving to town; while they were not scheduled to be tag partners, they were to meet each other in the ring. It was welcomed news for Beyer, personally and professionally. Having his wife's sister and her family near his own, made the transition to Texas easier on Willy and the kids, now 5 and 2, but just as important was the fact that he and Billy worked well together and he looked forward to a program with him.

After several months of travelling the Texas loop, the brothers-in-law were scheduled to face each other in a tag team match in Beaumont. Beyer always travelled with an inventory of Destroyer masks in the car, but rarely had the opportunity to sell them directly to the public. Lyons told him he had an idea and, on the local televised studio wrestling show a week before the Beaumont tag match, Lyons told the viewers "I will be wrestling against The Destroyer next week, and if anything drives him crazy it's seeing fans at the matches wearing Destroyer masks; he thinks he is the only one allowed to wear a mask in the arenas; I will be selling masks near ringside before the match… get yours so we can get him" Lyons took the 300 masks to ringside and sold them all. The Destroyer entered the ring and looked around the arena – most everyone was wearing a Destroyer mask. He complained loudly, jumped up and down, pointed to the crowd and said to the referee "Tell them to take the masks off…I am the only one good enough to wear it…that's an insult!" The crowd resisted the faint warnings by the referee and heckled the masked man incessantly. It was a masterful marketing ploy by Lyons and at $3.50 a piece, the in-laws made a little extra cash from the masks that evening to go with their match pay.

During a week early in 1966, Beyer and Lyons were on opposing sides of another type of team match known as a chicken fight. The two men wrestlers were to transport around the ring two female wrestlers perched on their shoulders; the females were to engage each other in combat from their shouldered positions. Lyons was first to hoist his female partner onto his shoulders and they awaited the challengers in the center of the ring. Beyer as Destroyer had as his partner a female wrestler who carried considerably more weight on her frame than her counterpart. The woman wrestler tried to mount onto The Destroyer's shoulders from varying positions, but found the going tough; after several attempts, The Destroyer put his female partner into the corner ropes and instructed her to stand on the top rope at the turnbuckle; he backed into the corner and took one leg and then the other until he had her on his shoulders. But things went south from there. As the large female sat into position, she inadvertently grabbed the mask and twisted it so that the holes were misaligned and Beyer was unable to see. Her weight was a surprise and took him off balance to where he was unable to control her body on his shoulders. Beyer staggered around the ring like a town drunk, his vision blocked by his mask askew of his face and his partner's large thighs pushed up against his neck chocking off his airway. The sight of the masked man and his oversized partner trying to regain balance all over the ring was too much for Lyons and his female partner – they broke down in extreme laughter so much that the entire bout had to be improvised. It was their first, and last, chicken fight.

Another tag partner was later assigned by the Houston promoters to expand awareness of the mystery man. With Clyde Steeves as the Golden Terror, The Destroyer and his partner won numerous team matches along the Texas route including the February 8th match in Dallas against Antonio Inoki and Duke Keomuka for the World Class World Tag Team title. It was the only title held by Destroyer/Golden Terror during their Texas tenure, but a significant addition to the team titles earned by The Destroyer since 1962.

The Destroyer, Billy Red and assorted wrestling talent played to sellout crowds including several in San Antonio for local wrestler/booker Joe Blanchard. Blanchard, one evening, was agitated and highly anxious prior to the scheduled match between Billy Red Lyons and The Destroyer, due to a published wrestling magazine article that mentioned the in-law relationship of the two wrestlers. Approaching them in the dressing room Blanchard, looking nervous and shaken said, "You two killed my town." When asked what he meant, Blanchard replied, "That article said you were in-laws…that will kill business for us." Both Beyer and Lyons tried to reassure him that little would come of the article, as both continued to dress and warm up before the bout. Blanchard wouldn't listen and stormed out of the dressing room and headed outside to check on ticket sales. He was stopped cold in his tracks; as he got near the ticket window, he saw a line of people that stretched around the corner and out of sight. In disbelief, he stood on the sidewalk when a woman, standing in the long line, walked over to him and said, "I wouldn't miss this match for anything …there is nothing better than a good in-law fight!"

Some matches were promoted as blood and guts wars, two men in the ring with nothing on their minds except the complete annihilation of their opponent through torture and punishment. One such match was scheduled between The Destroyer and relative newcomer Ox Baker, a big 6'5" 340 pound, slaughterhouse. At the North Side Coliseum in Fort Worth, Baker, who had, of all people, Billy Red Lyons as his corner manager for the night, looked like a beast of a wrestler with black, bushy eye brows that curled up at the ends, a large moustache, a bald head, and menacing stare. His appearance alone was enough to frighten off most people. Baker entered the ring to the hushed sounds of the crowd gazing in awe at the human embodiment of evil and carnage. Once The Destroyer was stationed in the ring, the two locked in combat and provided the fans with an early display of unrestrained defacement, that is, until a cockroach landed on the surface of the canvas. Beyer spotted the creature and called timeout; as The Destroyer, he picked up the bug and started to walk toward his huge, hulking opponent to show him when Baker bolted, ran around the ring, hands in front of his body to ward off his opponent from getting any closer, yelling in obvious fear of the little roach that had invaded their work space. This was something completely spontaneous, and Baker's reaction overwhelmingly hilarious. Beyer was not about to let this go without adding to the fun; he caught Baker and placed the bug in his backside trunks – the bug was dead, but Beyer did not tell Baker that important detail, as the wooly wrestler jumped around the ring trying to extricate the creature from his pants by shaking out his trunks without touching the bug. The scene was something to behold

– Billy Red, and indeed the entire crowd was in convulsive laughter, and The Destroyer endeavored to remain stoic but even he had to stop and laugh. Baker was a good sport afterwards and chuckled about it… a little.

After nearly a year in the Houston territory, Dick Beyer felt compelled to move on; more than anything, he never wanted The Destroyer to outlive his welcome wherever he worked. Beyer and his family had enjoyed their stay and the Texas hospitality shown them was warm and generous. He could not say enough good things about Morris Sigel, Paul Boesch, and the local bookers and promoters on the circuit, and especially the wrestling fans who took to the heel exactly the way Beyer needed them – venomously and with contempt. Willy called her family in Buffalo and told them, "We'll be there for dinner in three days but staying longer…Dick is going to work from home."

CHAPTER **14**

OVER THE NEXT thirteen months, and for one of the few times in his professional career, Dick Beyer lived in one territory and worked in others. From his farmhouse in Akron, New York, Beyer travelled to outlier regions of the country, invited by promoters to wrestle short and mid-range programs. In the four years since he first donned the mask, Beyer had earned the respect of every promoter, tag partner, and opponent he worked with, not to mention the legions of fans who, while hating the cantankerous rule breaker, loved his technique and intelligence for the ring. Volumes of articles in wrestling publications and newspapers made The Destroyer known to a wider audience; sales of his masks and cigarette lighters, advertised in national wrestling and boxing publications, did well, making Beyer one of the first pro athletes to promote and endorse his own products. The masked heel was a sensation no matter who or where he wrestled; he knew how to generate fan interest and cash at the box office, so good was he as a villain, but to promoters he was a saint.

In addition to the circuits of Los Angeles, Portland, Houston, Nashville, and Indianapolis, Beyer travelled to Detroit, Windsor, Ontario and Las Vegas; he faced wrestlers Pat O'Connor, Terry Yorkson, Bobby Managoff, Ernie Ladd, Bobo Brazil, Magnificent Maurice, Mark Lewin, The Preacher, Moose Cholak, Jose Betancourt, Buddy Austin, Lou Thesz, and other names large and small. Some business trips were quick one-night stays, others were three to four week excursions. Though the money was very good, it proved to be a more challenging lifestyle for Willy and Beyer; he didn't see his family as often, but he never short-changed his kids on time and activities when he was home. Willy was busier, yet lonelier, without her husband; although living in her hometown with family support helped ease the burden, it didn't ease the longing. They had moved every year since they were married, sometimes twice in a short span; she knew moving around was part of the profession but the recent relocations she quietly regarded as disruptions since they undercut the community roots she wanted for her young children. She coped with it as best she was able, and nurtured her two children while her husband went on the road.

During this time, Beyer bought additional property adjacent to his original 85 acres in Akron. He heard from his cousin who worked with the landowner at the telephone company that the property, another five bedroom farmhouse on 35 acres of land, was for sale; speaking directly with the owner, Beyer was asked what he thought the property was worth; he replied $18,000. After conferring with his lawyer, Beyer went back to the owner and said "Short of an appraisal, maybe $16,000," but after another meeting with his lawyer, Beyer visited the owner a third time and offered $15,000, in cash. The transaction was swiftly completed. Owning 120 acres of land and two five bedroom farmhouses gave Beyer a measure of comfort and solitude, away from the crush and crowds of his business, to protect his wife and children; it felt reassuring to him, in a way like the Osaka and Hamamatsu castles guarded the ruling clans, but as the history of those castles proved, not everything, and not everyone, was secure from time and events.

Beyer's sixth trip to Japan for Shohei Baba placed him in the JWA 9th World League Tournament, that was to begin in April. Other non-Japanese participants included Paul Vachon, Dan Miller, Mike DiBiase, Pampero Firpo, Duke Keomuka, and Waldo Von Erich. Over six weeks the tournament roamed through various cities and regions of Japan, giving residents of remote areas rare opportunities to experience the matches in person and witness the dastardly *gaijin* wrestlers get their payback from homeland heroes. The tournament culminated with the finals in Yokahama, as Baba defeated the masked Destroyer for the championship. By now, Baba and Beyer were close friends, and Beyer impressed his colleague with a few Japanese phrases he had acquired on each successive trip. Beyer continued the tradition started under Rikidozan and never took off his mask while in Japan; this also pleased Baba and thrilled the people on the streets whenever they saw the American wrestler dining out or visiting their points of interest. *De-stroy-yaa* was a commonly heard exclamation that, on the streets of Japan, Beyer was always delighted to hear, and he played to it.

Back home, Beyer, on several occasions, worked the Indianapolis territory that had been acquired within the last few years by wrestlers – turned - promoters Dick Afflis and Wilbur Snyder. Beyer knew the promoters well; all three had collegiate football backgrounds as well as pro wrestling experience; each had worked with the others. Like Afflis, Snyder also played professional football as a top placekicker in the Canadian leagues before going into wrestling full time. The 'Bruiser/Snyder' promotion, known as the World Wrestling Association, had a talent exchange arrangement with the AWA that enabled Beyer to land a match in Chicago against AWA champ Verne Gagne. The Destroyer/Gagne match was intense from a fan perspective but seamless from the participants' point of view. The two worked well in the ring, giving the other opportunities to showcase his specialties, and rewarded the fans with a memorable bout.

At the end of the match, impressed by Beyer's ring performance under the hood, Gagne, who also co-owned the Minneapolis promotion, invited Beyer to meet him for drinks at the Playboy Club in downtown Chicago. Beyer accepted, and met the champ at the well-known nightspot. Gagne was blunt and to the point. "Dick, I want you to come out to Minneapolis for a spell but not as The Destroyer." He told Beyer that he believed most everyone knew The Destroyer's identity was Dick Beyer and, because of it, didn't want *that* masked man, but he wanted *another* masked heel on the circuit with Beyer's credentials. While Beyer disagreed with Gagne about the extent of

◄ **MASKED DECISIONS**

The Destroyer's known identity, telling him, "Who the hell is Dick Beyer anyway?...he never made any money," he was interested in working for him, knowing Gagne to be a good payout man and respected owner with partner Wally Karbo; together, Gagne and Karbo had strong talent rotation and a territory that stretched west and north from its Minneapolis base. Beyer called his wife in Buffalo to tell her of his meeting with Gagne and the offer – he forgot to tell her where they met for drinks. The two discussed the decision by phone. From Gagne, Beyer requested and was given the latitude to work other territories as The Destroyer from time to time; he did not want to retire the mask, convinced that there was a future for The Destroyer, but he needed to replace the masked man with another character while he worked the Minneapolis territory.

In August of 1967, the Beyer Family took to the road again, this time to the mid-west and Minneapolis/St. Paul. On the journey to their next port of call, Beyer thought of several ways to create a new masked identity so that any resemblance to The Destroyer would be remote. Settling into their new home near 60th and Penn, on the south side of Minneapolis, Beyer called wrestling equipment supply firm Karl & Hildegard to discuss his ideas for a mask and accompanying accessories. The new masked man would appear diametrically opposite from the original one – like a distorted negative of a photograph. Where The Destroyer wore mostly white, the new character would be cloaked in black; he'd remove the white boots to lace up the new character's black high-tops; from wrestling no-shirt to wearing a black singlet, black tights and trunks; the white mask would be exchanged for a black mask with a molded beak to hide the shape of Beyer's bent nose, and the eye and mouth holes designed smaller so that less facial area was visible. The final versions, shipped from Karl & Hildegard- shoes, tights, trunks, singlet, and masks- met Beyer's expectations and, when fully attired, rendered the wrestler's appearance more beast-like and sinister; accordingly, he fashioned a new walk- a longer, foreboding stride and added sweeping arm gestures as if playing to the last row in the theatre. Beyer recognized that since the mask was not as pliable as the girdle masks and because no emotions were detectable, the character in black needed more body language to exhibit his dark virtues and deliver his malevolent message. The personality and ring traits of the new villain, while exaggerations of the original masked heel, were fresh and contemporary, with a hefty dose of cheating, a box of bully, and two cups of intimidation.

Gagne's directions to Beyer were unusual but simple – for the first three weeks of the televised *All Star Wrestling* matches, Beyer, in street clothes, was to sit in the audience near ringside wearing a bag over his head. He cut eye, nose, ear, and mouth holes sufficient to see, breathe, hear and speak, but he did not engage anyone nor attempt to provoke any wrestler in the ring. Beyer sat unassumingly in the crowd and caught the attention of fans, the camera, and television announcers. During the second week, the interviewer, with microphone in hand, walked to the unknown patron and, on camera, asked "Sir, what are you doing, you can't sit here with that bag on your head." Beyer replied "What do you mean…who are you to tell me… see that woman, she has a hat on her head…see that man, that's a wig he's wearing…so why can't I wear a bag on my head?" "Are you a wrestler?" the interviewer questioned; the bag man replied, "None of your business what I do." The televised exchange created the buzz about the man in the bag at the studio matches, and viewership shot upwards in the initial few weeks of Beyer's participation.

At the mid-August televised arena match between John Pesek and Verne Gagne, a bagged Beyer was seated in the second row from the ring, in full view of the inquisitive crowd, and not unnoticed by the television announcers. The match was proceeding well, with Gagne having the upper hand and looking to take full control of the bout. As Gagne was leveraging for victory, suddenly the man with the bag on his head ran up to the ring, jumped over the ropes, and began pummeling Gagne with furious elbows and knee kicks, dropping the popular wrestler to his back, at which point the mystery man clamped the figure four leg lock on Gagne. In pain, Gagne rose up slowly, requested the ring microphone, and spoke directly to the bag man. A challenge match was issued by the AWA champion to the man of unknown identity. From underneath the bag an ominous voice thundered "If I'm gonna pick on someone, it might as well be the world champ." The crowd roared hoarse concurrently wondering *who is this guy in the* bag mask....if he could do that to our champ, what else could he do...what was he up to? As the bag was slowly removed, the black mask became visible to the crowd and television audience; the mysterious man turned clockwise to face each section of the arena, as a collective gasp echoed from the hall; Gagne's gauntlet was accepted – the bag man agreed to wrestle. The ploy to expose the new masked man to Twin City fans of wrestling worked the way Gagne had envisioned it; fans were hooked by the mystery man and desperate to see what he could do in the ring. Beyer was now in the lineup and needed to find a name for his new creation.

For the first few matches under the new hood, Beyer was promoted in the ring as simply the Masked Man. There were no identifying symbols on the black mask or outfit and no signature characteristics, yet his brute strength, athleticism, and killer mentality made the new heel one of the more compelling and violent villains the Minneapolis territory had ever seen. He didn't just defeat his initial opponents - he beat and rendered them unconscious. A new name for the new nemesis came about quite unexpectedly. Reggie 'Crusher' Lisowski, another friend of Beyer from his Chicago days, was a star on the circuit both in individual and tag team with partner Dick 'The Bruiser' Afflis. Prior to a scheduled match in St. Paul with the new heel, Lisowski said during a televised interview "Look at that new guy...he looks like a duck with that beak; he must be a doctor, a quack...I call him Doctor X...he's a quack doctor." Lisowski got it across that the heel was a quack; he enlisted the support of the fans to chant 'quack quack' at the matches; they quacked and like baby ducks following the mother, they lined up to buy tickets, selling out arenas wherever this menace called Doctor X was to perform. Beyer just accepted the moniker that was bestowed on him by happenstance, and later added a large letter 'X' to the forehead area of his masks. He proclaimed to the fans that he would not reveal his identity until he lost two pin or two submission falls. Not since Dr. Bill Miller who wrestled as Mr. M, was a masked man so riveting to Minnesota wrestling fans.

Beyer as Doctor X bulldozed his way through the territory that first year and in his wake left indelible memories of unrelenting force against the likes of Rene Goulet, Igor Vodik, Kenny Jay, Cowboy Bill Watts, Luke Brown, Dutch Savage, Wilbur Snyder, and several notable run-ins with Verne Gagne. Doctor X won by dominating the majority of his bouts, usually referred to as squash matches, often in brutal fashion, occasionally using a foreign object to provide an unfair advantage over his opponent and draw crowd reaction. He became the most vilified heel to come into the territory in memory. As much as the fans adored their champion Gagne, they feverishly hated Doctor X. Gagne, Karbo and Beyer made big money from the developing story. They paired the Doctor with heels Harley Race (former AWA tag champion with partner Larry Hennig) and Mad Dog Vachon in tag team matches to provide additional storylines and defeats to set up other angles. 'Handsome' Harley Race was methodical and deliberate in the ring, but not on the road. He had a penchant for fast cars. Beyer was travelling with Race back to Minneapolis one night after a match; on Interstate 80, his speeds reached near 100 miles per hour. Beyer was panicky and asked Race several times to slow down, but Race continued full metal to the floor. At a truck stop for gas, Beyer grabbed his wrestling bag, got out of the car, and told Race he would get a ride to the city with a truck driver. Race tried to talk him back into the car but to no avail; Beyer hitched a ride on a truck and arrived in town later but safe. The team of Doctor X and Harley Race faced Bill Watts and Snyder then Watts and Crusher; when paired with Vachon, Doctor X and the 'Mad Dog' tangled with Igor Vodik and Luke Brown, Joe Scarpello and Kenny Jay, Watts and Haggerty.

◂ **MASKED DECISIONS**

The program reached a crescendo when Gagne and Doctor X wrestled for the AWA World Title in August of 1968. The match, held in Bloomington, Minnesota, contained all the key elements fans craved in championship bouts – speed, power, holds, aerial maneuvers, suspected wrong-doing, cliffhanger moments, classic good versus evil, only this time evil triumphed; the malicious Doctor X surgically removed the belt from Gagne to claim the AWA World Title. It was the only title Beyer's Doctor X held during his time in the Minneapolis territory; he didn't hold it for long, losing in the built-up rematch fourteen days later to eventual ten time champion Gagne.

Beyer was having more fun and making more money than he expected; he spoke with Gagne and Karbo about an angle he had in mind; they liked it; the opponent was asked to come to the territory – Billy Red Lyons said yes. Beyer and Lyons had great success working their program in California and Texas, and Beyer had a hunch it would work well in Minnesota. Lyons, who had finished up in Texas and moved on to new opportunities in Oklahoma, was delighted by the invitation, and soon moved his family near the Beyer household in south Minneapolis.

Beginning the fall of 1968 to early 1970, Doctor X and Billy Red Lyons worked their angle and the circuit, travelling far and wide. Unlike other territories that were mainly confined to a region or state, the Minneapolis territory included Minnesota, Michigan, Illinois, Wisconsin, Iowa, North Dakota, South Dakota, Nebraska, Colorado and some cities in Canada. With such a vast area, talent rotated frequently, allowing storylines to develop and mature over longer periods of time; a wrestler could work a match in January in a particular city and not return to work the angle for another month or more.

October of 1968 brought another change to the Beyer constellation - the arrival of son Richard Ward Beyer. Kurt, 8, and Kris, 5, were impatient, and wanted desperately to train their younger brother in the art of protecting the family's secret identity. Experience prompted their desire; taunting and fighting, instigated by peers who told them wrestling was fake, were part of everyday life now for Kurt and Kris; they didn't want the same for their younger brother. Giving Willy a break from all three, Kurt and Kris were often taken to the local matches by their father and positioned near the ring with arena staff to watch over them while dad worked his match. There were times when others, having seen the children with the masked wrestler, approached the two kids and asked their names, expecting to learn the identity of the masked man; Beyer's daughter always gave the same answer "My name is Krissy X."

One of the best photos in pro wrestling history, according to many

MASKED DECISIONS

In addition to Lyons, Doctor X wrestled other big names and lesser known talent – Pete Memco, Mike Bowyer, Jose Acosta, Bob Lewis, George Gadaski, Mark Starr, and Hank Meadows among the many. One time Minnesotan Rolland 'Red' Bastien, who had won team championships with partner Lou Klein in 1960 and 1961, entered the territory with a reputation as a tag expert, but soon was headlining with Doctor X in what turned out to be some of the most highly regarded matches recorded in the territory. Bastien at 5'10" and 200 pounds was a master of anticipation and loved aerial acrobatics. He and Beyer first tangoed in Los Angeles during Beyer's second tour as The Destroyer; it only took seconds for Bastien to realize that Beyer was a natural. "Where have you been all my life?" he gushed to Beyer after their initial lockup in the ring; Bastien sensed when and where his opponent was headed and, with perfect timing, introduced a move or maneuver that made for a smooth transition and flow from one hold to another. Bastien and Doctor X performed in Duluth, Winnipeg, Davenport, Milwaukee, Minneapolis, and other cities around the expansive territory to ecstatic crowds thrilled by Bastien's air superiority with his flying head-scissors and Doctor X's ground attack with his strong-arm battery and the figure four leg lock.

Doctor X, to the fans, was pure evil, and their contempt for him strong, so strong it spilled over to real life. Leaving the ring after a heated match in a high school gymnasium, Beyer as Doctor X walked up the aisle headed toward the dressing room door, when a fan pulled on his mask from behind and another burned his back with a cigarette. In a reflex action, Beyer swung around to clear himself from the fan's hand on his mask, when he hit the left ear of a fourteen year old, caught up in the fan melee. The boy was not involved in the attack on Doctor X; he was innocently standing nearby when accidentally hit by Beyer. To many fans, it appeared the wrestler deliberately clipped the boy, whereupon scores of fans surged toward Beyer and chased him into the dressing room. Police secured the quarters and guarded the wrestler. The mob eventually disbursed when additional police forces arrived. Beyer had to provide an official statement which was later released to the press, and the story made its way into the newspaper that weekend. The boy was not injured but his mother was very upset, not with Beyer, with her son. Beyer was not charged but the incident was another in a series of fanatical reactions that wrestlers like Beyer had to often endure.

Beyer as The Destroyer made two trips to Japan in 1969 to further his commitment to Baba and help keep the JWA and professional wrestling moving forward. Bull Ramos, Frank Holtz and Jim Osborne rounded out the foreign team that faced Kintaro Oki, Baba and Antonio Inoki. Baba had forged good working relationships with several of the NWA promotions in the States, and the imported foreign talent enabled JWA to retain vitality in Japan. Baba and Inoki had developed into a formidable tag team in recent years but not without drama. Since the death of sensei Rikidozan, dojo classmates and best friends Inoki and Baba pushed on with the JWA, however, Inoki found himself working in a supportive role to the more well-known Baba. In 1966, seeking to establish a higher profile, Inoki joined upstart promotion Tokyo Pro Wrestling, but within the year was back with JWA when the competitor folded. Together, Inoki and Baba dominated tag team competition as the 'B-1 Cannon' and won multiple NWA World Tag titles.

The second trip to Japan, that began in late September and ended in early November, promoted The Destroyer with Ben Justice, Mexicans Black Gordman and Francisco Flores, Mr. Atomic (former Golden Terror Clyde Steeves), Buddy Austin, and New Zealander Steve Rickard. Beyer, since the late 1950s, had worked the ring with wrestlers from other countries and had been tested by many of the greats from Japan, Canada, Mexico, and Europe. He enjoyed squaring off against foreign grapplers to hone his skills and learn from the experience they brought to the mat. Within the group, Beyer and Rickard developed a solid friendship during their stay; it was to be a significant relationship for Rickard, and an even more important one for

Beyer. He finished the tour and while preparing to leave Japan, Beyer chewed on an idea of wrestling more foreign wrestlers…in their native countries.

A cold, wind-swept but very excited Minnesota awaited Beyer when he returned home during the beloved Vikings' march to the NFL championship with a 12 game winning streak in hand and a date with the Cleveland Browns at Metropolitan Stadium in Minneapolis on January 4, 1970. The Vikings defeated the Browns 27 to 7 to earn their first-ever appearance in the Super Bowl. One week later, head coach Bud Grant's 'Purple People Eater' defense was unable to stop the Kansas City Chiefs and Minnesota suffered a hard 23 to 7 Super Bowl IV loss. Beyer, still a fan of the Buffalo Bills, said to Willy, "The Vikes will go back again and win the big game …they can't lose them all." Willy told him of a new soap opera that debuted on television that month – All My Children. "The title got my interest, but it's like the others and probably won't last." "Are you clairvoyant?" Beyer asked his wife; "No, I'm Willy Beyer."

Doctor X resumed making house calls to the cities and towns that comprised the Minnesota wrestling community, carrying in his bag a lethal dose of bad medicine for those who dared oppose him. For several tag engagements, the promoters linked him with Black Jack Lanza, a relatively new heel, who made his mark in the St. Louis territory with manager Bobby Heenan. A February 1970 match in Minneapolis became a 'Black versus Red' pairing, as Black Jack Lanza and black clad Doctor X faced Red Bastien and Red Lyons. On that night, two reds were better than one, and got the best of Lanza and Doctor X.

As promised by Gagne, Beyer was given a few dates out of the territory to dust off his white mask, polish his white boots and wrestle as The Destroyer. Invited to Texas, he faced Billy Spears and Roberto Soto and was reunited, for the first time professionally, with Tim Woods. Beyer had beaten Woods (then known as Tim Woodin) in the 1954

Niagara AAU heavyweight finals match that qualified Beyer to go to San Diego for the nationals. Now a top ranked professional, Woods was working as the masked babyface, Mr. Wrestling. The two former collegiate rivals talked about their separate paths to the professional level with Woods telling Beyer, "Even though you beat me, you told me some good things that helped me get here." Beyer told him, "You had the talent I just confirmed it...now let's go out there so I can beat you again." Neither masked man won as they fought to a draw. It was a memorable reunion and it brought back memories of many other wrestlers Beyer had worked with since he first stumbled into the sport in college. It got him thinking about his life; he wasn't getting younger, and there were places he yearned to see and things he wanted to experience and desired for his family. Then it dawned on him; what if I could wrestle my way around the world and take *my family on the journey?*

For several weeks, Beyer discussed the notion of a world tour with Willy who, while not exactly in love with the idea, gave it consideration since it appeared to mean so much to her husband. She was hesitant at first, given the number of moves they had made since first married and, more importantly, since the children, and she desperately wanted to settle down and provide them stability. But this trip was one of those once-in-a-lifetime opportunities and she said to her husband "If you don't go now, you will be too old to go." He assured her that the kids- 10, 7, and 2- would benefit from the one-year exposure to sights and cultures of different lands.

Arriving at consensus, not without trepidation, Beyer began making phone calls to promoters to assess the potential for matches, length of stay, compensation and travel arrangements. He was quickly able to set up tours in Hawaii, from late September to mid-December, and in Japan for April and May of 1971. With these early successes, he went to see Verne Gagne to inform him of his ideas and plans and determine whether his departure was going to be problematic. Somewhat surprisingly, Gagne was supportive of

MASKED DECISIONS

Beyer's request for a year's leave of absence to travel the world, telling Beyer, "That's something I always had in mind." Beyer said he wanted to return to Minneapolis immediately after the trip; Gagne agreed, and the two discussed storylines to provide Doctor X a plausible exit strategy. When Beyer mentioned that he had a gap in his preliminary schedule from January to March, Gagne replied that Jim Barnett, the promoter in Australia, had been after him for years to send good talent down under; "This might be a way to finally get him off my back," and picking up the phone, Gagne called Barnett and offered him the chance to work Doctor X, The Destroyer, or Dick Beyer in Australia, January to March. Barnett told him, "Wonderful, I'll take The Destroyer." With Gagne as arbiter, a deal for $750 a week was struck; Beyer was now on the clock for a September departure from Minneapolis, but there was some unfinished business that had to be addressed in the ring.

For tag team matches, promoters Gagne and Karbo were unsure with whom to pair Dr. X in the stretch run to late summer. Beyer suggested Jim Osborne, one of the wrestlers he met on his trips to Japan in 1969. Not much was known about him, but Osborne was in town and available, having toured Arizona in recent months. "If you give him to me, I will make him my partner; I'll call him… Double X." It was worth the gamble to conceal a relative unknown to carry out the plot they had devised.

Doctor X and his secret masked partner Double X drew the curiosity and ire of wrestling fans for their cheap tactics and underhandedness as they crisscrossed Minneapolis and St. Paul, laying waste teams like Joe Scarpello and Kenny Jay, Edouard Carpentier and Pepper Gomez, Joe Scarpello and Beau Brunelle, and other combinations. Fans became increasingly agitated and clamored for someone to stop the evil doctor. It appeared their prayers were about to be answered when it was announced that masked Mr. M was returning for a loser-takes-off-mask bout with Satan-incarnate Doctor X in July. Mr. M had been a terror in the territory years earlier, but after an unmasking, left for other parts unknown. Many were unaware that Mr. M was Dr. Bill Miller, and others didn't care, what they knew was the 6'6" wall of steel was more than capable of causing severe bodily harm to the black-shrouded Doctor X.

On a mid-July evening in St. Paul, Mr. M stood in a corner of the ring awaiting the entrance of Doctor X. In customary black disguise, his opponent entered the ring to the jeers of the large crowd; the match was underway. It was a battle for control from start to finish and several times Mr. M, clearly the crowd favorite, appeared to be headed for an ignominious loss. When things seemed to be at their worse, a sudden shift in momentum gave Mr. M the upper hand and before anyone could catch their breath, Doctor X stood in the ring, defeated. Fans were unable to contain their joy; the din was ear-piercing. Mr. M walked over to the vanquished Doctor X to remove his mask, as per the rules of the match. As the black mask was removed, another mask was visible - one associated with the newcomer Double X. Mr. M, and the wrestling disciples of St. Paul, were double crossed by Doctor X. The opponent Mr. M defeated was a decoy. The second mask was ripped off, revealing that Double X was, in fact, Jim Red Osborne, but the mystery identity of Doctor X remained for yet more matches to come.

The finale was set. Weeks of anticipation ended with a scheduled tag match in Minneapolis, pitting partners in crime Doctor X and Black Jack Lanza against Red Bastien and Pepper Gomez. The menacing duo took charge early with a barrage of body blows to Bastien and Gomez. At one point late in the bout, a disagreement developed between the bad guys, evidenced by wild gesturing, yelling and finger-pointing. Unexpectedly, Lanza turned on his tag team colleague and began punching away at the Doctor, to the surprise of the fans and the two opponents. Lanza's manager, Bobby Heenan, climbed into the ring to gang up on the masked man. When the fracas cleared, a deliriously angry Doctor X demanded a match with the traitor Lanza and was granted his wish on the spot; the crowd roared when Doctor

X loudly declared that, should he lose a single fall, unlikely as it was, he would voluntarily unmask.

One time thick-as-thieves partners Black Jack Lanza and Doctor X met at the St. Paul Auditorium before a push and shove crowd that was expecting a blood bath. They got it and more. When the bell rang for the last time, it was Lanza who stood victorious. How ironic for the fans to witness the downfall and destruction of the most hated heel in recent times at the hands of his former teammate and friend. The mask was pulled off revealing the face of the doctor of darkness for the first time, but in what became an inside joke his name was announced as Bruce Marshall. Beyer had given the fake name – made up from the names of two local sportscasters – to the announcer ahead of time. It felt odd to Beyer to be standing in a ring with his face fully exposed to the elements, as the crowd looked on in a brief and largely disinterested moment. He wasn't certain what they had expected, and their reaction was atypical by most standards. In a way their reaction was strangely disappointing to him; it seemed like a quiet stillness had descended upon the auditorium, so he climbed through the ropes and disappeared from the scene. They had no way of knowing that the wrestler they despised above all, whose face they had seen, would return in a year to completely upend the staid order of their wrestling world.

Only a few of the places and countries were confirmed, leaving Beyer no choice but to sew up other matches and details on the fly. Willy worked out arrangements with the kids' school so that they would have lesson plans for the year; family members lent a hand to move furniture and belongings into their basements for safe keeping while the Beyer family was away. Domestically, things were well in hand. Beyer booked a short tour for Mexico City that would preface their 3 month stay in his favorite place on earth, Hawaii. He needed to pick up visa papers at the Mexican embassy in Chicago, but when he arrived, the papers were not there; he went back a second day to the embassy and the answer was the same. Boiling angry, he cancelled the Mexico tour, and hastily made arrangements for Las Vegas and a short vacation before flying to Honolulu. "Maybe the Mexicans are getting even with you for beating Pepper Gomez," Willy said with a smile. "Willy, fasten your seatbelt, we're going around the world… manyana."

CHAPTER **15**

TO SAY THE desert playground of Las Vegas didn't hold much interest for the Beyer children- outside of the pool at their hotel- couldn't be said for Beyer and his wife. The couple fixed their astonished eyes on the new resorts that had sprung up along the strip in recent years as they cruised down the neon-shadowed roadway, past the names of Elvis, Bobby Darin, Liberace, and other stars of show business on the large marquees, denoting the entrances to the hotels, nightclubs and casinos. "This place keeps getting bigger," Beyer said to his family in the car; from the back Kurt shouted, "So does my appetite, can we eat now?" Stopping for dinner at a small restaurant not far from Caesars Palace, Beyer told Willy he was concerned that he hadn't lined up more matches in other countries and the problems the lengthy layovers might pose. "You will…you just need to talk with the boys and promoters and things will be OK. Remember how you felt when we first arrived in L.A. in '62, looking up at the Hollywood sign in the hills…you had confidence, so trust your judgment and it will all work out." The family retired early for the night in order to get a quick start on their trip to Los Angeles; Beyer slept like a nervous poker player unable to call a bet.

The following day, in the dressing room of the Olympic Auditorium in L.A., the only day he was to be in town, Beyer was introduced fortuitously to Pita Maivia, a native of Western Samoa, former NWA Hawaiian tag team champion, and cousin of Hawaiian Neff Maiava, whom Beyer had met in Honolulu. In town for that evening's matches, 'High Chief' Pita Maivia knew Beyer's stellar reputation as Destroyer, and was eager to learn what the American star was doing back in L.A. After Beyer explained his plan for wrestling around the world that was to begin with a morning departure to Hawaii, Maivia took a deep interest; he told Beyer he was planning to travel home to Samoa – his first trip back to the capital, Apia, in fifteen years - and asked Beyer if he was interested in wrestling him in his native land. Samoa was not on the original radar screen, but since it was only 4000 miles from Australia, it was practically in the neighborhood. Beyer agreed; Maivia gave him the name and telephone number of the promoter/wrestler in New Zealand who would book the match for them in Samoa. That name was Steve Rickard. Astounded, Beyer told Maivia he met Rickard on a tour of Japan in 1969 and had enjoyed his company; it also surprised Beyer to learn that Maivia received all his formative wrestling training in New Zealand at the hands of Steve Rickard – the American and Samoan shared a New Zealander as a degree of separation. A more optimistic Beyer said to Maivia "I'll call Steve and see you in Apia so we can talk samoa." Though the pun may have been lost, the chance meeting turned into an opportunity to extend Beyer's time in the South West Pacific before going into the Australian outback. *Willy was right again*, he conceded.

The islands of Hawaii were as beautiful and welcoming as ever; the kids couldn't wait to get to the soft, sandy beach; their father couldn't wait to make a phone call to New Zealand. A pleasant telephone conversation with Rickard, held moments after arriving in Waikiki, yielded an agreement to book a match for The Destroyer and High Chief Maivia in Apia, Western Samoa, the week before Christmas. As a bonus, Rickard also booked him in New Zealand the last full week of December for towns on the South Island. Beyer took a deep breath as additional stepping stones were now in place but a few more were needed to complete the trip. For the three months they made Waikiki home, the Beyers lived as normal a life as was possible for the family of a professional wrestler; the two oldest kids, Kurt 10 and Kris 7, were enrolled at Jefferson Elementary School in walking distance from the Beyer's rented apartment. The family enjoyed being together on the beach, and Beyer especially loved taking Kurt and Kris out onto the surf to ride the waves back to the edge of the sands till sunset. Kris stood on her father's shoulders as he balanced on the board looking very much like the veteran surfer he had become, riding next to the athletic Kurt. At night, Beyer and Willy played cards with their kids, not only to amuse, but to teach them math skills and the lessons of competition; the teacher never stopped teaching; cribbage was added later to the family game list that kept them occupied and together. The bonds between the children and their father were tight and growing stronger with every experience, every year.

In late September, 1970, the NWA North American Heavyweight Championship (Hawaii version) was on the line in Honolulu in a match that featured current champion Pedro Morales against The Destroyer. It was Morales who took the WWA title from The Destroyer in March of 1965, the last time the masked heel held that title on the west coast. Retribution was the motivation spoken by The Destroyer to hype the rematch as the fans bought into the championship. A turn-away crowd at the Civic Auditorium was treated to a spectacular performance by the two wrestling titans, won by The Destroyer. In the ring, promoter Ed Francis presented The Destroyer with the North American belt, emblematic of NWA wrestling supremacy. The belt looked awful; weathered, tarnished and beat up, it resembled an old cheap prop from a bad superhero movie. Beyer wanted to take the belt on the road and wear it around the world, but that particular strap was an embarrassment. He contacted well-known belt maker Reggie Parks who designed and shipped a classy piece to Beyer with the inscription 'United States Heavyweight Wrestling Champion,' a designation Beyer created to differentiate it from the North American title. He now had a belt to display and a title to defend.

Midway through the month of October, Beyer received a letter from promoter Jim Barnett. The Oklahoma native Barnett had played a huge role in the development of professional wrestling not only in the States but also Australia. The former wing man to Fred Kohler in Chicago, Barnett was a savvy businessman who was credited with inventing the studio wrestling show. When the letter arrived, Beyer assumed it was details on his upcoming tour of Australia that was put together with the help of Verne Gagne. Jolted by the contents, Beyer was informed that Barnett, no longer in need of a masked man, had cancelled his January through March tour. "He can't do this," he told Willy "I'll write back and tell him I don't need to wear the mask, I'll go in as Dick Beyer." A second letter arrived several weeks later, telling Beyer the promotion in Australia had booked too many wrestlers for early 1971, and the original decision remained. 'Thank you, but I will not need you at this time' were Barnett's final words. "Isn't this great…I'm halfway around the world and now a quarter of my tour is cancelled." Beyer was convinced there was more to the story, but he was unable to uncover the details. Willy had not seen her husband that upset since his mother and Rikidozan died weeks apart; she had a hard time getting him to accept the cancellation and to find new opportunities. Beyer was in a foul mood.

Days later, Beyer met up with a few wrestlers at the beach front bar of the Moana Hotel in Honolulu. Still reeling from the loss of a three month engagement, Beyer told his woes to the guys at his table. Drinking with him were Nick Bockwinkel, his fishing buddy from Portland, who was in Hawaii on vacation from his wrestling work in Gagne's Minneapolis, Wahoo McDaniel, the ex- Oklahoma Sooner and former professional football player with the Dolphins, Jets and other teams returning from a wrestling tour of Japan and Billy Robinson, a British amateur wrestling champion turned professional making his Hawaiian debut. They listened to Beyer's plan to wrestle round the world and commiserated with him on the loss of the Australian leg. Robinson, who had wrestled throughout Asia and Europe, told the boys that, not only was this his first trip to Hawaii, he had never wrestled on the mainland. Beyer, who was scheduled to wrestle Robinson in tag and singles matches, saw in the Brit a kindred spirit of sorts, both looking to experience new lands. Forgetting about his own travel dilemma, Beyer left the table and called Verne

Gagne to see if he could use Robinson in Minneapolis. Robinson's amateur experience was the kind of background Gagne loved, and he gave Beyer the go-ahead to invite Robinson to his territory. Robinson didn't know what to say. Though he and Beyer had never met until that afternoon, he was impressed that the American took time from his issues to help him land work in the United States. So appreciative was Robinson that he went back to his hotel room and returned with two names and phone numbers for Beyer – one was John DaSilva, a well-connected, champion wrestler in New Zealand, and the other was Gustl Kaiser, the promoter in Germany. "Call them, perhaps they can be of assistance to your journey," Robinson said to Beyer. With mutual respect and appreciation for each other's help, they shook hands and departed from the bar.

Before going home that day, Beyer had a pre-arranged meeting and photo shoot onboard the U.S.S Preble, the American destroyer vessel stationed at Pearl Harbor. The meeting, arranged in cooperation with the United States Navy, was positioned for publicity as 'one Destroyer meets another.' Beyer was invited by the ship's skipper, Captain Masterson, to eat with the crew, to inspect the ship, and even to engage in a tug of war with crew members on deck. Photos of The Destroyer's activities aboard ship were taken for a future edition of *Wrestling Revue* magazine.

After several months of individual and team matches with talent that included Sam Steamboat, Frank Allman, The Sheik, Johnny Barend, Frankie Laine and others, The Destroyer lost the NWA North American title to England's Billy Robinson on December 16, 1970. The Destroyer handed Robinson the title but not the new belt, even though promoter Ed Francis tried hard to get it. Beyer was taking that belt, his self-created U.S Heavyweight Wrestling Champion title, and his family on the next stop of their tour – Western Samoa.

Situated roughly halfway between Hawaii and New Zealand, Samoa was to be a five-day stop for some rest, shopping, and a payday match with High Chief Maivia. Beyer took the kids to lunch while Willy took off to get in a little Christmas shopping for the family. Later, the family toured the harbor town of Apia, on the northern coast of Upolu Island, famed as the last residence of Scottish novelist Robert Louis Stevenson. A short rest preceded Beyer's match in the little performing hall in Apia. The place was oversold, with hundreds more turned away from the event; many had come to witness their first wrestling match and shouted support for their countryman, Pita Maivia, the moment they arrived at the venue. In the small narthex that served as a dressing room, Beyer heard the volume build in the crowd's emotion; he knew he was in for a tough night. He as The Destroyer entered the ring to the quiet stares of the Samoan crowd, followed by the deafening cheers for High Chief Maivia. The hall was so packed that many of the Samoans sitting ringside were sardined together, their arms pushed up onto the perimeter of the ring, causing Beyer to exercise caution when warming up in the corner to avoid stepping on limbs. As the big match unfolded, the crowd roared its delight with every hit Maivia put onto the masked villain, while giving The Destroyer life-threatening glares whenever he landed an arm bar. The hostile environment prompted Beyer to rethink his original plan for a draw, so he found a way, after fifty-five minutes, to get Maivia's hand raised as the winner. Utter joy filled the hall as the partisan fans saw Maivia hold up the shiny new belt of the United States Heavyweight Champion and a title he now claimed for himself and his countrymen.

The following day, to show his appreciation and gratitude, Pita Maivia invited the Beyer family to attend a traditional Samoan wedding ceremony on a remote island off-limits to tourists. Inhabited solely by Samoans, the island had no electricity, no running water. The people lived in grass huts and wore tralatitious wraps to the ceremony; to the Beyer family, it was like taking a giant step back in time, and they were absorbed by it. Welcomed as family, they were honored to be included in the wedding formalities. Afterwards, a guide took them on a brief tour during which they saw banana trees, cashew trees, and captivating, indigenous life. The Beyer kids played with the native children in the crystal clear waters washing up on the island while the adults gathered in the central part of the small village to conclude the celebration. The impressions and lessons occasioned by this side-trip were instructive and humbling.

Back in Samoa, on the final night of Beyer's visit, Pita Maivia displayed the belt he had won around the town and at dinner so that everyone could see the spoils of his victory. Late that night, Beyer's rental car drove up to the back of the restaurant. At the appointed time, Maivia came out the back door, handed the belt to Beyer, shook his hand, wished him well on his journey, and returned inside the restaurant.

The Beyer family, and the belt, landed in Fiji for a cup of coffee and a bathroom visit before arriving in Wellington, New Zealand at 3:00 pm Christmas Eve 1970; wrestler/promoter Steve Rickard greeted them at the airport. Rickard could not have been more gracious or hospitable; he drove them through some scenic spots on the North Island before dropping them at their hotel. As he did, he told Beyer and Willy he would return on Christmas Day at 4:00 pm and take them to his home "for tea."

Shopping that afternoon and evening Beyer found nearly impossible. Most everyone in Wellington had gone on holiday and it was Christmas Eve, but he managed to locate a decorated artificial tree, about twelve inches high, and snuck it into the room. Early the following morning, the three kids were treated to Christmas in New Zealand – not much in quantity but not lacking in love. The few presents in boxes, purchased during Willy's time in Apia, overpowered the small tree and caused Kris to comment, "The tree is under the presents!" That afternoon around 2:00 pm, the family went for a walk and stopped for a large lunch, returning to the hotel just before 4:00 pm, when Rickard was to pick them up. When they arrived at the Rickard home, they discovered that, in New Zealand, "tea" meant more than tea, it meant dinner. Not wanting to appear ungrateful, the

MASKED DECISIONS

Beyer family consumed their second large meal within two hours of the first and thanked Rickard and his wife for a wonderful Christmas dinner. The Destroyer's shiny new belt suddenly felt a little tighter.

Rickard was scheduled to leave New Zealand a few days before the New Year for a wrestling tour in Japan; he accompanied the Beyer family on the ferry to the South Island for Beyer's first four matches, the last scheduled for the city of Christchurch on the South Island's east coast. The Destroyer matches were overwhelming successes; wrestling fans and curious bystanders were caught up in the versatility and personality of the visiting masked man from America. Rickard was very pleased. In Christchurch, The Beyer family walked the center city to see the Anglican cathedral of Christchurch in Cathedral Square, built in the 19th century. After touring the city, Beyer went inside the wrestling venue to assess the setup for his final match; the floor of the ring was as hard as the Canterbury stone that buttressed the cathedral he had visited earlier in the day. There was nothing more than a piece of canvas stretched out on the unforgiving floor of the stage; the posts were inserted into the stage and there were ropes tied to the posts. If the event were boxing, it would have been appropriate for the purpose, but for wrestling, it was a different matter entirely. During the referee's instructions in the center of the ring that night, Beyer whispered to his opponent "This is gonna be a standup match," and neither wrestler fell to the floor much that night. Still, it was a riveting performance given by The Destroyer that delighted Rickard, who said he would keep in touch, and after the match departed for Japan.

With the Rickard-arranged matches concluded, Kurt asked his father what they were going to do next. "Kurt, we are going to do what the New Zealanders do…go on holiday." They boarded a train from Christchurch to the southernmost city in the country, Invercargill, and spent New Year's Eve learning about the region's Scottish lineage, a lineage shared by Willy, and punctuated by the fact that many of the streets in Invercargill were named after rivers in Scotland and the

United Kingdom; Willy, whose father was from Motherwell, Scotland, was intrigued; the kids fell asleep.

Renting a car on New Years' Day 1971, Beyer and his family set out to further their New Zealand experience, travelling north along the west side of the South Island, finding Queenstown in the southwest by early evening. The resort town was full; it looked as though every citizen of New Zealand had checked in, and no rooms were available at the first several hotels Beyer checked out. He said to his wife "It's time you put your Scottish brogue to work;" Willy stepped out of the car, walked into the very next hotel, and within five minutes returned with the manager of the inn, who explained where they could get a place for the night. They drove up toward the outer reaches of town, slowly made their way through a darkened field occupied with what appeared to be hundreds of sheep, to a farm house managed by an elderly couple as a bed and breakfast. The innkeepers welcomed the new arrivals, and prepared a light snack for the family before they bedded down for the night. Bedded was not exactly how they were accommodated. Dick and Willy slept on the floor, Richie in a cot, with Kris and Kurt spread out on church benches along the wall. Beyer pulled out his movie camera to record the primitive sleeping arrangements before taking up his position beside his wife. At 4:00 am, he was awakened by the sound of an angry rooster that must have known an American wrestler was in the house and wasn't going to let him sleep, Beyer surmised. Shortly after dozing off again, the breakfast bell rang and Beyer slowly rose from the floor along with the rest of his family to restart the journey, with sore backs and little sleep. "I tried counting sheep," Kris told her family; her father replied, "So did I...I looked out the window but they kept moving."

Having compensated the elderly couple for breakfast, adding an autographed Destroyer photo, back on the road the Beyer family drove, catching sight of the vast tracts of uninhabited land as they motored north. Several hours into their drive, Beyer noticed a sign along the side of the road indicating '150 Kilometers of Metal Road Ahead.'

MASKED DECISIONS

Beyer was not familiar with the term, but the words seemed to imply hard smooth surfaces, so he continued north and did not bother mapping a detour. Big mistake; he learned the hard way that a 'metal road' in New Zealand was a gravel and dirt road. So for several hours, the family car bounced and created clouds of dirt and gravel in its wake. They eventually arrived at one of the key tourist attractions along the west coast of the South Island – Franz Josef Glacier. The glacier, a throwback to the ice age, stretches down from the Southern Alps through a rainforest, creating dramatic iced valleys and icefalls, and extends almost to sea level. The three Beyer children enjoyed being on the ice, sliding and skating wearing only shorts and tee shirts. The dichotomy was not lost on them.

Beyer decided at that point, facing twelve weeks with no work in sight until Japan and with nothing to lose, he'd call John DaSilva – one of two contacts Billy Robinson gave him when Beyer met the Englishman in Hawaii in December, to see if the wrestler/promoter might have some ideas for him. Beyer had never met or spoken with DaSilva, but one would never guess judging from the friendly telephone conversation that took place. Before Beyer hung up the phone, DaSilva had booked a match for the two of them, given him the name of a sports writer to contact, and told him where to stay when Beyer got back to Wellington. It was a lucky break for Beyer and it came at just the right time.

From the upper west side of the South Island, the family navigated north then east to Picton, near the northeast corner of the island, where they boarded another inter-island ferry, sailed around the Marlborough Sounds and across to Wellington, the capital city at the southwest tip of the North Island. They checked into the motel recommended by DaSilva, and the following day Beyer took his entire family to see the newspaper sports writer, to talk about Beyer's impending match with John DaSilva.

DaSilva was quite happy that Beyer had suggested he come into the match as himself, rather than either of the two masked alternatives, and he wanted Beyer to tell his story to the local news publication for promotional purposes. In the sports department of the Wellington newspaper, Beyer met the writer and discussed his credentials as a former Syracuse University football and wrestling star in town to wrestle the New Zealand great, John DaSilva. On the day of the match, a large photo of Beyer appeared on the front page of the newspaper with an article on Beyer and the scheduled bout with DaSilva. That same morning, Beyer received a call from Steve Rickard who was still touring Japan. Having been informed of the Beyer/DaSilva match, he told Beyer to not let DaSilva beat him. Rickard was to return in two weeks and wanted Beyer to remain unbeaten until he arrived back home; Rickard also told Beyer he'd set up a series of matches for him with other New Zealand talent that would lead up to their confrontation. Another stroke of good fortune had brushed Beyer. "Looks like 'tea' was worth it," he told a smiling Willy. Beyer and his family took to the streets of Wellington that day to promote the match. They carried copies of the newspaper with the photo of Beyer and write-up. Beyer, Willy, and the kids signed the newspapers. The extra personal promotion time they put in plus the newspaper publicity pushed the event over the top – a sellout crowd of more than 2000 New Zealanders filled the arena and netted Beyer a $500 payday – big money thanks to DaSilva, with more matches on the docket thanks to Rickard. Things were looking up down under.

After the unforgettable match with DaSilva in Wellington, Beyer and his family drove to Auckland. There, he sought out wrestling referee and promoter, Ernie Pinches. Pinches, pleasant and congenial, agreed to set up a match for Beyer. When Beyer asked about local lodging, Pinches recommended renting a cottage on the beach, about 30 kilometers north of Auckland, while waiting for Rickard to return from Japan. Beyer found the location, and an available cottage, in Orewa Beach on the Hibiscus Coast. The little bungalow was situated about a block from the shoreline. Nearby, the area offered shopping, services, facilities and a school for his kids. Kurt found the school different from any he had attended previously. Unlike other schools, where students 'endured' class, the students in New Zealand seemed enthralled with whatever the teacher had to say. It was infectious and soon Kurt was enjoying class for one of the few times in his life. Orewa Beach became home for three months, an ideal location for the surfing and swimming Beyer family.

Pinches worked hard to line up a match for Beyer with the New Zealand heavyweight champion, Frank Lipanovich, set for Monday night, January 25, at the roomy YMCA Stadium in Auckland. Since it had worked well in Wellington, Beyer, this time disguised as The Destroyer, went to the local newspaper, the Auckland Star, and spoke with a sports reporter about the scheduled match. He took his family with him and gave an account of their travel and destinations. The January 22, 1971 edition of the Star that promoted the match between Lipanovich and the masked American also carried a large photo of The Destroyer with his family and the story of the family's journey around the world. The publicity lit up the town, and The Destroyer became an overnight sensation in Auckland; everyone inquired about the masked man from America and flocked to him, and his beautiful family, whenever they spotted them in town or on the beach. Beyer remained under the hood both in and out of the ring. The Destroyer and Willy used their celebrity to return the affection bestowed on them by the public. They visited businesses, hospitals, and even conducted class in a small elementary school in Orewa that generated publicity for the school.

The match with Lipanovich was an enormous success. The New Zealand Herald reported that the near capacity crowd "went wild" as the two wrestling titans fought to a draw. When Rickard returned, he kept his word and booked a number of matches for Beyer in Auckland and Wellington. Through his drawing power and the performances he delivered, The Destroyer helped change the way wrestling was promoted in New Zealand. Before he arrived, matches had never been scheduled in January or February, but after The Destroyer's tour de force, he convinced Rickard and Pinches to run matches six nights a week until he was to depart the country in March. The Destroyer faced New Zealand stars Ricki Wallace, Bruno Bekkar, Skull von Neumann, Tau Paa Paa, Mo Sakata, and took on Mario Milano in a match that became the largest promotion in New Zealand since Earl McCready wrestled Ed Don George – Beyer's mentor – in the 1930s. Beyer acknowledged and appreciated the historical relevance. These matches, with attendant publicity, served as prelude to the final match that stacked The Destroyer against New Zealand homelander, Steve Rickard.

Back in Wellington for the closing bout, Beyer once again took his family to the same sports department of the Wellington newspaper, but unlike the previous visit, he donned the mask. He met with a different reporter and gave an interview as The Destroyer, in town to defend his U.S. title against leading heavyweight, Steve Rickard. The office personnel, photographer, and others at the newspaper whom they had met on their first visit were completely unaware that the masked man was Dick Beyer, the man who had given a similar interview, accompanied by the same family, weeks earlier.

The Rickard/Destroyer match, staged at the Wellington Town Hall and promoted as 'The fight of the decade,' was one that not only attracted hard core wrestling fans, but also those curious enough about the masked man to buy a ticket and see him in the ring. As he had learned in Japan, wearing the mask in public was one of the best forms of advertising and promotion. Fans followed and witnessed a superb performance by their countryman, Steve Rickard, and a memorable display of skill and showmanship by the masked and mysterious Destroyer.

New Zealand was a rare and fantastic opportunity for the family Beyer. The countryside and cities they found to be extraordinary, matched only by the sincerity of the people they met. John DaSilva and Steve Rickard helped save the mission and, in fact, sweetened the pot; instead of the $750 a week he was to make in Australia, Beyer earned close to $1500 a week when factoring in the last several weeks of the promotion on the North and South Island. It was the right place, right time, right people and the right decision by Beyer. Just before Beyer's departure, New Zealand writer Dave Cameron wrote in a wrestling publication - "I personally have been watching wrestling since 1946 and have seen many top Americans in those years. I rate the Destroyer tops as a wrestler, showman and as a person…He created a lasting impression and did an enormous amount for wrestling in New Zealand."

As Beyer and his family packed for the next leg of the journey, he received a phone call from Australia – it was Jim Barnett. The promoter heard about the sold-out cards in New Zealand and the storm of publicity Beyer and The Destroyer had kicked up, and re-invited Beyer to work Australia. He told Beyer: "Come on over, Dick, and work as yourself or The Destroyer." Beyer had planned to take his family to see the outback, but due to Barnett's cancellation, he hadn't planned on working there. Deciding whether to accept Barnett's new offer, his answer came swiftly, borrowed from Barnett's own words: 'Thank you, but I will not need you at this time" and he hung up the telephone. As he did, he decided he wasn't quite through with Barnett.

From New Zealand, the family had two weeks before they were scheduled to be in Japan; as promised, Beyer first flew them to Australia. He arranged a flight into Brisbane, a transfer to a smaller plane, then on to Brampton Island, at the southern end of the Whitsunday Islands, in the heart of the Great Barrier Reef along the Queensland coast. The one-story resort, a quaint, charming and laid back retreat, offered all ground-floor rooms with direct access to the palm tree lined beach. The family checked in, attended an orientation on the event schedule for the week that was to include snorkeling, hiking, and water skiing, joined others for dinner and eventually turned in for the night. Kurt was often the first one up in the morning; he loved to explore new surroundings and after putting on a pair of shorts and a tee shirt, he opened the door to begin his early morning scouting trip. There, directly in front of him, stood a towering live kangaroo, as still as night, looking down at the boy. Kurt, frozen for seconds and terrified by the sight, slammed the door and yelled. Beyer jumped out of bed and ran to his son near the front door; Kurt, as best he could in a frightened state, told his father about the encounter. Beyer tried to reassure his son, and the other two children who had been awakened by the scream, that the resort surely would not allow dangerous animals to approach guests and to not be afraid. He opened the door with Kurt, Kris and Richie standing in line behind him, but the animal was no longer there. They searched left and right and looked out to the beach but there was no sign of the kangaroo. It was later that day the family learned that kangaroos, koala bears, and a variety of exotic birds roamed freely on the island and lived peacefully, however, they were instructed to leave the koalas alone. Feeling more secure, Kurt, Kris and Richie made it a daily habit of going to the beach early to eat coconuts that had fallen from the trees during the night. One of the island crew members told them of how the coconut trees were planted many years earlier on the largely uninhabited island in order to help stranded and shipwrecked seamen survive, and he instructed them on how to choose a coconut and open it, using a spike that had been cemented in place on the beach for that very purpose. These little lessons in resourcefulness and independence were never to be forgotten by the three kids.

The Beyer family flew to Sydney to prepare for their departure for Southeast Asia. The day before they were to leave, Beyer learned that a wrestling card, with promoter Jim Barnett, was to be held that evening in the city. He waived a taxi and arrived at the wrestling venue, purchased a ticket, and with Destroyer mask on, walked into the arena and sat down. For the entire undercard and main event, he sat as though an average spectator, never got up to cause a scene, but his very presence, in mask, made for quite a stir in the building and, without doubt, made an emphatic point to the promoter Barnett.

Southeast Asia, with its exotic locations, produced lessons and experiences the Beyer children would never find in a standard classroom. In Bali, Indonesia, the family was taken deep into the

◄ MASKED DECISIONS

countryside to witness a traditional Indonesian dance; in Singapore, the smallest nation in Southeast Asia, they visited Tiger Balm Gardens, originally built to teach Chinese values and mythology through its many statues and tableaux, where the Beyer kids held a boa constrictor and watched a snake charmer coax a cobra from a straw box. In Hong Kong, they boarded a traditional Chinese junk boat and toured Hong Kong harbor; the kids were fascinated by the chaos created by hundreds of boats sailing in seemingly different directions yet each navigating safely through the morass. It was during this period of the world tour that young Richie was toilet-trained onboard the multiple airplanes they took from country to country. Beyer told his wife, "I hope I don't have to convert our bathroom into a smaller one with a folding door." It was an educational and exhilarating ten days through six countries for his family, and Beyer as the masked mystery man continued to dazzle people wherever they landed with his intrigue and engaging personality. As The Destroyer, he signed autographs, gave press interviews, promoted amateur and professional wrestling, and caused a scene everywhere he went. While the Beyer family discovered the world, the world was discovering The Destroyer.

Around the world as Destroyer's family

"*Ohayo Gozaimasu,*" the pretty Japanese woman greeted the Beyer family as they arrived mid-morning at Haneda airport near Tokyo. Although it was the ninth trip to Japan for Beyer, it was the first for his family, who finally got the opportunity to see why the country held such a magical spell over him. It didn't take long. As his family waited in the airport lobby, Beyer went into the men's room. When he returned, he had his signature mask pulled down over his head, and a group of people following him snapping pictures and requesting autographs. He said to his wife, "They weren't all in the men's room." Kris said to her mother, "Dad is a big time celebrity here," as she watched her father yield to those who intercepted him. The family was accustomed to people's reactions to The Destroyer, but to see throngs of people, sometimes four or five deep, rushing up to say hello or take a photo with him was a newer experience. To the kids, there was no doubt that their father, The Destroyer, had captured the attention and imagination of the Japanese people through his personal appearances and his televised matches over the eight year span. Most *gaijin* were ignored by Japanese when recognized on the street, but The Destroyer was viewed differently. Still a heel, his scientific approach and captivating ring personality connected with the Japanese, who appreciated good wrestling technique, as in their national sport of sumo, and personas that transcended a sport, like top players in their fast developing affinity for baseball.

Giant Baba was delighted to meet The Destroyer's family; he showered them with gifts and foods and assured their stay would be pleasant and comfortable as he described for Destroyer the tour and matches that were ahead of him in April and May. The cities on this tour included Nagaoka, Hamamatsu, Yamagata, Fukushima, Iwaki, Nagoya, Toyama, Komatsu, Kobe, Osaka, Hiroshima, and others. Beyer had a good grasp of the circuit and remembered a number of the cities from previous visits. He thought it a wise move to revisit some places each year and to add new cities to the tour to generate more awareness for the business. Beyer felt at ease with Baba, and at home in Japan.

MASKED DECISIONS

With his family ensconced in a suite at the Hotel New Japan, located in the same neighborhood as the Latin Quarter where Rikidozan was stabbed years earlier, The Destroyer, Baba, and the wrestling brigade that included foreigners Killer Karl Kox, Abdullah, Gordon Nelson, Man Mountain Mike, Ray Mendoza, Joe Leduc and Angelo Mosca, made the rounds to the wrestling halls and left fans with memories for a lifetime. During his off time, Beyer as Destroyer escorted his family on visits to cities and villages in Japan; He got the sense that the Japanese people showed him more respect on this particular tour than on previous excursions through Japan. He wondered if the sight of his wife and children accompanying him humanized his character and perhaps rendered him more mortal in their eyes. Regardless of the speculation, Beyer knew he had to work hard as the masked villain to help Baba maintain pro wrestling vitality in the country. The Destroyer wrestled well to numerous wins and a few losses, mostly in team matches, but he was troubled by what he perceived as a loss of spirit in Antonio Inoki, Baba's tag partner in several championships, whose performances Beyer assessed as half-hearted. Inoki had returned to JWA following a defection to a start-up rival and its short-lived operation, and had recently wrestled John Tolos in Los Angeles, where he won the NWA United National Heavyweight title. Beyer thought Inoki may have been fatigued by the travel and grueling schedule of the Japanese wrestlers, and chalked it up to exhaustion.

In Omuta, during a stop along the southernmost end of Fukuoka, Beyer decided to phone the other contact Billy Robinson had given him, Gustl Kaiser in Germany. He knew it likely was a long shot, but wanted to ask the promoter, whom he had never met, if there was work available for a masked man in Europe for the summer and, if not, he needed to make other plans soon. Beyer didn't need to make other plans. Kaiser had received advanced word on Beyer's sensational work as The Destroyer – from Billy Robinson – and invited him to participate in several tournaments that were to be held in Germany from June to August. *"Wunderbar,"* he said to Beyer upon hearing The

Destroyer was invading central Europe. Robinson's good word had resulted in another several weeks of work for Beyer in Germany, and another part of the world for his family to experience.

The Japan tour wrapped up in mid-May, and provided Baba the bump needed to move the promotion forward. Beyer, satisfied with the tour and energized by the response of the Japanese, arranged visits to several other countries on the way to Germany. At the departure area of Haneda airport, Beyer in mask, ushered his family through the terminal toward their gate, but this time several Japanese approached Willy and the kids for photos and autographs; "I won't mind coming back here again," Kurt said to his parents as he signed several autographs 'Kurt Destroyer.'

For the next phase of their world tour, India, Italy, and Switzerland occupied their travel itinerary and attention. In New Delhi, Beyer hired a taxi to take him and his family to Agra. Midway on the hours-long journey through barren landscape, they came upon a herd of cattle that had stopped to rest on the roadway. Kris asked the driver why he stopped and to blow the horn; the driver told her it was 'bad to make the cows move' that when they were ready they would get up and go, and he shut off the engine to wait. Eventually the cattle dispersed, and an hour later, in the distance, the family caught sight of the Taj Mahal, standing as a majestic, solitary structure in the middle of the barren land. The Beyers were given a tour of the magnificent white marble structure that was built between 1632 and 1648 on orders by Emperor Shah Jahan in honor of his wife, Mumtaz Muhal, who died in childbirth, and later was entombed in the lower chamber. The 'Crown Palace' became symbolic of a man's love for his wife. They spent the following day in New Delhi, touring and sampling Indian cuisine; Beyer had a number of photographs taken of himself as The Destroyer along the tree-lined avenues of the capital city before they departed for Italy. He had additional photos taken in a gondola floating on the waterways of Venice, standing in front of the Roman Coliseum in Rome, at the base of the Alps in Switzerland, and at other points of interest as crowds of onlookers, who had gathered to observe the white-masked visitor to their lands, walked away smiling from their exposure to the ambassador of good will from America. No matter the language, 'Destroyer' had become universally understood.

The family arrived in Germany in the town of Krefeld, a port on the west bank of the lower Rhine River and known as a center for textiles. Promoter Gustl Kaiser greeted Beyer and provided information on the tournaments and on hotels and campgrounds where many of the wrestlers were staying during the tournament. Beyer bought a camper and a car and headed to the campground for the two-week stay with his family's blessings; they preferred to inhabit natural surroundings rather than a stuffy hotel in town.

The timing could not have been better; the outcome could have been much worse. Within days of arriving in Krefeld, Kris celebrated her eighth birthday and later told friends she was almost drunk on her special day. The circumstances began as a group of wrestlers staying at the same campground heard of Kris' birthday and, out of respect for fellow competitor The Destroyer, wanted to make the day special for his daughter. They insisted on bringing a cake to the celebration. That evening, before the candles were lit, Kris took a small piece of cake and as she bit into it, a peculiar expression came over her sweet, innocent eight-year old face. Her mother, concerned the cake might be spoiled, broke off a small piece, tasted it, and a similar facial expression, though not as sweet and innocent, appeared. The cake was loaded with so much rum Willy was afraid it might burst into flames from the candles now lit atop of it. Quickly, the candles were plucked and the children were given other birthday treats while the wrestlers devoured the cake before the last candle had extinguished. Spiked cake aside, what made the day special for Kris were the stories of events and people told by the wrestlers that kept her enraptured for hours…she didn't miss the cake or icing one lick.

The tournaments in which Beyer participated were spread over five German cities during June, July and August of 1971. Fourteen of the best wrestlers from around the world – from Spain, Hungary, England, Germany and the United States - were invited to compete in the two and three week tournaments; to win, a wrestler had to square off against every wrestler entered in the tournament and either win every match or register the best record. Each one of the hosting cities – Krefeld, Cologne, Wiesbaden, Nurnberg and Munster - held its own 20 consecutive-day tournament. The rules were tighter than pro wrestling in the States and based on the round system: eight five-minute rounds and in the event of a draw, another ten minutes were added to the match.

Beyer and the multi-nationals toured the five cities and gave the German wrestling audiences superb performances that helped to fuel stronger interest in professional wrestling cards in the country. Crowds in Krefeld, Cologne and Wiesbaden erupted into German song during the matches that seemed to intensify during The Destroyer's bouts as they sensed something special in the ring. At each stop on the tour, Beyer told Gustl Kaiser to introduce him in the ring as 'The Intelligent, Sensational, Destroyer'; Kaiser, every time, introduced him as "Dick Beyer, The Destroyer." Questioned by Beyer, Kaiser's reason for doing so was "These people must be told you are German." The main event in every city was the same - The Destroyer against German favorite, Horst Hoffman. Before heading to the ring for each card's finale, Kaiser, the 6'2" and sartorially resplendent promoter, always said to Beyer, "Maybe the German boy wins tonight." Only in Munster, the last town and the last match of the tour, did Kaiser say to Beyer, "Maybe you win tonight," but before they entered the ring, Kaiser whispered "Maybe the German boy wins," and Beyer knew what he had to do. Pleased with the shows and overall results of the tournaments, Kaiser told Beyer it was great having another German on the card and confessed that he leaked information on Beyer's heritage to the press prior to each tournament. "And I thought it was my skills and personality," he said to Kaiser in regard to the enormous fan response generated. Heritage notwithstanding, Beyer had made a remarkable impression on the German people, especially with his matches against Hoffman; those matches, practically overnight, grew to mythical proportions with the wrestling fans in Germany, and put The Destroyer into elite company as a masterful technician and performer they would not soon forget.

Germany turned out to be a three month highlight reel on their trip around the world, not only for Beyer, but for his family. They enjoyed visits to Germany's major cities interwoven with side trips to shops, stores, parks and museums. After each match, Beyer made a routine of taking his family to dinner; one of their favorite establishments in Krefeld, Manfried's, captivated the hearts and palates of Kurt and Kris for the roasted chicken and potato pancakes the restaurant served up hot. Several of the wrestlers from the tournament often joined the Beyer family for dinner, and afterwards regaled the kids with stories about wrestling and interesting facts about the countries from which they came. It was an advanced class in European history and culture told in a very personal way that the kids looked forward to each evening.

At the conclusion of the last tournament in Munster, Beyer saddled up the family gear and mapped out the final segment of their world trip that was to take them through the flower fields of Holland to France, and across the channel to England and Scotland. The major cities of Amsterdam, Paris, London, Edinburgh and their unique historical attractions served as backdrop for the family's snapshot moments, and there were many. At a restaurant in Paris, Beyer was introduced to Andre Roussimoff, a physically imposing figure making a name in pro wrestling. Beyer's kids were shocked to watch the large wrestler throw dishes at a wall in the restaurant – a custom familiar to Parisians but foreign to Kurt and Kris. In London, they visited Madame Tussauds Wax Museum, Big Ben and Buckingham

Palace. Kurt and Kris learned more about the cities and countries they visited than any history book they had read. Toward the closing days in Scotland, of particular interest was a drive through the town of Motherwell, south east of Glascow, and birthplace of Willy's father. The time spent in Motherwell helped Willy place into perspective her family roots and lineage; it was an emotional climax to a most eventful journey. At dinner, she tried out her best Scottish brogue, in response to a challenge issued by her husband and children, who muffled laughs as they watched her order from the menu, rolling her 'R's and refusing to sample the haggis. "You should have served this at Dim's" she said to Beyer who replied, "Customers would have called it a sheep trick."

After a tour that included twenty countries, more than 50,000 miles, took 368 days, that earned him $25,000 and cost $23,000, Dick Beyer arrived in New York City on September 4, 1971, with a world of experiences under his heavyweight belt and, for his wife and children, a lifetime of memories. As a family, they were closer having shared moments few could match. Willy, despite her initial hesitation, loved the time spent with her husband and children, even though much work was required throughout the year to educate and raise three children while moving around foreign lands. All learned a great deal about the world, each other, and themselves as a result, but the bottom line for them, unanimously, was that it had been a fun and thrilling adventure. In the weeks that followed, friends from around the world sent them copies of newspaper and magazine articles describing the visits by The Destroyer and his family. The Destroyer had made headline news in every country, and had achieved a celebrity status that rivaled many movie idols, recording artists, and athletes of the time. For Dick Beyer, it seemed the best of times were ahead.

CHAPTER **16**

DICK BEYER ALWAYS believed that every person had the capacity to make other people happy…some by arriving, others by leaving. Heading back to Minneapolis, he crossed his fingers in hopes that wrestling fans there would welcome the return of the 'reformed' Doctor X.

With his family safe at their farmhouse in Akron, New York, Beyer planned to tarry another year in the Minneapolis territory. He rented a small apartment in Minneapolis for his frequent two to three week gigs. His plan was to work the fourteen to twenty-one day territorial schedule then fly home to Akron for several days to spend time with Willy and the kids before repeating the routine. Having been so close to her husband the past year while touring the world, the return to the previous lifestyle was not an easy adjustment for Willy to make, in fact it was a most difficult one. Three children, lonely nights, and a husband home only a few days a month wore on her in the harsh gray winter of late 1971.

On his first day back in the Minneapolis territory, Beyer was questioned by Verne Gagne in his office for nearly two hours about the places he visited and the matches he wrestled on his year's sabbatical from the territory. Gagne vicariously enjoyed the travels, experiences, and bouts Beyer vividly described; he also thanked Beyer for sending Billy Robinson to the territory the previous September; he was angry to hear about the cancellation of the Australia tour by Barnett, but glad to have dastardly Doctor X back in town. "About that bad ol' Doctor X," Beyer began his next sentence, and for an hour presented an idea about how to use the Doctor's healing powers in the ring; Gagne listened; a new plan was prescribed.

◄ MASKED DECISIONS

Even though they witnessed the unmasking of Doctor X the year before, at the hands of former partner Black Jack Lanza, and were told the fake identity of the Doctor (Bruce Marshall), none of that mattered to the fans; they were only interested in seeing others get even with evil Doctor X; fans never heard of Bruce Marshall and couldn't care less about him – they wanted the Doctor's license to practice in the ring revoked through physical punishment.

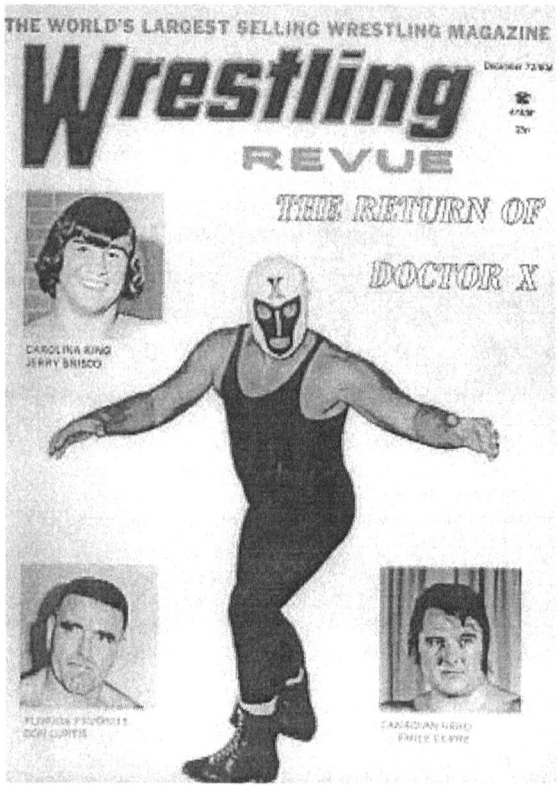

Doctor X was the most compelling masked wrestler in the Midwest

One of the first matches upon his return was a territorially televised tag team bout that paired Doctor X and Larry 'Pretty Boy' Hennig against Bill Howard and George Gadaski. During this match, teammates Hennig and Doctor X, two ultimate heels, had a significant falling out that resulted in a 'turn' and a 'swerve'; Doctor X turned baby face, completely swerving the storyline and putting him on the side of good. This change meant Doctor X was to wrestle other heels who previously were his allies; a feud quickly ramped up between former ring partners Ray 'Crippler' Stevens and Doctor X. Fans were stunned at the sudden shift in direction. Adding to the surprise was the addition of a new mask and outfit modifications by Doctor X. Gone was the solid black mask, replaced by a white mask with a black overlay that covered the area near his eyes, nose and mouth, and a large letter X in the middle of his forehead. He balanced the white mask with white trunks over the black tights and occasionally wore a white tee shirt instead of the black singlet with the imprint of his white mask on the front. The changes softened his appearance in the ring and supported his transition to good guy wrestler who sought revenge for the evil deeds of the heels in the territory. One of the outlaws had become a member of the posse. Wrestling fans, having hated him so long, welcomed his epiphany.

For eight months throughout the vast Minneapolis territory, good Doctor X took on the ill-willed likes of Hennig, Lars Anderson, Chris Markoff, Ivan Koloff, Dusty Rhodes, and teamed with Red Bastien, Wahoo McDaniel, The Crusher, Billy Robinson, Bull Bullinski, and Don Muraco to tackle Bockwinkel/Stevens, the Hennig/Anderson team and others. Sales of his masks and tee shirts – with the face of Doctor X on the front – grew. The transformation took hold. No longer reviled, Doctor X was revered. However the forty-two year old Beyer, wrestling since he was nineteen, grew concerned about pain he began to experience in his right leg. His knee was giving him trouble especially as he endeavored to clamp on the figure four leg lock. A visit to a physician and an x-ray revealed that reconstructive knee surgery was required. Since this was to take him out of action nearly all summer of 1972, the promoters created a scenario to excuse the doctor and provide an appropriate alibi.

Televised on the Minneapolis territory All Star Television Wrestling Network, a grudge match between Ray Stevens and Doctor X drew very strong attention, as the super villain and ex-villain grappled all over the ring. Toward the latter part of the match, Stevens managed to get the right leg of his opponent tangled up in the lower rope as Doctor X dangled precariously out of the ring over the hard surfaces of the floor. With the leg completely exposed and vulnerable to attack, Stevens unleashed an assault of kicks, punches, and even hit the knee with the timekeeper's bell. There was no escaping the beating from the enraged Stevens. At that moment, other wrestlers came down to the ring to assist the Doctor and stop the punishment he was absorbing. Disentangled from the rope, Doctor X lay on the canvas writhing in agony; wrestling colleagues helped carry him out as the Doctor pulled up on his mask to breathe more comfortably. It was reported that he was taken to the local hospital, where he was to undergo surgery and rehabilitation for several weeks.

The storyline in place in Minneapolis, Beyer returned home to Akron to have the reconstructive knee surgery performed at a hospital in Buffalo. He checked into the hospital, underwent surgery, and later recuperated and rehabbed at his farmhouse. Kurt 12, Kris, 9, and Richie 4 helped their father recover by fetching him the morning *Courier Express* newspaper, coffee, and staying just out of reach as their dad chased them around the farm land. By late summer, his knee was better and Beyer was ready to return to the ring; Willy wasn't quite ready to let go.

Doctor X reclaimed momentum on the Minneapolis trail, defeating Pete Carlos, Hans Herman, Dusty Rhodes, Bobby Van, Mike Spangler, Great Hamaguchi, and others, showing fans and opponents that his knee was better than ever, as was his appeal. Beyer was also given a few different combinations of tag partners that included Crusher Lisowski, Bull Bullinski, Wahoo McDaniel, and even Mad Dog Vachon, but was never able to pull the AWA tag title away from Stevens and Bockwinkel. Perhaps the most intriguing partner he had during the fall of 1972 was an enormous Frenchman who had come to North America as a work-in-progress for champion wrestler Edouard Carpentier, and was making a giant name in many territories throughout the States. Andre Roussimoff stood close to seven feet tall and weighed within a few pounds of four hundred. His size and strength made it difficult to maintain and match him with opponents in any one territory, so he was rotated frequently around a number of territories. Beyer first met Andre in France in 1971 during Beyer's world tour and later in Springfield, Illinois, where both were working a card; since they were also scheduled to work the next stop in Chicago as a tag team, they decided to travel to Chicago together in Beyer's car. Before the trip was underway, they picked up some beer, a bottle of vodka and some snacks. Beyer and Andre got along well during the drive but every so often, Andre turned to Beyer and said "Boss, we need beer." Every-so-often turned into very frequently and before he knew it, Beyer had made multiple stops for beer; the trip took longer than the original three plus hours it was to take and Andre had consumed, by Beyer's calculation, approximately forty-two beers and the entire bottle of vodka…and never asked to stop for a restroom. Beyer was dumbfounded watching Andre, who without any physical signs of overconsumption, got out of the car in Chicago, grabbed his luggage, and said "Let's go drink." Andre's reputation, in the business and in the bars, became legendary.

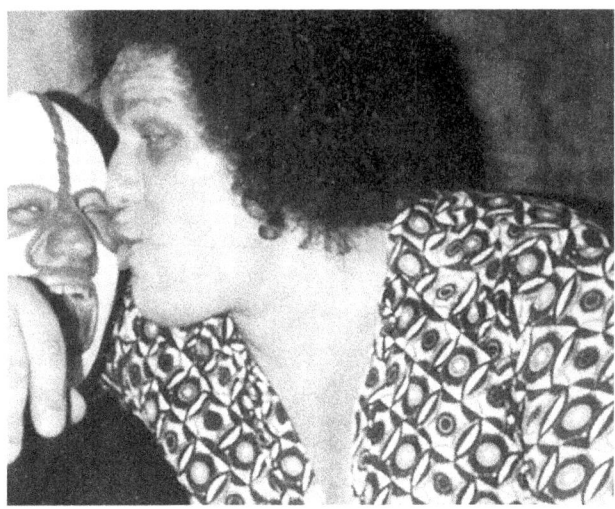

Andre was a legend in many ways

MASKED DECISIONS

It had been a year of volatility for wrestling in Japan. Only hours after Beyer and his family departed Tokyo for Europe the previous May, Antonio Inoki requested from the Japan Pro Wrestling Commission an opportunity to wrestle away the NWA International Heavyweight title held by teammate Giant Baba. The Commission deferred the matter to the jurisdiction of the JWA which, in turn, ruled that the request was premature and denied Inoki's shot at Baba's title. In early December, Inoki and Baba lost their international tag team title to the Funk Brothers; one week later, Inoki was fired from the JWA for allegedly plotting to take over the promotion. This stunning development caused a rift in the Inoki/Baba relationship that lead to Inoki forming a rival promotion, New Japan Pro Wrestling. As Inoki's business took flight, JWA disintegrated. A contract with NTV for the exclusive air rights to Baba's matches was breached when JWA allowed rival network NET to broadcast a Baba bout. NTV broke away from airing JWA matches and soon Baba decided he had enough; he vacated his NWA International Heavyweight title, resigned from JWA and formed his own promotion, All Japan Pro Wrestling, with partner NTV granted the broadcast rights. Rikidozan's star students, Inoki and Baba, once close as brothers in rekindling JWA after Rikidozan's death, became enemies and drew off the remaining talent from JWA, effectively setting the stage for the dissolution of the former dominant wrestling association in the country.

Since his last match with Inoki in Osaka, Beyer had a hunch something was amiss with the star Japanese wrestler, so it came as little surprise that Inoki was no longer with JWA, however, the rest of the story was big news to Beyer. He knew his friend Baba well enough to know that things must have been very difficult for Baba to decide to leave JWA and form his own promotion. These developments in the Far East came to light at a time when Beyer was scheduled to end his term as Doctor X in Minneapolis, in December, and depart for his tenth tour of Japan as The Destroyer. Preparations for his trip were underway when he received a phone call from friend Charlie Iwamoto, who was working the Los Angeles territory as a booker, asking if he had interest in working with him for the territory in which his Destroyer had become a huge star. With no definitive plans once he was to return from Japan, Beyer agreed to the offer and begin his official duties in January of 1973. In November 1972, Doctor X wrestled Dusty Rhodes in Fargo, North Dakota; with well-wishes from Verne Gagne, Beyer departed the AWA and the Minneapolis territory, leaving behind for wrestling fans bold contrasting memories of the evil and good Doctor X, the greatest masked man in AWA history, one of the most beguiling and compelling wrestlers ever to work the territory, and a duality that was never to be seen again.

The news was a prayer answered for Willy, who viewed the booker job as a way for her husband to downsize his schedule and find more time for her and his family. She went so far as to believe that they would make Los Angeles home for a longer period this time around. What followed next was something neither she nor her husband expected, much less imagined.

Beyer flew to Japan and was shocked and saddened to see the state of Baba's promotion. The corps of wrestlers that had joined with Baba was not a caliber that would attract fans and hold their interest for lengths of time. It was a team with one star and Beyer knew from his years of experience that no promotion could grow and sustain itself without several good heels and baby faces. What kept Baba afloat to that point were the foreign wrestlers who, like Beyer, had come to Japan to help spur on Baba's new promotion.

Beyer had choices. He was welcome to remain with the JWA, such as it was, and tour till it shut down or hold out for an offer from Inoki's New Japan Pro Wrestling which was gaining popularity throughout the country. He could return to the States, work as a booker in L.A. and, from time to time, pick up additional work in other territories as

MASKED DECISIONS

The Destroyer. Assessing the talent, or lack thereof, that Baba had put together for his series, and the dim long range survival prospects for Baba's new promotion, Beyer intuitively recognized his choice. With thoughts of Shibuyu Station and the story of the faithful dog Hachiko, Beyer had long ago placed his own loyalty with Baba. The decision was a natural. When Baba asked him to join his promotion and forego work with the others, he unhesitatingly accepted. For the short term, Beyer would visit Japan a few times a year and wrestle for Baba, but for the long term, Baba's promotion required a transfusion, and Beyer knew where to find a donor. The next step was the tricky one.

With help from Baba and his associates, Beyer arranged a meeting with Akira Hara, a high-ranking executive of NTV, the network that agreed to partner with Baba in his All Japan Pro Wrestling venture. Banking on his popularity and celebrity as The Destroyer, and his credibility and expertise in the wrestling business, Beyer said to the Japanese television executive, "You need me." Asked to explain, Beyer replied, "You need me –The Destroyer- as Baba's wrestling partner." For the balance of the afternoon, Beyer articulated a well-crafted rationale, storyline, and timetable that, in the end, would prove to be a substantial investment in All Japan Pro Wrestling and an enormous publicity grab for the promotion. The executive was reluctant to go all in; Beyer was unrelenting. The verbal exchanges were heated and by late evening the two exhausted men had found common ground.

At the television studios of NTV during its weekly broadcasted wrestling show, The Destroyer got in front of the camera and presaged what was to come: "I will wrestle Baba on television; I am so confident I will win that I stake this claim - if I can't beat him, I will join him; I will become his tag team partner and remain in Japan for one year." The do-or-die announcement, with the stipulation that a loss meant The Destroyer had to become a full-time wrestler in Japan, caused a murmur among the wrestling faithful, and even those generally less enthused by the business were hooked by the angle. The news spread throughout the country. Ordinary Japanese asked 'if he loses, would the masked American really join forces with *archrival Baba?'* Beyer had placed all his eggs in one basket and relied on his star quality in Japan to put the story over and help give Baba the foundation he needed to succeed.

The final step for Beyer was the trickiest of all – telling Willy.

The long distance phone call Beyer made to his wife was expensive in several ways. She did not immediately buy into the plan as an investment and, in fact, retained a large percentage for emotional bad debt. She was less than ecstatic by the proposed shortened term in L.A. in exchange for the extended stay in Tokyo. "After a year, then what?" she said to Beyer's details about working in Japan. The nomadic existence of a professional wrestler and his family was tough enough in continental United States; the prospect of living abroad- after a year's world travel- on top of the series of relocations since 1959, placed Willy and her husband at one of life's intersections without a yield sign. The ensuing discussion was tense, terse and troubling. The final answer, decided more by capitulation than consensus, was not without Willy's reservations duly noted.

On December 19, 1972 in Niigata Japan, the birthplace of Shohei Baba, a wrestling war unlike others unfolded in the ring between Giant Baba and The Destroyer. The sold out arena and millions watching NTV were privy to what Beyer later called "Another hell of a bout" between the two gargantuan personalities. The match undeniably was a ratings and publicity success for NTV and All Japan Pro Wrestling– few Japanese were unaware of the consequences while most pulled for their hometown hero to render the popular masked American a migrant worker for Japanese wrestling. The technical superiority of the wrestlers was on full display that evening; both jockeyed for positional control and provided many moments of impending doom followed by edgy anticipation for those watching. At its conclusion, though neither opponent achieved a dominant advantage, Baba was declared the winner by a count out of the ring on The Destroyer.

MASKED DECISIONS

Absolute frenzy broke out in the arena. The television cameras caught the ecstatic crowd in full celebration before zeroing in on the defeated masked American, who in center ring took to the microphone and said, "I don't like the way things turned out…he didn't beat me and I didn't win…but I'm a man of my word…since I didn't beat him, I'll join him." Baba and The Destroyer shook hands, cementing their agreement and, in effect, making The Destroyer an indentured servant in Japan; the crowd exploded.

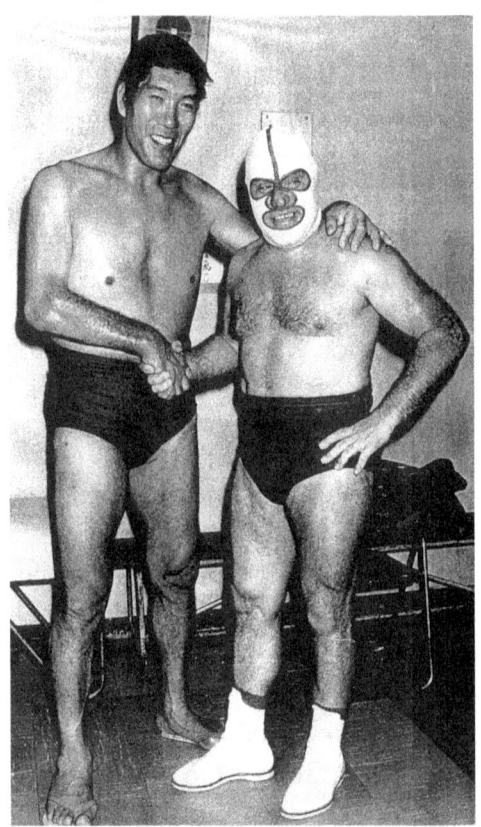

Baba and Destroyer dominated Japanese wrestling

In the world of wrestling, it was a seismic event. Former enemies from different countries had become partners. An American masked wrestler was about to wrestle *for* the Japanese. It marked the first time in history an American wrestling star committed to performing full time in Japan. More importantly, it was the first time any American wrestler had ever joined forces with the Japanese team to fight other *gaijin*, from the U.S. or other countries. New history was being written. The ring announcer informed the audience that Moose Morowski and Cyclone Negro -two former tag partners of The Destroyer during this tour - demanded to battle the Japanese/American team; the match was set for Korakuen Hall. Less than 24 hours later, the newly formed alliance of Baba and 'De-stroy-yaa' had beaten the *gaijins* handily for what was to be the first of many wins for the supremely regarded wrestling powerhouse. The Japanese fans, overwhelmed by the popularity and civil union of the new dynamic duo of Japanese wrestling, carried Baba and The Destroyer out of the arena on their shoulders like conquering crusaders. Beyer's pop celebrity as The Destroyer was large, but nothing compared to what was to come.

The significance of the partnership of Baba, Destroyer, and NTV that emerged in December of 1972 carried well beyond the wrestling ring. Nothing like it had been seen before in American pro wrestling or in Japanese 'Puroresu'; in fact, it was rare in any sport. Many likened it to imagining the Bill Russell-led Boston Celtics of the 1960s signing Wilt Chamberlain – two big dominant players on the same club. For the Japanese it was unusual and irregular behavior. They had never accepted a foreigner as honorary Japanese, let alone a masked heel from America. For Dick Beyer, the experience was even more profound.

He instantly recognized the irony; an empire he long ago feared and abhorred, a land that infatuated him, a country he had grown to love was about to become his home. Turning pro in 1954 was a nodal event that put Beyer on a winding path. Eight years later in the Los Angeles territory, he was presented a gift, which he eventually decided to accept – to be a masked man. Throughout his lifetime, Beyer made plenty of momentous decisions ranging from college and fraternity selections to embracing amateur wrestling, grad school, teaching, marriage, from moving his Destroyer character into new territories, creating Doctor X, to working from home. These choices - or masked decisions as he later called them - were complex puzzles whose solutions and outcomes were crucial to his future and which triggered unforeseen repercussions. Beyer made the tough calls, sometimes under intense pressure, with the best available information guided by his values. He was decisive. To him it was the only way. The one-year commitment he made to Baba, to work for and alongside him as one of the good guys in Japan, was a decision that did not come without consequences, immediate and unplanned. He knew that too. He also had never worked as a baby face Destroyer and had never before entered into an arrangement quite like this one. It was all so unfamiliar.

CHAPTER 17

FROM WHAT SEEMED like a never-ending, tornadic, 'to do list' written in January of 1973, Beyer and Willy pushed through the vortex of activity and by mid-March found themselves in a rented house near Ichigaya Station in central Tokyo, in walking distance to the main broadcast facilities of NTV, for which Destroyer was to do wrestling shows when his job with Baba commenced.

Packing and making arrangements for a trip around the world was a wing's worth of chicken meat in comparison to what it took to bring this move forward for what was expected to be only a year's stay in Japan. There were so many things to get done. As usual, Willy bore the brunt of addressing the domestic details for her family. It was not easy on her. Perhaps it was the layered years of uprooting or the thought of another lengthy stay abroad that contributed to her unsettled mood, but for the first time in their marriage she was not fully committed to a change of territory. On the day before Beyer had called her to tell of Baba's offer to work in Japan, she had secretly placed a down payment on another contiguous 85 acres of land that Beyer had coveted for years and that she believed would anchor him more to Western New York; the land – with 2,000 feet of road frontage on Sandhill Road, 3 barns and a generous wooded area – had a posted 'sold' sign that Beyer was shocked to see when he returned from Japan and asked Willy if she knew who bought the property; she replied, "Yes, you did." While the purchase of the prized property delighted Beyer, he was oblivious to the underlying reason for his wife's actions, and it did nothing to alter his plans for the move. Unusual for her, Willy felt listless and harbored a queasy sense of foreboding. Despite her misgivings, she conveyed only positive regard for the upcoming trip to her children and had most everything in order

MASKED DECISIONS

by the time Beyer returned to Buffalo from his commitment as a booker for the Los Angeles territory. It was an abbreviated stint, but Beyer used his time wisely to schedule himself as Destroyer into several matches for a few good paydays; the boys didn't mind – they knew the crowds would be larger. While in L.A. he even hooked up in the ring again with old buddy Freddie Blassie, but Beyer's mind was on Japan, and once he finished his three-month booker job, he flew to Buffalo to help with final preparations. Beyer made arrangements for the maintenance of his property and handled the legal paperwork for living abroad. As family and friends bade farewell to them at the airport, Beyer and his wife shepherded their children onboard the airplane for another family adventure. Unlike their previous trips however, this one held hidden seeds of disharmony.

Like summer in Buffalo, time was short. The extensive tour of Japan, arranged by Baba's new enterprise, was scheduled to begin within days of the Beyer family's move to Tokyo and last weeks. Beyer did not want to be on the road so soon and away from his new home and family, but knew it was essential for the tour. He longed to start his full time job as Baba's partner for television and regional matches in June; so did Willy. Before his departure, Beyer helped Willy settle into their short-term rental home and enroll Kurt at St. Mary's International School and Kris at Seisen International School, both private institutions attended by children of other expatriates. They scouted the area for shopping, services, and medical facilities, and found support from several nearby Americans. One of those Americans, Clark Hatch, a Minnesotan and former Army serviceman, had opened a fitness center in Tokyo eight years earlier and, from its colossal success, expanded his business to Seoul, South Korea. Hatch invited Beyer to workout at his facility and within no time a friendship emerged, followed by others, that buttressed Beyer and his family. It appeared that, in a number of ways, their entry into the Oriental lifestyle was better than expected.

Beyer departed for the tour with Baba and his associates, joining foreign talent that included King Iaukea, Baron Scicluna, Mark Lewin,

Mad Russian, Tony Parisi, George McCreary, Cyclone Negro, and Moose Morowski. This tour originated in Tokyo before making stops in Shibukawa, Ninohe, Kuji, Futaba, and numerous other Japanese cities and towns, and ended in Fukui where Baba defeated Lewin to win what was called the Carnival Tournament. The Destroyer was feted to a royal welcome in every hall and arena in every city and village, especially since turning baby face and working with, not against, national hero Baba. Interest in The Destroyer as a scientific wrestler and underneath the hood deepened now that the Japanese had him on their side as a full-time employee; what made him special to them beyond his wrestling acumen was his respect for their traditions and his unique way of engaging and communicating with them. Beyer committed himself during this particularly arduous tour to creating a new tone and tenor in his matches; he wanted to punctuate each performance with superb wrestling technique and showmanship, so that fans clamored to see more of the masked man; leaving them wanting was his way of thanking Baba for the opportunity.

When Beyer returned home from the long tour, he was contacted by executives from NTV to come to the broadcast facilities for a meeting. Beyer thought the meeting was to discuss the televised wrestling matches; he was wrong. The Destroyer's move to Japan had been extensively covered by the media and his arrival on their shores was headline news. NTV had launched a new musical comedy show on Friday nights whose ratings were not doing well. The producers were searching for something to help it along and thought that bringing on The Destroyer as a featured guest that week could do no harm. A one-time appearance was negotiated between Beyer and NTV. Beyer went home and talked it over with his wife and kids who gave him unanimous approval. Friday night, the show aired live. Willy and the kids sat in front of the television set watching the bizarre antics unfold. Kurt and Kris could not understand a thing. Though each had Japanese dictionaries in their hands, the Japanese cast members spoke so fast that nothing could be deciphered. But whatever The Destroyer did, the audience seemed to love, and the cast of the show laughed hysterically. But no one was laughing in the network executive suite – they had a decision to make.

At his rented home, Beyer asked his family to be seated at the kitchen table, where all serious matters were discussed, to assess their adaptation to living in Japan. He worried that, in order to make him feel better, they were holding back their true feelings about living overseas. "Tell me honestly how you like it here," he said to his two older children. Thirteen-year old Kurt and ten- year old Kris told him they were adjusting well; they found friends in their English-speaking school and were eager to learn Japanese; four-year old Richie stayed home with his mother where she taught him basics. Willy took Richie during the day to explore nearby neighborhoods; two blocks from Azabu Juban - the old world foothills south of the city- near San-No-Hashi, she found an apartment in a twelve-story residential building known as Mita House. The apartment building housed a grocery store, barber shop, and other amenities on the ground level and, on clear days, the vacant sixth floor, three-bedroom apartment offered a captivating view of Mount Fuji, located sixty miles to the southwest. She thought it would be idyllic.

The family moved into Mita House in September, three months after Beyer had begun his new duties that included weekly television appearances on Baba's Saturday evening wrestling show on NTV. Three or four times a week, he travelled by car or train to an arena to work for Baba's All Japan Pro Wrestling promotion. Baba and Beyer months earlier had agreed to a compensation and expense plan that placed Beyer in an enviable position to that of other wrestling stars.

Adapting to the new culture and environment was more perplexing for Willy. With the children occupying most of her time, she was not in the company of other adults or bi-lingual Japanese, and thus not in position to absorb the language or societal mores as quickly as her family. She was a stay-at-home mom in the truest sense, and it cost her social currency. Beyer, while home most nights, worked more hours so that Willy actually saw less of him and, as a result, their interactions began to decline. Without complaining to him, she felt disaffected. Both knew that with his work schedule expanding, their time together and relationship would be further tested; just how much they soon discovered.

NTV's broadcast of professional wrestling each Saturday evening from 8:00 pm to 9:00 pm was earning mostly marginal ratings. Baba used his sway with promoters in the States, Australia and Europe to attract the best wrestling talent and keep that talent flowing into Japan, and his business. Aside from signing The Destroyer and Jumbo Tsuruta, the influx of *gaijin* heels helped put his promotion on track and into the collective awareness of the Japanese. Beyer lauded Baba - known in Japan as *'Touyou no Kyojin'* or Giant of the Orient- for his foresight in recruiting international wrestling stars. They kept the arena and television productions fresh. To further aggrandize the shows, Beyer as Destroyer used his masterful skills on camera and with the microphone to articulate scenarios of what fans could expect at the matches or on the next broadcast. He spoke directly to the television audience; using an interpreter, he told them, "I appreciate your letters and support for Baba and me…and if you write me a letter in English, I promise I will write back to you." After weeks of wrestling, promoting and marketing, his fan base responded, and he began writing many more return letters.

From The Destroyer fan mail and other mail received at the television studio, Beyer and Baba, with help from the network, analyzed the Japanese wrestling fan demographic; the conclusion was that while the base appreciated and understood wrestling, the number of fans watching the television show wasn't growing on the trajectory they had hoped. In addition, Inoki's New Japan Pro Wrestling and Kokusai International Pro Wrestling promotions were formidable competitors with loyal supporters. The question became how to grow the fan base and what business model or means should be used. Beyer knew that in the public eye The Destroyer was closely linked to Baba, and he reasoned that a higher profile for Destroyer meant more awareness for the TV show and Baba's business. He had inclinations of asking NTV for more appearance opportunities, but that approach was likely to be rejected by the network and Baba as too self-serving. Beyer hatched a brilliant idea - let the request come from the viewers.

As he wrote back to the scores of letter writers, he asked them to call NTV and request to see The Destroyer on other types of television programs. Beyer's plan was designed to get Destroyer onto mainstream television shows so that fans less inclined toward wrestling would become aware of the personality of the masked man, and with their curiosity piqued, drive them to Baba's matches and televised wrestling shows. He thought that if he could get 100 or more callers to ask for The Destroyer's appearance on other shows, he might have a chance to convince the executives, earn spots on regular programming, and help develop and attract new fans to Baba's wrestling enterprise. It wasn't necessary – the volume of calls was overwhelming. Soon thereafter, The Destroyer had made guest appearances on a noontime cooking show, a game show, and other programming where, in limited Japanese, he drummed up interest for Saturday night wrestling on television and Baba's arena shows. Those who knew of The Destroyer saw him under very different circumstances and enjoyed it, telling others in the process; word spread fast; those who were not wrestling followers were intrigued by this personable masked wrestler. The response from the Japanese viewing audience was so positive it moved NTV to find imaginative ways to slot The Destroyer into selected programs.

One of the most popular live shows on Japanese television in the early 1970s was a musical format known as *Kohaku Best 10 Show*; similar to America's 'Your Hit Parade' of the 1950s, it featured a selection of top tunes of the week sung by various performers on a large stage in front of thousands of people. NTV executives, recalling their earlier experience with the burly masked wrestler, took a chance and inserted an off-beat segment.

During one episode, a teenage singer named Sakurada Junko was positioned in front of a tranquil bay set as she sang a popular sweet melody about a bluebird, *Aoi Tori*. Midway through the delightful song, five ruffian dock workers (trained stuntmen) crowded around the singer, cut off the song, and frightened the teenager. As they slowly closed in toward her, she yelled out in Japanese, "Oh, Destroyer, save me!" When the television camera panned slowly up a fifteen-foot flight of steps, the curtain at the top parted to reveal The Destroyer standing in his familiar arms-cross-his-chest pose, staring down and shaking his head at the evil doers. The audience gasped and applauded at the sight of the towering masked man surrounded by barrels and dock ropes on his perch high above the stage. On television, it looked much more dramatic. The Destroyer quickly descended the steps and on live television with no rehearsal, grabbed two gangsters and pushed them down, picked up another and airplane-spun him, tracked down another climbing up the steps and tossed him into the arms of the other gang members standing on the floor below – the bad guys fled. With the hoodlums dispatched, Junko resumed her song as her hero The Destroyer sat beside her to protect against further intrusion. It was a touching scene. Japanese television viewers loved the spot as did the television executives of his improvisational work. That the valiant American masked wrestler acted to protect a young Japanese girl, and by inference Japan itself, so ingratiated The Destroyer with the Japanese public, their emotional response became indicative of the deferential regard in which they held him. The following week, NTV featured The Destroyer in a different segment with five comedians. The Japanese viewing public again was enthralled. Viewer reaction pushed the needle to its limit. NTV discovered it had a burgeoning television star - cloaked in a mask, white boots and short trunks.

How did all this happen? Beyer, early each morning, sat at home over coffee in amazing disbelief of the whirlwind of TV appearances and fuss over his Destroyer character by the Japanese. What began as a way to nurture a new base of fans for Baba's wrestling promotion had, as an unintended consequence, skyrocketed The Destroyer into a media sensation. The family was excited by the hot spotlight of attention and curiosity shone onto The Destroyer; they enjoyed it on two levels – the second-hand recognition as the family of a celebrity and the pride of achievement for the man under the mask, the real Dick Beyer. They had the best of both worlds…without the mask, they were a normal expatriate family in Japan taking in the cultural, social and entertainment experiences of the country; with the mask, Willy and the kids became the family of a star and were accorded the trappings of the status. Beyer was particularly careful in these early stages not to let the sudden rise of fame adversely impact the children. He spoke to them often and counseled them against getting 'too big for their britches' as his father used to tell him during his successes in school sports. He was fully aware of Willy's strong insistence on as 'normal' a life as they could provide for them. For her, all the commotion was put into the bracket of 'it comes with the territory' and she believed it would end sooner than later, in fact, she pined for it.

Behind the walls deep within the belly of the network compound, executives at NTV were in furtive discussions about their weekly musical comedy series whose ratings surged in popularity after the one time appearance by the American wrestler. With a new title - *Uwasa No Channel* – and modeled loosely after the 1960s American television legend *Rowan and Martin's Laugh-in*, the show was formatted to showcase some of Japan's emerging musical and comedy artists – singer and actress Akiko Wada, teenage singer/model Maggie Minenko, actor Mitsuo Senda, and comedian Masayuki Uhara. Another name under serious consideration for the show was a masked wrestler - The Destroyer. Despite the hour-long length of the late night Friday show, NTV officials believed, with the Japanese cast they had assembled, the addition of the masked Destroyer, who at this point was not fluent in conversational Japanese, nonetheless gave the show broader appeal and latitude, especially in comedic situations, with a way in and out of completely outrageous skits.

Beyer was dyspneic by the offer; *they want me, an American wrestler, on a weekly variety TV show*! Since it meant a change to his Friday wrestling schedule, he dashed over to request permission from Baba to do the program before returning to the television offices to firm up the deal and enter into planning meetings for bits and routines. Baba knew of the offer in advance from network officials and gave Beyer his tepid approval. Beyer told his family he had signed on to the weekly show; the kids were thrilled, Willy smiled and though happy, told him she was concerned about the impact on his wrestling career – a concern shared by her husband who told her, "I will approach each sketch carefully; I will not put myself in situations where my wrestling image might diminish in the eyes of the public." She hesitated for a moment…then nodded; she held back from him her true personal concern.

Production began shortly after Beyer was contractually signed. On the first day of rehearsals, Beyer was introduced to Carol Abe, a woman from Hawaii, who was to serve as his official interpreter with cast and crew. She laughed during their first meeting, telling Beyer that when the producers asked her to be the interpreter for The Destroyer, she thought they meant an entire ship! Unfamiliar as he was to her, the cast was largely unknown to Beyer, but all interacted well and played off each other's talents, as the show took on the situation comedy format of a household, the Japanese were cast as family members with Destroyer as a house guest; special guest stars were to be invited weekly to round out the show's variety. Teen singing sensation Maggie Minenko, an American model of Japanese and Russian heritage, fluent in Japanese, and who would go on to record two hit singles (*Moeru Boom Boom* and *Namida no Kawa*) within the year, became close to the Beyer family, especially Willy, and spent many nights at the Beyer home as a houseguest. In a reversal of sorts, life was truly imitating art.

Uwasa No Channel re-debuted in October of 1973. During the first several episodes, Beyer as The Destroyer appeared in comedy bits for

MASKED DECISIONS

which he memorized his Japanese lines phonetically. To the viewer, his pronunciations sounded funny, but his delivery made his communications endearing and enormously entertaining; few people realized he was actually learning to speak Japanese, not in a formal classroom setting, but by casual conversation with Abe, cast, crew, and others willing to listen and help him. As his Japanese speaking ability improved and became more discernable, the television executives asked him to relinquish the formality and revert to his original 'broken Japanese' on camera, since it had developed into a special part of the show's appeal. Beyer obliged but continued his Japanese lessons behind the scenes.

Rehearsals were held every Friday morning at 10:00 am; the ensemble ran through ideas for the live opening, then taped several hours of comedy bits from which the best twenty minutes were chosen for air during the early part of the show; that was to be followed by another live segment featuring musical or comedy guests. Beyer drove from Mita House to rehearsals, at times as The Destroyer to jack up public awareness on the street, at other times without the mask to find solace from the recognition. On his way to the studios, he occasionally stopped by the working class neighborhood of Azabu Juban; it always gave him a sense of what old world Tokyo must have been like. More importantly, seeing the people perform their everyday tasks sensitized him to remain cognizant and respectful of their traditions and values. With his career flying, his ego was tethered by his observations of their simple yet noble work. Beyer liked to stop by the Palace Restaurant, next door to Tanimura's Appliance Store, located on a narrow side street in Azabu Juban. The restaurant earned a reputation as a gathering spot for American expatriates and visiting foreigners staying up the hill in nearby Roppongi - home to numerous embassies - in addition to its abundance of good Japanese and western style comfort food. Beyer had come to know and respect the owners of both the restaurant and the appliance store, and the feeling was mutual. Beyer was drawn by the story of the Palace's owner, known simply as Master

– so named for his culinary skills- and his wife Masako. Masako Hada was one of three daughters of a father whose surname, Hada, was to be discontinued once the three daughters married, as he had no sons. In honor of and respect for her father and his heritage, Master took Masako's surname at their wedding ceremony – rather than have her adopt his surname – so that the Hada lineage would continue in Japan uninterrupted. Beyer found the story appealing for the sacrifice, loyalty and devotion it carried. As poignant a story as it was, a much different circumstance led Beyer to his relationship with the appliance store owner, Mitsuaki Tanimura.

In 1964, Beyer was in Tokyo for a friend's wedding, and had ordered from the Duty Free store several watches to be delivered to his room; Tanny was the delivery boy. Having never heard of The Destroyer or Dick Beyer, Tanny proceeded to the hotel room to deliver the package. Once inside the room, he was told by Beyer to sit and wait while he attended to another delivery of shirts. Tanny overheard Beyer say to the shirt deliveryman, "These shirts are the wrong size…I cannot wear them to the wedding…please bring me a larger size shirt or I will throw you out this ninth floor window." Tanny caught a wink in the large American's eye and knew he was not serious with the threat, but the deliveryman, who was tipped off that Beyer was the evil Destroyer (also known to the Japanese as *Wanakeeko* or White Devil) was frightened out of his skin, and nervously laughed as he exited, backwards, from the hotel room, returning within minutes with many larger shirts…but remained near the door and never crossed the threshold. Tanny, who over the years learned to speak more than eight languages, developed a close relationship with the American wrestler during tours by The Destroyer and became a trusted confidant.

Each *Uwasa No Channel* episode began with the cast strutting in line onto the stage from the wings snapping their fingers and moving their arms up and down, in the manner of a big band singer, with The Destroyer bringing up the rear. It became common place during the show for Akiko and other cast members to hit The Destroyer over the head with folded paper fans and various objects; it never ceased to generate enormous laughter as the masked man reacted to the blows with wide-eyed surprise and animated gestures. Readying the cast to move out to the stage one night, the prop man, as a lark, placed a German army helmet on The Destroyer's head. Beyer immediately thought of Arte Johnson's character Wolfgang the German soldier from 'Laugh-in' and wanted no part of the helmet. Just as he was about to remove it, live television forced Beyer as Destroyer to go out on stage with the helmet low on his masked head. The audience, and even the cast, roared at the sight of the large well-known American wrestler with the German helmet over his trademark mask, in his short white overalls and white wrestling boots. From that moment forward, the helmet became a staple of his on-stage wardrobe. The Destroyer as a television performer, with a comedic presence that delighted and fascinated audiences, had emerged.

Within the course of three months, *Uwasa No Channel*, the Japanese cast, and The Destroyer became familiar, recognizable, everyday names throughout all Japan. Though the program gave viewers opportunities to see the very top artists of Japan – Pink Lady, Sakurada Junko, Yamaguchi Momoe, The Four Leaves, Go Hiromi, Goro, Downtown Boogie Woogie Band, Southern All Stars, Char and others – it was the cast that stole the attention. They were the weekly headlines and cover stories. They were on the minds and on the lips of the Japanese. Those who had not been exposed to the wrestler's identity before the show gravitated to his mask, mannerisms, comedy antics, and sideways delivery of Japanese words. The show and ensemble shot to stardom. By December of 1973, *Uwasa No Channel* was the most popular program on TV and the number one rated show in Japan, garnering an unbelievable 37% television rating.

The show's popularity grew, and as it did, it made The Destroyer, already a wrestling star, such a mega celebrity his personal appearances rivaled those of movie, governmental, sports, and other public figures with years of fame behind them. It didn't matter that he was not Japanese…to the Japanese he was an adopted son, not *gaijin* to be ignored, or anything other than a television and wrestling personality they simply adored. The Destroyer was theirs and, like his own family, they protected him as one of their own. At a time when foreigners were not well regarded, The Destroyer's ascension to superstar status was remarkable and unprecedented. His popularity, in turn, uplifted the attendance at Baba's All Japan Pro Wrestling events – an original goal of Beyer's plan had been fulfilled. Baba, however, was troubled; he had visions of Destroyer's wrestling matches turning into circus acts with buffoonery and clowning. In measured, quiet, almost bitter tones he said to Beyer during a meeting, "You make people laugh," referencing the television program. Beyer responded, "You don't have to worry…I will not let any match become a comedy…like you I take wrestling seriously…and will always wrestle the way it's supposed to be done." The frank exchange between Beyer and Baba was necessary for both; it focused them on keeping the matches good contests that the Japanese wrestling public would appreciate and support by their attendance. It reaffirmed for both that wrestling was number one. It brought them closer.

The television show and the wrestling went on, mutually reinforcing their respective popularities. Masayuki Uhara left the show and was replaced by the Osaka-based comedy duo *Anonenone* – popular funnymen Harada and Shimizu; singer Maggie Minenko also left *Uwasa No Channel* after one year. The show's hold on Japanese television viewers, however, did not abate with changes in the cast so long as Akiko Wada and The Destroyer remained. Baba's fears were allayed, The Destroyer wrestled fiercely, the wrestling promotion was solid and advancing, network executives were happy, Beyer as The Destroyer was the most recognizable face – such as it was– in the country. The Japanese television industry tuned in and took notice, honoring the television show with a photo of The Destroyer and Akiko Wada on the cover of the *Japanese TV Guide* magazine; no foreign wrestler, let alone many Japanese television stars, ever made it to such heights. For his role on the top rated television program in the country, Beyer as The Destroyer won a TV Guide Award, similar to an Emmy Award in American television. Offers deluged his mailbox and telephone. Beyer was patient. He balanced his good fortune by chairing charity fundraisers and events in Japan and making personal appearances at hospitals and schools, where he taught students some wrestling moves and English; he loved all of it. His creation was more well-known than ever before, but he never lost sight of his roots or code of conduct. He continued to keep himself in superb condition and was athletically more fit and in better shape with more energy at forty-four than men half his age. Stressing the importance of physical exercise, the scholar athlete authored a book – translated into Japanese - on fitness routines with illustrations depicting The Destroyer, his wife and kids performing the exercises. It sold quite well.

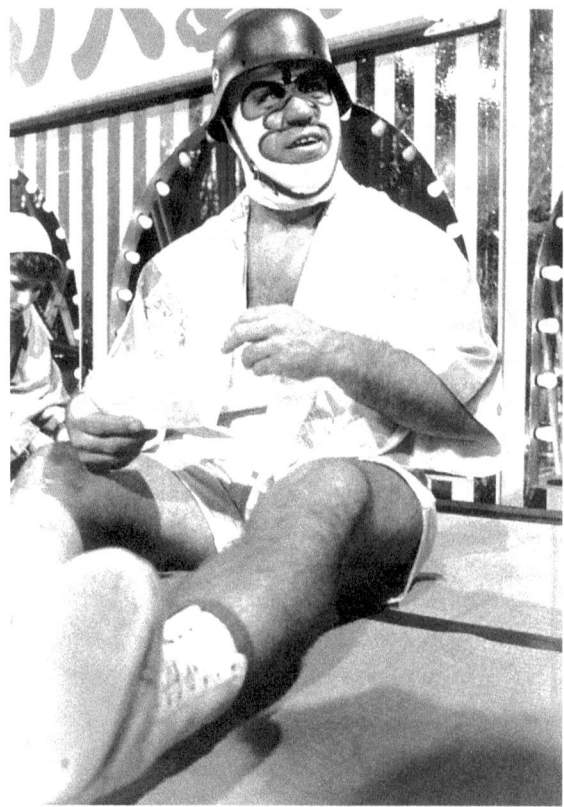

Beyer as Destroyer on the set

Wada and Destroyer on the cover of TV Guide

What began as a one year commitment to wrestle had mushroomed beyond a year and far beyond wrestling. Arenas and personal appearance venues packed to standing-room-only crowds around the country. The Destroyer squared off in what was to become a customary total of 200 or more matches each year, an extraordinary schedule when weighed against his busy television and endorsement work. Most Japanese magazines and feature publications including *Sports Illustrated* at one time or another had The Destroyer prominently displayed on their covers; a typical Tokyo citizen could not walk three city blocks without seeing a representation of the masked celebrity. Television commercials, billboards, and print ads for Fugi Film, Cheetos, Drain-O, and even McDonald's contained images of The Destroyer endorsing their products. It may have been Japan, but it was truly the land of the rising masked man. The Intelligent Sensational Destroyer evolved into more than a popular wrestler - he became *Ichiban* (number one) and was promoted in publicity photos complete with raised index finger and boasts of "De-stroy-yaa Ichiban" that paralleled the flamboyancy of Mohammed Ali. Beyer as Destroyer had become the talk of the country and was in heavy demand. Away from home much more than ever before, his life was non-stop Destroyer appearances. No one was more keenly conscious of his drawing power than Willy. She had sacrificed to help him get to this level and, while overjoyed by his success and thankful for all that had accrued from it, she lamented the closeness they had lost. It was to get much worse.

The Destroyer and family enjoyed a celebrity lifestyle but lived down to earth

Beyer was in a section of Roppongi one evening with several executives from NTV. It was late in 1974 as the Christmas shopping season was about to get underway. At a country and western music bar called 'Mr. James' that he and Willy had often frequented, Beyer began singing 'Jingle Bells' with a few Japanese words thrown in. The rendition was surprisingly entertaining. Several of the executives encouraged him to record it and other Christmas songs. Beyer laughed off their comments, knowing he did not have a pleasant singing voice, but during the following week those same people contacted officials at RCA recording studios about the idea. RCA was interested. Seemingly overnight, Beyer as The Destroyer, with Willy singing melody or harmony to parts of songs, recorded ten Christmas classics, mixing English and Japanese, that included stories and comedy interludes. The album cover in Christmas motif depicted The Destroyer in scenes from the television show, and on the back a photo of Destroyer with Willy. By the end of the year, the album had become the number one selling Christmas record on the RCA label in Japan, and earned Beyer a music award for its success.

There was no apparent limit to the masked Midas in any of his endeavors, and especially in the wrestling ring. Destroyer took on foreign heels and won more than 90% of his matches over visiting talent that included Abdullah the Butcher, Mr. Fugi, Bob Backlund, George Steele, Dick Murdoch, Otto Manheim, Len Sherry, Don DiNucci, Jimmy Snuka. For partner Shohei Baba, Destroyer was ringside as Baba defeated Jack Brisco to become the first Japanese to win the NWA World Heavyweight title. It was a signal to the wrestling world that Japanese wrestlers were on par with the best, and it boosted Baba and his promotion up the ladder; it was a great time to be wrestling in Japan and Beyer knew it. Destroyer and Baba took on the top foreign teams of the time and with the third leg of the stool, Jumbo Tsuruta, the three gave fans extraordinary matches against renowned wrestlers that lifted them to legendary status among wrestling enthusiasts in Japan.

Between 1974 and 1976, interspersed with regularly scheduled cards throughout the country, All Japan Pro Wrestling, with sponsorship from *Tokyo Sports Press*, Japan's reputable daily sports newspaper, promoted a series of matches that pitted The Destroyer against ten of the world's greatest masked wrestlers. In battles to retain hidden identity, The Destroyer took on the masked marauders in both team and singles matches before capacity crowds captivated by the spectacle of The Destroyer and other hooded giants engaged in mask to mask combat.

Mascaras and Destroyer fought in multiple countries and thrilled millions

The Destroyer's most famous bouts were with nemesis Mil Mascaras – Mexican movie matinee idol Aaron Rodriquez- that developed into heated feuds, originating in Japan and spilling over to matches in the States. Beyer and Rodriquez (whose ring name Mil Mascaras translates into Man of a Thousand Masks) became great friends away from their disguises despite their ring behaviors toward each other and a language barrier. Mascaras at 5' 11" and 240 pounds, achieved international stardom for his *lucha libre* (free fighting) style and repertoire of high flying maneuvers. Beyer as Destroyer always got fired up for his matches with Mascaras because Mascaras had a reputation of not giving anything away; opponents had to work hard against Mascaras – something many wrestlers abhorred, but Beyer found very appealing, and their mutual affinity for 'bring your best' wrestling was often on display in their bouts as fans fixated on the aerial acrobatics of the *luchador* and the adroit power attack of the masked Destroyer. In July of 1974 in Tokyo, with the Pacific Wrestling Federation U.S. Heavyweight title on the line - the title Destroyer brought to Japan that was later sanctioned by All Japan Pro Wrestling - Destroyer and Mascaras gave fans a thrilling headliner performance. The title was successfully defended and retained by The Destroyer.

Later that same year, a singles match with superb worker The Tornado (Dick Murdoch) was followed by two tag team matches, one that featured the Avenger (Minnesota territory colleague Moose Morowski) and the other showcased the Barracuda (Mario Milano). Cyclone Negro, as The Caribbean Hurricane, blew through the territory in January of 1975 and mid-year a reunion match was held with Mr. Wrestling (Tim Woods); Beyer was pleased by how well Woods' career under the hood had progressed and the two former amateur opponents had a great time in Okayama during their stay. The Spirit (Texas friend Karl Kox) and Black Devil (Manuel Soto) made summer appearances in 1975. Dan Miller as the Blue Shark cruised onto the scene early in 1976. The last match of the 'greatest masked wrestlers' series fittingly pitted The Destroyer against the Super Destroyer (Don Jardine). The angle for the final masked match read - a win for The Destroyer puts a halt to Super Destroyer's use of the name in both the *U.S. and Japan*. In the end, The Destroyer vanquished each member of the masquerade party, an unusual string of wins by any wrestler let alone a hooded baby face American working for the Japanese. Having beaten all ten masked greats, *Tokyo Sports Press*, in a rare move, bestowed the title of 'World's Greatest Masked Man' on The Destroyer, complete with a new trophy and a commemorative plaque; Beyer added a new belt; more importantly, the title became symbolic not only of how the Japanese felt about his wrestling, but about him.

The groundswell of publicity amplified by the series of masked matches and general 'Destroyer-mania' throughout Japan occasioned a surge in popularity by fans for Destroyer masks. To that point, Willy handmade all the masks for her husband's use, for autographed giveaways, and the moderate mail order business, but the dramatic climb in demand for masks outstripped her manual ability. Beyer needed to find an industrial solution. He turned to a friend, Hirotoshi Otani, who worked for Osaka-based Descente Limited, one of the largest manufacturers of fine sportswear. Through Otani's intervention, Beyer convinced Descente to produce Destroyer masks, and afterwards, with larger quantities, he was able to go big with commercial sales. The relationship with Otani was fortuitous in another way. In the lobby of Descente's main office, located in front of Osaka's Momodani Station, Beyer met and befriended Los Angeles native Marty Keuhnert who was Descente's assistant to the managing director. Keuhnert had forged a solid reputation as a baseball executive in California and Japan. The two Americans instantly bonded and Keuhnert's home in the Kansai area became a sanctuary for Beyer on his wrestling trips to Kobe.

During the mid-1970s, the aura of celebrity enwrapped the entire Beyer family. The masked American made a brief cameo appearance in a Japanese movie starring his fellow television cast member, singer Akiko Wada. A book on The Destroyer was written by Toshiyuki Kuramori, a respected Japanese sportswriter. NTV produced a 90 minute special called 'The Destroyer Show' that provided an insider's look into the life of the masked man as he went about his daily routine, wrestling, show preparations and family activities, all while remaining under the hood. At no time did he allow himself to be photographed or seen as Dick Beyer when in Destroyer mode. The show presented The Destroyer in an 'everyman' scenario – a married family man earning a living, albeit masked as a professional wrestler and television personality.

The exposure tightened the bond the wrestler had with the Japanese; they had come to appreciate and admire his technical abilities in the ring and later found joy and laughter in his television work. Subsequent to this expose' and other broadcast and print interviews, whenever people spotted the masked man in the streets, they felt as though they had peeked under the mask and caught a brief glimpse of who he really was. Beyer as The Destroyer was always on his best behavior in public and gracious with everyone who came up to him in an arena, restaurant, while shopping, or travelling. So celebrated was he, and so recognized was his family, that his mask had become a permanent fixture whenever he stepped out in public with his children and wife. Gone was the anonymity that existed before fame took control. In an odd way, his family's celebrity forced him to hide behind the mask. In the community, he had to be The Destroyer full-time. Even then, he modeled the out-of-ring demeanor he wanted his children to adopt, but there were moments that defied logic for them all.

Twelve-year old Kris found it odd at first when others asked her if she had 'ever seen Mr. Destroyer's face.' She initially told them yes, but over time the absurdity of the question grew to where it was more fun to reply, "No, I have never seen his face, I tried once when he was asleep but he caught me!" Not even Willy was immune to the question; several had the audacity to ask if she saw his face during sex. She, too, took it to a punch line "No, but I always wondered."

When his kids accompanied him to the matches, they, along with the Japanese fans, cheered for *De-stroy-yaa san*; the three remained patient as their father signed dozens upon dozens of autographs, always with the now-familiar 'D' in Destroyer containing two circled eyes and an up-curved smile - a caricature of his well-known mask. Younger son Richie, who turned seven in 1975, became a favorite of the Japanese with his platinum blonde hair and diminutive stature; he went on tour with his father during summer vacations and, like his older brother and sister, saw the entire country of Japan as most citizens never had. Because his father was a national celebrity, he became a minor one. To him it was fun to tell fans at the arenas, "I'm the son of the Destroyer" to which they replied "*Uso*" (no way) with Richie responding, "*Honto*" (it's true). This always provoked an enthusiastic "*Honto*" by the Japanese, and many even asked the young boy to sign his autograph in their wrestling programs – and he did – right beside his father's picture – with the 'R' in Richie containing two circled eyes and an up-curved smile.

At school, Kurt, Kris, and Richie were known as the children of a wrestling and television star, but to their credit they kept it well in hand and never used the status to advance self-interests. With core values and respect for others, they also had learned at early ages that life with dad the wrestler was normal -for them, just as normal as the lives of kids whose fathers worked in offices. What they found in Japan was that it was easier to maintain and defend 'real wrestling'- and the family secret- than it was in the States. Here, their friends included children of company presidents and executives, entertainers, sports figures, embassy employees, and others with parents in higher profile positions, and because their father was so well known and respected, they were never subjected to the severe taunting and teasing they experienced in America. The environment was more conducive to learning and maturing – and the children thrived in it.

Together and separately over several years, the Destroyer brood made numerous appearances on television game and musical shows, conducted interviews for magazines and radio programs, and made personal appearances at schools, hospitals, and special events; they were celebrities with or without their masked head of household. The family entertained on several televised Christmas specials performing holiday songs in Japanese; hearing tunes sung in their native language by the adopted American family delighted and drew warm responses from the viewers. "If we're not the first family we are at least the Von Trapp Family of Japan" Beyer jokingly told his kids. Willy wanted her children to enjoy these occasions, but monitored them closely to guard against being spoiled or overindulgences. For herself she wanted to keep a lower profile, but that was not always possible. In addition to being a talented artist, the thin, pretty brunette in glasses was a good singer and musician who, when prompted, sang with her husband at the Tokyo country and western bar, and who later joined with other performers to entertain in public, providing accompaniment on guitar, harmonica and ukulele. Willy preferred to stay out of the limelight and only took the stage sparingly, but when she did she was a showstopper.

The conventional, quiet family life Willy so desperately relished for her children had sailed off course a few degrees; she worked to keep it upright and steady since most of her children's time was spent with her while her husband worked long hours and nights away from home. By all measures, she was successful. For as much grounding as she achieved for her celebrity children, she slowly found herself unable to sustain the same results with her husband. Quiet nights alone were followed by quieter nights when Beyer was around. The kids received the bulk of his attention during his short stays home, and it was getting harder for her to be 'Mrs. Destroyer' in public at all times. She felt detached. She was getting tired of hearing about her husband's appearances or travel schedules from others. She saw more of him on television than at home. He wanted his kids to know his love was always there even when he wasn't, but found it impossible to reach that objective with Willy. They became disconnected, barely communicative, and regressed to neutral corners.

From Willy's perspective, the one year pledge to Japan had become a four year blur. By 1977, despite the explosive success that, in many ways brought them happiness, their marriage developed a fissure with cracks that metastasized through its foundation. It manifested itself insidiously by a decline in real, everyday communication and the 'George and Gracie' style relationship they had outwardly displayed. Time, busy schedules, television appearances, wrestling around the country, travels, any and all were initial suspects identified as driving a wedge between husband and wife, not that Beyer and Willy allowed or wanted it to happen, but in their environment, like a snowball rolling downhill, they were simply unable to stop the cumulative effect that distance, both mental and physical, had quietly imposed. Both had retreated deep into their respective parental roles and responsibilities but at no time did they disagree on the direction they had chosen for the children. Each of the kids was sheltered from the increasing marital disengagement and they were never deprived of the love, attention, time or activities they had come to appreciate. Whatever minor behavior changes they may have observed they considered speed bumps, not major hurdles. They never heard arguments – there weren't any – but the silence between Beyer and Willy was a language only husband and wife understood. Beyer was torn. The constant demands for his work in the ring and on the screen were evidence of a very successful career, one that others in his profession admired and envied, and one that he and his family fought many battles to attain. The Destroyer was an international star, idolized everywhere he travelled, yet for Beyer the one relationship he had come to rely on, the most important of all, was no longer holding together.

Beyer was not the type to talk openly of his problems with anyone. Like his face in the ring, he kept his private matters shielded, revealing only what needed to be seen. He tried thinking his way through the trouble, as he often did when confronted with personal or business issues. But this one was far more emotional and his skill set not as equipped to handle it. He took longer walks before arriving for work, usually slow, methodical, head-down strolls through the winding, stone streets of Azabu Juban, past the familiar noodle restaurants, *taiyaki* shops, *onsen* (hot springs baths), *tatami* mat huts, and other local offerings in old Edo tradition. He politely acknowledged those inside the Palace Restaurant but kept his visits short. These were the places he and his family had enjoyed, where they spent much time together, and the shopkeepers knew them all by name. It was home turf. He searched his soul for answers on his sojourns, quietly contemplating options to resolve the escalating interpersonal strain. When no means of mediation were immediately identified, he felt defeated and found himself dragged deeper into the work as the masked man.

Each of the children kept busy with school and their own pursuits, unaware of their parents' difficulties. Kurt wrestled and starred in a variety of sports and theatre; Kris swam and developed an interest in fitness; both of the older children formed independent, strong-willed personalities than most others their age. They toggled between mom and dad without playing one against the other. Richie joined little league and played basketball; still very young, he remained under the close supervision of his mother. All three children became conversant in Japanese and had any number of friends at whose homes they could stay when they wanted a night out from Mita House. Kurt, who loved the nightlife on the streets of Tokyo, was often guided or given alternatives on where to go in Tokyo by another resident of Mita House – Nick 'Nicola' Zapetti – the same Zapetti from whom Rikidozan borrowed money to establish his wrestling promotion. Zapetti's background and ties to the *Yakuza* were unknown to Kurt and overlooked by Beyer since Zapetti proved to be very neighborly and good to his family. There was never a hint of dark-side activity and Zapetti always went out of his way to welcome the Beyer family at his restaurants. For whatever shadowy reputation he may have had in certain Japanese circles, his relationship with the Beyer family was in stark contrast; Zapetti helped to keep Kurt safe on the streets of Tokyo.

Willy and Beyer were of one mind when it came to their children's happiness; regardless of their personal battle, their kids would not become collateral damage. Willy, too, maintained a hectic schedule mostly with her kids' activities and, late at night, with the kids asleep, she allowed herself to ponder her marriage, like her husband lost and unsure of what to do to repair the broken pieces. Despair shaped her silhouette.

It wasn't that Beyer and Willy had come to hate each other - protracted separation and a diminished connection proved to be too much over the latter part of their eighteen year union; they could not reignite the embers to flame up under their relationship – in months, the marriage irreparably cooled. With no hope of reconciliation, they knew what had to be done.

On February 8, 1977, as young Kris and her brother Kurt returned from school, she said to her mother, "Happy Birthday, Mom." Willy, who was readying dinner, turned to her daughter and said, "Thank you honey, but it's not going to be a happy one." Neither Kris nor Kurt understood the significance of the comment until after dinner and after Richie was put to bed, when they were summoned to the kitchen table. Usually these discussions were about adapting to life in a new city, or deciding to move, or a contract extension for The Destroyer; as they pulled chairs up to the table, this one felt different. Kris and Kurt listened as each parent spoke of their love for them and then were told that their parents were divorcing. Neither child ever saw this coming. Both reacted to the shocking news in different ways. Kris's thoughts went back a week earlier when she and her friend, Diane DeSchane, talked about what perfect marriages their parents had, how they joked, danced, sang, played cards, drank beer, never argued. She sat in stunned silence, looking straight ahead at nothing. She was unable to cry – only blank stares and expressionless eyes conveyed her feelings. After several minutes, the pin-dropping quiet in the room was interrupted by a slow, guttural expression of pain that rose up in intensity from deep within Kurt. The muscular six-foot sports star erupted into tearful sobbing without shame or embarrassment, unleashing his emotions, his head cradled in his hands. For all, that night was the most difficult night of their lives.

Consoling their children during this heart-wrenching time, Beyer and Willy waited until both Kris and Kurt regained some control and clarity of mind before describing the next course of action. Beyer told his children he had decided to leave Japan and return to their home in Akron, New York; Willy was to remain in Tokyo. The two children were given a choice – stay with Mom or return with Dad. With love expressed for both parents, Kris said she wanted to stay and help with Richie; Kurt wanted to leave. A few weeks later, a medical emergency changed everything.

Kurt had returned to Tokyo from an unprecedented school-sponsored trip to the Soviet Union with a serious illness – meningoencephalitis. He was within hours of dying. A sharp, interested physician diagnosed it accurately, and the fifteen-year old rallied. Hospitalized two full months, Kurt began to realize the closeness of the friendships he had developed in Japan and now wanted to stay and graduate high school with his classmates. He was faced with a dilemma. When his father came to visit, Kurt asked him to sit down and listen. He explained everything to his father who looked on intently. Kurt expected his dad to be miffed by his sudden change of heart, but after a short silence Beyer told his son "OK. I will stay in Japan for two more years, until you graduate, and then I will go back to the States."

It was a decision she agonized over, but Willy told her husband *she* was moving out. Though highly unusual, it made sense to her. They both believed Richie was too young to be told of their decision to divorce so they agreed to a plan, supported by the older two, in which Willy was to be at the apartment every morning to see the kids off to school and be there when they returned and to put Richie to bed. Over time, they would tell Richie about their separate living arrangements and what it all meant. Since Beyer was mostly at work or on the road, he could devote all his time to the kids during his days off without uprooting them to travel to another location, and that's what made the decision for Willy easier to make. She found an apartment within a few blocks of the family's home and relocated so that she and her older kids had only a short commute to and from Mita House. She and Beyer also agreed that whenever he was on an extensive road tour, she was to move back into Mita House temporarily to stay with the kids. The arrangements were not perfect, but bought additional buffer time while the divorce settlement was being worked out and more importantly, reinforced for the children that they were foremost in the minds of both parents.

As the months moved forward, reality descended hard on Willy. Her living circumstances proved to be more emotionally challenging when the children weren't around. For the first time in her life she was alone, without extended family, few friends, and in a country that knew her personality, not her as a person. She cried more often. To this point, she had been wife to The Destroyer. With their divorce final in 1977, she became a single woman but still recognized in public as part of The Destroyer clan. No public announcement of the divorce was revealed and no press release issued. It was a sad, frightening and anxious time for her, the end of one journey and the start of something uncertain. Where do I go from here? What can I possibly do? She was wrestling with her own future.

Beyer hid his emotions and delved deeper into his work to compensate for the loss he experienced. The mask that brought The Destroyer such recognition provided cover for Beyer. Those close to him – Master and Masako, Tanny, and to an extent Baba – recognized his struggle and gave him the space and time to do whatever helped him cope with the aftermath. Kurt, Kris and Richie were his sources of energy and inspiration and just as they protected his identity, so too they protected the divorce; the kids agreed that it was privileged information, another family secret to watch over. They did what came naturally to them - they closed ranks and circled the wagons. Few people outside the immediate family were aware of what had taken place between husband and wife. Beyer was careful to shape and limit the personal appearances of his children, each of whom recognizable figures in the public eye, so that fans or press did not draw conclusions about Willy's absence. Beyer's own schedule became so overloaded that his time off evaporated and forced another decision – Willy moved back into Mita House to look after the kids, and Beyer moved out.

He relocated to a small flat in nearby Azabu Juban. As the year progressed, the split-up and its by-products were items never discussed with anyone, at any time.

Sadly, their dissolution was not to remain a hushed, private, family matter for long.

No one knew for certain how some details on their divorce leaked out. Neither Beyer nor Willy wanted any news disseminated, and if it were reported, they wanted to personally clear it and exert control over its content to protect the children, and Destroyer fans, from misrepresentation and erroneous reports. Beyer worked with officials from NTV and the wrestling promotion on public relations safeguards for his television and personal appearances. His persona was so recognizable, his reputation so large, that Beyer as Destroyer had much to lose from false accusations or poor impressions. So, too, NTV and All Japan Pro Wrestling. It was late one evening, many months after the final decree, when Beyer received a phone call at his apartment from a reporter telling him the newspaper was going to publish information on his divorce in the next day's edition; alarmed, Beyer called the editor and vehemently objected, but to no avail. He was apoplectic. He immediately informed his ex-wife and his children of the paper's intentions. They were prepared for the story, but not for what was printed.

The following morning, the newspaper's front page garishly displayed a family photograph of The Destroyer, Willy and the three children accompanied by a blistering, scandalous report on the couple's divorce. It shocked and angered Beyer. While the article defended him as a hard working wrestler and celebrity, well respected and admired throughout the country, the inferences toward Willy as an awful woman were unjustly harsh and critical. The article indicted and vilified her, impugned her character, intimated other relationships, and unflatteringly portrayed her worse than some heels on the wrestling circuit. In essence, the paper placed full culpability for the breakup on Willy. Beyer was livid over the story. To be sure, he and Willy had differences, but the paper's report created a tabloid scandal that went beyond the bounds of decency and accuracy in details. The toxic story made its way around the country.

Near school, Kris happened by a copy of the paper with her family's photo on page one. Though she clearly knew the story was to be about the divorce, she asked a classmate what the article said. Her friend, Noriko Akiyama, grabbed the newspaper out of Kris's hands yelling "Lies, nothing but lies" and never gave the paper back to her. Similar acts of protection by friends enveloped the other children and Beyer. Those close to them rallied to their side and helped brush back the media and public onslaught that was boiling up from the sensationalized report. The same could not be said for Willy. Though her family knew the truth, the damage was too great for her to recover in the same way. There was nothing she could convincingly say or do to remove the unwarranted cloud of suspicion that hung over her. She lost friends, was rejected by store merchants, was the object of finger-pointing, was the target of ridicule. Whenever she ventured to the stores or an outing with the children, she felt the icy glares from strangers and former friends. Tough as it was in the wake of the divorce, the upshot from the scandal basically ostracized her from all normal interactions. Few rallied to her side. Beyer himself could do little to mollify the tumult. If he were to sue or make a strong public comment, it could ruin his reputation or prolong the bitter aftertaste for Willy and his children – with either result he was unwilling to take the gamble. He privately feared that his wrestling and television career would be too damaged to maintain. They had to wait it out, stay under the radar, and move on with everyday life.

For the next two years, Beyer and Willy lived separate lives in Tokyo, coming together only for birthdays, graduations, and other events involving the children. It wasn't cursory or perfunctory behavior on their part, they conversed and interacted civilly and the three kids appreciated their efforts to make things pleasant for everyone. Willy remained with the children in Mita House, venturing out less and less, closeting herself from a society that had turned on her. The kids were given everything necessary to succeed, especially unconditional parental love, and succeed they did, escaping any residual adversity from the uproar. Kurt's achievements revolved around music, theatre, and several athletic championships, both in team sports and in wrestling. Kris excelled in swimming and training while precocious Richie enjoyed his own celebrity. All three earned high marks in school and the enduring friendship of many. Beyer stayed the course as The Destroyer and found his appeal hadn't diminished in the ring or on television. The Destroyer was venerated, sentiment and respect intensified; to many Japanese, his problems were no different than their own. His life was mortal but his identity mystic. To his amazement, his celebrity star never tarnished in their eyes.

After a Friday television show rehearsal, Beyer sat down in the dressing room and looked at himself in the mirror, losing track of time. It had been two years since Akiko Wada left the show to concentrate on her singing and entertainment career. Beyer had intended to leave the show, and Japan, after he and Willy agreed to divorce, but held on to keep life structured for his kids. As it turned out, despite the newspaper scandal, it was a good decision. However, time and circumstances changed his thinking and he informed NTV executives he was next to leave. He had made history with the television show, extended his fame throughout all Japan, and simultaneously helped his partner Baba forge a lucrative and healthy wrestling enterprise by his TV appearances. No regrets. Beyer also knew that he could not move his Destroyer to another long running show without losing credibility or damaging future wrestling opportunities. It was the right time to disembark from the television program. NTV officials had nothing but high praise for his work. As he thanked them for the opportunity of a lifetime and took a final on-camera bow, he had one more 'masked decision' to make.

In late summer of 1978, Destroyer lost, and regained, the Pacific

Wrestling Federation U.S. Heavyweight title, a title he earned for a record fifth time. Beyer had been in Japan nearly six years – twice as long as any territory he worked in the States – and travelled many times to every prefecture in the country. Through television, personal appearances, and media publicity, his Destroyer was known everywhere. He sat down with Baba and explained that, like all masked good guys in western movies, he wanted to 'go out with his boots on.' Wrestling 200 or more matches each year had significant ramifications for both the wrestler and the wrestling fan. Beyer always sensed the right time to move on; he never wanted The Destroyer to be thought of by fans as fading or stale. Baba understood. The two, close as brothers, agreed on The Destroyer's farewell series of matches.

For the remainder of his time in Japan, Beyer met up with some of old friends in the ring, imported courtesy of Giant Baba. Billed for return engagements with The Destroyer were stars Bobo Brazil, Dick Murdoch, Billy Robinson, Dory and Terry Funk, Black Jack Lanza, Nick Bockwinkel, Curtis Iaukea, Fritz Von Erich, Gene Kiniski and Billy Red Lyons. The final bout of his six-year run in Japan was reserved for his boss, Giant Baba. The match was hyped as a victory by Destroyer terminated his working association with Baba. On June 14, 1979 in Tokyo, Destroyer beat Baba, and with the win, earned his unconditional release to return to the United States. Even beating treasured Baba and disclosing his relocation plans did not sour the Japanese toward the masked American; the public was reverential in their regard for what The Destroyer had brought to their arenas, homes, and lives. Through television, he had entered their living rooms each week and left them with fond memories. Like family, he was welcome to return anytime; the key to their hearts was under the tatami mat. Baba gave Beyer carte blanche to wrestle in Japan whenever he desired; Beyer assured him that, in support of his promotion, he would make the trip to the Far East every July for the summer tournaments.

In tribute to his friend, Baba retired the Pacific Wrestling Federation

Heavyweight title, leaving Destroyer as the only five time title holder, and its last.

Beyer walked over to the apartment in Mita House early in April, 1979, to discuss the preparations for his departure to the United States and short term plans for his children. Everybody, including ex-wife Willy, participated in the talks around the table. It seemed most everyone was on the move. Kurt, a recent high school graduate, had decided to attend Chaminade University in Hawaii; the islands were his father's favorite place on earth. Beyer was happy for his oldest son, telling him he'd visit more often than most other parents and to "keep an extra surf board ready for when I get there." Kris and Richie were to travel to Buffalo with their father for the summer, but return to Japan for the fall school schedule. Any plan for the children had to be signed off by both parents – that's the agreement Beyer and Willy had made. Beyer was surprised, however, to hear Willy say she had decided to stay in Japan indefinitely, not just for the kids' upcoming school term. She had weighed her options carefully – a divorced woman in her forties returning to the States after a six year hiatus would have difficulty obtaining immediate employment. While never spoken, she may also have thought it easier to avoid the 'what happened to your marriage' questions she inevitably would have had to field back home. In spite of the torturous, shoddy treatment she was forced to endure, she believed it was better to remain in Tokyo, a place she had come to know, and try to reassemble her life and care for her two children. To Beyer she appeared stoic and resolute, but privately she trembled at the daunting task before her. The former draftsman and amateur artist had limited skills to rely upon to secure work. The divorce settlement addressed the children's future and living arrangements but what financial resources she had remaining would only sustain her for a short time. She knew she had to find a job. Her odyssey was only beginning.

Beyer left Japan having reached the apogee of a career he never imagined. With his two younger children at his side, he settled in for the half-day plane ride back to Buffalo, fulfilled as only those who achieve iconic stature can be. The price he had paid for his achievements was exacting and tragic – a failed marriage. Beyer conceded his failures and shortcomings. He recognized his role in the deterioration of his marriage to Willy, learned from his mistakes, and reconciled to move ahead. Something else came into focus. He confessed he was torn between two loves. As he looked to the near future, he was occupied by a driving desire – a need that had been brewing slowly over years – a necessity unrecognized until now - to bridge his love for America and his love for Japan, somehow, someway.

CHAPTER **18**

AS THE SUMMER weeks of 1979 faded away and the circled departure date to Japan on the calendar drew nearer, newly-licensed Kris, 16, took her brother Richie, 10, on several rides around and through their Akron farmland in the 1973 Oldsmobile '98 Beyer kept on his property. The kids enjoyed the freedom to travel the countryside as it was not a luxury afforded them in Tokyo's restricted urban lifestyle. One day in August, they were in the car talking, not about the traditional ways of Kayfabe, or the masked identity, or other family secrets, but about their parents and how Dad was going to be in Akron alone. Living in Tokyo the last six years, for them, had been a magical experience; even after the divorce, they had the benefit of both parents' involvement since one or the other lived nearby. The love and devotion they had for their parents was strong and binding and even at such tender ages, Kris and Richie felt invested in them and their happiness. The reality of their father's future hit them hard and the thought did not sit well with either one; it was not the Beyer way.

The heartache of divorce never weakened their definition of family. Kurt attended college in Hawaii but was not considered distanced from the clan. With Kris and Richie scheduled to live with Mom in Tokyo, Dad would be back in Akron, without anyone. Each of the Beyer children had been raised in the shadow of their father's career. They had lived a nomadic existence, a herding society that moved on when time or circumstances prompted. Due to their father's profession and shrouded identity, they were brought up to watch his back, defend the industry, and protect the family enterprise, and each other. It was what they knew best. Their tribal instincts were well-honed.

MASKED DECISIONS

Before they arrived back at the farmhouse, Kris stopped the car and said to her brother, "Richie, we need to make a pact. We can't leave Dad alone." Richie replied, "What do we do?" Kris looked deeply into her younger brother's blue eyes and said, "Since I'm the oldest here, I will stay with Dad and you will live with Mom." "But we're both supposed to go back, Kris." "I know, but this is something we have to do...like losing a match in the ring, you win another time when it counts." Richie understood the metaphor. He looked out the window toward the corn fields, paused, with misty eyes turned to his sister and said "I'll take care of Mom, right Kris?" Kris replied "…and I'll take care of Dad, right Rich?" They cried and consoled each other with the belief that their sacrifice was justified. As the last tune played on the car radio, brother and sister shook hands, securing their pledge, then tried to do a 'brotherhood' style hand shake they had seen black people do, but their hands became tangled and awkward and both broke out in giggles.

Beyer was surprised and a little unnerved. Hearing his daughter say she wanted to stay in Buffalo with him was not something he expected or planned for. He knew she had a very close relationship with Willy and loved her life in Japan, so this declaration was out of the blue to him. In the divorce settlement, Willy had been granted custody of the children, but both Kris and Kurt were given the option of remaining with their mother in Japan or living in the States with their father; while Kris's initial decision was to stay in Japan and help look after Richie, her sincerity on the matter convinced Beyer that a serious discussion was required. He called Tokyo; Willy was not in agreement. Kris and her mother exchanged several letters and engaged in a few lengthy telephone conversations – as did Beyer with his ex-wife. Once Beyer had a plan in place that was acceptable to Willy, Kris was finally given permission to remain in Buffalo. Richie returned to Japan. Two households, and four lives, were unexpectedly reshaped by a summer agreement between two siblings.

The decision to allow Kris to remain with him was made not without caveats. School, activities, work, and other expectations were clearly and unambiguously outlined for her – it was either agree to all, or forfeit and return to Japan. Kris agreed to every stipulation. Beyer, too, made conciliatory changes; after twenty-five years he had grown tired of life on the road; now that his daughter was living with him, he cut his wrestling schedule back to part-time with a contract clause that any travel must be in driving distance to Buffalo. Sufficient monies, through savings and wise investments, made the decision practically a no-brainer. He comprehensively analyzed everything he had, needed, and wanted, concluding it was time for Dick Beyer to finally do what he set out to do after college – what he was finally able to afford to do.

Wrestling – with travel restricted to short drives- remained a joy for Beyer, with promoters in the States and Canada happy to have him work their territories. From his home base in Buffalo, Beyer made day trips to Montreal and Toronto, where he wrestled other big names of the business including former travelling companion Andre the Giant, Ric Flair, Bob Backlund, Dory and Terry Funk, fishing buddy Nick Bockwinkel, Ed Carpentier, Mad Dog Vachon, Superstar Billy Graham and others. What made it more enjoyable was that, for the first time, he was able to wrestle as the masked Destroyer in his backyard. The long-standing rule prohibiting masked wrestlers from working Madison Square Garden in New York was lifted while Beyer lived in Japan. During this prohibition, Beyer worked only as Dick Beyer in New York State, and thus never got the Big Apple opportunities or the big press from the New York media machine. Beyer's amigo, Mil Mascaras, had become the first masked wrestler to work MSG in the early 1970s, and the ban was eliminated shortly after that match. Though Beyer never before worked under the hood in his home state, fans, aware of the masked man's reputation and acumen, lined up to see his work as The Sensational Intelligent Destroyer in arenas in New York as well as in Michigan, Ohio, and eastern Canada. It was worth the wait for them to marvel at his still-edgy repertoire that belied his years.

MASKED DECISIONS

At forty-nine years of age, Dick Beyer heard -and dismissed- the footsteps of time creeping up behind him; still a superbly conditioned athlete for one approaching his fifth decade, he understood his limits, more importantly, he recognized his limitless aspirations. At night when Kris finished her homework and went off to bed, he sat by the table in the kitchen of the farmhouse and wrote out the things he still wanted to achieve – a list he eventually whittled down to a select few. It included working with kids, teaching, mentoring, and coaching them to reach higher as he did in his life; it included bridging his devotion to America and Japan, and finding ways to show his gratitude to both for giving him the opportunities he had to succeed. From his list he saw the common threads that connected each of his bulleted items – not so much surprise as affirmation – the consistent themes were 'engage' and 'giving back.' It was what he had always believed he was about. Beyer could hear his father's voice inspiring those actions; he could see in his mind's eye the elder gentleman on the train and hear his words of advice; he engaged and gave back through his work as an Eagle Scout, and throughout his professional career. However, wrestling, as great as it had been for him, was to be his penultimate career. Through it he gave all he had as an athlete, performer, and entertainer and, as he looked ahead, would use all the good that came from it to achieve his latter yet loftier goals.

Beyer didn't waste any time. He contacted people in school districts around Buffalo, but it was Fred Machemer Jr., son of the man he considered a second father, the man who had recruited Dick to Syracuse and helped him land summer jobs while in school, that brokered an appointment for Beyer to meet Donald Munson, the principal at Amherst High School, a large public school within short driving distance from Akron. The high school needed a wrestling coach. Beyer interviewed with Munson and a few school officials who were impressed with his credentials, especially his amateur wrestling background and lifelong interest in developing kids. He met the requirements and soon was coaching boys on the mat; Beyer felt comfortable yet stimulated;

it was the kind of opportunity in which he fit well, and by wrestling part-time and with no financial pressures, he could afford to be a high school coach. "I might not be the biggest or the strongest," he told his wrestlers "but I'm the quickest and the smartest." They soon found out he was also the toughest.

Across the Pacific, Willy struggled. Though several years had passed since the humiliation of the newspaper expose' and the public shunning she sustained, the process of re-assimilation to Japanese society sputtered. She worked hard to learn more of the language and harder still at multiple jobs she held to support herself and her son. The money Beyer provided helped, but the cost of living in Japan outpaced her ability. Life had become an uphill climb, yet she never wavered in her resolve to see a better day. Richie grew taller, and basketball occupied most of his after-school hours. Eventually, Willy moved into a smaller apartment near her son's school, and after several attempts, with little background other than her draftsman career, got a job as an assistant in the school's art department, and also taught typing. What little money she made from the school was augmented by the little money she made from an Amway distributor business she started. Kris and Kurt stayed in close contact with her from thousands of miles away. Willy told her daughter she and Richie would be in Akron for Kris' high school graduation; Kurt, too, planned to be there, but first had to tell his mother and father about another plan – a plan to leave Chaminade University and attend the University of San Francisco. He explained by phone to both that USF's curriculum gave him more opportunities – and, by the way, his high school sweetheart was also at the school. In the end, Kurt's transfer proved to be a good move, and for the right reasons.

After a meeting with Munson about the wrestling team budget, Beyer walked the halls with the principal and met several teachers and administrative staff. Near the end, Beyer was introduced to the school nurse, a tall, beautiful woman with salt-and-pepper hair. "Coach Beyer, meet Wilma Maurer." Beyer was startled by her first name;

apart from his ex-wife, the only other Wilma he had ever heard of was Wilma Flintstone. He took her hand, turned to Munson and said, "I was married to one of these once." Nurse Maurer assumed he had been married to a nurse. "Oh, was she an LPN or an RN," she asked. Beyer, emphasizing each letter, replied, "She was a W-I-L-M-A."

Forty-six year old Wilma Blake Maurer worked at the school since 1974 and had been recently elevated to her current position. She enjoyed the work, but found nursing to be a twenty-four hour calling, as her husband Don, a plumber, was diagnosed with pancreatic cancer and not doing well at home. Wilma's daughter, Patty, married and expecting her first child, helped her mother with the care of her father, and provided Wilma a sounding board and a shoulder. The two were very close. Wilma, born in Flint, Michigan, had lived in Buffalo since she was five; the eldest of three sisters, her mother died when she was very young; her father later remarried. Caretaking was something Wilma learned early on. She devoted every spare hour to her husband's medical needs, but in February of 1980, Don Maurer passed away. It was a sad close to a chapter in her life – a most unusual one was about to open.

The high school wrestling season was ratcheting up late in 1980 with boys trying out in various weight categories. Each week, the boys lined up according to Coach Beyer's instructions, stood on the scale, and were told their weight numbers. Assuring the validity and accuracy of the readings was Wilma Maurer, school nurse. It was a joy for her to participate in this ritual; the boys ribbed and joked with each other about their respective gains or losses, and their coach barked out details to each in his gruff, gravelly voice. As she got to know the boys, she felt vested in their outcomes, and soon began attending the matches, cheering and rooting for the Amherst squad. Beyer appreciated her attendance and interest, but was sensitive to her loss from earlier in the year. Still, he thought she was one attractive woman. It had been three years since his divorce. It was time. He made the first move. One night after a match, as the two were walking out of the gym, Beyer said to Wilma, "How long do I wait before I can ask you out?" Before the last snowflake had fallen that winter season, they had shared a pizza and talked at length over coffee.

Wilma Maurer hadn't been on a real date since the early 1950s. Something about the wrestling coach fascinated her; she heard him yell at the wrestling boys countless times but knew his bark betrayed his bite, and witnessed how much he cared for each one of them. A young, eager wrestler named Mark Ragin caught Beyer's attention early. Ragin had all the attributes to be a successful high school grappler, and he eventually reached the finals in the state competition, but in his career two episodes of hyperventilation during matches cost him victories. Beyer never wavered in his support for Ragin; Ragin admired Beyer and sought his advice on how to get to the professional ranks after he graduated. They remained lifelong friends. Wilma observed how Ragin, and many other boys, gravitated to Beyer. She saw the heart of the man, and it drew her in. With time, she learned more. That he was a professional wrestler was common knowledge, but what was not known to her was that he still wrestled. It was a matter of weeks before he asked her to go with him to one of his matches. She happily agreed. The following weekend, a car pulled up to her home with two men inside– one was Beyer, the other man was unknown. "Wilma, this is my buddy Lloyd, he will be your body guard tonight." Wilma stepped into the car haltingly; Beyer never mentioned another person was to be with them that night, and the mysterious 'body guard' comment was puzzling and arresting. Beyer drove, Wilma sat in the front passenger seat with Lloyd seated directly behind her; she was fidgety and uneasy. Beyer spoke most of the way en route to the arena in Niagara Falls, Ontario, Canada, just over the Rainbow Bridge that crosses the Niagara River and separates the U.S. and Canada. He made her feel relaxed with his quips and jokes and descriptions of wrestling matches from prior years and in Tokyo. So comfortable had Wilma become, she forgot Lloyd was in the back seat. Her complacent demeanor was jolted into alarm when, just before reaching the arena, Beyer pulled into a side street across from a bank, stopped the car, and pulled a mask down over his head. Her first thoughts were *they're staging a robbery and they're going to kill me* but Beyer, seeing the blood drain from her face, was quick to inform her this was his wrestling disguise and persona as a bad guy in the business, and he always took precautions when arriving at the venues to hide his true identity from wrestling fans with his ring identity. She sighed in deep relief, but her attention shifted to Lloyd's role for the evening. Seated near ringside during the matches, Wilma quickly surmised his *raison d'etre*. During most of the undercard and especially during Beyer's Destroyer match, the fans reacted to the wrestling and outcomes by fighting, throwing items into the ring and at each other, and other outbursts and disturbances; Wilma was happy Lloyd was there to shield her, and deeply touched by Beyer's concern and the safeguard he initiated for her protection. A highly unusual first date, but it was not to be the last Destroyer match she attended with her masked wrestler gentleman friend. Another match, months later, caused their date to run longer than expected; Wilma arrived home in the early morning hours, slowly opened the front door and gingerly tip-toed into the living room, only to find her daughter Patty sitting up with her own daughter; Pointing to her watch, Patty turned to her mother and said, "Mom, you're grounded."

In the spring of 1981, Kris graduated from high school and announced that she was following her father's footprints to Syracuse University to major in engineering. Beyer was extremely proud of her. She had grown into a bright, self-assured young woman who carried herself with grace and with a 'don't mess with me' attitude; people loved her. At the reception Beyer arranged for her at the farmhouse, family and friends gathered including Kurt who, without girlfriend, flew in from the west coast, along with Willy and Richie from Japan; it was the first time Beyer had seen Willy since he left Japan, and the first time since then the entire family had been together. Beyer and Willy were cordial and friendly to each other, setting the mood for a festive celebration with the family. It was also the first meeting between Willy and Wilma. In what could have turned into an awkward and most disquieting situation for everyone, Willy and Wilma made it a special occasion. The two seemed to recognize and appreciate the moment – former spouse meeting current girlfriend – and to their credit, they moved passed the potential clumsiness by sitting down and connecting eye to eye, woman to woman; a simple, mutual, gesture of respect born out of enormous class. This was to be no short-lived, disingenuous, empty interaction, but a true friendship in the making.

As Kris prepared to enter Syracuse University, a young man named Mike Rotunda prepared to graduate from the same institution and search for a career. Beyer kept tabs on all graduating wrestling and football athletes from SU and, in some ways, Rotunda reminded Beyer of himself. A two-time AAU All-American who wrestled and played football, Rotunda was big – 6'3" and 240 pounds – and Beyer saw the raw potential for a pro career in the young grappler. He called Rotunda and invited him to Canada to explore the professional wrestling scene. Once the young amateur wrestler experienced the spectacle and fan reaction, he was hooked. Beyer took him under his wing and worked the rookie hard to prepare for life in the ring. Rotunda learned fast and, in the fall, travelled to Germany with Beyer on an all-expenses-paid trip to get on-the-job training. Beyer and Rotunda wrestled some fine European and American talent including Beyer's pals Dick Murdoch and Moose Morowski; the experience for Rotunda was no less than baptism by fire. Beyer, on his way to Japan from his two-week stint in Germany, convinced the German promoter into extending Rotunda's stay for October and November with the proviso that both would work the early December tour when Beyer returned from Japan. The promoter consented to the deal, and the extra work paid off for Rotunda, who developed into an all-around professional.

MASKED DECISIONS

For Beyer, the fall tour in Germany and Japan was long and, for the first time in many years, he longed for the companionship of a woman - one particular woman. He phoned Wilma Maurer and asked, "How would you like to spend Christmas in Japan?" "Will Lloyd be coming along?" she replied with a trace of laughter in her voice. He liked her repartee.

It turned out to be a wonderful, snowy Christmas season in Japan that year. Beyer was excited to show his new woman around his familiar haunts and introduce her to his friends at the Palace Restaurant and throughout Azabu Juban, Roppongi, and the Ginza in Tokyo, Asahikawa to the north, and elsewhere. Wilma learned more about the man and witnessed first-hand the love and admiration the Japanese held for him. In one respect it melted her heart, in another it was a revelation to see her boyfriend, Dick Beyer, put on the mask of The Destroyer and be treated with such adulation as throngs surged toward him for autographs and photos wherever they went; *Now, I know what Yoko must have gone through with John.*

Knowing Richie was out of school on winter break, Beyer arranged for the three to head up the mountains for some skiing; the afternoon was a perfect day for alpine. After a few runs, Wilma's hip was feeling sore, so she begged off the remainder of the day and left father and son to enjoy the slopes together. The next day, Wilma decided to call Willy. Late in the day, the two women met for tea, then shopped and walked before realizing they'd been out for hours. Willy and Wilma created a bond and a connection that was unique and was especially satisfying to Beyer. He never expected a relationship to form between his 'two Wilmas.' Because of it, everyone was at ease in their company, and Beyer knew he had found someone who just might become more than a steady date.

Back home from Japan, Beyer drove north to Canada and met up with Rotunda; the two worked Montreal, where Rotunda came to the attention of a recruiter for the North Carolina territory – whose booker was

Beyer's friend, former wrestler and football player, Wahoo McDaniel. It didn't take long for Rotunda to agree to move south. Before he left for North Carolina to further his career, Rotunda drove to Akron and, as payback to Beyer, helped him build a twenty-feet by twenty-feet portable wrestling ring in Beyer's backyard. Developing young talent excited Beyer, but he had something in mind to attract more to the sport.

Beyer not only coached wrestling at Amherst but also helped out for a year with the high school football team. He hadn't been on the gridiron since his coaching years at Syracuse. Interacting with the kids injected a pure high into his system and he couldn't get enough. He returned to Japan for All Japan Pro Wrestling's summer series – a promise he kept to Baba and would keep for years to come. Though he didn't always work the main events, Beyer as Destroyer was a mentor to many younger wrestlers coming up in the business and he helped develop them into solid performers. Baba was grateful for his insights and his willingness to mold young talent; Beyer made more money by his participation in the summer series than by working a year in the school district…but the money was not important, fellowship with Japan and building interest in wrestling was.

With the portable ring he and Rotunda built in his backyard, and having applied for and received his promoter's license from the New York State Athletic Commission, Beyer set out to create a higher level of awareness in amateur and professional wrestling. He bought a truck and purchased a ring trailer, loaded the ring on the back, and with his vast contacts and circle of amateur and pro friends, he and Wilma drove the highways of western and upstate New York, taking wrestling to the people. He was convinced that more could be lured to the sport if properly introduced to both the scientific and the showmanship sides of wrestling. He promoted in Erie, Pennsylvania and up into New York's southern tier in Jamestown and Olean, to Massena and Watertown in northern New York State, and over to the Adirondack Mountain region to Plattsburg, and points along the way. Grueling, exhausting, and yet exhilarating, the work was more a mission for fifty-two year old Beyer, but he persevered for two years, wrestling and promoting, recruiting friends and new wrestlers to work his ring, exposing many to the ancient art form and the old-school professional variety. Beyer as Destroyer claimed one last professional wrestling title during this time, when he defeated Billy Robinson in Montreal to win the Canadian International Heavyweight Championship, the highest level singles title in the Montreal-based promotion. For his career, The Destroyer had held titles in several countries and multiple territories and had travelled the world and made lasting impressions with his charisma, communication style and technical abilities - but the aging hero to millions wanted to be a regular guy to one – and bring about one more change in title.

On a wickedly cold night in the winter of 1983, Beyer asked Wilma to become Mrs. Beyer. "Are you sure you want another Wilma?" "Are you sure you want a masked husband?" Assurances given, they decided to stage the wedding, for ease of process and proximity for many, in Las Vegas in April the following year. The wedding and reception were well attended by the Beyer and Maurer families and many friends from the west coast. The couple also held summer receptions in Buffalo and in Tokyo for those unable to attend their wedding. At the receptions, Dick and Wilma proudly displayed photos from the wedding – two sets of photos – one with Beyer in Destroyer mask, one without. How could it be otherwise? Wilma's daughter Patty, who was on the squad of the Buffalo Jills, the cheerleaders for the Buffalo Bills football team, told her friends that her mother the nurse had married a masked wrestler "so she has no idea what he looks like", but in reality Patty adored Beyer and Beyer adored his step-daughter and new bride. Kurt, Kris and Rich saw the happiness Wilma brought to their dad and they welcomed her into their sacrosanct community. Beyer had found that special someone again, in a strange twist, with another Wilma.

Wilma #2 and Beyer wed in 1984

Weeks after his wedding, as the itinerary shaped up for his annual trip to Japan, Beyer received a phone call from California-based Red Bastien. The wrestler was aware of Beyer's overseas trip schedule from contacts in Japan, and knew he was to be in Los Angeles before heading to Tokyo. "Dick, how would you like to work a movie?" Beyer said, "I'm too old to be a ticket taker" but intrigued, told Bastien he would meet him to discuss the offer after he landed in L.A.

At a bar near the Los Angeles motel were Beyer was staying, Bastien handed over a script. "Looks like this masked wrestler is in a lot of scenes...how am I supposed to do that in a couple of days?" Beyer

MASKED DECISIONS

asked. Bastien replied, "Dick, you're not the masked wrestler." The film, entitled 'Grunt! The Wrestling Movie' was written as a mock documentary and comedy about a heel wrestler who supposedly kills himself but who many believe returns as a masked baby face. Beyer had just assumed from his own life's work he was playing the masked man, and in a way felt foolish, but a bit relieved. "You'll work Wednesday and Thursday and get about two grand…and you'll be working with Dick Murdoch in your scenes," Bastien told Beyer. That sounded just fine to Beyer – he always enjoyed his matches with Murdoch and looked forward to working with him on the set. "Red, where have you been all my life," Beyer jokingly said to Bastien; both laughed at the reference to their initial encounter in the ring.

The first scene shot for the movie was an interview segment between the sportscaster and the Grunt Brothers (Murdoch and Beyer). During this scene, both 'brothers' were to describe the mayhem and punishment they planned to dish out to their opponents in an upcoming match. Murdoch and Beyer gave it their all, playing to the rolling camera and selling every pounding syllable with matching body language. Beyer relied on his experience with the microphone and having done thousands of interviews as The Destroyer to bring out the best in his role. After the first take that included shoving props and breaking a few things on the set, the actors congratulated each other on a good performance, but the director wasn't fully satisfied and called for a second take. Beyer was surprised and told the director, "You're not going to get it better than that." The director shot back a nasty reply and once the set was restored, curtly signaled for the next take. The two wrestlers looked at each other and instinctively responded as they had done so many times before on camera during in-studio matches.

Murdoch and Beyer turned up the heat and not only delivered their lines convincingly, they actually tore up the set, deliberately destroying props and set pieces so that there would be no way to film a third take. The director was nearly hit by flying debris as the wrestling giants bore down on the set pieces. It worked; after hearing 'cut' they left the set for some drinks and didn't return until the director was ready to film their wrestling scene, and what eventually became the last in Beyer's movie career. As they say in the motion picture business, this movie wasn't released – it escaped. 'Grunt the Wrestling Movie' debuted inauspiciously in the fall of 1985; it was a quick takedown; no rematch, no red carpet, no sequel.

Returning to Akron, Beyer told his wife all about his fleeting movie career as well as his recent trip to Japan. Wilma took the opportunity to ask him what he wanted to do more than anything else. "Teach the kids" was his reply. No sooner had he told her his desire, Wilma informed him of a job opening at the Akron Elementary School and the potential for coaching roles with the Akron High School athletic department. He was out the door before she finished telling him all about the jobs and, late in the day, he returned as the new physical education teacher at Akron Elementary and the assistant football coach and varsity swim coach at Akron High. The bright beam in his blue eyes assured Wilma that her husband had found the connecting road on his life journey. Actually, it was the original road but he detoured for thirty years through a career in professional wrestling. He also came to a realization about his part-time professional wrestling schedule. He was in fantastic condition; he was still in demand; he was fifty-five years old. To satisfy himself, his commitments, and time, Dick Beyer announced his 'semi-retirement' from professional wrestling – choosing only to work summers as The Destroyer in Japan for as long as he remained healthy and Baba wanted him. He knew it to be the right decision at the right time. He also saw the writing on the wall. Territorial wrestling as Beyer knew it had declined in recent years due to the rise in national promotions like the WCW and WWF. Regional territories could not compete for the talent with the nationals and their large cable television power bases. Some territories were demoted to 'farm clubs' for the national promotions and eventually lost the interest of the fans as more were drawn to the televised version. In a way, wrestling enabled television, again. As the medium struggled in its infancy during the 1940s and 1950s, wrestling shows caught the eye and attention of the new viewer; as cable television looked to expand its reach in the 1980s, wrestling provided a willing audience. Beyer never walked the national wrestling stage in the U.S. as he had in Japan; nevertheless, he was content with his achievements, success, and decisions.

The Beyer offspring were busy making life-changing decisions of their own in the mid-1980s. Kurt graduated from the University of San Francisco, returned to Japan, and worked as a writer and editor for one of the country's leading newspapers, *The Daily Yomiuri*, in addition to marketing and advertising work for the Tokyo-based Odyssey Corporation. Following the lead of his older brother, Rich graduated from St. Mary's International School and decided to attend the University of San Francisco and major in hotel and restaurant management. A year after Kurt's return to Japan, Kris graduated with honors from Syracuse University with a Bachelor of Science degree in electrical engineering.

Beyer caught his second wind. He and Wilma sold the farmhouse, and the house she owned during her first marriage, to design and build a new, knotty cedar home on Sandhill Road, on acreage located around the corner from the old farmhouse in Akron. Downsizing was right; still, Beyer and Wilma owned so many acres of land around the new house they leased portions of it to nearby farmers to help expand their crop yields. In addition, to honor the land and a people that adopted him, Beyer hired a master craftsman he met in Japan, Mr. Arakawa, to build a room in his new house dedicated to the heritage of Japan. The addition was authentic, complete with *Fusuma* sliding door, *Shoji* screen, and genuine artifacts; he decorated the room with many mementos from his wrestling tours and television appearances in Japan.

Teaching physical education, coaching football and the swim team, and involvement in kids' amateur wrestling programs ignited a rocket of energy and enthusiasm that burned white hot everyday inside the man kids and parents came to know as Coach Beyer. The work was every bit as rewarding as wrestling. Beyer approached teaching like being 'on stage,' always mindful of delivering quality presentations as a teacher the way he had as a wrestling performer. In many ways teaching became more personal as he developed relationships with the kids, helped them grow and achieve, and was with them and their families during difficult and sometimes tragic circumstances. Brought forward from his childhood during the Great Depression, Beyer was sensitive to the pain and misfortune many of his students endured. He set out to help his students and others in the community in direct, impactful ways – volunteering to chair fund raising events, blood collections sites, medical equipment needs, food drives, and other events large and small but always meaningful. Everyone in the little town of Akron, New York and surrounding communities knew Coach Beyer and his wife Wilma because of their tireless efforts on behalf of many. They were the people who showed up first and departed last. Beyer was giving back – in ways even he found unimaginable – and it all felt right.

His life in retirement became busier than when he worked full time, but no complaints from Dick Beyer; he did what he wanted to do. He took full advantage of the opportunities given to work with kids and engage the larger community. Now he set his sights on the one goal that, to date, had eluded him – how to bring about something of value between Japan and America… as a lasting endowment of gratitude.

Each summer, unfailingly, Beyer and his wife flew to Japan for Baba's summer wrestling series. Over several weeks, Beyer as Destroyer worked the ring with seasoned professionals and rookies getting their start in the business. Crowds came out to see the pros and new upstarts, but it was The Destroyer who remained a joy and, for many, a privilege to watch. The name drew reverence and people to the arenas. They knew he was older, but with the mask and his superb physique, he looked like The Destroyer from yesterday, just a little slower. Quite by accident, in the dressing room toward the end of the series, Beyer overheard a conversation between two of the younger Japanese wrestlers, one of whom, Yoshiaki Yatsu, was on the 1984 Japanese Olympic wrestling team. Yatsu described his work with a fledgling amateur tournament devoted to kids of various ages – boys and girls. Beyer's curiosity prompted him to ask questions about the tournament, its structure, format, and organization. It interested him. He was invited by Yatsu to meet the kids, the few people involved with the project, and to offer his suggestions. Beyer was smitten by what he saw; it reminded him of his work with youth during his Chicago days and it sparked an idea – what if I brought American kids over to compete with *the Japanese kids…*

He and Wilma returned to Akron with thoughts of the children's tournament never leaving his head. The more he ruminated on the idea the more he liked it. It appeared to incorporate all the elements he sought - learning, fellowship, competition, sportsmanship, cultural exchange. *If it is put together right, everyone benefits*. Beyer got to work, familiarizing himself with travel guidelines, tournament organization, lodging and food requirements, and a myriad of details. The one key item on his list that he circled several times was the most thorny– money. He chose not to burden families by asking them to put up the money since some would not be able to afford to send their son or daughter and he was not going to say no to anyone and certainly not a child. Beyer stood up from his chair at the kitchen table and said to Wilma, "The only way is fund raising so that everyone goes or no one goes." He realized what he was saying and the forecast for uncertainty; Akron and the neighborhoods surrounding it were not large, highly affluent communities, and it made fund raising that much more daunting. It was the only option that made sense to him, but one that would require several money-generating activities over many months. He and Wilma were neck-deep into various charitable fund raising endeavors and they asked each other if they had the capacity to adopt one more cause; neither hesitated.

In 1988, after selling hot dogs, pizza, washing cars and a string of other events spread out over ten months, Beyer and his pioneers of young amateur wrestlers, 17 boys, 1 girl, 8 chaperons, mostly from nearby Clarence, arrived in Tokyo for the first of what would blossom into an annual event for kids from Western New York. Everyone was awe-struck. The kids pinched themselves and each other, to be sure they were in Japan, but nothing could have adequately prepared them for what they observed of Coach Beyer. Yes, they knew he was popular; yes, they knew he wore a mask when he wrestled; no, they did not realize he would be wearing the mask when they got to the Haneda Airport terminal and for the duration of their stay. Like a superhero they had seen in the movies, Coach Beyer, not in a phone booth but a restroom, transformed into the Intelligent Sensational Destroyer. This group of kids and each succeeding group that, with Beyer's help, raised its own money and travelled with Beyer to Japan, saw a new side of their coach and gazed in complete amazement as The Destroyer strolled throughout Japan with scores of people shouting 'De-stroy-yaa' and asking for autographs, pictures, or just to shake his hand. Beyer often heard at least one of the kids say to him, "Coach, you really are important to these people" to which Beyer always replied, "No, they are important to me."

Without the full cooperation and assistance of the tournament committee and its sponsors in Tokyo, Beyer's groups could not have enjoyed the experience to the full measure they did. His good friend, Tanny, became invaluable helping put together the itinerary and post-tournament plans for the groups; Beyer relied on him heavily and the wily Tanny always came through; Beyer considered him a 'friend at the factory' for his ability to do things others were unable to accomplish. Over the years, each group of athletes, wrestlers and later swimmers, developed a composite personality that Beyer classified into categories. Some groups were docile while others were more

◄ MASKED DECISIONS

aggressive, yet every member of each group did his or her best in competition and building relationships. As Beyer had done early in his wrestling career, he afforded his athletes an opportunity to be tested by competitive athletes from another country, learning lessons in the process. In representing themselves well, they represented their country well. This was key to Beyer's plan; teams from two countries in competition, playing by the rules, arriving at a better understanding of others…and themselves. He finally discovered the 'something of value' he had been searching for by melding his love of two countries, sports, children, competition and learning.

Beyer's gift transcended sports and travel. He became ambassadorial in furthering productive international relations between the U.S and Japan through his children's program. Governmental officials in Japan took part in his tournament ceremonies largely out of respect for his devotion to children's physical development; they realized the value and substance he brought through his program and they helped pave the way for an expansion of his U.S. – Japanese activities for the children. The Japanese officials and people not only held Beyer in high regard for all he had done, but for all he was doing.

During his 1990 trip to Japan, Beyer met his son Kurt for lunch as he often did during these trips. Unlike previous occasions, Kurt dreaded this particular meeting; he had something to tell his father and obsessed over his dad's reaction. Father and son sat down at the Palace Restaurant, ordered fish and beer. They talked about Rich, who graduated the previous year from the University of San Francisco with a degree in hospitality management and had returned not to Japan, but to Buffalo, anticipating his assignment in the Army; as a senior, Rich signed up for Reserve Officers Training Corps (ROTC), graduated with the Distinguished Military Graduate distinction – awarded to only the top five percent of all cadets nationwide - and needed to fulfill his active duty obligation. Rich's decision to enlist was a proud moment for his father; Beyer did not expect nor encourage his son to take on such ambitious responsibility but, like his own father when a young Dick Beyer entered pro wrestling, Beyer told his son to make his best choices during the most uncertain of times. In the meantime, Rich went to work at Ilio DiPaolo's Ringside Restaurant south of Buffalo, awaiting official word from the Army and a departure date. Kurt's sister, Kris, also became a topic of conversation. After graduating from Syracuse University, Kris was recruited to a division of General Motors Corporation to work research and development, designing solenoid actuated flow control valves for finer heater core resolution, and later vehicle and HVAC component testing. But last year, after getting married, she transferred to Japan and worked in the Tokyo office covering the Asian-Pacific market as a technical liaison. So within the same year, Rich moved back to Buffalo, and Kris relocated to Tokyo.

Kurt found an opportunity to segue from the conversation about family to tell his father an important message, a message he had rehearsed a thousand different ways in his mind, but at the moment of delivery blathered out in a rush, "Dad, I'm quitting my job and going into pro wrestling." The thirty-year old Kurt anxiously looked at his father, waiting for his reaction and reply…and waiting…and waiting; none came for several minutes. The elder Beyer finished his meal, took a few slugs of beer, cleared his throat, looked directly at his son and said, "I'll give you one month – I will train you. If you are good enough I will recommend you to another trainer, but answer me this – why didn't you tell me when you were twenty-four and just out of college – you're thirty and have, or should I say had, a good career." Kurt wasn't certain how to respond; it was a surprise to hear his father say he would train him, but another to hear him ask why he was making a wholesale change now. "I can do this, Dad, and besides, like you, I think I have what it takes." "You wanna be like me? Marry someone, father three kids, and get beat up in a ring six nights a week travelling from place to place…" Kurt nodded contritely; point well made.

Kurt Beyer hurried around Tokyo to make all the necessary arrangements. He moved to Buffalo and began working out with his father, his brother Rich, and a friend at The Destroyer Wrestling Academy in

Blasdell, a gym converted for wrestling training, near where DiPaolo's restaurant was located. The restaurant was a frequented stopping point for Beyer and Wilma; the food was the best in all Western New York and Beyer and DiPaolo, over the course of forty years, had become best of friends. It was a blistering August and the workouts were intense; Rich actually showed much promise but was not of the mind to get into the business; besides, he was to be shipped off to an Army barracks soon. The 6'4" 230 pound Kurt caught on fast and showed surprising agility and maneuverability for a big man; Beyer worked him over and harder than he worked Mike Rotunda, Jumbo Tsuruta, or any other upstart; Kurt's amateur wrestling experience from high school helped, and having seen his dad in the ring thousands of times, he had memorized some nifty moves from his observations of The Destroyer and his opponents. After thirty-one days of hard grueling work, Kurt was sent to Dean Malenko's School of Wrestling in Tampa, Florida, where he was joined by his brother (who remained in training for the Army) and another friend. Dean's father, Boris, put the three through weeks of tough maneuvers, all as a courtesy to Dick Beyer. Excited and relieved after completing Malenko's training, Kurt told his father he wanted to enter the All Japan Pro Wrestling Dojo in Tokyo, which was managed by Kenta Kobashi, one of the great Japanese wrestlers and trainers. That was not going to be an easy feat and both father and son were acutely aware of it. All Japan's dojo did not accept many foreigners into the school, reputed to have one of the toughest training schedules in the world and take several years to complete. Kurt was one of the fortunate few to get in, but he soon found out how justly deserved the school's reputation was. He had never worked harder and longer at anything in his life; he prayed nightly that he would make it through the following day; many others did not. He leaned on the advice and example of his father and eventually found his way to finish the exhausting training requirements.

In early 1993, two significant though diametrically opposite events occurred in the Beyer family. Kurt, now a professional wrestler, made his pro ring debut in Japan. His father, a pro wrestler for nearly forty years, announced his retirement from the ring. To honor The Destroyer, Giant Baba scheduled a series of 'farewell' matches in multiple cities throughout Japan; these matches were to take place during the traditional summer wrestling program. It was a smart decision by Baba to arrange these matches; The Destroyer name was still a brand beloved by the Japanese and the people wanted to say goodbye and thank the man who had given them so much and so much of himself over twenty years. Baba, too, wanted to thank him and what better way to conclude the final match of The Destroyer's illustrious career than a six-man tag team event featuring the team of The Destroyer, Baba, and young Kurt Beyer.

One last decision made without reservation. Nearly 8500 matches, a nose broken six times, multiple contusions, many sore muscles, knee surgeries, and millions of miles around the world were enough for one career and two masks. Besides, he loved teaching, coaching, working with the kids, accompanying them to Japan each year for his cultural exchange program, and with his many charitable endeavors, he needed to make room for more. At age sixty-three, he conditioned himself for his final summer matches with the same vigor and intensity he had when he was twenty-three. He was ready physically and mentally. He packed, deliberately choosing what he wanted to wear for the final match; he stowed away several carefully selected Destroyer masks, drove to the airport with Wilma and boarded the plane to Japan to begin his sayonara tour.

Kurt self-described his new career as "entertaining…for some". In January, he had made his professional debut, wrestling as an unmasked Kurt Beyer, against Masao Inoue, in Shimonoseki City. Though Kurt towered over his first opponent, Inoue, the fan favorite, pinned the rookie Beyer. Kurt had thoughts of wearing a mask after his inaugural bout "just to hide" but fought on in subsequent matches, many of which were held at the venerable Budokan in Tokyo, the 14,000 seat auditorium originally built for the judo competition of the 1964 Olympics. Since then, Budokan Hall hosted a variety of events including the first rock concert in Japan by The Beatles as well as shows given by stars ranging from Dylan to Abba to Clapton however its main use was for Japanese martial arts and professional wrestling. Kurt loved the Budokan; he saw many matches and several of his music idols in concert at the auditorium and it was an honor for him to be wrestling in the hall. Though he lost to Dory Funk in February and with tag partner Al Perez lost to Doug Furnas and Dan Kroffat in June, the thrill of performing in the Budokan was unmatched. He drove to the airport early in July to pick up his father and step-mother, welcomed them both, and told his father the details of his initial matches. The elder Beyer roared with laughter at Kurt's descriptions all the way into downtown Tokyo, but he was feeling very proud of his son's work ethic and, more importantly, his humility.

Baba scheduled twenty-two matches for The Destroyer, the first and last in Tokyo and the others spread throughout the country in order to give fans a final opportunity to see his friend, their adopted hero, perform one last time in person. Tumultuous crowds in each city and venue greeted the masked American. From Hamamatsu, Tottori, Imabari and Hiroshima to Kagoshima, Hakata, Shirahama and Hitachi fans cheered, clamored for autographs and photos, wept, and applauded as the Intelligent Sensational Destroyer, with mask in place looking as young as ever save for a bit more girth, defeated each foe on his journey to the final professional wrestling match of his astounding forty-year career.

Momentum had been building in Japan since word spread that The Destroyer's wrestling swan song was imminent. The Japanese press followed him around the country and provided unprecedented coverage of the American wrestler's tour. At the conclusion of each match, crowds gave The Destroyer a rousing send-off of cheers, toasts, and well-wishes befitting one held in the highest regard in their society. Beyer was moved to tears at every stop during the tour, his masks damper than usual. Having racked up a perfect 19-0 record, The Destroyer proceeded to the final three matches.

The first was held in Kanazawa, fittingly, since this Japanese city was designated in 1962 a sister city of Beyer's hometown of Buffalo, New York. The Kanazawa match became noteworthy for another reason – it was the first time in Japanese history a father-son tag team performed together in a match. The Destroyer and Kurt, two Buffalo guys, wrestled together – as partners- in Buffalo's sister city -and won. But history wasn't through being written…not by a long knee-drop.

Next, The Destroyer and Kurt Beyer travelled to Yokohama, south of Tokyo, to do battle against Giant Baba and his partner for the match, Mitsuo Momota. That The Destroyer would again face Baba was not the main buzz for this match – it was that The Destroyer and his son would be tangling with Momota, the son of Rikidozan. An odd feeling – sort of a coming full circle – enveloped Beyer as he prepped for the match in the locker room with Kurt, Baba and Momota. He could not help but recall his 1963 trip to Japan to wrestle Rikidozan in what would become the most watched television program to that point in Japanese television history. Beyer also reflected on the untimely death of the father of Japanese professional wrestling and the long-nagging helpless feelings he endured afterwards. Beyer had always credited his matches with Baba and Rikidozan with giving him the opportunities he had to succeed in Japan in both the wrestling ring and in entertainment media. He saw in Momota's face the countenance of his lost father and idol to millions of Japanese and knew he had to give a strong performance that evening. At sixty-three years of age, Beyer was acutely aware of every ache and pain in his body; he summed up the will and energy through the knowledge that his own son - and the son of Rikidozan - were in the ring with him. Destroyer, Kurt, Baba and Momota were superb. Though the team of Destroyer and Beyer won, those in attendance gave standing ovations to all four wrestling stars. As he stepped down from the ring, Beyer as Destroyer spotted his daughter in the front row snapping pictures. He hugged her, then picked her up and carried her up the aisle. The crowd applauded wildly. It was on to the finale in Tokyo.

Thursday, July 29, 1993. The stage was the Budokan in Tokyo, a forum full of warm memories and good karma for Dick Beyer and his son. It was the final match in the career of The Destroyer and a complete sellout in the 14,000 seat arena assured. The Japanese media – news writers and sports reporters – were densely packed into the media sections to cover the event for newspapers, magazines and television news and sports. Anticipation and excitement pulsated in every corner of the octagonal building. The spectacle began with ceremonial fanfare reserved for the most respected and honorable events. Following the arrival of the opponents, the announcer intoned and Giant Baba made his way to the ring cloaked in his traditional Japanese kimono in colors gray, black, and white, with red trim. The crowd bellowed and chanted "BA-BA, BA-BA." A short time later, with the lights out, the first few bars of the United States National Anthem played as the crowd's roar picked up in intensity and excitement. To the announcement of "The Destroyer" the masked wrestler and his son Kurt, accompanied by former tag partner Don Manoukian, who flew to Japan to honor his old friend, made their way down the aisle to the rhythmic claps of the fans with people on both sides of the aisle jockeying for position to shake hands with or pat the back of the admired wrestling star. The Destroyer clapped along with the fans and enjoyed his last entrance to the stage. Reaching the ring, The Destroyer entered through the ropes, walked over to Baba and exchanged hand slaps as Baba smiled and laughed. Seated near ringside were Wilma and Kris; Rich, a U.S. Army Airborne Ranger stationed in Korea, was unable to obtain a furlough but sent a warm loving telegram to his father and brother. Beyer as Destroyer was dressed in a white mask with red piping. For the pre-match ceremony, he wore a white warm-up jacket with blue and red bars on the front, and the letters 'USA' prominently displayed. His trunks and shin pads were red; in Japan the combination of red and white signifies a happy, festive occasion – exactly what Beyer had in mind when he chose those items.

The Destroyer took the microphone and in English introduced his friend Don Manoukian to the appreciative crowd. The event, covered live on Japanese television, was hosted by Japanese television star Kazuo Tokumitsu, known as the Johnny Carson of Japanese TV. The bell rang out, the ring announcer intoned. Introduced as the challengers was the team of Haruka Eigen, Masa Fuchi, and Masao Inoue; it was Inoue who pinned Kurt Beyer in his opening professional bout six months earlier, setting up another dramatic theme to this event. The announcer introduced a bearded Kurt Beyer who, dressed in dark trunks and boots, raised his hand and walked to center ring looking lean, fit and focused. In his years working as Baba's tag partner, Destroyer had always been introduced before his boss, so he began to strut out next to pose in his traditional arms folded over his chest posture, but instead of hearing his name, he heard Baba's; the tall, lanky Japanese superstar, dressed also in red trunks, grabbed Destroyer's arm to hold him back and had a wry smile on his face as he stepped forward and stood center ring, sheepishly glancing over at The Destroyer as the fans yelled in approval. Beyer was surprised and moved by the act of his friend, who had obviously made prior arrangements to have him introduced last – a position of honor normally reserved for the top man. As the announcer finished the introduction with a loud and rhythmic 'DE-STROY-YAA' a raucous standing ovation followed that seemed to reverberate endlessly throughout the auditorium.

The match had begun. People sat on the edge of their seats expecting to witness a wrestling match for the ages. The Destroyer was in first, moved patiently, stalked his prey and delivered body blows with such force the impact could be felt in the upper rows; he was a creature in his natural habitat. As he circled the ring in a style similar to Mohammed Ali, he looked like he had not lost a step. At one point, as his opponent readied a kick to his midsection, Destroyer was coming off the ropes toward his opponent when, spotting what was awaiting him, he hung back; he stopped short, broke out into a strut around the ring waiving his finger back and forth as if to say 'no, you're not getting me with that.' The crowd broke up. Kurt, standing on the ring apron, watched his father prowl the canvass like the champion wrestler he had seen as a youngster. All the childhood images came flooding back; Kurt remembered the matches in which his father appeared to be in trouble and his rambunctious attempts to help him restrained by ring personnel. He recalled grabbing the ring hammer and hitting the toe of Uncle Charlie (Mr. Moto) so hard he broke it, only to be lectured by his father and Moto in the locker room. All the long-ago memories of wanting to help his famous father were vivid and clear if only for a fractious moment. Then, after all the years, tribulations, training, and agony, everything washed away with one simple tag of his hand by his masked father. Kurt jumped in the ring. He was on.

The sheer joy of the tag could be seen on Kurt's face. He was living out a boyhood dream that few are ever granted. Time and reality seemed to move in slow motion – like an out-of-body experience - as he tangled up with Fuchi, then Inoue, then Eigan, but he savored every second. Kurt Beyer, son of The Destroyer, stood center ring, protecting and defending his hero and icon to millions. The Budokan, and Kurt, changed forever that night. Working the ring with his father and Baba was a fantasy come to life. He was a thirty-four year old man but that evening, an exuberant eight-year old boy wrestled alongside two of the best the world had ever seen.

Baba, too, enjoyed the match in a way rare for the Japanese mega star. While the night clearly belonged to The Destroyer, Baba fought formidably and every now and then flashed a smile that reflected he was having a fun night-out with the boys. He tagged in and out with Destroyer to the delight of the fans, who were visibly amazed when The Destroyer, on the canvas with his head caught in a leg scissors, did a headstand maneuver that disentangled him from the hold, displaying the agility of a man half his age.

MASKED DECISIONS

The match moved along to its climax as each of the six wrestlers took turns locking up in battle, pounding, twisting, maneuvering, assaulting from the air and ground, giving wrestling fans thrills beyond comprehension. As all six positioned themselves in the ring, they paired off for the last tussle; the crowd sensed a wild impending finish and rose up with thunderous cheers and applause. Baba held Fuchi in an abdominal stretch; as Kurt wrestled Eigen and The Destroyer engaged Inoue, father and son clamped the famous figure-four leg lock onto their respective opponents. The bell rang furiously. The match was over. A career had come to an end.

The ovation in the Budokan muffled any attempt to speak or be heard by fans. All anyone could do was observe. The referee stood between The Destroyer and Kurt, hoisting their arms aloft in victory with Destroyer holding Baba's right arm with his left. The noise never abated. A brief ceremony followed with representatives from newspapers, magazines and television presenting gifts to The Destroyer that included framed photographs of several matches and his visits around the country, trophies, flowers, artwork, and other signs of affection and appreciation. Television announcer Kazuo Tokumitsu presented him with a framed photo of The Destroyer and cast members from the Uwasa No Channel television show. Beyer kidded with him in the ring and was humbled by the sentiments and respect. After the gifts, everyone left the ring except Kurt and Manoukian who waited in corners; The Destroyer then took center stage. The lights were turned off but for one spotlight that shown down onto the masked icon. The sight of the celebrated disguised wrestler standing alone, center ring, was mesmerizing; the crowd in a hushed silence. The wrestler's body glistened from the perspiration; his red trunks and knee pads gave a regal appearance; his mask seemed self-illuminating as it emitted a white glow against the stark, black background. The Destroyer stood, head slightly bowed, hands at his side, as the Japanese ring announcer spoke overhead; translated, he said: *"In 1963, after living in the States for eighteen months, Giant Baba met an extraordinary masked wrestler, a man who had recently arrived in Los Angeles and quickly became the WWA Heavyweight Champion. He was the masked, white devil – The Destroyer. Bringing his finishing move, the figure-four leg lock, he arrived in Japan in May of 1963. Together with the now-departed Rikidozan, they changed the face of pro-wrestling. Now thirty years after his historic debut in Japan, he has made Japan his second home and left us with innumerable great matches. From the time All Japan Pro Wrestling first raised its flag, he and Giant Baba teamed up to make a great U.S.- Japan partnership, fighting the likes of Abdullah the Butcher and Mil Mascaras. Then, from 1974 to 1976, he took on the world's top masked wrestlers and earned the title – World's Greatest Masked Man. Today, July 29, 1993, The Destroyer puts a period on his illustrious thirty-nine year career. However, we will remember his name, along with his famous figure-four leg lock, for a long, long time to come. Thank you and Sayonara, The Intelligent, Sensational Destroyer!"*

The final match and an honor bestowed on only the revered

Kurt, Wilma, Kris and Destroyer salute Japan

The Destroyer raised his arms triumphantly and in appreciation for all the Japanese had given him. Thunderous applause broke out. After bowing to the crowd, Destroyer walked over to Baba and hugged him in a manner that conveyed respect and honor. In the far corner of the ring, Kurt wept uncontrollably, not like the night he was told of his parents' impending divorce, but tears of gratitude and pride. Into the ring entered Wilma and Kris to congratulate them and share the final episode; Kurt stood to the right, Wilma and Kris occupied the center, and The Destroyer took up the left for a very unusual family photograph with arms raised to signify their unity, more importantly, to show their undying love and gratitude to the crowd and the Japanese at large. A song, recorded by Beyer's television co-star Akiko Wada, played over the public address system:

> 'I am happy to have met you. You have the aura of hope. Even though you may stumble, get hurt or cry out. You still have an aura of hope. The city is asleep (referring to apathy). You are

the one to ring the bell. The people are in a fog. You are the one to ring the bell. I am happy to have met you. My faith in love has returned. Together we can feel the kindness returning. The city is mired in a desert wasteland. You are the one to ring the bell. The city is filled with loneliness. You are the one to ring the bell.'

It was an emotionally laden moment. Under the mask Beyer released tears of bittersweet happiness. The time, and decision, was right. The champion wrestler and iconic figure stood for one last look around the arena knowing he had never lost his mask nor had anyone, over four decades, beaten his finishing move, the figure four leg lock, to lay claim to the bounty he anted up when he first pulled down the mask tight over his face.

With Kurt holding the ropes open for his family, The Destroyer was last to leave the ring when he spotted Tokumitsu behind his television desk, crying. Without hesitation, The Destroyer walked over to the desk and hugged him. The exchange was a spontaneous, one-of-a-kind television event. Many others in the standing room only auditorium were seen with tears streaming down their faces. Afterwards, Kurt, with the help of two trainers, lifted his father onto his shoulders. To the ecstatic applause of the crowd, Kurt carried The Destroyer out of the hall, shouldered like a benevolent emperor from a far-away land.

Beyer as Destroyer patiently answered all the questions posed by the media at the post-match press conference. When the inquiries were through, with the camera lights spotting directly on him, Beyer, for the first and last time, removed his famous mask, showing the lines, wrinkles and receding gray hairline of an aging former wrestler, and in one move handed the mask to his son, who was to continue his career in Japan under the name of Destroyer Junior. Cameras caught every sensitive moment. That evening, news of The Destroyer's retirement was headliner material. The NTV network covered it in full on

◄ MASKED DECISIONS

its nightly World News program. Newspapers and magazines raced the clock to get their editions out before first light and deadlines.

Friday morning at the airport prior to boarding a flight to Buffalo and the Akron house he loved, Beyer picked up several newspapers and magazines to read on the flight. With publications in hand, he sat in the plane scanning the material… and his eyes began to tear up. In each of the newspapers and magazines, and in the written accounts of the preceding night's television newscast, despite the hundreds of snapshots and yards of newsreel tape, no photos of Dick Beyer were displayed, only those of the revered Destroyer. The Japanese media and the Japanese people had made one final masked decision of their own.

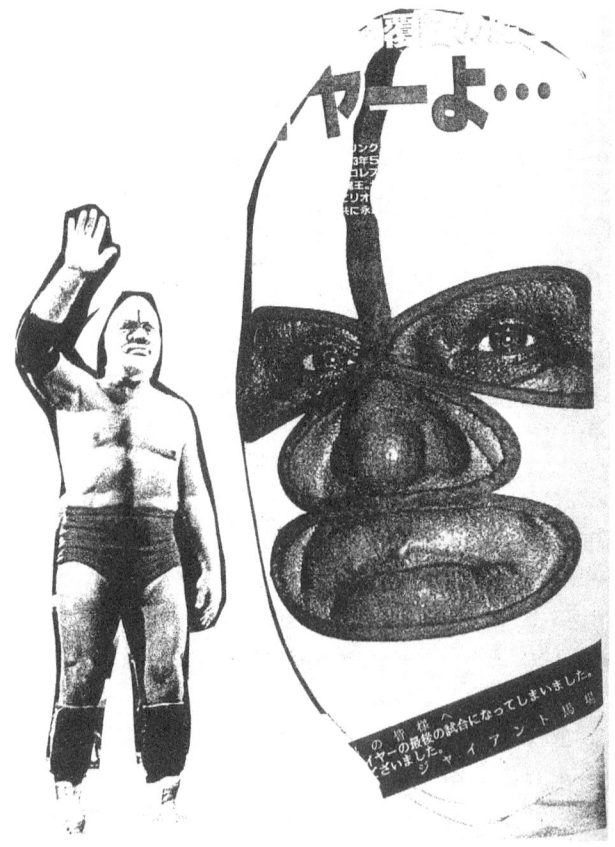

Epilogue

"A few words in recognition of those who richly and unselfishly contributed to my life and my life's work…"

Fred Blassi: "Remained a close personal friend for many years; He gave me the big breaks I needed in this business." After retiring from an illustrious ring career, Blassie managed other wrestlers including George Steele and Hulk Hogan. He entered the World Wrestling Federation Hall of Fame in 1994; in 2004, a year after his death, he was inducted into the Professional Wrestling Hall of Fame.

Vic Christy: "Vic maintained his reputation as the ultimate practical joker in the wrestling business but he was a good wrestler too." Christy passed away in 1995 at age 83.

Dewey and Celia Beyer: "My parents never let on that we were poor. They gave me and my sisters the best childhood and upbringing we could ever have and they gave us the unconditional love that we continue to pass on to our children and grandchildren."

Jean Beyer/Frank Martinke: "My eldest sister and her husband had a wonderful marriage that lasted more than fifty years. I will never forget her and the good times we had building the boat in their garage. They had three daughters, Karen, Sandy and Lori. Frank died in 2006 and Jean passed away in 2010."

MASKED DECISIONS

Dorothy Beyer/Roger Stoessel: "My sister Dorothy and her husband Roger lived in Rochester, New York, and had three sons and a daughter, Mark, David, John and Lynn. They built an ice rink in their yard so the kids could learn to skate and play hockey and the kids were good. When they retired, they moved to Leesburg, Florida, and played a lot of golf together. Dorothy, who was in a nursing home the last few years, died in 2010 and Roger passed away in 2011."

Shirley Beyer/Steve Clergy: "Steve worked as a rigger at Bethlehem Steel and died from cancer several years ago, so Shirley moved to Oregon to be near her three daughters, Sharon, Linda and Mary Ann, on the west coast. Mary Ann was born the same day as my son Kurt. My sister and I are still close and always will be."

Chet McMahon: "Chet's work with kids had an influence on me that helped shape my desire to coach." McMahon's children became high ranking bowlers in Buffalo.

Fred Machemer Sr.: "He became my 'father' at Syracuse University and looked after me in much the way my own father did. I owe a lot to Fred." Machemer served as a detective in the Buffalo Police Department before he retired.

Charlie Stiemke: "If Fred was my SU 'father', Charlie was my SU 'grandfather' who later became my personal lawyer."

Les Dye: "Les once told me I was 'too nice' as a freshman football player and that I needed to 'get mean.' I took his advice. He was a great coach and a Phi Gamma Delta Fraternity brother." Dye passed away in 2000 at age 84.

Ben Schwartzwalder: "As a coach he was tough, but always honest. He changed my way of thinking and my life changed because of it." Schwartzwalder, in his 25 years at Syracuse University, led the team to seven bowl appearances and one national championship.

After Jim Brown and Ernie Davis, he recruited and molded many outstanding players including Floyd Little, Larry Csonka, Rick Cassata, Tom Coughlin, Jim Nance, and others. He retired from coaching in 1973 and was inducted into the College Football Hall of Fame in 1982. Schwartzwalder passed away in 1993.

Ed 'Yips' Yaple: "Ed really got me interested in pinochle and was at the table the night Howie Tice came in and asked me who was the next wrestling heavyweight." Yaple returned to Pennsylvania and taught school for many years.

Bill Kliber: "Bill didn't know it but without him I would never have joined the fraternity and found my destiny." Kliber became a minister and worked in Montana and also served as interim minister at Hendricks Chapel at Syracuse University in the early 1980s.

Bernie Custis: "Our team's quarterback during my sophomore year, he became one of the first black quarterbacks to play professional football in the Canadian League." Custis had a stellar career as a college football coach and was elected to the Canadian Football Hall of Fame in 1988.

Jim Ringo: "Playing next to him on the line was great; he was probably the best offensive blocking center in the history of the game." Ringo played in 3 NFL championship games, 10 Pro Bowls, was selected to the NFL All-Decade Team of the 1960s and inducted into the NFL Hall of Fame in 1981. Ringo coached and developed the 'Electric Company' offensive line for the Buffalo Bills; that line enabled O.J. Simpson to become the first running back to reach 2000 yards in 1973.

Joe Szombathy: "Joe is a great guy and supporter of everything at SU; we have been friends for sixty years." Joe coached at Syracuse and served as athletic administrator for years; the 'Joe Szombathy Special Teams Award' at Syracuse University is given annually in his honor.

MASKED DECISIONS

Howie Tice: "He came in to the card game that Yaple and I were playing and said I was the next heavyweight on the wrestling squad; I never wrestled before, but I did a lot afterwards. Maybe he instinctively knew I would like the sport because I roughhoused a lot in the fraternity house." Tice later coached wrestling in the Lehigh Valley region of Pennsylvania.

Enzo Marinelli: "Enzo gave me my introduction to wrestling the night of the card game; he was a terrific amateur wrestling mentor, roommate and friend." Marinelli taught, coached, and became school principal in New Jersey.

Nick Caivano: "Nick showed early on his remarkable artistic talent and was a great guy to have as a roommate and friend." Caivano became a successful artist and sculptor, had his own studio and taught art at the high school and college level in New Jersey. He died in 2009.

Bill Skyinskus: "If Bill hadn't blown out his knee, I would never have ended up on the wrestling team. The timing was just right and for that I will always thank Bill, and his knee." Bill 'Sky' coached high school football and became principal at a school in Carthage, New York.

Joe McDaniel: "During my first two years in college wrestling, I could never beat my coach in practice, even though he weighed only a hundred and fifteen pounds. He was instrumental in guiding my early wrestling experiences." McDaniel eventually returned to his home state of Oklahoma and in 1990 was named the recipient of the Gallagher Award, given annually to an Oklahoma State University wrestling alumnus who exemplified the spirit and leadership shown by champions.

Don Beitelman: "Don was another great wrestler from Buffalo and the match we had in college helped get me noticed." After changing his name to Don Curtis, he joined fellow Buffalonian Mark

Lewin and became a top tag-team of the Golden Era of Wrestling. He retired in 1981 and promoted wrestling in Florida for a time. He died in 2008 at age 80.

Ed Don George: "I owe my professional career to Ed Don George; everything started with him." George, who passed away in 1985, was posthumously elected to the International Wrestling Institute and Museum in 2002 and the Professional Wrestling Hall of Fame in 2006.

Les McClelland: "With Les to my right and Jim Ringo to my left, how could I lose? We had a great offensive line with Carl Karilivacz, Nick Rahal, Bob Fleck and Joe Szombathy." An Air Force ROTC at Syracuse, McClelland's service career led him to a fifteen year term as a pilot aboard Air Force One.

Pat Stark: "Pat and I were on the coaching staff for the '59 Syracuse team that won the national championship." Stark later became head football coach at the University of Rochester. He was awarded the Syracuse Letter Winner of Distinction honor in 1991 and inducted into both the University of Rochester and Syracuse University Hall of Fame.

Jim Brown: "The best ball carrier I ever saw in college and professional football." Brown excelled in several sports and holds a rare distinction of having been inducted into the College Football Hall of Fame, Lacrosse Hall of Fame, and the Professional Football Hall of Fame. The *Sporting News* in 2002 named Brown the greatest football player of all time. Brown became an actor and an activist after his playing days.

Tim Woodin: "We wrestled in Japan five months before he survived a 1975 plane crash. His career ended shortly afterwards; Tim was a great talent." After changing his name to Tim Woods, he worked professionally as the masked 'Mr. Wrestling.' Woods was inducted into the Tragos/Thesz Professional Wrestling Hall of Fame in 2001.

Eddie Albers: "Ed was my first professional training partner and my first professional match opponent. He was big and went on to a very good career." Albers was an original 'Mr. Clean' and used the moniker for a time because of the uncanny resemblance. After leaving pro wrestling, Albers became a successful real estate agent in San Jose, California.

Dick Hutton: "Dick was not only a great professional wrestler but a champion collegiate grappler. I learned a lot from him while training in Columbus in 1954." Hutton was inducted into the NCAA Hall of Fame, and the Tragos/Thesz Professional Wrestling Hall of Fame. He died in 1980.

Don Eagle: "Don was a Mohawk from Canada, an outstanding draw and great champion. He, too, helped in my formative years in Columbus." Eagle died at age 41.

Fred Atkins: "Fred was one of the toughest and strongest wrestlers I ever faced." Atkins, from New Zealand, not only wrestled, he trained Giant Baba among others and later worked as a trainer for the Buffalo Sabres hockey team and the Toronto Maple Leafs. He died in 1988.

Lenny Montana: "Lenny was just an all-around fun guy to be with." Montana finished his wrestling career with several individual and tag team championships and found fame as an actor playing the role of Luca Brasi in the hit movie classic 'The Godfather.' He passed away in 1992 at age 66.

Penny Banner: "We were friends but never anything more...she was one beautiful girl." Banner enjoyed a successful wrestling career, dated Elvis Pressley several times, later competed in the Senior Olympics in swimming and served as the commissioner of the Professional Girl Wrestling Association until her death in 2008.

Ken Marshall: "Ken and his brother Joe booked a tag match for me and Johnny Gilbert in the Kentucky territory and that match helped me get into the Chicago territory were Johnny came from; it was shortly after that I was named 'Rookie of the Year' in 1955.

Al Karasick: "Al gambled on a young rookie named Dick Beyer and through him I found Rikidozan and reconnected with Fred Blassie who got me into Los Angeles, where I found my destiny. Thanks to Al, my professional life took off." Karasick influenced the careers of many others.

Bill Ziegler: "Managing Dim's hot dog stand with him was a great experience and we made good money for a couple of punks. He remained in Buffalo and provided estimates for a cleaning company that specialized in fire and water clean-up and restoration."

Dick Afflis: "Bruiser helped me learn the nuances of the business in Chicago; he did well with Wilbur Snyder when they owned the Indianapolis territory and he also won titles with Crusher Lisowski." Afflis passed away at age 62.

Reggie Lisowski: "We had some great times in Chicago in the 50s and 70s; Crusher was a real working man's wrestler." Lisowski and Afflis were inducted into the Professional Wrestling Hall of Fame in 2005.

Angelo Poffo: "Poffo was great working a program and we had a humdinger in Buffalo in the 60s." While a good wrestler, he was noted for being the father of two wrestling greats, Randy 'Macho Man' Savage and Leaping Lanny Poffo/The Genius.

Lord Blears: "Without Blears teaching me the figure four leg lock, I would not have had a great finishing hold." Blears acted, promoted, and worked as a representative for Giant Baba's PWF promotion. He was known as the voice of '50th State Wrestling' and remains a legend in Hawaii.

Gene Kiniski: "Gene was a tough opponent, a good partner with

Blears, and we had some great times together; he attended Baba's tribute with me in Japan." Kiniski was inducted into the Tragos/Thesz Professional Wrestling Hall of Fame in 2004 and the Professional Wrestling Hall of Fame in 2008.

Rikidozan: "Seventy million people watched our match on TV in 1963 and it made me well known in Japan since there were approximately one hundred million people in Japan at that time. My career in Japan is directly linked to him." Rikidozan was inducted into the Professional Wrestling Hall of Fame in 2006.

Roy Simmons: "Not only a great football coach, he coached boxing and made Syracuse lacrosse a powerhouse; I learned a great deal about scouting a team from Simmy." Simmons was inducted into the Lacrosse Hall of Fame in 1964 and passed away in 1994 at age 94.

Billy Red Lyons: "A close brother-in-law, great opponent and tag team partner." After Lyons retired from professional wrestling he worked as a television interviewer for Maple Leaf Wrestling and coined the phrase "Dontcha dare miss it." He passed away in 2009.

Ilio DiPaolo: "My best friend in wrestling was Ilio." DiPaolo became synonymous with charitable endeavors in Western New York. His business, Ilio DiPaolo's Restaurant and Ringside Lounge in Blasdell, New York, is a favorite among residents, visitors, and even the Buffalo Bills' organization. The DiPaolo Scholarship fund was established to help deserving high school students who excel not only in athletics but in academics and in family and community endeavors; the 'Destroyer Wrestling Award' is part of the scholarship fund and honors the community work of Dick Beyer and his relationship with Ilio DiPaolo. DiPaolo died in 1995 after being struck by a car. He was posthumously honored with the New York State Award from the Professional Wrestling Hall of Fame in 2003.

"I've known Dick Beyer for many years through my relationship with Ilio DiPaolo. They are two of the finest men I've had the opportunity to meet in Buffalo."

- Jim Kelly, retired quarterback, Buffalo Bills,
University of Miami and Pro Football Hall of Fame.

Gorgeous George: "Looking back, I'm glad I was able to help him when he needed it; our 'hair versus mask' matches in California became classics. He had an influence on the business like no other." George was posthumously inducted into the Professional Wrestling Hall of Fame in 2002 and the WWE Hall of Fame in 2010 for which Dick Beyer was asked to present George's nomination.

Ernie Davis: "Ernie was as inspirational off the field as he was on." Davis was drafted by Washington then traded to Cleveland and was to be in the same backfield as Jim Brown but at age 23 Davis died of leukemia before he could play in the NFL. Davis was inducted into the College Football Hall of Fame in 1979.

Baron Gattoni: "Baron went to Japan with me in the mid-1960s; one of the strongest men I ever saw." Gattoni remained a hero in his native Argentina while wrestling mostly in the U.S. He died in 1982.

Bobo Brazil: "As a tag partner or an opponent, Bobo gave a great show and everybody loved him." Brazil worked in the restaurant business for more than twenty years before his death in 1998. He was inducted into the Professional Wrestling Hall of Fame in 2008.

Maurice Mad Dog Vachon: "When we left Hawaii for the States in the early 60s, I became The Destroyer in California and he became Mad Dog in Portland; must have been something with those dastardly names." Vachon and his brother Paul won numerous titles and were inducted into the Canadian Wrestling Hall of Fame and the Professional Wrestling Hall of Fame.

Dean Ho Higuchi: "I trained often at Dean's gym in Waikiki and he was very good to me, so I helped him learn pro wrestling." Higuchi often wrestled under the name 'Dean Ho' in North America, won several tag team titles, and had a marathon run in Vancouver which became his home. Higuchi was acknowledged by the Cauliflower Alley Club as a Men's Wrestling Honoree in 2010.

Tosh Togo: "Many people don't realize he won a silver medal in weightlifting for the United States in the 1948 London Olympics." Togo (Harold Toshiyuki Sakata) adopted an acting career while still wrestling; his most famous role was Oddjob in the James Bond movie, 'Goldfinger.' He died in his native Hawaii in 1982.

Mr. Moto (Charlie Iwamoto): "Charlie was a close friend and godfather to my daughter. We had some great fishing trips together, even had to fish for his pole that flew out of the boat when a fish hooked the line and took it under…funny stories too numerous to mention. He loved to frequent Las Vegas and became very popular there as well as in Los Angeles. He died in 1991."

Curtis Iaukea: "From Prince to King, he became known for his 'Hawaiian Splash'. He did well in Australia and Japan." Iaukea later managed Kamala and Sika in the WWF promotion.

Nick Bockwinkel: "One of the best workers in the business but one of the worst fishermen I ever saw. He is still a good friend." Bockwinkel was known as one of the best 'heels' ever and was popular not only in the Northwest but won titles in the South and Midwest. He remains active with the Cauliflower Alley Club and resides in Las Vegas.

Don Owen: "By far Don was the best promoter in the business; well regarded. He allowed me out of our initial agreement so I could work L.A. and because of that, I became The Destroyer." Owen died at age 90.

Art Michalik: "Art became my tag partner in Oregon after his football years with the San Francisco 49ers." Michalik enjoyed a successful ring career and later served thirty-two years as a school administrator and coach.

Lou Thesz: "Lou was a truly great champion who taught me plenty." Thesz is universally regarded as a wrestling innovator, technician, and greatest champion of all time. He died in 2002.

Don Manoukian: "We were the best tag team Strongbow ever saw. Don came out to my final match in Japan; He is a great guy and a close friend." After wrestling, Manoukian worked in real estate development in Reno and Las Vegas.

Giant Baba: "Without the three matches we had in L.A. I would not have come to Rikidozan's attention and would not have had the success in Japan. He made it all happen for me there and I have fond memories of Baba; a great competitor and a great friend. At the memorial tribute they held for him in Tokyo after his death, his wife placed his boots in the center of the ring and I was given the honor of retrieving them from the ring and returning them to his wife. I hold Baba in the highest regard." Shohei Baba drove All Japan Pro Wrestling to become the number one promotion in the world in the 1990s. He passed away in 1999 and was posthumously inducted into the Professional Wrestling Hall of Fame in 2008.

MASKED DECISIONS

Don Leo Jonathan: "Don was the best big man in the business." The Utah native Jonathan settled in Canada where he became a legend in professional wrestling. He was inducted into the Professional Wrestling Hall of Fame in 2006.

Killer Kowalski: "Telling me to slap him in the ring in Japan helped put me over with the Japanese and I will always be grateful to him." Kowalski had a legendary career and eventually opened a wrestling school and trained several top stars. He was inducted into the Professional Wrestling Hall of Fame in 2003 and the National Polish-American Sports Hall of Fame in 2007. Kowalski passed away in 2008.

Danny Hodge: "Pound for pound the toughest wrestler in the business. We had some great times in Japan and I saw him squeeze apples in his hand and turn them into mush; he had an unbelievably strong grip." Hodge was inducted into the Wrestling Institute Hall of Fame and the Professional Wrestling Hall of Fame.

Antonia Inoki: "One of the better Japanese wrestlers and workers; despite his split with Baba, he did well and wrestled some big names; he is considered a national hero alongside Rikidozan, Baba and few others." In 1976 he participated in a mixed match with boxing great Muhammad Ali; while the match ended a draw, many consider that match the root of the Ultimate Fighting Championship craze. Inoki was inducted into the Pro Wrestling Hall of Fame in 2009.

Regis Philbin: "Without me putting the mask on him and appearing on his San Diego TV shows in the early 1960s, he would be nothing today!" Philbin entertains audiences around the country singing solo and duets with wife, Joy, and hosts a daily national talk/interview show called 'Regis and Kelly Live' on which he often mentions the Golden Age wrestlers that appeared on his early television shows.

Mike Mazurki: "Mike was a giving person and a good friend for years." Mazurki, in addition to an outstanding ring career, appeared in numerous movies and television shows including the 1945 and the 1990 versions of 'Dick Tracy', 'Some Like It Hot', 'Love, American Style' and 'Charlie's Angels.' Mazurki founded the Cauliflower Alley Club as a non-profit organization comprised of former wrestlers, boxers and actors to raise money for deserving young athletes and support for retired wrestlers. His ear appears as the logo for the club; he died in 1990. The Cauliflower Alley Club gives its highest honor – the Iron Mike Award - annually, and is considered the ultimate honor among wrestlers. In 2005 he was recognized with the New York State Award from the Professional Wrestling Hall of Fame.

Verne Gagne: "Gagne knew how to wrestle and was a superb champion; as a promoter he gave me a big break in Minneapolis and because of him Dr. X was born; I will always appreciate what he did and how well he treated me there." Gagne trained some of the biggest names in pro wrestling including Ric Flair and Ricky Steamboat and helped to develop Jesse 'The Body' Ventura. He was inducted into the Pro Wrestling Hall of Fame in 2004.

Harley Race: "Great wrestler, tough competitor, lousy driver…way too fast." Race competed against the best in the business and held numerous titles and belts in several promotions. He later joined the WWF as Handsome Harley Race. After active wrestling, he managed the likes of Lex Luger and Vader and developed close associations with Mick Foley and Steve Austin. The Professional Wrestling Hall of Fame welcomed him in 2004.

Red Bastien: "Red and Billy Red Lyons, my brother-in-law, made a great tag team; Red could really fly and had great reaction and a sense of timing. The picture of me as The Destroyer holding Red high in the air is considered by many the best action wrestling photo of all time. I think so too." Bastien was selected in 2007 to the International Wrestling Institute and Museum.

Pita Maivia: "High Chief and I had a celebrated match in Western Somoa during my world tour; I found a way to get his hand raised and it saved my life...from his fans and countrymen." Maivia's grandson is former wrestler turned movie actor Dwayne 'The Rock' Johnson. Maivia died from cancer at age 45 in 1982.

Wahoo McDaniel: "Well respected because of his athletic ability; he was one of the first great Native American wrestlers; when he played football at Oklahoma and I was on the coaching staff at Syracuse, I had to choose a player to represent Wahoo on the practice team – and it had to be our best player." McDaniel died of complications from diabetes in 2002.

Billy Robinson: "Billy enabled me to get booked in Germany after telling Gustl Kaiser about me and I helped him get into the Minneapolis territory. It worked out well for both of us." Robinson was a star on several continents and eventually trained several martial arts legends. The International Wrestling Hall of Fame inducted him in 2003.

John DaSilva: "One of the toughest international competitors I faced; he promoted in New Zealand and was instrumental in getting me booked there; I owe a debt of gratitude to John." After retiring, DaSilva worked with disadvantaged youth in his native New Zealand.

Moose Morowski: "Terrific wrestler, terrible cribbage player; he put me over in Minneapolis and in Japan." Morowski spent much of his later years volunteering his time to a variety of organizations.

Clark Hatch: "Clark was one of the first people to welcome me to Japan and remains a close friend." A fitness pioneer, Hatch established more than a hundred fitness centers in fourteen different countries and is a health and sports advocate, author, lecturer, and international fitness adviser.

Maggie Minenko: "Maggie was a great kid on the show in Japan and became close to my kids and to Willy." Leaving 'Uwasa No Channel' after a one-year stint, Minenko returned to New York City, worked as an interpreter and for Major League Baseball, raised a family and currently resides in Los Angeles. She reconnected with the three Beyer siblings and plans to see them on travels east.

Akiko Wada: "A wonderful woman, the best entertainer in Japan, and a great cast member." Wada hosted television and radio programs and released 33 record albums. Her 30th anniversary concert featured Ray Charles. In 2008, for her 40th anniversary in show business, she made her first solo appearance at the famed Apollo Theater in New York with The Destroyer and his wife in the audience.

Master/Masako Hada: "They owned and operated the Palace Restaurant, the official Destroyer fan club center in Tokyo, until they sold the enterprise in 2009. They are good friends to Wilma and me."

Tanny: "Tanny is still my best friend and associate in Japan. He helps to keep the Figure Four Club in the spotlight and is a valuable resource every time I take students to Japan. He also helps me organize my appearances during the Azabu Juban Festival each August in Tokyo."

Mil Mascaras: "One of the best masked wrestlers I faced and because we both liked good wrestling, we always gave the crowd their money's worth." Mascaras became one of Mexico's all time box office attractions with over 30 action movies to his credit, wearing the mask in each.

Marty Kuehnert: "Marty introduced me to many great ballplayers and sports stars in Japan and remains a close personal friend." During Kuehnert's three decades in Japan, he worked as a sports journalist for print and broadcast media, pioneered the sports licensing business, and introduced the first sports bar in Japan through his chain of 'Attic' restaurants. Considered one of the foremost authorities on sports in Japan, he made history when named the first foreign General Manager of a Japanese professional baseball team. The author of six books, Kuehnert currently hosts a TV sports journalism show in Japan and is a professor and Vice President at Sendai

◀ MASKED DECISIONS

University where he teaches courses in sports management, marketing, and media.

Dory and Terry Funk: "They were the best brother tag team in the business and they helped Baba establish All Japan Pro Wrestling by agreeing to wrestle for his promotion." Both Dory and Terry Funk were inducted into the Professional Wrestling Hall of Fame within one year of each other.

Ric Flair: "He had the talk but I taught him the walk…that strut he used was mine. He certainly had the talent and achieved a great career." In 2006 Flair was inducted into the Professional Wrestling Hall of Fame.

Fred Machemer Jr.: "Like his father, he helped me when I wanted to get into high school coaching; a great guy." Machemer taught science and coached basketball at Amherst Central High School.

Mark Ragin: "Mark had a great high school wrestling career and eventually fulfilled his dream of making it to the professional level." Ragin worked for Baba's All Japan Pro Wrestling, married, and relocated to Las Vegas where he works in the security field.

Mike Rotunda: "He had all the ability and made a good career for himself; I may have taken him under my wing, but he made the best of what he had; he did well in Japan too." Rotunda took on work as a road agent for the WWE and occasionally makes personal appearances under his ring name Irwin R. Schyster (I.R.S.).

Wilma (Willy) Thomson Beyer: "Willy was a good mother and wife who helped my career in many ways, not just making the first masks I used as The Destroyer. More importantly, she did all the things that kept us as a family and for that I will always be thankful." After their divorce, Willy's Amway distributor business in Japan eventually became very successful and she was able to devote more time to teaching and art. From her early start instructing typing and art classes at St. Mary's

International School for boys, Willy used her draftsman background to develop a mechanical drawing program; this led her to introduce an architectural design course which she managed on her own to get certified and accredited for college-level credits for students. Many students pursued degrees and careers in architecture as a result of her program. As her life in Japan improved, so did her interest in and knowledge of the Japanese language and culture; she not only learned to speak Japanese but also loved to collect Japanese style furniture. Having honed her painting skills in a variety of media, she began to paint numerous portraits, landscapes and other subjects from her fascination with all things Japanese. So renowned did she become, she was hired as an image/art consultant by a number of Japanese companies including a highly respected fashion school; subsequently, her program was adopted by the school worldwide. Willy's art was exhibited at a number of prestigious galleries in Japan. She returned to the United States in the late 1990s to be near her two sons in the Washington D.C. area. There, she continued her artwork. Willy later moved to Michigan and lived with her daughter Kris. In 2004, Willy passed away from leukemia without fulfilling her desire of opening an art gallery. Her three children, in tribute to her legacy and dream, designed and posted an online gallery www.wilmathomson.com to showcase the wonderful collection of art she lovingly bequeathed to the world.

Kurt Dewey Beyer: "Kurt is an intelligent young man with a heart of gold as large as his 6'4" frame. Because he was the oldest, he always looked out for me, even as he was growing up and he continues to do so today." The year after his father's final match, which featured the first father-son tag team in Japanese wrestling history, Kurt participated in the 1994 Summer Action Series in Japan as part of a 10-man American contingent; he lost his match in front of a sellout crowd in Kurashiki but won the 6-man tag team event at Budokan Hall in the final match of the series. During the latter part of the 1990s, Kurt wrestled in the Catch Wrestling Association in Germany before returning to the United States and settling in Washington D.C. near his brother. He continued to train and wrestle professionally, a few times as Destroyer Jr., and in 2002 Kurt won the IAW TV Championship defeating 'Flying' Andy Chene. He later moved to Michigan, became a certified personal trainer, and worked with his sister Kris at her gym. After his mother's death, Kurt eventually relocated to Buffalo and currently serves as international sales manager for ATTO Technology Inc. for which he uses his fluent Japanese language skills to make sales presentations on frequent business trips to Japan.

Mona Kris Beyer: "Kris is a wonderful daughter and apple of my eye. She doesn't talk about herself much but she was an excellent swimmer at Syracuse University and her love of fitness and athletics gave her a great career when she left engineering." While working in Japan for a U.S. Big Three automotive company, she met an athlete whose relationship sparked an interest in bodybuilding and physical fitness. Kris developed into a champion body builder, started her own fitness business in Michigan, and in 2004 graduated from the California University of Pennsylvania with an MS degree in Exercise Science. When her mother moved to Michigan, Kris and her brother Kurt served as caregivers until her death. Certified as a fitness professional and personal trainer, Kris offers fitness, conditioning, weight loss and nutrition coaching services nationally and operates studios in Brooklyn, Michigan and in Akron, New York. Additionally, for the last several years, Kris coaches the girls' swim team at Akron Central High School in Akron New York alongside her father who coaches the boys' team.

Richard Ward Beyer: "Richie was a favorite of the Japanese when he was growing up. He fell in love with basketball and was a high school Far East basketball All-Star. From there his life really took off." After college, Richard began his military career as an officer in the U.S. Army Infantry where he was responsible for the training, morale, and professional development of more than fifty infantry soldiers. He graduated from the military's toughest leadership schools and earned the coveted Airborne Ranger tab. Later, Richard was placed in charge of the U.S. Army Old Guard 'Honor Guard' and captained the U.S. Army Drill Team that performed throughout the country and abroad; he led wreath-laying ceremonies at the Tomb of the Unknowns in Arlington, Virginia, as well as those at the White House and Pentagon and participated in numerous ceremonial parades in Washington, D.C. After six years in the Army, Richard attended The George Washington University, earning his Masters' in Business Administration; while in Washington, D.C. he met his wife, Amy. Richard progressed through his management career serving as Regional Manager for Aramark and later worked as Division Director for Robert Half Inc. - both fortune 500 firms. He currently runs a company called R3Global, an international training, promotions, and events planning company. Richard and Amy reside in Jacksonville, Florida, with their three children – Grace, Grant, and Lucy, who refer to their wrestler-grandfather as 'Beepa.'

Patti Maurer Schrenk: "Patti is a wonderful step-daughter and added a great deal to our blended family. As a former Buffalo Bills' cheerleader, she has been a vocal supporter for the things in which Wilma and I are involved…without the megaphone." From her first marriage, Patti brought daughters Lisa and Kelly Murray and with second husband Marc Schrenk, extended the Beyer family to include stepchildren Laurene and Brent. Patti wrote a wonderful and heart-warming letter of recommendation for Dick Beyer's nomination to a Buffalo hall of fame, helped her step-father apply to Toastmasters' International, and was involved, along with step-sister Kris, in 'Wrestling Legends of the Aud' - the final event held at Buffalo's Memorial Auditorium that benefitted the Ilio DiPaolo Scholarship Fund and Children's Hospital.

Wilma Maurer Beyer: "To find another great woman to share my life with was unbelievable; that her name was Wilma was even more remarkable. She is not only my wife, but my best friend." After fourteen years, Wilma retired from her work as a nurse at Amherst Central High School and worked as a dental assistant for a short time before joining her husband in his wrestling promotions throughout Western New York. She travelled to Japan several times each year with The Destroyer, attended many Japanese wrestling shows and got to know her husband's friends in addition to seeing the countryside. Wilma served as her husband's administrative assistant, corresponding secretary and travelling companion as he forged ahead with his voluminous activities. She was score keeper for his swim team, workout partner for him at the Village Glen fitness center, and assisted him with the Syracuse University Alumni functions and fund raisers. For the last ten years, she worked with her husband on the Relay for Life, a fundraiser for the American Cancer Society. Wilma continues to work by her husband's side in the numerous charitable endeavors they adopted both at home and abroad and lovingly remains his primary supporter and caregiver.

Dick Beyer: After he left the wrestling ring in 1993 at age sixty-three, Beyer returned to teaching and coaching at the Akron Central school district. Though he retired from the classroom in 1995, he continued to coach the boys' high school swim team and to make yearly sojourns to Japan. He became active with Buffalo's sister city program in Kanazawa, and very involved with multiple fundraising activities for the Japanese Red Cross and earthquake relief efforts after the 1995 Japan earthquake, taking quilts to Japan shortly after the catastrophe. In addition, Beyer became associated with the Akron Masonic Lodge #527, Boy Scout and Little League activities as an advisor and coach, played Santa Claus for hospitals, nursing homes, disabled children centers and orphanages, chaired the *Buffalo News* 'Kids Day' paper sale to benefit Children's Hospital, joined Toastmasters International and spoke at various charitable functions and service organizations.

Beyer's dedication to young people has been recognized in many ways. He was given the Appreciation for Service Award by the Boy Scouts of America #159, the Distinguished Service and Personal Contribution Award from the Masonic Lodge #527 and the Service to Youth Award from that same organization. Additionally, he received the Personal Contribution and Support of Wrestling Award from the Ladies

International Wrestling Association and had, in his name and honor, an annual award designated by the Ilio DiPaolo Memorial Foundation. For his devotion to and support of Syracuse University, Beyer was chosen for the J.Michael Heinke Memorial Award, the Letter Winners of Distinction for distinguished career and community service, and the Outstanding Alumni Officers Award. In 1999, Beyer was named 'Citizen of the Year' by the Akron Chamber of Commerce. He and Wilma found other ways to contribute their time and talents; they joined Literacy Volunteers and read to young children, helped with the Lothlorian Therapeutic Riding Center, Special Olympics, and the exchange student program of the Rotary Club for which they hosted a boy from Mexico.

Beyer's legendary contributions to wrestling and to humanity were acknowledged on national levels beginning in 1996 when he was chosen the recipient of the 'Iron Mike Award' – the most prestigious and coveted award given by the Cauliflower Alley Club, the service organization started by Mike Mazurki. That same year, he was selected to the inaugural class of the Wrestling Observer Newsletter Hall of Fame. In 2002, Beyer was inducted, alongside his mentor Ed Don George, into the International Wrestling Institute and Museum in Waterloo, Iowa. A year later, Beyer was elected to the Greater Buffalo Sports Hall of Fame in Buffalo, New York and earned the New York State Award from the Schenectady, New York based Professional Wrestling Hall of Fame into which he was enshrined in 2005. During his induction, eldest son Kurt gave a moving tribute to his father.

Having wrestled in more than 8500 matches, travelled over two million miles, worked in Asia, Europe, the Pacific Southwest, Canada, Hawaii and most U.S. states through a career that spanned 40 years, The Destroyer never had his famous figure four leg lock broken by anyone, and still has the original $5000 he anted up. He remains the most successful masked wrestler of his era, and arguably, any era. So, too, his legend and popularity remain in his beloved Japan where he visits several times each year and spends days seeing old friends and greeting new ones, at the annual Azabu Juban Festival in Tokyo.

MASKED DECISIONS

The respect and admiration the Japanese people have for him is equaled only by the love and high esteem in which the kids from Western New York and Japan hold him, as he continues to foster meaningful interpersonal relationships between the two countries, through his sports program and his Figure Four Club of Tokyo. This 'Children's Ambassador' uses his program and network to promote playing by the rules, good sportsmanship, competition and learning, just as he did while in the classroom, out of the ring, and as a father. Dick Beyer's life – and his life's work – is sui generis.

> *"I am a guy who was in the right places at the right times, and found myself around great people who made me better than I was. But it was the decisions I made when I got to those places and times that linked the outcomes together. I didn't let the mystery of the unknown block me from being decisive, and just relied on my upbringing and education. My dad was right – whatever you put into your head, nobody can take away from you, but it is what's in your heart that you can share with anyone."*

www.ingramcontent.com/pod-product-compliance
Lightning Source LLC
Chambersburg PA
CBHW052035230426
43671CB00011B/1656